AF806600

Atypical Interaction

Ray Wilkinson · John P. Rae ·
Gitte Rasmussen
Editors

Atypical Interaction

The Impact of Communicative Impairments within Everyday Talk

palgrave
macmillan

Editors
Ray Wilkinson
Department of Human Communication Sciences
University of Sheffield
Sheffield, UK

John P. Rae
Department of Psychology
University of Roehampton
London, UK

Gitte Rasmussen
Department of Language and Communication
University of Southern Denmark
Odense, Denmark

ISBN 978-3-030-28798-6 ISBN 978-3-030-28799-3 (eBook)
https://doi.org/10.1007/978-3-030-28799-3

© The Editor(s) (if applicable) and The Author(s), under exclusive license to Springer Nature Switzerland AG 2020
This work is subject to copyright. All rights are solely and exclusively licensed by the Publisher, whether the whole or part of the material is concerned, specifically the rights of translation, reprinting, reuse of illustrations, recitation, broadcasting, reproduction on microfilms or in any other physical way, and transmission or information storage and retrieval, electronic adaptation, computer software, or by similar or dissimilar methodology now known or hereafter developed.
The use of general descriptive names, registered names, trademarks, service marks, etc. in this publication does not imply, even in the absence of a specific statement, that such names are exempt from the relevant protective laws and regulations and therefore free for general use.
The publisher, the authors and the editors are safe to assume that the advice and information in this book are believed to be true and accurate at the date of publication. Neither the publisher nor the authors or the editors give a warranty, expressed or implied, with respect to the material contained herein or for any errors or omissions that may have been made. The publisher remains neutral with regard to jurisdictional claims in published maps and institutional affiliations.

Cover illustration: © Alex Linch shutterstock.com

This Palgrave Macmillan imprint is published by the registered company Springer Nature Switzerland AG
The registered company address is: Gewerbestrasse 11, 6330 Cham, Switzerland

Acknowledgements

This work was supported by an Economic and Social Research Council Research Fellowship Award to Ray Wilkinson [RES-063-27-0144].

Contents

Notes on Contributors

Charles Antaki is a Professor of Language and Social Psychology, and a member of the Discourse and Rhetoric Group (DARG) at Loughborough University, UK. Among his publications is the edited volume *Applied Conversation Analysis* (Palgrave Macmillan, 2011).

Peter Auer received his academic training at the universities of Cologne, Manchester and Constance, where he also worked as an Assistant Professor of General Linguistics. From 1992 to 1998, he was Professor of German Linguistics at the University of Hamburg. Since 1998, he has held a chair of German Linguistics at the University of Freiburg (Germany). From 2007 to 2013 he was one of the directors of the Freiburg Institute for Advanced Studies (FRIAS). Peter Auer has done extensive research on bilingualism, on dialectology and sociolinguistics, on phonology and prosody, on interaction and on spoken language from a syntactic point of view, as well as atypical conversation (particularly aphasia). He has published more than 200 articles in linguistic journals and edited volumes and is the author/co-author of six monographs, among them *Aphasie im Alltag* (with Angelika Bauer).

Scott Barnes is a Senior Lecturer in the Department of Linguistics at Macquarie University, Australia. His research uses conversation analysis to explore the interface between the organization of interaction, language, cognition, and related impairments. With this research, Scott aims to improve speech pathology assessment and intervention for people with communication disorders, with a focus on aphasia, traumatic brain injury, and right hemisphere damage. Scott is especially interested in turn-taking and repair organization, and issues of measurement in speech pathology practice.

Angelika Bauer received her academic training at the universities of Constance, Brussels and Freiburg. From 1981 to 2008, she worked as a speech and language therapist at a Neurological Rehabilitation Clinic, as lecturer (neurolinguistics and aphasia therapy) at the University of Basel and the Fachhochschule Nordwestschweiz (FHNW), and participated in a research project at the University of Freiburg (Germany). Since 2009 she has been head of the school of speech and language therapy in Freiburg.

Steven Bloch is an Associate Professor in Language and Cognition at University College London, UK. With a clinical background in speech and language therapy his research interests include conversation analysis and its application to telephone-mediated healthcare interactions and to conversations involving people with progressive neurological conditions. He is currently working on end of life interactions: how healthcare professionals interact with family members and how oncology teams discuss prognostication. He is Editor-in-Chief of the *International Journal of Language and Communication Disorders.*

Katie Ekberg is a Research Fellow in the School of Health and Rehabilitation Sciences at The University of Queensland, Australia. Her research interests involve conversation analysis and healthcare interactions. Her previous research has involved examining communication in a range of healthcare environments, including: Cognitive Behavioural Therapy sessions for clients diagnosed with depression, calls with specialist nurses on a major UK cancer helpline, consultations with neurologists and patients suffering from seizure disorders, and most recently, interactions with people with hearing impairment, their families, and clinicians.

Christopher Elsey is currently a Lecturer in Health and Well Being in the School of Allied Health Sciences at De Montfort University, UK. Methodologically his research primarily utilises video recordings to investigate work-place practices, activities and sites of learning, informed by the sociological research traditions of ethnomethodology, conversation analysis and symbolic interactionism. The worksite settings analysed to date include medical consultations (e.g. GP, Memory Clinics), air force communication and military inquiries, and an educational setting for adults with learning difficulties. Currently he is researching professional sport and mental health, and medical neutrality in armed conflict situations.

W. M. L. Finlay is a Reader in Psychology at Anglia Ruskin University, UK. His research interests include intellectual disabilities, interaction, and political communication in conflict situations.

Simone Girard-Groeber is a Scientific Collaborator at the Institute for Integration and Participation at the University of Applied Sciences Northwestern Switzerland (School for Social Work). She has a doctorate in Applied Linguistics from the University of Neuchâtel. Her main research interest is in interactional competence understood as the methodic use of semiotic resources for accomplishing social actions. In this respect, she is interested in spoken and signed language interactions as well as more generally the multimodal design of interactional practices. More broadly, she is concerned with the challenges and opportunities of people with disabilities in communication and participation.

Louise Hickson is Associate Dean in the Faculty of Health and Behavioural Sciences and Professor of Audiology at The University of Queensland, Australia. She is recognized internationally as a research leader in audiological rehabilitation for adults and children with hearing impairment and their families. She has over 250 publications including 5 books and 20 book chapters and is committed to the transfer of knowledge into practice. In 2013 Prof. Hickson received the International Research Award from the American Academy of Audiology.

Ina Hörmeyer studied Linguistics at the University of Münster and the University of Freiburg, Germany. From 2012 to 2014 she worked for the project "Interactive Conditions in Augmentative and Alternative Communication (AAC)" at the University of Freiburg (Linguistics Department). Since 2017 she has worked for the project "Interaction-based Intervention in Augmentative and Alternative Communication (AAC)" at the Catholic University of Applied Sciences, Freiburg.

Minna Laakso is a Professor in Logopedics (speech-language pathology) at the University of Helsinki, Finland. Her research focuses on interactions involving participants with differing competencies (e.g. children and parents, participants with aphasia and their familiar and professional interlocutors, and people with hearing loss in clinic and home). In particular, she has studied repair practices in connection with communication disorders. Her research projects include 'The child's developing interaction' and 'Communication with the help of a hearing aid: A comparative study of persons with acquired hearing loss within their interactions in private settings and with hearing health practitioners' funded by the Academy of Finland.

Christopher Lind is an Associate Professor in Audiology at Flinders University, Australia. Christopher has practised, taught, and researched in adult rehabilitation for over 30 years. The focus of Christopher's work is to understand the client experience in adult-onset communication difficulties, particularly adult hearing impairment, and to provide situationally relevant intervention(s) that address clients' functional needs arising as a result.

Douglas W. Maynard is the Maureen T. Hallinan WARF Professor at the University of Wisconsin–Madison, USA. He is the author of *Bad News, Good News: Conversational Order in Everyday Talk and Clinical Settings* (2003), and co-editor (with John Heritage) of *Communication in Medical Care: Interaction Between Primary Care Physicians and Patients.* His current work includes co-editing (again with John

Heritage) a volume entitled *Harold Garfinkel: Praxis, Social Order, and Ethnomethodology's Legacies* (forthcoming with Oxford University Press), and writing a monograph co-authored with Jason Turowetz on the testing and diagnosis of Autism Spectrum Disorder (forthcoming with University of Chicago Press).

Lisa Mikesell is an Associate Professor in the Department of Communication and associate faculty at the Institute for Health, Health Care Policy and Aging Research at Rutgers University, USA. With a focus on neurological and psychiatric disorders, she studies practices of patient engagement in community and clinic contexts to provide an ecological lens on everyday functioning and person-centered communication.

Sarah Morris is a specialist speech and language therapist working for Worcestershire Health and Care NHS Trust, UK. She currently works in mainstream schools and a range of specialist settings including language class, special school and autism bases.

Francesco Possemato is a Research Associate in the Department of Linguistics at Macquarie University, Australia. His research addresses language and social interaction in a variety of contexts. Francesco completed his Ph.D. at the University of Sydney, exploring classroom interactions using Conversation Analysis. He is currently the project manager for the *Conversational Interaction in Aboriginal and Remote Australia* (CIARA) project led by Dr. Joe Blythe. Francesco is a principal investigator for the *Students Flourishing Through Italian Classroom Interaction* project (LaTrobe University), and is the organizer of the *Conversation Analysis in Sydney* (CAIS) group.

Julie Radford is an Associate Professor of special and inclusive education at UCL Institute of Education in London. Her research focuses on classroom and peer interactions with children who have special educational needs. She has published over 30 peer-reviewed papers and book chapters in this field. She has a special interest in topic management in classroom discourse and how repairs are organised. She is a co-author of *The Teaching Assistant's Guide to Effective Interaction*. Her most recent research project involved an intervention in 100 schools to improve the interactions of teaching assistants.

John P. Rae is a Reader in Psychology in the Department of Psychology, University of Roehampton, London. He has a B.A. in Philosophy and Psychology and a Ph.D. in Psychology, both from the University of Leeds. He is interested in how people use talk and visible action in social interaction.

Monica Ramey is a Psychology graduate from the University of Roehampton, UK, with an interest in teaching and supporting children and adults with Autism Spectrum Conditions. She has received a PG certificate in intellectual and developmental disabilities from the University of Kent and is currently working in a special needs school for children with autism in London.

Gitte Rasmussen is a Professor of Social Interaction in the Department of Language and Communication, University of Southern Denmark. Her research interests concern how people organize social activities and interactions and how they design their talk and visual actions in accordance with their assumptions about each other's knowledge.

Charlotta Saldert is a Professor of Speech and Language Therapy at the Institute of Neuroscience and Physiology, University of Gothenburg, Sweden. Her main area of research is interaction analysis of everyday communication including people with stroke-induced aphasia and progressive neurogenic communication disorders and their communication partners. Current research includes work on interactions and lived experiences of anomia in everyday communicative interaction including adults with more subtle neurogenic communicative difficulties.

Jason Turowetz is currently a Postdoctoral Fellow at Siegen University, Germany. His research interests include social theory, cultural sociology, race, and health and illness. His publications include "The interactional production of a clinical fact in a case of autism" (2015) and "Discovering culture in interaction: Solving problems in cultural sociology by recovering the interactional side of Parsons' conception of culture" (with Anne Rawls, 2019). He is currently working on a monograph on how clinicians assess/diagnose autism (with Doug Maynard, forthcoming with University of Chicago Press) and another monograph on the Milgram "obedience" experiments (with Matthew Hollander, forthcoming with Oxford University Press).

Chris Walton is a Lecturer in the Psychology department at Lancaster University, UK, and lectures on social psychology and qualitative research methods. He is a member of the Social Processes research group and he researches interactions in social and health care settings.

Ray Wilkinson is a Professor of Human Communication at the University of Sheffield, UK. He has a clinical background in speech and language therapy. His research interests focus on everyday social interaction, in particular where participants do not have the communicative resources available to neurotypical adult native language speakers.

Transcription Symbols

These are the main conversation analytic transcription symbols used within this volume.

Some chapters use, and provide descriptions of, additional symbols.

[[	⌈ ⌊	The simultaneous occurrence of one utterance or non-verbal action with another is marked by left-hand brackets at the point where the simultaneous occurrence begins
]]	⌉ ⌋	Right-hand brackets mark where the simultaneous occurrence or two or more utterances or non-verbal actions ceases
=		An equals sign marks where there is no interval between adjacent utterances
(0.5)		Silences are marked in seconds and tenths of seconds
(.)		A full stop in single brackets indicates an interval of around a tenth of a second within or between utterances
:		A colon indicates a prolongation of the immediately preceding sound (the more colons, the longer the prolongation)
.		A full stop indicates a stopping fall in tone
,		A comma indicates a 'continuing' intonation
?		A question mark indicates a rising inflection
!		An exclamation mark indicates an animated tone
↑ ↓		Upward or downward pointing arrows indicate marked rising or falling shifts in intonation respectively
hhh		'h's indicate discernable aspiration, sometimes laughter

.hhh	'h's preceded by a dot indicate discernable inhalation
£	The pound sterling sign indicates 'smiley voice'
WORD	Capital letters indicate talk that is spoken notably loudly compared to surrounding talk
°word°	Degree signs surround talk which is spoken more quietly than surrounding talk
word	Underlining indicates emphasis
>word<	The 'greater than' sign first indicates talk that is produced at a faster speed than surrounding talk
<word>	The 'lesser than' sign first indicates talk that is produced at a slower speed than surrounding talk
word-	A dash indicates an abrupt cut off to a word or part of a word
(word)	Single brackets before and after talk indicate that the transcriber is unsure if this is what was said
( )	Single brackets with no talk transcribed within indicate that the transcriber was unable to produce even a best guess at what was said
(( ))	Double brackets before and after text indicate that this text is the transcriber's description of something in the interaction

List of Figures

List of Tables

1

Atypical Interaction: An Introduction

Ray Wilkinson, John P. Rae and Gitte Rasmussen

Talking with others is central to many areas of daily living, including one's professional, educational, family or social life, and for most people this ability to talk is a taken-for-granted competence. Many individuals, however, have an atypical capacity for talking within everyday social interactions. This book contains a collection of empirical studies of 'atypical interaction', that is naturally-occurring conversation or other forms of social interaction where at least one of the participants has a

R. Wilkinson (✉)
Department of Human Communication Sciences,
University of Sheffield, Sheffield, UK

J. P. Rae
Department of Psychology, University of Roehampton, London, UK

G. Rasmussen
Department of Language and Communication,
University of Southern Denmark, Odense, Denmark

© The Author(s) 2020
R. Wilkinson et al. (eds.), *Atypical Interaction*,
https://doi.org/10.1007/978-3-030-28799-3_1

communicative impairment which impacts upon the interaction. These impairments are linked to particular conditions or disabilities, including (to mention those in this collection) autism spectrum disorder, learning disability, schizophrenia, dementia, aphasia, developmental language difficulty, stammering, dysarthria or hearing impairment.[1]

Much of what we know about people with these conditions and disabilities comes from a long tradition within medical and psychological practice of testing them in various ways, particularly using formal assessments (e.g. Goodglass et al. 2001; Lord et al. 2012). By highlighting and focusing on the impairments and on what those taking part in the tests cannot do, or find difficult to do, such testing can be useful in a number of ways. These include diagnosing the presence of the condition (e.g. aphasia) and the type of condition (e.g. Broca's aphasia), highlighting deficits in order to target treatment, and allowing for re-testing, for example following treatment, to capture possible change. Another set of methods used in the assessment/investigation of people with these conditions involves the use of interviews or questionnaires, where the

[1]A note on terminology. The field of communicative impairments/communication disorders is one which has been the focus of attention from a number of different disciplines, with medicine (including psychiatry), psychology (including neuropsychology, clinical psychology and developmental psychology), linguistics, and speech pathology and therapy being among those which have had most influence on the field. While social science perspectives, such as that in the current volume, have perhaps been less in evidence historically, this has changed somewhat in recent years, with, for example, the social model of disability (Shakespeare 1998) becoming influential. Overall, therefore, there is a wide range of perspectives and terminology within the field. The approach in this volume is primarily a descriptive one, aiming to capture aspects of the talk and other interactional conduct of the participants in these interactions, while at the same time retaining an awareness that at least one of the participants has a particular condition or conditions which are impacting on their talk and/or conduct. In the vast majority of cases, these conditions will have been assessed or diagnosed by a medical or other professional. The interactions here are 'atypical' in that they display differences in systematic ways to the practices that have been described by conversation analysts in relation to 'typical' interaction (i.e. here, in people without communicative impairments). We use the term 'impairment' to refer to aspects of the condition which impact on talk and interaction. These can be, for example, linguistic, cognitive, motor or sensory in nature and are often only evident in mundane interaction through their impact on talk or conduct. The term is not used here in the sense of the talk/conduct being 'impaired'. To take one example: the use of sign language is 'atypical' in that its use of the visual-manual channel as the primary mode of communication makes it different from spoken talk, the most common form of human face-to-face communication, which uses the auditory-vocal channel. While sign language is by no means an 'impaired' form of communication, it can be used when the person has a hearing impairment (see Girard-Groeber, this volume).

person affected, or those with knowledge of them such as family members, are asked for their perspectives on the condition and its impact (e.g. Hilari et al. 2003; Lee et al. 2008).

The research studies within this book provide analyses of data which were collected neither through eliciting linguistic or other communicative behaviour via testing, nor through eliciting some form of personal report via interview or questionnaire. Rather the data are of social interactions which were (a) recorded—usually video-recorded—within everyday settings such as the home, care home, the street or the classroom; (b) generally do not include the researcher; and (c) would typically have occurred even if they were not being recorded (i.e. they are 'naturally-occurring' and do not, for example, contain any pre-arranged topics suggested by the researcher).[2]

Until around 30 years ago there was very little naturalistic observational research published on how people with communicative impairments actually communicated within their everyday life environments and how social interactions involving these participants differed in systematic ways from those of 'typical' participants (i.e. without communicative impairments). For example, in a pioneering 1982 observational study of people with aphasia (a language disorder acquired following brain damage) in family interactions at home and in other daily settings, the author was able to remark that while 'systematic field observation' was used in many areas of social and behavioural science, including in studies of language acquisition, it was 'used less in the study of language problems, and few if any studies exist of language problems and communication usage in natural environments. To my knowledge, no published observational studies of aphasic patients' natural communication are currently available' (Holland 1982, p. 50).

Holland's study used trained observers who were present when the interactions were taking place and who used a set of pre-determined categories to guide their observations, which they made in real-time. One development since the time of Holland's study has been that recording devices, including video-recording devices, have become far

[2]This is not to deny the risk of the interaction being affected in some manner by the participants' awareness of being recorded i.e. the 'observer's paradox' (Labov 1972). For some ways in which this type of research attempts to overcome, or at least minimize, these risks see Goodwin (1993).

easier for the researcher to access and use, and the studies in this collection draw upon (often extensive) sets of recordings of people with communicative impairments within everyday social interactions. These recordings can be made in various ways, with common methods including the researcher either leaving the recording device (sometimes over a number of weeks) with the participants in order that they can record themselves, or remaining within the same space as the participants during the recording but typically not being part of the interaction (for example, following the participants around while video-recording them). Recordings have some obvious advantages compared to real-time observational note-taking and scoring, including the fact that they provide a record of the 'raw data' for the researcher to repeatedly return to and use, and for others to potentially access and examine.

Another development over this period is that more powerful analytic tools and methodologies have been applied within studies of atypical participants' social interaction. One such approach has been that of systemic functional linguistics (Eggins 1994) which has been applied to a number of communication disorders (e.g. Togher and Hand 1998). Other developments (e.g. Angeleri et al. 2008) have drawn on work within the field of linguistic pragmatics, including speech act theory (Searle 1969) and Grice's (1989) maxims of conversation. All the studies in this collection, however, draw on a different and distinctive approach to social interaction which has been increasingly applied over the last 25 years to the talk and social interaction of people with communicative impairments: that of Conversation Analysis (henceforth, CA) (Clift 2016).

In the following section we will provide a brief introduction to CA. Following this, by way of introducing each of the chapters in the book, we will outline some of the main themes and findings of research carried out over the last couple of decades that has used CA to investigate the impact of different types of communicative impairment within social interaction. In the final section of this Introduction we discuss the status of atypical interaction as an area of study, including what we see at this stage in its development as its main contributions to the fields of (1) communication disorder research, and (2) conversation analytic research, as well as how it may develop in the future.

Conversation Analysis

CA emerged during the 1960s and 1970s, primarily through the work of Harvey Sacks in collaboration with his colleagues Emanuel Schegloff and Gail Jefferson. The development of CA was influenced by particular strands within American sociology at the time, in particular Garfinkel's (1967) work on Ethnomethodology and Goffman's (1964) research into what he came to term the 'Interaction Order'.[3]

CA examines talk and other aspects of conduct within naturally occurring social interaction in general and conversation in particular. It does so based on close analysis of recordings (audio or video) of social interactions, and relatively detailed transcriptions of those interactions, making use of a transcription system originally developed by Gail Jefferson (see Jefferson 2004). A distinction (although not necessarily always a rigid one) is drawn between conversation (involving friends, family members, colleagues, strangers and so on) and other types of social interaction, including forms of 'institutional interaction' (Drew and Heritage 1992), such as those between doctors and patients or teachers and pupils.[4] Conversation constitutes the basic speech-exchange system and the form of interaction within which talk developed, both ontogenetically and phylogenetically (Schegloff 2006).

CA aims to uncover the 'machinery' of interaction, that is the structural organizations of practice that participants within a social interaction draw upon (with various levels of conscious awareness) in order to produce talk and other conduct that is perceived as meaningful, coherent and orderly (Heritage 1984). In particular, there is a focus on how talk and other resources (such as gesture, gaze and other aspects of body movement) are drawn upon by participants to produce talk and conduct which are recognizable by recipients as particular actions (such as requesting, offering, directing, informing, complaining, questioning etc.).

[3]For further details of the development of CA, see Schegloff (1992a).

[4]The term 'talk-in-interaction' is used to refer to talk within social interaction generally, thus including both conversation and institutional interaction (Schegloff 2007).

Some of the organizations of practice that CA focuses on and which are particularly examined in the analyses in this collection include:

Turn organization and turn-taking organization: for example, the practices involved in how turns-at-talk, and the turn-constructional units (TCUs) that make them up, are progressively produced item-by-item, and how turns are exchanged between participants, typically with little gap or overlap (Schegloff 1996; Sacks et al. 1974).

Sequence organization: for example, how successive actions can be formed up to constitute a course of action, with common forms being adjacency pairs (Schegloff 2007) such as questions-answer sequences or greeting-greeting sequences.

Overall structural organization: for example, how beginnings and endings of interactional events are structured and how this informs what might be placed there and how that will be understood by a recipient (Schegloff and Sacks 1973); how topics are launched, developed or closed down (Button and Casey 1984).

Repair organization: for example, the practices involved in highlighting and possibly resolving ('repairing') troubles in speaking, hearing or understanding (Schegloff et al. 1977).

In general, each of the chapters in the collection draws upon relevant conversation analytic work in order to highlight some of the ways in which the particular form of atypical interaction being analysed is distinctive or different to interactions involving typical speakers. As such, the relevant findings from CA work on typical speakers are included in each chapter. It may be useful at this point, however, to provide some more detail about repair organization in typical speakers since repair practices are a central theme in many atypical interaction studies, including several in this collection.

A distinction can be drawn between two aspects of repair activity: the initiation of repair and its outcome (i.e. the repair itself, or abandonment of the repair attempt). Repair activity deals with some trouble (or 'trouble source') in speaking, hearing or understanding of talk. Trouble sources need not necessarily be errors. Both initiation of repair and the repair itself can be produced by 'self' (the participant whose talk contains the trouble source) or 'other' (another participant). Self-initiation of repair can be concerned with certain repair operations such as the speaker searching for a word or replacing a word or bit of talk that they have previously produced. Other-initiation of repair often highlights some bit of talk produced by another participant (usually in the immediately prior turn) as something which the current speaker has had difficulty in hearing or understanding. Repair can also be launched to deal with misunderstandings in talk (termed 'third-position repair' and 'fourth-position repair': Schegloff 1992b).

There are a number of preferences that have been highlighted concerning repair.[5] For example, self-initiation of repair is preferred to other-initiation of repair (Schegloff 1979), and self-repair is preferred to other-repair (Schegloff et al. 1977). There is also a preference for progressivity in relation to repair activity; since all repair delays the current turn and/or sequence in which it occurs, there is an expectation that the repair activity should be completed quickly, such that the talk that was underway can then resume.

The Impact on Social Interaction of Particular Types of Communicative Impairment

Starting in the late 1970s and through the 1980s, a few isolated studies were published which used findings from CA's research on typical conversation to investigate the nature of social interactions involving people with communicative impairments.[6] Two groups to be investigated in these early studies were people with aphasia (Lubinski et al. 1980; Schienberg and Holland 1980) and people with a learning disability (Price-Williams and Sabsay 1979; Abbeduto and Rosenberg 1980; Yearley and Brewer 1989).

Around the mid-1990s, CA started to become established as a method for examining the interactions of people with communicative impairments and their interlocutors, with studies published on, among

[5]For an outline of conversation analytic work on 'preference' see Pomerantz and Heritage (2013).

[6]A related strand of ethnomethodologically-inspired work on communicative impairments and disability more generally should also be noted here. See, for example, work on interactions between children with severe learning disabilities and their family members (e.g. Pollner and McDonald-Wikler 1985; Goode 1994), and Robillard (1999) on the lived experience of motor neurone disease. For reflections on ethnomethodological studies of disability, see Goode (2003).

others, aphasia (Goodwin 1995), autism (Local and Wootton 1995), sign language (McIlvenny 1995), learning disability (Rapley and Antaki 1996) and people with cerebral palsy using augmentative and alternative communication (AAC) (Collins et al. 1997). Since that time there has been a rapid growth in the field, with many individual studies and collections of papers applying CA to particular types of communicative impairment. The collections include analyses of aphasia (Goodwin 2003), dementia (Mates et al. 2010), hearing impairment (Egbert and Deppermann 2012) and AAC (Norén et al. 2013).

The current volume is, however, the first set of conversation analytic studies which investigates communicative impairments from across the spectrum of types of atypical interaction, including both congenital/developmental disorders (i.e. occurring from birth or during development in childhood) and acquired disorders (occurring after the person has developed communication, often following brain damage). Forms of communicative impairment are discussed here within four main groupings (cognitive impairments, language impairments, fluency impairments, speech or hearing impairments). These groupings are not meant to be rigid or absolute, but rather are designed to allow some broad similarities and differences to be explored across them. In practice, the same type of communicative impairment can present quite differently in different people due to factors such as the severity of the impairments or changes over time (in developmental or degenerative conditions). It should also be noted that any individual can present with a range of different types of impairments (for example, someone with dementia may also have dysarthria and a hearing impairment).

The Impact of Cognitive Impairments on Social Interaction

Autism spectrum disorder, learning disability, schizophrenia and dementia are in many ways a heterogenous group of conditions, but speakers with these conditions (and others which are not able to be focused on in this volume due to reasons of space, such as traumatic brain injury) who present with communication difficulties are regularly described as having problems at the level of pragmatics i.e. the rules governing how language is *used* (Levinson 1983).[7] While the factors underlying these pragmatic difficulties and other features of these conditions are, in many cases, not yet well understood, it is typically considered the case that in these conditions cognitive functioning is generally in some manner impaired, with deficits in, for example, memory, attention or executive functions (e.g. Stopford et al. 2012).

Within social interaction, one common way in which these pragmatic difficulties present is in the form of atypical actions, where actions (such as questions or informings) or other conduct produced by people with these conditions may regularly be oriented to by co-participants as inapposite or inappropriate in some way (Wilkinson 2019; cf. Denman and Wilkinson 2011).

We will now present short summaries of each of the chapters in the book on these conditions, preceded by some brief descriptions of relevant previous conversation analytic work.

A number of pioneering case studies using CA to examine interactions involving children with *Autism Spectrum Disorder* (ASD) appeared in the 1990s and focused on echolalia, the tendency of some children with autism to produce utterances that reproduce expressions that they have previously heard (Local and Wootton 1995; Wootton 1999; Tarplee and Barrow 1999). In the last 20 years a large number of studies on a range of phenomena involving children with ASD have appeared. One focus has been on the distinctive capacities and competences of children with ASD (e.g., Muskett et al. 2010; Stribling et al. 2007; Sterponi et al. 2015). Another line of research has focused on clinical testing (e.g. Maynard and Turowetz 2017; Korkiakangas et al. 2016) or on ASD within medical settings (Solomon et al. 2016). A further line of research has examined the interactional provision of support for children with ASD (e.g. Stribling and Rae 2010). Whilst most of the research has focused on children with autism, the interactional use of formulas in an adult with ASD was examined by Dobbinson et al. (2003).

[7]While this difficulty with pragmatics appears to be a central feature of the communication problems of people with these conditions, in many cases other aspects of language (such as lexis and grammar) or speech may also be affected.

In this volume, **Maynard and Turowetz** examine encounters between people with autism and a person carrying out institutional responsibilities. More specifically, they focus on actions which the professional party interprets as unwarranted and problematic. Two cases are examined. First, an encounter between a young man with autism and a police officer in a public park; second an interaction between a nine-year old boy being assessed for autism by a clinical psychologist. In each case, video records of the interactions are examined in detail. Also, additional evidence in which the professional party talks about, or reports, what happened is analysed. The analysis proposes that the professional party's interpretation of the problematic action (attempting to run away from the police officer, not cooperating with a psychological assessment) arises from their particular understanding of sequencing of the unfolding actions and event. Thus, rather than seeing the young man's backing away as a response to the police officer's conduct, the police officer sees the young man engaging a new course of action—setting out to run away; rather than seeing the boy as resisting the psychologist's directives, the psychologist sees the boy as not cooperating with the test. A specific methodological feature of the analysis is that in addition to examining records of the interaction, other sources of evidence, such as the police officer's report are also considered.

By contrast, **Rae and Ramey** consider domestic interactions involving a child with autistic spectrum disorder (ASD). They present a case study of an extended episode in which Ben, a 12-year old boy with ASD and his father interact while using a construction kit. Drawing on multiple sequences from within this episode, they examine the interactional resources through which the father and son participate with each other. First, they show how the father makes use of directives to organize Ben's activities, and they delineate the supportive practices that the he draws on. In particular, they show how the directives are multimodal, that is they draw on talk, gestures and the use of objects, in order to facilitate Ben's ability to respond to them. They further examine how the father assists Ben in responding, for example by using prompts. Second, they examine how the father orients to situations that arise when Ben engages in other activities, some of which are apparently extraneous. They show how the father's responses to these activities are selective, on some occasions closing down these activities, or on other occasions co-participating with them. For example, there are two instances of father-son play that are initiated by Ben that are separate to the construction game.

Whilst most of the CA work on ASD has focused on children, most CA work on *learning disability* has tended to focus on adults. One concern here has been to draw on CA and related approaches in order to re-examine the notion of learning disability (notably, Rapley 2004). A further line of research has focused on the challenges to the autonomy of people with learning disabilities (e.g. Rapley and Antaki 1996; Jingree et al. 2006) and on the potential for personal assistants to provide support (Williams et al. 2010). Here, **Walton, Finlay, and Antaki** examine interactions between people with intellectual disability and members of staff in two residential settings and a day-care setting. The study delineates a range of challenges faced by people with intellectual disability in initiating interactions, maintaining and progressing interactions, and closing interactions. The analysis shows how the communicative competence of people with intellectual disability is not solely related to their capacities considered in isolation, but rather depends on the people with whom they are interacting. In particular, Walton et al. show how partners' reliance on conversational resources from typical interaction can lead to difficulties. For example, when a partner does not understand something said by a person with intellectual disability and initiates repair, this can pose a challenge. A further challenge which can intersect with this is that staff members often have a need to fulfill institutional agendas and may orient to these rather than to the person with intellectual disability's immediate interactional concerns. Walton et al. suggest that the atypicality of these interactions is thus an interactional outcome.

Symptoms of *schizophrenia* can include hallucinations, delusions and confused thought patterns. Much of the previous conversation analytic work in this area has been focused on clinical interactions involving people with schizophrenia, including their engagement in clinical consultations (McCabe et al. 2002), the understanding of others' mental processes within clinical interactions (McCabe et al. 2004) and the effects of psychiatrists' questions on the therapeutic alliance (Thompson et al. 2016). In contrast, **Mikesell** presents a single case analysis of a person with schizophrenia engaging in his daily activities. The participant, Kevin, a 49 year old man, was recorded for a total of 15 hours in the course of a study that aimed to draw on video ethnography to assess neurocognitive and functional measures of psychological functioning. The study examines a particular utterance used by Kevin, "like I say", and presents his in situ usage of this expression in interactions with the recording ethnographers. "Like I say" is a cohesion marker which speakers commonly use to address the relationship between something that they are about to say and something that they have said previously. Kevin uses this expression with atypical frequency. Nevertheless, Mikesell shows that, when examined in context, his use of this is expression is sensitive to the real-world settings in which he is speaking. Mikesell's analysis thereby has implications for how we understand practices that appear to be atypical, as well as for the linguistic analysis of cohesion.

There are various forms of *dementia*, including Alzheimer's disease, frontotemporal dementia, vascular dementia and dementia with Lewy bodies. CA research carried out on specific types of dementia includes that by Kitzinger and Jones (2007) and Jones (2015) on Alzheimer's disease, Mikesell (2009) and Kindell et al. (2013) on sub-types of frontotemporal dementia, and Lindholm (2015) on vascular dementia. Much of the CA work in this area discusses how particular features of dementia, such as memory problems or confabulations, may impact on conversation and how interlocutors may respond to these impacts.

Rasmussen's chapter presents a single-case analysis of episodes in which Nancy, a 90-year-old woman with severe dementia, breaks into a song during the course of an interaction with Rita, a visiting researcher. Rasmussen discusses previous research concerning how persons with dementia or other memory disorders may show a capacity to perform previously well-learned activities, such as playing musical pieces. A distinctive feature of Rasmussen's analysis is her demonstration of how Nancy's singing is apparently responsive to the immediate interactional setting in which it occurs. She shows that there is relationship between the lyrics of the song and something that was said in the immediately prior talk. The previously-learned song thereby serves as resource for making an interactional contribution. Rasmussen further examines how Rita joins in singing the song and how the song thereby becomes a resource of interacting together. Rasmussen suggests that, in focusing on capacities retained by a person with dementia rather than on what they have lost, singing might be an important ability.

Elsey focuses on interactions recorded in a memory clinic as part of a larger study which aimed to explore how the patients' underlying condition might manifest itself in their talk. His chapter focuses on history-taking encounters. These involve a neurologist, the patient and an accompanying person who is commonly a relative of the patient. Whilst the neurologist's questions are generally addressed to the patient, these are triadic interactions in which, for example, the accompanying person occasionally disagrees with something that the patient says about themselves. The details revealed in these disagreements can be consequential for the neurologist's diagnosis. In examining sequences in which such disagreements occur, Elsey points out that one feature of these settings is a practical dilemma for the accompanying person; on the one hand they show a concern with seeking to ensure that their relative's difficulties are fully represented to the neurologist, while at the same time they face the challenge of doing this in a way that risks challenging their relative's own account.

The Impact of Language Impairments on Social Interaction

Aphasia is an acquired language disorder which occurs following brain damage, commonly caused by stroke (Sarno 1998). Developmental language disorders first present in childhood though in more severe cases impacts can remain into adolescence or beyond (St. Clair et al. 2011). In both acquired and developmental language disorders, the deficits primarily concern the linguistic system, with, for example, lexical or grammatical abilities impaired. Reading and writing can be affected as well as spoken language and the understanding of others' spoken language.

CA studies of aphasia have highlighted how the linguistic impairments associated with the condition can result in repair activity which is both more frequently initiated and, once initiated, more prolonged than in typical interaction (Wilkinson et al. 2003). One common form of repair is repair which is self-initiated by the person with aphasia, often either in the form of a word search or in an attempt to replace an error (Helasvuo et al. 2004). Another common form is other-initiation of repair (for example in the form of an understanding check) produced by an interlocutor as a result of the PWA's turn being difficult to comprehend due, for example, to its compacted agrammatic form (Heeschen and Schegloff 1999; see also Goodwin 1995).

CA-based research has also highlighted how people with aphasia and/or their interlocutors can adapt their talk and conduct in systematic ways which regularly result in the person with aphasia's message being articulated with less repair and other forms of disruption or delay than would otherwise be the case. As such, conversations may be organized in ways that differ from the organizational patterns of ordinary social interaction. So, for instance, actions or turns that might be produced by a typical speaker are, in the case of aphasia, systematically co-constructed by two or more speakers. One form this can take is adapted forms of turn-construction by the speaker with aphasia, including some, such as telegraphic speech in non-fluent aphasia, which may prompt adaptation by the interlocutor in the form of co-construction of what the person with aphasia was attempting to convey (Heeschen and Schegloff 2003). In producing their contributions to the interaction, the person with aphasia may also make significant use of resources such as gestures, gaze and body movements, as well as resources within the local environment, such as objects and pictures. These may be used in various ways and in various combinations, including simultaneously with talk (or, at least, vocalisation) to allow the person with aphasia to convey what they wish to communicate (Goodwin 2000; Wilkinson et al. 2010; Rasmussen 2017).

The chapter in this collection by **Barnes and Possemato** analyses how familiar conversation partners of speakers with aphasia attempt to scaffold the production of the speaker with aphasia through the use of test questions and designedly incomplete utterances (DIUs). The test questions elicit noun phrases which the co-participants work towards saying subsequently. Barnes and Possemato's study shows how test questions are regularly followed by DIUs which aim at isolating the correctable items. The DIUs are designed to elicit responses, and, as such, are used to construct individual TCUs across turns and speakers. Finally, the conversation partner regularly repeats the item following its production, especially when solicited through the use of DIUs. Barnes and Possemato note that, in one way, test questions and DIUs can be seen as supportive of the talk of the person with aphasia since they provide resources for production of the TCU. At the same time, however, they create a highly constrained sequential environment for the speakers with aphasia, which makes failures visible and accountable. In the light of these findings, Barnes and Possemato suggest that these practices might be more fruitfully explored in terms of issues concerning 'agency' rather than that of 'pedagogy'.

Laakso pursues her previous work on repair organization as she interestingly compares sequences of repair in different times and circumstances of life, i.e. when individuals are becoming fully competent in language use and when they have lost some of their previous competence due to brain injury. The chapter analyses how children and parents organize repair of troubles in talk produced by the children in early stages of their language development, i.e. between 1 and 3 years, as well as repair organization in interactions between speakers with aphasia and family members or speech and language pathologists. The study demonstrates a parents' continuum from co-constructing the child's talk to initiating repair on it, and how parents' behaviour relates to the child's stage of language development and probably serves to enhance it. By comparison, speakers with aphasia indicate awareness of their problems and initiate self-repair operations on it. Indications of problems with completing the repair make it relevant for conversational partners to, for example, complete word searches, offer candidate understandings or even correct errors, thus orienting to the progressivity of the interaction. This is supported by the speaker with aphasia who confirms the conversational partner's contribution rather than, for example, repeating it as does the child who is engaged in language learning.

Compared to CA-based studies on aphasia in interaction, studies involving children with *developmental language disorders* in interaction are relatively few in number. Tykkyläinen (2010) investigated how children initiated repair of problems in interactions with speech-and language therapists that stemmed from hearing, attention, or understanding difficulties. By comparison, typically-developing children's repair targeted processes of task-solving (Tykkyläinen 2010). In another study of the ability to initiate repair, Merrison and Merrison (2005) found that children with developmental language (pragmatic) disorders were less skilled in initiating repair, as compared to a mainstream group of children. Finally, a single-case study (Rasmussen 2013) of a training session between a speech and language therapist (SLT) and a boy with severe language impairments showed how the boy engaged in training and learning signs to support language development. The training was based on a story about his whereabouts during the weekend which his foster mother had described in a letter to the SLT. The boy oriented towards the SLT's repairs on his signs, thus accepting them as appropriate expressions, whereas he resisted repairs that resulted in a description of his experiences that he did not agree with.

Radford examines classroom interactions involving teachers and children with specific speech, language and communication needs (SLCN). She points out that classroom talk involves characteristic asymmetries in the teachers' and students' authority, that is, their rights or entitlement to speak. Yet Radford suggests that it is particularly desirable for teachers to increase the authority of SLCN children. Her analysis considers data arising from two classroom activities. In one task, the topics of talk concerned picture books or exercise books with pictures of personal interests. In another task, the topics of talk concerned the children's audio-recorded ideas for writing a story together, or picture boards for writing individual stories. Radford examines two interactional practices. First, the ways in which opportunities for talking within these tasks are created for, or by, these children; second, how troubles, for example phonological or grammatical errors in their talk, are addressed. Radford shows how the interactional practices for identifying topics to talk about in the classroom tasks are related to those that have been identified through previous CA studies on conversation. Teachers may, for example, use *topic initial elicitors* which invite the child to identify a topic, or *itemised news enquiries* which ask the child about a specific issue. On the other hand, children may use *news announcements* to propose a topic. With respect to the correction of problems in children's talk, Radford shows how different practices used by the teachers are responded to differently by the children. Radford's study contributes to discussions of how CA may be used to study language development (see also Samuelsson 2009) with the purpose of developing intervention programmes and strategies.

The Impact of Fluency Impairments on Social Interaction

The most researched type of fluency impairment is *stammering* (or 'stuttering' as it commonly referred to in many parts of the world). Stammering most commonly begins in childhood, and common symptoms include prolongations and repetitions of sounds, and 'blocks' where the speaker has difficulty in producing the next due sound or item (Guitar 2013). Compared to other forms of communicative impairment, there has, however, been relatively little conversation analytic research into the impact of stammering on social interaction. Published work in this area includes Tetnowski and Damico (2001), Acton (2004), and Lind and Sønsterud (2014).

From research so far it appears clear that an important focus of analysis concerns how stammering impacts on the turn-at-talk and what the interactional risks or consequences of this impact might be. Tetnowski and Damico (2001), for example, highlight two interactional methods (one used by the person who stammers, and one by the conversation partner) which appear to be used within interaction to mitigate the possible risk of the person who stammers losing their turn when dysfluent. In the case of one dyad within their data, Tetnowski and Damico (2001) note that the person who stammers regularly looks away from the recipient during dysfluency, and they suggest this behavior may be seen as a means of maintaining speakership and retaining the turn at a point where the turn is vulnerable to incursion by another participant. In another dyad they observed that the conversation partner would regularly produce various forms of recipient display at points in the talk when the speaker with a stammer was being dysfluent. They suggest this may be a method by which the interlocutor displays that they are maintaining 'recipient' mode and are not going to move into speakership and attempt to take the floor at these points when the turn of the person who stammers is potentially vulnerable to incursion.

The chapter by **Wilkinson and Morris** in the current volume shows that a primary impact of stammering is a disruption to the progress (Schegloff 2007) of the turn in general and to turn-constructional units (TCUs) (Sacks et al. 1974), such as sentences, in particular. There is a preference for progressivity in conversation (Schegloff 2007) which in relation to TCU production means that TCUs are expected to progress relatively smoothly item-by-item to completion (Lerner 1996). Stammering means that the TCUs of affected speakers will regularly not display this preferred form of TCU production. The disruption to progressivity can result in another participant entering the turn space of the person who stammers. One form this takes is the conversation partner producing a turn completion (cf. Lerner 1996). Another form is other-initiations of repair (Schegloff et al. 1977) by the conversation partner which are produced while the ongoing turn of the person who stammers is still ongoing and incomplete. This sequential positioning of other-initiation of repair is therefore different to that seen between typical speakers where the repair initiation regularly occurs not only following the hearable completion of the prior speaker's turn, but in addition is regularly withheld slightly beyond that completion point (Schegloff et al. 1977). As Wilkinson and Morris show in the phone calls they analyse, speakers may mention towards the start of the call that they stammer, and this self-presentation as someone who stammers generally appears to function to alert the call recipient (someone who does not know the caller) that the caller will need more time than a typical speaker would to produce their turn-at-talk.

The Impact of Speech Impairments or Hearing Impairments on Social Interaction

The speech impairment which has been most analysed using CA is *dysarthria* (sometimes termed 'anarthria' in severe cases). Dysarthria is a motor speech disorder (Freed 2000) which can be present in childhood (linked to conditions such as cerebral palsy), or can be acquired at some point during the lifecycle (following a stroke or as part of degenerative conditions such as Parkinson's disease or motor neurone disease). Damage to the nervous system can impact on one of more of the speech subsystems of respiration, phonation, resonance and articulation, impacting on the ability to produce speech which is intelligible and/or of normal speed. The main forms of *hearing impairment* are sensori-neural hearing loss, where there is damage to the auditory nerve and/or inner ear, and conductive hearing loss, where some condition interferes with sound passing from the outer to the inner ear (Sataloff and Sataloff 2005).

Conversation analytic work on interactions involving participants with dysarthria or with a hearing impairment has highlighted that in each case a major way in which the impairment can be seen to impact on the interaction is in the form of other-initiations of repair (Schegloff et al. 1977), disrupting the progressivity of a series or sequence of turns. In the case of dysarthria, a recurrent feature of interactions is that the recipient may produce an other-initiation of repair in order to try to understand what the person with dysarthria has said (Bloch and Wilkinson 2009). In hearing impairment interactions, the difficulty in hearing what the other person has said may result in an other-initiation of repair, with open-class other-initiations of repair (Drew 1997), such as 'pardon?' being common (Pajo 2013).

In this volume, the chapters by Bloch and Saldert on dysarthria, and Ekberg, Hickson and Lind on hearing impairment each provide further evidence about the nature of other-initiations of repair in these atypical interactions. **Bloch and Saldert's** chapter focuses on an aspect of talk that appears to be a relatively common form of trouble source in the conversation of people with dysarthria i.e. names. One reason they suggest for this is that even when recipients of talk by people with dysarthria are having trouble in making sense of something the person with dysarthria has said, they may be able to use the context to predict or otherwise interpret the problematic item(s). Names may be an element of talk that are more problematic in this regard since their relative uniqueness makes them less predictable from the context, and the recipient therefore has to rely more on phonetic decoding to make sense of them. Bloch and Saldert display some of the ways in which names may create difficulties for the recipient in making sense of the name and also the turn within which it occurs. These range from a quite simple checking of the name, to more complex instances where, for example, trouble with understanding the name, or that the linguistic item is a name, is tied up with understanding other aspects of the turn in which the name occurs, such as what action it is carrying out. **Ekberg, Hickson and Lind** analyse how in the environment of people with hearing impairment producing other-initiations of repair to indicate difficulty in hearing an interlocutor's talk, the responsibility for that trouble may be negotiated. While it could be assumed that both participants might treat the hearing-impaired participant as bearing responsibility for the breakdown because of their hearing difficulty, in practice there is regularly a more subtle negotiation of responsibility. The person with the hearing impairment may, for example, display in their talk that they are holding the other participant responsible for not sufficiently adapting their talk (and consequently, for example, speaking too fast or not speaking loudly enough). In their data of interactions between people with hearing impairments and audiologists, Ekberg et al. show that in this situation the audiologists regularly respond by subsequently adapting their talk accordingly, thus implicitly taking some responsibility for the trouble. In contrast, in their data from conversations between people with hearing impairment and familiar conversation partners, the partners less commonly adapted their subsequent talk and thus did not so clearly assume responsibility for the trouble. Ekberg et al.'s chapter is important in highlighting how participants in interaction can display an assumption, at least in some cases, that it is an ongoing responsibility of the interlocutors to adapt their talk and conduct in order to mitigate the possible impact of the communicative impairment on the interaction. It is also important for showing how repair can raise particular issues for the moment-to-moment relationship between the participants within atypical interaction.

Another feature that dysarthria and hearing impairment have in common is that in the case of more severe forms of impairment, the participants may rely partially or largely on other modes of communication that make significant use of the visual-manual channel. In cases of severe hearing impairment and deafness, for example, a participant may use sign language. In cases of severe dysarthria, the participant may use some form of alternative and augmentative communication (AAC), such as a voice output communication aid (VOCA) whereby the participant can, for example, choose letters or symbols in order for the device to produce electronic speech. There have been conversation analytic studies of both these forms of interaction, each of which shows marked differences to typical talk-in-interaction. Wilkinson et al. (2011), for example, note that the use of VOCA devices structurally separates out the participation roles (Goffman 1979) of the 'author' of the message, who has selected the words (the person with dysarthria) and the 'animator' of the message, by which means those words are physically produced (the VOCA device), with implications for aspects of the interaction such as eye gaze. For example, both participants may regularly be gazing at the VOCA during message preparation and output. CA research on sign language has focused largely on how signed turns in many ways appear to function similarly to spoken turns-at-talk, such as orienting to the 'one-party-at-a-time' rule (McCleary and Leite 2013). At the same time, there are some features which are distinctive to the visuo-spatial aspects of sign language, such as the importance of having a recipient's eye gaze in order to successfully self-select to take a turn within the interaction.

In this volume, **Auer, Bauer, and Hörmeyer** provide an analysis of interactions involving (1) participants with dysarthria/anarthria using AAC, and (2) people with aphasia. Drawing on Goffman's (1979) work on participation roles, they show how, in each case, the participant with the communicative impairment can still retain the role of the principal (Goffman 1979) of the utterance, being held responsible by others as a social actor who is conveying something within the interaction. This is even the case when the participant is significantly compromised by their communicative impairment in fulfilling the roles of author or animator of their message, with an interlocutor having, for example, to provide a significant amount of communicative assistance in an effort to co-construct what the atypical communicator was trying to convey. Auer et al's chapter is important in drawing out similarities in the interactional impact of different forms of communicative impairment and in highlighting how the (at least partial) success of the conversation relies on participants adapting their interactional conduct and co-constructing the interactional contributions of the participant with the communicative impairment.

Girard-Groeber explores the interactional practices of school students with prelingual hearing loss who are fluent in a signed language and a spoken language and are thus bilingual and bimodal. In their school, these students take classes where the medium of instruction is nominally exclusively one of these languages. Focusing on the design of repair initiations, Groeber examines interaction in these two settings. Drawing on recent conversation analytic cross-language comparative work on the initiation of repair (Dingemanse et al. 2015), she first presents an analysis of the distribution of instances of restricted and unrestricted other-initiations of repair in the two classroom settings. The analysis suggests that whilst these two types are roughly equally distributed in the signed language setting, unrestricted types are more common that restricted types in the spoken language setting. However, Girard-Groeber cautions against concluding that the use of repair resources are simply determined by the setting. She presents a detailed interaction analysis of repair sequences involving finger-spelling, a practice drawn from sign language, showing how these bilingual-bimodal students can creatively combine different linguistic resources in order to address specific interactional contingencies.

The Field of Atypical Interaction

We noted above that there has been a rapid growth over the last 25 years or so in CA investigations of the impact within social interaction of particular communicative impairments, such as those associated with autism, aphasia, dementia and so on. The chapters in this collection add to our knowledge in these areas, focused as they are, on the whole, with one of these types of communicative impairment or communication disorder. While such work will and should continue, research in this area has now reached a stage where it is possible to gain some overview of 'atypical interaction' as a field and to start to highlight some generic aspects of how communicative impairments impact on social interaction. The chapter by Auer, Bauer and Hörmeyer in the present collection takes one step in this direction in comparing participation roles (principal, author and animator) in interactions involving people with aphasia and with anarthria (severe dysarthria).[8] As such, as well as gaining insight into the recurrent interactional features of particular forms of atypical interaction, we are now in a position where it is possible to start to compare these different forms of atypical interaction to each other in order to highlight similarities and differences between them and, more generally, to uncover features of atypical interaction as a distinct form of talk-in-interaction.

An aspect of talk-in-interaction that is evident across many different forms of atypical interaction is that there are *delays in progressivity* in the interaction, often in the form of participants' practices concerned with highlighting and attempting to resolve trouble sources and other kinds of difficulties in talk. Many of these trouble sources and difficulties can be seen to be linked to the presence of communicative impairments.[9]

In the case of many types of atypical interaction, there are distinct patterns of delayed progressivity that recur across different speakers and conversations and that can be seen to be linked to the particular form of communicative impairment(s) present. One way of exploring these patterns is in terms of which position within the 'repair initiation opportunity space' repair is initiated from in relation to the trouble source that it is targeting (see Schegloff 1992b). For example, the impact on talk of certain types of communicative impairment will recurrently take the form *of first position repair initiations* (i.e. self-initiation of repair, typically in the same turn as the trouble source). People with aphasia who have anomia (a difficulty 'accessing' lexical items), for example, will regularly display word searches in their talk. Thus in these cases it is the participant with the communicative impairment (in this instance, aphasia)

---

[8]For other CA investigations which examine particular interactional practices in both aphasia and dysarthria see Bloch and Beeke (2008) and Wilkinson et al. (2011).

[9]It is important to keep in mind that not every trouble source in the talk of people with communicative impairments will necessarily be linked to those impairments (cf. Schegloff 2003). As is evident in the talk of typical speakers, repair can be initiated for a number of reasons, not all of which are to do with errors or infelicities in talk (Schegloff et al. 1977).

who themselves first highlights the problem and launches an attempt to resolve it (see Laakso, this volume). Another way to view this is that in such cases *the delay to progressivity is first occurring at the level of the TCU (here, of the participant with the communicative impairment)*. While the dysfluencies linked to stammering are rather different to the word searches of a speaker with anomia, they share a similarity in that in the first instance they delay the progressivity of the TCU of the person with the communicative impairment (Wilkinson and Morris, this volume).

This is in contrast to conversations involving people with dysarthria or with hearing impairment. In both these cases, the communicative impairments regularly lead to a pattern of other-initiations of repair (i.e. *second position repair initiations*) within talk-in-interaction (Bloch and Wilkinson 2009; Pajo 2013). In the case of dysarthria, these other-initiations of repair are commonly produced by the interlocutor to display a problem in understanding, or otherwise making sense of, the talk of the person with dysarthria (Bloch and Saldert, this volume). In the case of hearing impairment, repair is initiated by the person with the hearing impairment, treating a prior turn of the interlocutor as a source of trouble (Ekberg, Hickson and Lind, this volume).[10] In these cases, *the delay to progressivity is occurring at the level of the sequence or the series of turns*, with what might have been the next due turn delayed by the other-initiation of repair. Turning to a different kind of problem in interaction (and a different type of action for dealing with that problem), a co-participant may treat some aspect of the talk or conduct of the person with a communicative impairment as inappropriate or inapposite. This has been described, for example, in the case of a person with traumatic brain injury (TBI) (Denman and Wilkinson 2011) where the person with TBI's touching of a co-participant was treated by that co-participant as inappropriate (see also Maynard and Turowetz, this volume). More generally, it may be a feature of interactions where a participant has some pragmatic difficulty linked to a cognitive impairment.

[10] The talk of speakers with non-fluent aphasia (Kent 2004) can also regularly be treated as a trouble through an interlocutor producing an other-initiation of repair (e.g. Heeschen and Schegloff 1999).

As with other-initiations of repair, the type of sequence seen here is a retro-sequence (Schegloff 2007), with the action (such as a complaint) being produced in relation to an earlier turn and delaying some other action that may have occurred instead in that 'next turn' slot.

As well as delays in progressivity, another feature that is evident across many forms of atypical interaction is adaptation i.e. that one or more of the participants will adopt particular ways of talking or conducting themselves that appear to be part of attempts to cope with, or lessen, the impact of the impairments within interaction (see, for example, Rasmussen, this volume).[11] This can include, for example, the use of *practices of turn construction* by the person with the communicative impairment that differ from those used by typical participants in comparable environments. People with communicative impairments may rely on *indexical* resources such as pointing (and see, relatedly, Mikesell's chapter in this volume on the use of the cohesive marker 'like I say') or *iconic* resources such as iconic gesture or enactment. For example, both people with aphasia (Wilkinson et al. 2010) and people with dementia (Kindell et al. 2013) have been shown to make recurrent use of enactment in the form of combinations of direct reported speech and gesture/body movement (among other resources) to iconically depict an action or aspects of an event rather than relying primarily on verbal description. This use of depiction rather than description, (of 'showing' as opposed to 'telling'), whether in the form of iconic gesture or enactment can be seen to be a useful resource for turn construction in the case of these speakers in that it allows for the conveying of often relatively complex information while making use of limited linguistic resources. In other cases, the adaptive methods of communication adopted will be ones that have been more formally taught or introduced, such as the use of sign language by people with severe hearing impairment (see Girard-Groeber, this volume) or AAC devices by people with dysarthria (see Auer, Bauer and, Hörmeyer, this volume).

[11]It appears that these ways of talking and conducting oneself are not always consciously adopted by the participants (Heeschen and Schegloff 1999).

In atypical interaction, the interlocutor may recurrently be actively involved in co-constructing what the person with the communicative impairment is attempting to convey or in other ways acting to clarify what the person means (Goodwin 1995; Heeschen and Schegloff 1999). This feature of atypical interaction is evident in many of the chapters in this volume, including, for example, that by Auer, Bauer and Hörmeyer in relation to both interactions involving people with aphasia and also people with dysarthria (and see also Bloch and Beeke, 2008). Instances of adaptation by the interlocutor are often in some manner a response to adapted practices of talk or conduct adopted by the person with the communicative impairment (Heeschen and Schegloff 1999; Bloch 2005). As Heeschen and Schegloff (2003, p. 268) note, adaptation can often be a 'mutual phenomenon'. A recurrent feature of atypical interaction, then, is that *what might be achieved by a typical speaker alone is in atypical interaction regularly achieved by means of collaboration between the person with the communicative impairment and an interlocutor.*

In conclusion, we can briefly consider where the field of atypical interaction sits in relation to (1) other communication disorder research and practice, and (2) other CA research.

For communication disorder research:

- the application of CA provides a novel, *interaction-focused*, perspective, analysing the conversation/interaction as a social event which is the product of the concerted collaborative work of all the participants. This is in contrast to most other approaches within the field which generally adopt a more individual-focused approach, such as assessing the person within a clinic or laboratory setting.
- What is atypical about particular types of atypical interaction can be uncovered empirically through a form of comparative analysis (Drew and Heritage 1992), drawing on CA's accumulated series of findings about the organizations of practice involved in typical talk-in-interaction.
- A CA approach allows for the analysis of how the speaker's communicative impairments impact on real-life, real-time talk-in-interaction. The analysis can focus on trouble and other kinds

of difficulties evident in the talk and how the participants deal with them, and also on practices of adaptation and collaborative interactional activity by the participants which may function to potentially lessen these impacts.

- The comparison of different types of communicative impairments and communication disorders can provide novel perspectives on similarities and differences between them. For example, while dysarthria and hearing impairment are in many ways quite distinct (for example, one being a problem relating to the production of talk and one being a problem relating to its reception) they show some similar features in relation to the way that trouble is recurrently highlighted and worked on (i.e. through other-initiation of repair).
- These forms of analysis have already led to a novel form of intervention ('interaction-focused intervention': Wilkinson 2014) which uses the findings from CA investigations as the basis for planning targets for intervention and comparing conversational actions and practices post-intervention.

For CA research:

- As with the analysis of interactions involving children (Kidwell 2013) and second language speakers (Gardner and Wagner 2005), the analysis of interactions involving people with communicative impairments presents the analyst with a form of interaction which differs from those involving adult native speakers without communicative impairments that have formed the basis for CA's findings about social interaction. How child, second language and atypical interactions display systematic similarities and differences as regards those of typical adult native speakers, as well as regards each other (see Laakso, this volume), is a focus for future work.
- While talk-in-interaction data involving people with communicative impairments can be used for 'applied conversation analysis' (Antaki 2011) in that CA can be used to shed light on the impact of communicative impairments on interactive talk, such data can also be used to contribute to findings about practices and actions in talk-in-interaction generally (Schegloff 2003; and see also Drew and Penn 2016).

- Atypical interactions, perhaps particularly those involving participants with cognitive impairments, can provide naturally-occurring instances of occasions when a participant (the person with the impairment) is not acting with regard to the background assumptions that all participants in an interaction typically trust to be shared between them (Garfinkel 1963, 1967) and which thus form the basis for a world shared in common (Maynard and Turowetz, this volume; and see also Rasmussen 2018, Rasmussen et al. 2019). As such, a feature of these types of data concerns their *social* nature and a focus of interest is how participants may socially interact together when this shared tacit knowledge cannot be assumed.
- Atypical interaction also provides the possibility of investigating the interface between talk-in-interaction and the neural, cognitive, motor and sensory structures and processes that are implicated in its successful, taken-for-granted, production and reception. By examining what happens when one or more of these structures or processes is impaired, it is possible to start to explore its role in typical talk-in-interaction.

It is issues such as these that are likely to be central to future work at the interface of conversation analytic and communication disorder research in the years ahead.

References

Abbeduto, L., & Rosenberg, S. (1980). The communicative competence of mildly retarded adults. *Applied Psycholinguistics, 1*(4), 405–426.

Acton, C. (2004). A conversation analytic perspective on stammering: Some reflections and observations. *Stammering Research, 1*(3), 249–270.

Angeleri, R., Bosco, F. M., Zettin, M., Sacco, K., Colle, L., & Bara, B. G. (2008). Communicative impairment in traumatic brain injury: A complete pragmatic assessment. *Brain and Language, 107*(3), 229–245.

Antaki, C. (2011). Six kinds of applied conversation analysis. In C. Antaki (Ed.), *Applied conversation analysis: Intervention and change in institutional talk* (pp. 1–14). Houndmills, Basingstoke and New York: Palgrave Macmillan.

Bloch, S. (2005). Co-constructing meaning in dysarthria: Word and letter repetition in the construction of turns. In K. Richards & P. Seedhouse (Eds.), *Applying conversation analysis* (pp. 38–55). Basingstoke: Palgrave Macmillan.
Bloch, S., & Beeke, S. (2008). Co-constructed talk in the conversations of people with dysarthria and aphasia. *Clinical Linguistics & Phonetics, 22*(12), 974–990.
Bloch, S., & Wilkinson, R. (2009). Acquired dysarthria in conversation: Identifying sources of understanding problems. *International Journal of Language and Communication Disorders, 44*(5), 769–783.
Button, G., & Casey, N. (1984). Generating topic: The use of topic initial elicitors. In J. M. Atkinson & J. Heritage (Eds.), *Structures of social action: Studies in conversation analysis* (pp. 167–190). Cambridge: Cambridge University Press.
Clift, R. (2016). *Conversation analysis.* Cambridge: Cambridge University Press.
Collins, S., Markova, I., & Murphy, J. (1997). Bringing conversations to a close: The management of closings in interactions between AAC users and 'natural' speakers. *Clinical Linguistics & Phonetics, 11*(6), 467–493.
Denman, A., & Wilkinson, R. (2011). Applying conversation analysis to traumatic brain injury: Investigating touching another person in everyday social interaction. *Disability and Rehabilitation, 33*(3), 243–252.
Dingemanse, M., Roberts, S. G., Baranova, J., Blythe, J., Drew, P., Floyd, S., et al. (2015). Universal principles in the repair of communication problems. *PLoS One, 10*(9), e0136100.
Dobbinson, S., Perkins, M., & Boucher, J. (2003). The interactional significance of formulas in autistic language. *Clinical Linguistics & Phonetics, 17*(4–5), 299–307.
Drew, P. (1997). 'Open' class repair initiators in response to sequential sources of trouble in conversation. *Journal of Pragmatics, 28,* 69–101.
Drew, P., & Heritage, J. (1992). Analyzing talk at work: An introduction. In P. Drew & J. Heritage (Eds.), *Talk at work* (pp. 3–65). Cambridge: Cambridge University Press.
Drew, P., & Penn, C. (2016). On failure to understand what the other is saying: Accountability, incongruity, and miscommunication. In J. D. Robinson (Ed.), *Accountability in social interaction* (pp. 47–72). New York: Oxford University Press.
Egbert, M., & Deppermann, A. (Eds.). (2012). *Hearing aids communication: Integrating social interaction, audiology and user centered design to improve communication with hearing loss and hearing technologies.* Mannheim: Verlag für Gesprächsforschung.

Eggins, S. (1994). *An introduction to systemic functional linguistics*. London: Pinter.
Freed, D. (2000). *Motor speech disorders: Diagnosis & treatment*. San Diego, CA: Singular.
Gardner, R., & Wagner, J. (Eds.). (2005). *Second language conversations*. London: Continuum.
Garfinkel, H. (1963). A conception and experiments with "trust" as a condition of stable concerted actions. In O. J. Harvey (Ed.), *Motivation and social interaction* (pp. 187–238). New York: Ronald Press.
Garfinkel, H. (1967). *Studies in ethnomethodology*. Cambridge: Polity Press.
Goffman, E. (1964). The neglected situation. *American Anthropologist, 66*, 133–136.
Goffman, E. (1979). Footing. *Semiotica, 25*(1/2), 1–30.
Goode, D. (1994). *A world without words*. Philadelphia: Temple University Press.
Goode, D. (2003). Ethnomethodology and disability studies: A Reflection on Robillard. *Human Studies, 26*(4), 493–503.
Goodglass, H., Kaplan, E., & Barresi, B. (2001). *The Boston diagnostic aphasia examination (BDAE)* (3rd ed.). Baltimore, MD: Lippincott Williams & Wilkins.
Goodwin, C. (1993). Recording human interaction in natural settings. *Pragmatics: Quarterly Publication of the International Pragmatics Association (IPrA), 3*(2), 181–209.
Goodwin, C. (1995). Co-constructing meaning in conversations with an aphasic man. *Research on Language and Social Interaction, 28*, 233–260.
Goodwin, C. (2000). Gesture, aphasia and interaction. In D. McNeill (Ed.), *Language and gesture: Window into thought and action* (pp. 84–98). Cambridge: Cambridge University Press.
Goodwin, C. (Ed.). (2003). *Conversation and brain damage*. New York: Oxford University Press.
Grice, H. P. (1989). *Studies in the ways of words*. Cambridge, MA: Harvard University Press.
Guitar, B. (2013). *Stuttering: An integrated approach to its nature and treatment* (4th ed.). Baltimore: Lippincott Williams & Wilkins.
Heeschen, C., & Schegloff, E. A. (1999). Agrammatism, adaptation theory, conversation analysis: On the role of so-called telegraphic style in talk-in-interaction. *Aphasiology, 13*(4/5), 365–405.

Heeschen, C., & Schegloff, E. A. (2003). Aphasic agrammatism as interactional artifact and achievement. In C. Goodwin (Ed.), *Conversation and brain damage*. New York: Oxford University Press.
Helasvuo, M.-L., Laakso, M., & Sorjonen, M.-L. (2004). Searching for words: Syntactic and sequential construction of word search in conversations of Finnish speakers with aphasia. *Research in Language and Social Interaction, 37*(1), 1–37.
Heritage, J. (1984). *Garfinkel and ethnomethodology*. Cambridge: Polity Press.
Hilari, K., Byng, S., Lamping, D. L., & Smith, S. C. (2003). Stroke and aphasia quality of life scale-39 (SAQOL-39) evaluation of acceptability, reliability, and validity. *Stroke, 34*(8), 1944–1950.
Holland, A. L. (1982). Observing functional communication of aphasic adults. *Journal of Speech and Hearing Disorders, 47*(1), 50–56.
Jefferson, G. (2004). Glossary of transcript symbols with an introduction. In G. Lerner (Ed.), *Conversation analysis: Studies from the first generation* (pp. 13–31). Amsterdam: John Benjamins.
Jingree, T., Finlay, W. M. L., & Antaki, C. (2006). Empowering words, disempowering actions: An analysis of interactions between staff members and people with learning disabilities in residents' meetings. *Journal of Intellectual Disability Research, 50*(3), 212–226.
Jones, D. (2015). A family living with Alzheimer's disease: The communicative challenges. *Dementia, 14*(5), 555–573.
Kent, R. D. (2004). *The MIT encyclopedia of communication disorders*. Cambridge, MA: MIT Press.
Kidwell, M. (2013). Interaction among children. In J. Sidnell & T. Stivers (Eds.), *The handbook of conversation analysis* (pp. 511–532). Chichester: Wiley-Blackwell.
Kindell, J., Sage, K., Keady, J., & Wilkinson, R. (2013). Adapting to conversation with semantic dementia: Using enactment as a compensatory strategy in everyday social interaction. *International Journal of Language and Communication Disorders, 48*(5), 497–507.
Kitzinger, C., & Jones, D. (2007). When may calls home: The opening moments of family telephone conversations with an Alzheimer's patient. *Feminism & Psychology, 17*(2), 184–202.
Korkiakangas, T., Dindar, K., Laitila, A., & Kärnä, E. (2016). The Sally-Anne test: An interactional analysis of a dyadic assessment. *International Journal of Language & Communication Disorders, 51*(6), 685–702.

Labov, W. (1972). *Sociolinguistic patterns*. Philadelphia: University of Pennsylvania Press.
Lee, L. C., Harrington, R. A., Louie, B. B., & Newschaffer, C. J. (2008). Children with autism: Quality of life and parental concerns. *Journal of Autism and Developmental Disorders, 38*(6), 1147–1160.
Lerner, G. H. (1996). On the "semi-permeable" character of grammatical units in conversation: Conditional entry into the turn space of another speaker. In E. Ochs, E. Schegloff, & S. Thompson (Eds.), *Interaction and grammar* (pp. 238–276). Cambridge: Cambridge University Press.
Levinson, S. C. (1983). *Pragmatics*. Cambridge: Cambridge University Press.
Lind, M., & Sønsterud, H. (2014). Co-construction of turns at talk: Active listening or disruptions in conversation with persons who stutter? *Journal of Interactional Research in Communication Disorders/Equinox, 5*(2), 141–166.
Lindholm, C. (2015). Parallel realities: The interactional management of confabulation in dementia care encounters. *Research in Language and Social Interaction, 48*(2), 176–199.
Local, J., & Wootton, T. (1995). Interactional and phonetic aspects of immediate echolalia in autism: A case study. *Clinical Linguistics & Phonetics, 9*(2), 155–184.
Lord, C., Rutter, M., DiLavore, P., Risi, S., Gotham, K., & Bishop, S. (2012). *Autism diagnostic observation schedule–2nd edition (ADOS-2)*. Los Angeles, CA: Western Psychological Corporation.
Lubinski, R., Duchan, D., & Weitzner-Lin, B. (1980). Analysis of breakdowns and repairs in adult aphasic conversation. In R. Brookshire (Ed.), *Clinical aphasiology conference proceedings* (pp. 111–116). Minneapolis: BRK Publishers.
Mates, A. W., Mikesell, L., & Smith, M. S. (2010). *Language, interaction, and frontotemporal dementia: Reverse engineering the social mind*. London: Equinox.
Maynard, D. W., & Turowetz, J. (2017). Doing diagnosis: Autism, interaction order, and the use of narrative in clinical talk. *Social Psychology Quarterly, 80*(3), 254–275.
McCabe, R., Leudar, I., & Antaki, C. (2004). Do people with schizophrenia display theory of mind deficits in clinical interactions? *Psychological Medicine, 34*(3), 401–412.
McCabe, R., Skelton, J., Heath, C., Burns, T., & Priebe, S. (2002). Engagement of patients with psychosis in the consultation: Conversation analytic study [with commentary by J Skelton]. *BMJ, 325*(7373), 1148–1151.

McCleary, L., & de Arantes Leite, T. (2013). Turn-taking in Brazilian sign language: Evidence from overlap. *Journal of Interactional Research in Communication Disorders, 4*(1), 123–154.

McIlvenny, P. (1995). Seeing conversations: Analyzing sign language talk. In P. ten Have & G. Psathas (Eds.), *Situated order: Studies in the social organization of talk and embodied activities* (pp. 129–150). Washington, DC: University Press of America.

Merrison, S., & Merrison, A. J. (2005). Repair in speech and language therapy interaction: Investigating pragmatic language impairment in children. *Child Language Teaching and Therapy, 21,* 191–211.

Mikesell, L. (2009). Conversational practices of a frontotemporal dementia patient and his interlocutors. *Research on Language & Social Interaction, 42,* 135–162.

Muskett, T., Perkins, M., Clegg, J., & Body, R. (2010). Inflexibility as an interactional phenomenon: Using conversation analysis to re-examine a symptom of autism. *Clinical Linguistics & Phonetics, 24*(1), 1–16.

Norén, N., Samuelsson, C., & Plejert, C. (Eds.). (2013). *Aided communication in everyday interaction*. London: J&R Press.

Pajo, K. (2013). The occurrence of 'what', 'where', 'what house' and other repair initiations in the home environment of hearing-impaired individuals. *International Journal of Language and Communication Disorders, 48*(1), 66–77.

Pollner, M., & McDonald-Wikler, L. (1985). The social construction of unreality: A case study of a family's attribution of competence to a severely retarded child. *Family Process, 24*(2), 241–254.

Pomerantz, A., & Heritage, J. (2013). Preference. In J. Sidnell & T. Stivers (Eds.), *The handbook of conversation analysis* (pp. 210–228). Oxford: Wiley-Blackwell.

Price-Williams, D., & Sabsay, S. (1979). Communicative competence among severely retarded persons. *Semiotica, 26*(1–2), 35–64.

Rapley, M. (2004). *The social construction of intellectual disability*. Cambridge: Cambridge University Press.

Rapley, M., & Antaki, C. (1996). A conversation analysis of the 'acquiescence' of people with learning disabilities. *Journal of Community & Applied Social Psychology, 6*(3), 207–227.

Rasmussen, G. (2013). That's my story! Resisting disabling processes in a therapeutic activity. *Journal of Interactional Research in Communication Disorders, 4*(2), 273–298. https://doi.org/10.1558/jircd.v4i2.273.

Rasmussen, G. (2017). The use of pictures for interactional purposes and the grammar of social interaction. *Journal of Interactional Research in Communication Disorders, 18*(1), 121–145.
Rasmussen, G. (2018). On the social constraints of having a world. *RASK: International Journal of Language and Communication, 7*, 79–107.
Rasmussen, G., Andersen, E. M., & Kristiansen, E. D. (2019). Working out availability, unavailability, and awayness in social face-to-face encounters—The case of dementia. *Discourse Studies, 21*(3), 258–279.
Robillard, A. B. (1999). *Meaning of disability: The lived experience of paralysis.* Philadelphia: Temple University Press.
Sacks, H., Schegloff, E., & Jefferson, G. (1974). A simplest systematics for the organization of turn-taking for conversation. *Language, 50*(4), 696–735. https://doi.org/10.1353/lan.1974.0010.
Samuelsson, C. (2009). Using conversation analysis to study prosodic problems in a child with language impairment. *Child Language Teaching and Therapy, 25*, 59–88.
Sarno, M. T. (1998). *Acquired aphasia* (3rd ed.). San Diego: Academic Press.
Sataloff, J., & Sataloff, R. T. (Eds.). (2005). *Hearing loss* (4th ed.). New York: Taylor and Francis.
Schegloff, E. (1979). The relevance of repair to syntax-for-conversation. In T. Givón (Ed.), *Syntax and semantics* (Vol. 12, pp. 261–286). New York: Academic Press.
Schegloff, E. A. (1992a). Introduction. In H. Sacks, *Lectures on conversation* (G. Jefferson, Ed.). Oxford: Basil Blackwell.
Schegloff, E. A. (1992b). Repair after next turn: The last structurally provided defense of intersubjectivity in conversation. *American Journal of Sociology, 97*, 1295–1345.
Schegloff, E. A. (1996). Turn organization: One intersection of grammar and interaction. In E. Ochs, E. A. Schegloff, & S. A. Thompson (Eds.), *Interaction and grammar* (pp. 52–133). Cambridge: Cambridge University Press.
Schegloff, E. A. (2003). Conversation analysis and communication disorders. In C. Goodwin (Ed.), *Conversation and brain damage* (pp. 21–55). New York: Oxford University Press.
Schegloff, E. A. (2006). Interaction: The infrastructure for social institutions, the natural ecological niche for language, and the arena in which culture is enacted. In N. J. Enfield & S. C. Levinson (Eds.), *Roots of human sociality: Culture, cognition and interaction* (pp. 70–96). London: Berg.

Schegloff, E. (2007). *Sequence organization in interaction: A Primer in conversation analysis* (Vol. 1). New York: Cambridge University Press.
Schegloff, E., Jefferson, G., & Sacks, H. (1977). The preference for self-correction in the organization of repair for conversation. *Language, 53,* 361–382.
Schegloff, E., & Sacks, H. (1973). Opening up closings. *Semiotica, 8*(4), 289–327.
Schienberg, S., & Holland, A. (1980). Conversational turn taking in Wernicke's aphasia. In R. Brookshire (Ed.), *Clinical aphasiology conference proceedings* (pp. 106–110). Minneapolis: BRK Publishers.
Searle, J. R. (1969). *Speech acts.* Cambridge: Cambridge University Press.
Shakespeare, T. (1998). *The disability reader: Social science perspectives.* London: Continuum.
Solomon, O., Heritage, J., Yin, L., Maynard, D. W., & Bauman, M. L. (2016). 'What brings him here today?': Medical problem presentation involving children with autism spectrum disorders and typically developing children. *Journal of Autism and Developmental Disorders, 46*(2), 378–393.
St. Clair, M. C., Pickles, A., Durkin, K., & Conti-Ramsden, G. (2011). A longitudinal study of behavioral, emotional and social difficulties in individuals with a history of specific language impairment (SLI). *Journal of Communication Disorders, 44*(2), 186–199.
Sterponi, L., de Kirby, K., & Shankey, J. (2015). Rethinking language in autism. *Autism, 19*(5), 517–526.
Stopford, C. L., Thompson, J. C., Neary, D., Richardson, A. M., & Snowden, J. S. (2012). Working memory, attention, and executive function in Alzheimer's disease and frontotemporal dementia. *Cortex, 48*(4), 429–446.
Stribling, P., & Rae, J. (2010). Interactional analysis of scaffolding in a mathematical task in ASD. In H. Gardner & M. Forrester (Eds.), *Analysing interactions in childhood.* Chichester: Wiley-Blackwell.
Stribling, P., Rae, J., & Dickerson, P. (2007). Two forms of spoken repetition in a girl with autism. *International Journal of Language & Communication Disorders, 42*(4), 427–444.
Tarplee, C., & Barrow, E. (1999). Delayed echoing as an interactional resource: A case study of a 3-year-old child on the autistic spectrum. *Clinical Linguistics & Phonetics, 13*(6), 449–482.
Tetnowski, J. A., & Damico, J. S. (2001). A demonstration of the advantages of qualitative methodologies in stuttering research. *Journal of Fluency Disorders, 26,* 1–26.

Thompson, L., Howes, C., & McCabe, R. (2016). Effect of questions used by psychiatrists on therapeutic alliance and adherence. *The British Journal of Psychiatry, 209*(1), 40–47.
Togher, L., & Hand, L. (1998). Use of politeness markers with different communication partners: An investigation of five subjects with traumatic brain injury. *Aphasiology, 12*(7–8), 755–770.
Tykkyläinen, T. (2010). Child-initiated repair in task interactions. In H. Gardner & M. Forrester (Eds.), *Analysing interactions in childhood: Insights from conversation analysis* (pp. 227–248). Chichester: Wiley-Blackwell.
Wilkinson, R. (2014). Intervening with conversation analysis in speech and language therapy: Improving aphasic conversation. *Research on Language and Social Interaction, 47*(3), 219–238.
Wilkinson, R. (2019). Atypical interaction: Conversation analysis and communicative impairments. *Research on Language and Social Interaction, 52*(3), 281–299.
Wilkinson, R., Beeke, S., & Maxim, J. (2003). Adapting to conversation: On the use of pro-forms by aphasic speakers in the construction of turns at talk. In C. Goodwin (Ed.), *Conversation and brain damage* (pp. 59–89). Oxford: Oxford University Press.
Wilkinson, R., Beeke, S., & Maxim, J. (2010). Formulating actions and events with limited linguistic resources: Enactment and iconicity in agrammatic aphasic talk. *Research on Language and Social Interaction, 43*(1), 57–84.
Wilkinson, R., Bloch, S., & Clarke, M. (2011). On the use of graphic resources in interaction by people with communication disorders. In J. Streeck, C. Goodwin, & C. LeBaron (Eds.), *Embodied interaction: Language and body in the material world* (pp. 152–168). Cambridge: Cambridge University Press.
Williams, V., Ponting, L., Ford, K., Rudge, P., & (Skills for Support Team). (2010). Skills for support: Personal assistants and people with learning disabilities. *British Journal of Learning Disabilities, 38(*1), 59–67.
Wootton, A. J. (1999). An investigation of delayed echoing in a child with autism. *First Language, 19*(57), 359–381.
Yearley, S., & Brewer, J. D. (1989). Stigma and conversational competence: A conversation analytic study of the mentally handicapped. *Human Studies, 12,* 97–117.

Part I

The Impact of Cognitive Impairments Within Social Interaction

2

Sequence and Consequence: Transposing Responsive Actions into Provocations in Forensic and Clinical Encounters Involving Youths with Autism

Douglas W. Maynard and Jason Turowetz

Introduction

In her book *Thinking in Pictures*, Temple Grandin (2006, pp. 154–155) describes the problems that "rigid thinking" can create in the social lives of autistic adults. She recounts how one young man "became romantically interested in a girl and went to her house wearing a football helmet to disguise himself. He thought it would be alright to look in her windows. In his literal, visual mind he thought that since he would not be recognized, it was okay to stand outside and watch for her." To a neurotypical observer, the young man's line of reasoning would appear to defy commonsense. Like many people with autism, he does not seem to participate in what Garfinkel (1967, p. 37), following phenomenologists such as Schütz (1962), calls the "natural attitude," the set of

D. W. Maynard (✉)
University of Wisconsin-Madison, Madison, WI, USA

J. Turowetz
University of Siegen, Siegen, Germany

© The Author(s) 2020
R. Wilkinson et al. (eds.), *Atypical Interaction*,
https://doi.org/10.1007/978-3-030-28799-3_2

taken-for-granted assumptions and expectations that make up the background of social life. As Garfinkel (1963, 1967) suggested in his famous breaching demonstrations, actions that violate these expectations undermine the mutual trust on which the commonsense world rests, resulting in confusion, anxiety, and anger as people try to make sense of what is happening.

Although she does not say so, we can surmise that the story told by Grandin probably ended with, at most, informal sanctions for the young man: perhaps he was reproached for his behavior, or admonished not to do it again, or educated about why it was inappropriate. This is how most autistic breaches of commonsense end. It is easy to imagine, however, a less benign conclusion to the story: the police could have been called, and the young man arrested for trespassing or stalking. In that case, professionals, including police, social workers, and perhaps lawyers and judges, would have had to examine the young man's behavior, determine its motivations, and decide how to handle it. How would they have made sense of his actions, and with what consequences?

In this chapter, we examine two cases where individuals with autism engage in behavior that violates the commonsense order of everyday life in their interactions with professionals. In both cases, the professionals draw on protocols and stocks of professional knowledge to make sense of the autistic person's actions, producing accounts that attribute the behavior to dispositional and psychological factors. The first case involves an incident where a police officer arrested an adolescent boy with autism in a public park. While still in his police car, the officer notices the boy's odd-seeming behavior, particularly the way he is "stimming"—a common form of anxiety-reducing action that individuals with ASD may produce (Silberman 2015, p. 48)—by twirling a string in front of his eyes. The officer concludes that he is on drugs, stops the car, gets out, confronts the boy, and wrestles him to the ground, at which point the boy's caretaker arrives on the scene and explains he has autism. In the second case, a clinician is evaluating a nine-year old boy for autism. After several attempts by the clinician to solicit his participation in a test that requires him to demonstrate how he brushes his teeth, the boy abruptly gets up from the table where he and the clinician are sitting, walks over to a corner of the room, and kneels down behind a chair. Although the clinician eventually manages to re-engage him in testing, they never do complete the demonstration task.

While the cases occur in different settings, we show that the two professionals—a police officer in the first case, a clinician in the second—use similar practices to make sense of and account for the interactional violations committed by the individuals with autism. In particular, both professionals employ an accounting device we call *transpositioning* (see Maynard 2019), which involves reconfiguring the original interactional sequence, so that an action by the autistic person that was *responsive* to a prior turn is instead depicted as *initiating* an independent course of action. In other words, an action that was originally in second position is *re*presented as having been in first position. This accounting practice transforms the sense of the interaction in a way that allows professionals to attribute mental states and motives to the autistic person, making them appear responsible for what was initially a concerted achievement. It also supports and justifies interventions by various agents, from police and clinicians to teachers, social workers, and family members.

Our selection of cases from two settings that are, on the surface, very different, is meant to illustrate the generality of transpositioning while suggesting the relevance of our results for a variety of contexts where professionals and others interact with autistic individuals. Accordingly, we conclude the chapter by discussing the implications of our findings for people with autism, their families and communities, and the institutions that deal with those whose interactional style is atypical.

Autism in Interaction

Autism is a developmental disorder of childhood characterized by impairments in social communication and interaction, and repetitive, stereotyped behavior (APA 2013). Once considered a rare condition thought to affect 2 in 1000 children in the 1960s and 1970s (Fombonne 2018), as of 2018, this figure has grown to 1 in 59 in the U.S. (CDC 2018), and 1 in 160 globally (WHO 2017). Several factors have been implicated in autism's upsurge, including diagnostic substitution, or the replacement of other diagnoses like "mental retardation" (now called intellectual disability) with Autism Spectrum Disorder (ASD); accretion, which involves diagnosing autism in addition to other conditions (Eyal et al. 2010; Gernsbacher et al. 2005); broadened diagnostic criteria that encompass more cases (Grinker 2007; cf. Wing 1981); information diffusion through social networks (Liu et al. 2010); the mass deinstitutionalization of mental patients in the 1970s, which prompted the creation of new classification systems to accommodate people with special needs in the community (Eyal 2013); increased de-stigmatization of autism (Nadesan 2005; Silberman 2015); and demographic trends such as advanced parental age (Durkin et al. 2008).

Our interest is not in explaining this diagnostic upsurge. Rather in line with our larger project on the testing and diagnosis of ASD,[1] we address the *how* of autism's accomplishment—the ways in which it is constituted in social and interactional environments. As Hacking (1999) points out, autism is not a *natural kind* that is "indifferent" to humans or their ideas about it. Rather, it is an *interactive*, human one: the very act of diagnosis affects the behavior of the diagnosed and those around them, eventually "looping" back into the definition of autism itself. Moreover, we can add that autism is also an *interactional* kind (see Maynard and Turowetz 2019)—what autism "is" is inseparable from the concerted social actions and reactions by which people make sense together.

In recent years, a growing number of researchers have investigated autism as an interactional phenomenon—as a collaborative accomplishment rather than an inherent feature of brain or biology. Their studies show how behaviors that appear senseless or arbitrary to a commonsense observer can take on new meaning when analyzed for the actions they perform in a given sequential environment. For example, close analysis of echolalia—the verbatim repetition of speech—shows that some forms of "pure echoing," which seem to have no communicative intent, can display an interactional stance toward prior actions, such as

[1]Under the auspices of a U.S. National Science Foundation grant (#125706), the recording was made in 2014, during the course of a four-year field study we conducted at a large clinic specializing in autism and other disabilities of childhood, which we call Central Developmental Disabilities Clinic (CDDC), located in a medium-sized U.S. city.

questions (Local and Wootton 1995; Wootton 1999; see also Streponi and Fasulo 2010), while repetition of an immediately prior turn at talk ("immediate echolalia") can demonstrate an orientation to that turn and sustain joint focus (Stribling et al. 2007). Similarly, some of the inflexible and rigid behavior associated with autism may be used to maintain control over an interaction, for example by repeating a topic-initiating question ("Do you know what?") to prevent a co-participant from controlling play (Muskett et al. 2010; see also Maynard and Turowetz 2019, for an example of a child using counter-directives to control the course of a clinical exam). Researchers have also shown that children exhibit competencies in certain contexts that they appear to lack in others: thus, Solomon (2015) shows how a young girl with autism displays a level of social sophistication in her interactions with a service dog, and in conversations about the dog, that seem absent from her interactions with fellow humans.

Collectively, these studies capture the many ways that people on the spectrum exhibit what Maynard and Turowetz (2017) call "concrete competence," which refers to the set of fundamental interactional skills, e.g. asking and answering questions, directing and responding, repairing and correcting, that enable participation in more complex social activities. While all people possess concrete competence, Maynard and Turowetz (2017) argue that children with autism may use these competences differently from their neurotypical counterparts, and that their very mastery of concretely competent skills can interfere with or inhibit the development and/or display of the more abstract forms of competence (e.g. hypothetical thinking that is disembedded from any concrete setting). As Maynard (2005) puts it, the distinctive features of autistic reasoning, as displayed in interaction, reflect and reinforce difficulty grasping social gestalts—understanding situations holistically, rather than in terms of discrete parts. And yet, these forms of reasoning have a logic, coherence, and intelligence in their own right, which is all too easily missed by deficit-centered definitions of autism (Gernsbacher et al. 2005; Muskett et al. 2010; Turowetz 2015a).

Paying close attention to the interactional particulars of autism makes these otherwise invisible competences apparent. Conversely, a focus on individuals with autism outside of their interactional environments not only masks these competences, but can make them appear as incompetence: repeating a question over and over, outside its social context, suggests that one doesn't understand how questions work; repeating others' speech verbatim would seem to indicate ineptitude in language use and communication. Yet clinical, therapeutic, and other professional protocols tend to encourage attention to action, rather than *inter*action, and a corresponding tendency to individualize autistic behavior. Turowetz (2015a, b), for example, has shown how clinicians report findings in ways that minimize their own contributions, and those of the test environment, to children's performances, attributing symptoms to dispositional factors and obscuring situational ones. This reporting procedure comports with the demands of standardized test protocols, as well as those surrounding the content and structure of medical records (Turowetz and Maynard 2019).

Data and Methods

Our approach in this chapter is Ethnomethdological Conversation Analysis (EMCA). In our project on the testing and diagnosis of autism spectrum disorder, we have collected data ethnographically (by the use of observations, interviews, video recordings, and access to medical records). For the forensic encounter, we draw from online video and police records. Our chapter involves an approach of "limited affinity" (Maynard 2003, Chapter 3) between our EMCA analysis of interaction and the ethnographic information we also collected. Accordingly, we are examining *activities* rather than social settings as such, prioritizing the participant-produced orderly aspects of interaction rather than more abstract knowledge of wider arenas in which these activities are embedded. It is the participants' own orientations to such wider knowledge that we attempt to capture.

The first of our two examples involves of a young man with autism being arrested in a public park in Buckeye, Arizona. The incident received national media coverage and the video, recorded on the arresting officer's body camera, was made publically accessible through major news outlets, such as NBC. As such, it represents an instance of what

Jones and Raymond (2012, p. 112) call "institutional third party video"—recordings created for organizational reasons that become available to the public, including researchers, for other purposes. Because the identities of the participants are a matter of public record, we have not anonymized them or modified any details of the encounter. We also draw on media reports about the case and a police report that is publicly available through SCRBID, an online digital reading service. The second video involves a nine-year old boy being assessed for autism by a clinical psychologist at the CDDC.[2] We also draw on a recording of the clinicians discussing the case afterward during a "pre-staffing" conference—a meeting where practitioners review findings and decide on a diagnosis. We also consult the post-visit medical reports entered in the boy's records and later sent to the parents.

Case 1: Arrest in Arizona

Connor Leibel, a fourteen-year old boy with autism, made national headlines in 2017 when he was arrested by a police officer in a public park. His caretaker, Diane Craglow, had left him alone for a few minutes and, upon returning, found the boy screaming as a police officer pinned him to the ground and attempted to handcuff him. The incident is described in an op-ed piece published in the New York Times, September 19, 2017 (Silberman 2017):

> When Ms. Craglow returned, she couldn't believe what she saw: a police officer looming over the boy with his handcuffs at the ready, pinning him to the ground against a tree. Connor was screaming, and the police officer, David Grossman, seemed extremely agitated… Soon it became clear to Ms. Craglow that the policeman was unaware that Connor has autism, and had interpreted the boy's rigid, unfamiliar movements – which included raising a piece of yarn to his nose to sniff it repeatedly – as a sign of drug intoxication.

[2]Both cases, at a less granular level than we present here, have been analyzed, alongside another forensic instance, in a paper (Maynard 2019) addressed to social psychology. The clinic data in the present paper also are analyzed more technically in Maynard and Turowetz (Forthcoming), but not with regard to transpositioning or for comparison with non-clinical settings.

Officer Grossman interpreted Connor's unusual behavior as evidence that he was on drugs. However, as we see in the transcript below, Connor was using the yarn—which he calls "string" in his conversation with the officer—for the purpose of "stimming," a term that refers to stereotypic, repetitive behaviors by which people with autism reduce anxiety (Silberman 2015, p. 48). Connor and the Officer are not orienting the situation in the same way: they do not share the taken for granted background expectancies necessary for making sense together, so that, in Garfinkel's (1963) terms, trust conditions, and the reciprocity and mutuality they entail, are absent.

The interaction between Connor and Officer Grossman was recorded on the Officer's bodycam. The video begins while the Officer is driving in his police car. He sees Connor on the sidewalk, per the police report about the incident, "appearing that he might had been inhaling some type of substance from his hands." So Officer Grossman stops, gets out of the car, and confronts Connor, who is standing on the sidewalk. At line 1, as he exits his vehicle, Grossman asks a question that immediately treats Connor's actions as accountable. The question is hearable as a challenge and, following a delay, Connor initiates repair (line 3), clarifying whether he is the question's addressee. The Officer confirms ('Yeah'), then reformulates his question in a way that specifically targets what Connor (What*ya*) is doing (line 4).

Case 1: Connor Leibel and Officer Grossman

Off: What's goin' on? ((Spoken as Grossman exists the car))
(1.0)
Con: Me?
Off: Yeah, whataya doin?
(0.6)
Con: Good.
Off: Whataya doing?
(0.6)
Con: I'm stimming.
(0.5)
Off: What?
(0.6) ((Connor is backing away from the Officer))
Con: I'm do with this. ((Lifts string up to show Officer while still walking back and away from Off, who is walking toward him))
(0.2)
Off: What is that? ((Connor still walking backwards away from advancing Off, who extends his extends his right arm toward Connor))
(0.2)
Off: Stop walkin' away from me. ((Connor halts and lifts string to Off))
Con: It's a string.
(0.6)
Off: Okay. So why ya bouncin' around all the way.
(1.0) ((Connor stands still))
Off: Ya have ID on ya.
(0.5)
Con: NO. ((Connor abruptly turns to his left))
(0.8) ((Officer reaches with his right hand to grab Connor's right elbow))
Off: Don't go anywhere. ((Officer, holding the right wrist, uses his own left hand to turn Connor around further so Connor's arms and hands are behind his back as he faces away from Officer))
(1.2) ((With his left hand, Officer grabs Connor's left wrist))
Off: Arright just relax. ((Officer pulls both wrists together))

```
        (2.0)
Con:    Are you okay?
        (1.0)
Con:    I'm okay, I'm okay, I'M OKAY! ((Screeching cries))
        ((Officer wrestles Connor to ground and tells him not to move, as Connor continues to claim to be okay, until Connor's caretaker arrives.))
```

After another delay (line 5), which may signal a problem with the question (Schegloff 2007), Connor responds, "Good" (line 6). His self-assessment seems to treat the question as a how-are-you type greeting. However, the Officer repeats his question (line 7), indicating that Connor's answer was insufficient; his vocal emphasis on the verb *do* (doin') targets Connor's actions, rather than his personal state, as the question's focus. Connor answers that he is "stimming" (line 9), which occasions an open-class repair initiation ("What?") by the Officer (line 11). As Drew (1997) observes, these kinds of repairs do not simply target a specific feature of the prior turn as problematic, but treat the whole turn/move as troublesome. Connor starts to back away from the Officer (line 12) and, continuing to walk backward, answers, "I'm do with this" (line 13), indexing the string ('*this*') as he lifts it to show the Officer. Connor is doing one thing with his words and another with his bodily actions: his words satisfy the relevance constraints of the Officer's questions, and comply by answering them; however, his movements are resistive, and break the face-to-face formation (Mondada 2009) that is normative and expected in ordinary interaction.

The Officer, meanwhile, walks toward Connor (lines 13–14), and asks another question that locates the string as a problem (line 16). Conner continues walking backward, and the Officer issues a directive for him to stop (line 19). Connor complies (lines 19–20), then answers the Officer's question, identifying the item as "a string" (line 21). The Officer responds with an "okay" token that accepts Connor's answer, but then produces a so-prefaced "why" question (line 23) regarding his "bouncin." In this context, the so-preface indicates an unresolved issue that remains to be dealt with (Bolden 2006). More generally, such questions can embody "a type of suspension of Garfinkel's…notion of 'trust' by claiming that they [the speaker] cannot make 'typical' sense of the causes of, or motives for, the event" (Bolden and Robinson 2011, p. 96; cf. also Rawls et al. 2018).

After Connor's lack of response (line 24), the Officer asks if he has "an ID on ya" (line 25). Connor hesitates (line 26), then answers in the negative, with raised volume ('NO'), and abruptly turns to his left. It may look as though Connor is trying to escape or leave the scene, and Officer Grossman reaches for Connor's elbow (line 28), issues a directive, "Don't go anywhere" (line 30) and, holding Connor's right wrist, starts to put Connor's arms and hands behind his back. This is a turning point in the interaction both figuratively and literally: restraining Connor's movements provides the basis for the transpositioning that the Officer later performs in his accounts of what happened, both to Connor's caregiver and in his official police report. Although Connor's abrupt left-turn was responsive to Officer Grossman's question and encroachment on his personal territory, the officer's bald directive truncates Connor's movement from his vocalized accounts that have been in second-position. "Don't go anywhere" formulates Connor's bodily movements as a first-position action that warrants a remedial, second-position intervention.

As the Officer pulls Connor's wrists together and prepares to handcuff him, Connor asks him, "Are you okay" (line 36) and, receiving no answer, begins to scream, "I'm okay, I'm okay, I'M OKAY!" (line 38). In addition to their plaintive character, Connor's repetition of "I'm okay" is a kind of multiple saying (Stivers 2004) which proposes that no further action by a co-participant is necessary. Connor continues to repeat this phrase as he struggles with the Officer, who pins him to the ground and attempts to place him in handcuffs (lines 39–41).

As the Officer and Connor struggle, Connor's caretaker arrives on the scene (not shown on transcript). As she explains where she was, Grossman describes what happened:

Grossman: He's fine, he's breathing, he just started- … I was tryin' to talk to him. I wasn't sure what was goin' on, and then he started backing away from me, and then kind of pulled away from me when he seemed like he wanted to run away.

The Officer's account displays transpositioning. The officer writes that he was "tryin' to talk" to Connor, and that he "wasn't sure what was going on." This depicts a moment of stasis, as if, in their interactions so far, Connor were non-responsive. On this textual rendering, Connor's "backing away" is separated from turns of talk (see Case 1 transcript) that immediately preceded it. Indeed, the locution depicting this move suggests it was something Connor "started." Rather than being a response, in second position, to the Officer's questions and physical movements toward him, Connor's actions seem sudden and abrupt, and to be initiating a *new* action sequence instead of extending one already in progress. The Officer also imputes a motive to Connor, *wanting* to run away, as a candidate reason for his actions. This depiction would tacitly warrant a second-position responsive move on the officer's part.

The Officer's account suggests that he had trouble coming up with a commonsense interpretation of Connor's actions. He "wasn't sure what was goin' on," and inferred that drugs were involved. From a commonsense vantage point, "anyone"—e.g., readers of the officer's report (cf. Garfinkel 1967, Chapter 6)—could understand Officer Grossman to be doing ordinary, competent police work, detecting unusual behavior, attempting to engage the potential offender, and restraining him when he appeared to break away. For Connor, however, the Officer's action may have been accountable in itself—Connor was answering his questions as well as resisting incursions on his self-territory. The Officer did not accept his answers, switched focus to Connor's embodied conduct, and then physically contained him. The overall result was a failure of the reciprocity required for successful interaction (Rawls 1987). Insofar as Connor's use of jargon like "stimming" presumes knowledge its recipient does not have (Heritage 2012), it may constitute a failure of recipient design (Sacks and Schegloff 1979). Meanwhile, the Officer asks questions and pursues actions that, from the outset, have an accusatory edge. When he ceases dealing with the vocalized, substantive issue of what Connor was "doing" with the string to engage Connor's embodied actions, he effects transpositioning, both in the encounter and in his post hoc, written account of what happened. In particular, after describing his initial exchange with Connor, the Officer writes:

> I asked Connor if he had any identification with him which he stated no. During my brief conversation with Connor he was sweating profusely as sweat drops were coming off his face and he started to walk backwards away from me in what appeared an attempt to flee. I reached out and grabbed Connor's arms and attempted to detain him to investigate further is when he began to pull away from me and tried to run in the northwest direction.

A fuller, more detailed analysis of this report and the circumstances surrounding it can be found in Maynard (2019). For present purposes, we can observe how Connor's "start[ing] to walk backwards" is detached from the turns that preceded it, such that the Officer's next move ("I reached out...") appears as a second position response to a line of action, attempting to flee, that Connor initiated, with which his apparent nervousness (indicated by "profuse" sweating) would be consistent. As in the Officer's verbal report to Connor's caretaker, Connor's actions become signs of deviance and grounds for police intervention, their initially responsive, resistive features transformed into motivated efforts to flee from police.

The transpositioning in the interaction between Connor and Officer Grossman occurs frequently in encounters between people with autism and neurotypical individuals. That is, there may be a breakdown in mutual intelligibility that makes it impossible, in the absence of reparative work, for the parties to make sense together. In the next section, we examine a similar breakdown in a very different institutional setting, a clinic for developmental disabilities, where transpositioning becomes evident in a discussion between clinicians about a child's performance on a standardized assessment.

Case 2: The Demonstration Test

Dan Chapman was nine-years-old when he was evaluated for autism at Central Developmental Disabilities Clinic (CDDC) in the winter of 2014. Based on their findings and Dan's case history, a team of two clinicians, a Developmental Pediatrician we call Leah and a Child Psychologist we call Jennifer, diagnosed Dan with autism. The centerpiece of the evaluation was the Autism Diagnostic Observation Schedule, Second Edition (ADOS-II), a play-based instrument consisting of a series of activities designed to test children's social competence. The ADOS, alongside companion interviews and tests, is widely regarded as the "gold standard" in autism assessment. Although Dan and Jennifer completed the first two activities without incident, difficulties arose as Jennifer attempted to start a third one: a demonstration task where the examinee is asked to "show and tell" the examiner how to brush one's teeth. From the outset, Dan resists the line of action Jennifer is proposing, shaking his head multiple times in response to her directives. Below, we reproduce a portion of the transcript, paraphrasing the rest in the interest of space (for a fuller treatment of this case, see Maynard and Turowetz, forthcoming). After our analysis of the demonstration task, we examine the episode in which transpositioning occurs.

Seated at a table next to Dan and facing him on a diagonal, Jennifer introduces the test by assessing it as "kinda silly" (line 1), then issues a relatively entitled (Curl and Drew 2008) directive (line 2), which she elaborates at lines 3–4. Her assessment of the task, with aspiration particles on "okay(h)" and "So(h)" (cf. Potter and Hepburn 2010) displays anticipation that Dan may find her directive to be a departure from ordinary activities and, in a sense, perhaps childish. As she tells him to "watch this" at line 4, Dan produces a lateral headshake, indicating resistance to the proposed activity (line 5). This headshake and subsequent ones are marked with numbered arrows.

Case 2a:24.PYDX:156

Jen: All right. So the next thing I'd like to do is kinda silly. .hh I
want you to pretend that I don't know how to brush my teeth,
okay(h):? So(h) I want you to sho::w me and tell me how you brush
your teeth.[So watch this,]
Dan: [((Lat. head shake))] ←1
Jen: .hh So here's a pretend sink.
(0.7)
Jen: Here's the <hot water> (0.5) cold water (0.4) toothbrush (0.3)
toothpaste and a cup.
(.)
Jen: Can you show me and tell me how you brush your teeth?
(2.4) ((Dan shifts gaze downward from Jen to the table))
Jen: Pretend I'm an alien and I have no: idea.
(.)
Jen: [Keheh heh]
Dan: [((Lat. head shake))] ←2
(0.4)
Jen: You don't wanna try that?
(1.0) ((Dan does lat. head shake)) ←3

Jennifer does not acknowledge Dan's line 5 headshake. Instead, she sets up the task, pointing to the location of pretend bathroom items (lines 6–9). Then, she produces a modal directive (line 11), asking Dan to show her how he brushes his teeth. The directive is formatted as a yes-no question about ability ("can you"), with downgraded entitlement (Curl and Drew 2008). As Craven and Potter (2010, p. 437) formulate the matter, "can you"- type directives potentially orient "to the recipient's capacities and desires." There is a subtle, important distinction here between ability and motivation, as we will see. At this point, Dan shifts his gaze downward and away from Jen (line 12), maintaining this head posture as she produces a further instructional directive that tacitly characterizes the task as a playful one (line 13) and that has attached laughter tokens (line 15). During this utterance, Dan shifts his gaze back to Jen.

After the laughter tokens (line 15), Dan engages in a second instance of lateral head shaking (line 16). Next, Jennifer proposes his lack of compliance is motivationally-based (line 18), indicating that the directive at line 11 also implicated a motivational feature. She does this by way of a negative declarative—a request for confirmation—that goes up upward on the gradient of epistemic stance (Heritage 2012). That is, the source of Dan's refusal to do this task is within Dan's own epistemic domain, yet Jen (at line 18) is asserting knowledge of Dan's internal state by proposing that his refusal is attributable to not wanting to do the task. In that sense, this is a strong exhibit of clinical if not lay commonsense knowledge. It also is in line with how to handle a breach of commonsense conduct, such as the conditional relevance of an answer to a test question. As Garfinkel (1967) suggests, the inference is that there must be a motivational problem of some kind (cf. Heritage 1984a, p. 99). By inviting confirmation of what it declares, and in following a series of refusals, the form and placement of the sequence at lines 18–19 are closure-implicative, rather presumptively settling the matter of Dan's performance so far.

In her subsequent (pre-staffing) account of what happened, Jennifer will continue to speculate about what Dan wanted or felt, largely glossing over what he *did* during the interaction itself.

Jennifer proposes that they "do another one" and announces that she will show Dan how to drive a car. Here, Jennifer is following the test manual, which recommends that the examiner try a "driving" demonstration task with children who are having trouble with the test (lines 20–21). Although she solicits a go-ahead from Dan who responds with another headshake, "no," (line 22) Jennifer nonetheless launches into the demonstration, ignoring Dan's refusal gesture. Miming how to drive a car, she narrates the process (lines 23, 25, 28, 30).

Case 2b:24.PYDX:156

```
20   Jen:  How 'bout we do another one (0.9) I'll: show you: how I drive a
21         car, okay?
22         (0.8) ((Dan does lat. head shake)) ←4
23   Jen:  Tch (0.2) S:o firs:t:
24         (.)
25   Jen:  I:: (0.5)take out the  [key:: (0.2) and I put it in the ignition]
26   Dan:                         [wider lateral headshake                 ]
27         (0.2) ((lateral head shaking continues)) ↖
28   Jen:  [And I put it in the ignition, ]
29   Dan:  [lat. head shaking             ]←———— 5
30   Jen:  [And then I-       ]  ←
31   Dan:  [lat. head shaking]
32               (0.9) ((Jen twists wrist as if turning key))
33   Dan:  I know how [to learn to drive.]
34   Jen:             [turn   it        o]n:
35               (0.7) ((Jen finishes the turning-key gesture))
36   Jen:  You ↑do:? [(.) .hhh And then: I:::] .hh move it out of:=
37   Dan:            [((nodding with smile)) ]
38   Jen:  =↑par:k (1.1) and then I: put my foot on the gas pedal (0.5) and
39         then I tu:r:n the steering whee::l, (0.7) then I put my foot on the
40         ↑brake? (1.0) when I stop, (.) I put it back into park, (1.8) ↑turn
41         it off, (.) and take the key out. (0.2) Okay?
42               (0.9)
```

Dan responds with a further, lengthy headshake (lines 26, 29, 31), then announces at line 33, "I know how to learn to drive" (line 33). The claim is in simultaneity with Jennifer's enactment and talk about turning the car on (lines 32, 34, 35). Jennifer stops what she's doing and marks Dan's announcement as newsworthy (line 36). However, in contrast to a news receipt that would encourage elaboration by the first speaker (Maynard 2003), the "You do?" utterance is a newsmark that forestalls further development (cf. Heritage 1984b). In overlap with Dan's confirmatory nod and smile (line 37), Jennifer resumes the demonstration Dan had been resisting (lines 36, 38–41). Another preference to not give a recipient information they already have (Heritage 2012) is also ignored here. Instead, Jennifer carries on with the activity and tries to solicit Dan's participation. Over the next several turns, Dan continues to reject Jennifer's directives, until finally he stands up and leaves the table (not shown on transcript). As Dan walks away, Jennifer says, "You don't wanna try that one?" and proposes, "We'll do something else then." Again, she suggests that Dan doesn't *want* to do the activity, ascribing a motive for his behavior.

After they'd completed their evaluations of Dan, the clinicians met for a case conference ("pre-staffing") to discuss their results and decide on a diagnosis before presenting their findings to Dan's mother. As she communicates her findings from the ADOS to Leah and Leslie, a student trainee, Jennifer describes Dan's disengagement from the test as his "most atypical response" (line 1), a term that, in clinical settings, indexes ASD. It takes several more turns of talk for her and the student to recall the part of the test where it occurred:

Case 2c:24.PSTF

```
1    Jen:   I'd say the: the most a:typical response he had was that one time
2           when he (.) got up [and he: walked away to the corner.]
3    Les:                      [What  wuh-  what  was the question] (rather)
4           insisting and that he didn't like and he just got up
5           [and walked (0.5) I find it frustrating.
6    Jen:   [↑It was: a (little) hard question. ((looking at notes)) It was um-
7                 (0.3)
8    Les:   You said to do something and he just didn't wanted to do it.
9           (8.0) ((Leah asks for camera shift, while Jen reviews ADOS notes))
10   Jen:   It was the demonstration test? So: asking him to show me how he
11          brushes [teeth? I think it was just-        ] he felt on the spot=
12   Les:           [↑Y:e:::ah.  That would be (        )]
13   Jen:   =and so he just got up an:d (.) [walked away into the corner, but=
14   Leah:                                  [Walked away.
15   Jen:   =he ↑came back and I just brought out the break toys...
```

Notice how at line 8 the student, Leslie, depicts Dan as not wanting to participate, and Jen (at lines 11, 13) formulates Dan as feeling "on the spot" in a way that occasioned his abandonment of the demonstration.

Both interpretations of Dan's conduct target his psychological state—what he *wanted* or *felt*—rather than the interactional context where the behavior occurred. In the interaction, Dan was resisting Jennifer's directives in second position: he did so twelve times before getting up from the table (see Maynard and Turowetz, forthcoming). But, in Jennifer's and Leslie's post hoc accounts, there is no mention of directives or refusals, only a minimal reference to the questions that were asked ("So asking him to show...", line 10). As a result, Dan's behavior seems abrupt and unexpected, and to have been undertaken unilaterally. Rather than being the culmination of a chain of directive-response sequences, Dan's actions take on a first position character. They constitute a breach of sorts that requires explanation, which his commonsense interlocutors work to supply. In contrast with Officer Grossman, the clinicians' explanation is cast in psychological terms, not embodied ones; nonetheless, both accounts adumbrate or suggest first-position escaping moves on each boy's part, deploying the device of transpositioning to make sense of the person with autism's actions.

Discussion and Conclusion

We have shown how transpositioning operates in two distinct cases of interaction between neurotypical professionals and autistic individuals. In both cases, the person with autism committed an interactional violation that defied (neurotypical) commonsense, and for which they were held responsible. However, close inspection of the original interactions reveals that the professionals' accounts spotlight the actions of the person with autism while obscuring or muting the interactional environment in which those actions occurred. In their original context, these violations—disengaging from a test-in-progress, attempting to flee from police—were responsive to prior actions that could be taken as inapposite in their own right. Connor Leibel was resisting Officer Grossman's incursions into his physical space and an accusatory line of questioning that treated his actions as accountable from the outset; Dan Chapman was resisting a series of directives, which he did calmly and politely before finally walking away from Jennifer. Yet, through transpositioning, these second position actions were transformed into first position initiations that appeared to come from out of nowhere.

Because the meaning of an action is worked out in interaction and depends on its position in an interactional sequence, a first position action has different implications than one in second position, and lends itself to different accounts of "what happened." Accounts which center on individual action, rather than *inter*action, lend themselves to individualist, psychologistic explanations of those actions, and are consistent with popular arguments that the troubles people with autism experience derive from a "theory of mind" deficit (Baron-Cohen et al. 1985), weak executive function (Frith 2003), or biological predispositions (Baron-Cohen 2003). While there may be some truth to these accounts, they are fundamentally asocial, isolating "behaviors" as if they were phenotypic phenomena that emanate from interior cognitive or genomic states (Maynard 2019). In our view, social meanings and identities are produced cooperatively in interaction, not through individual cognitions or neurobiological conditions; the relevance of cognition and neurobiology is always embedded in a social-interactional environment. Thus, it is necessary to ask what practices actors are using to make sense together—or how they fail to make sense, as the case may be—and the ways in which sense-making provides for the accounts that subsequently symbolize, explain, justify, rationalize, or otherwise transform those practices.

In both cases we have examined, a co-produced outcome is retrospectively transformed into evidence of a problem with the autistic party. This is important not only because it personalizes social problems, stigmatizing the person with autism and contributing to a deficit-centric picture of dis/ability, but also because it becomes the basis for sanctions, formal and informal, that can have significant effects on the lives of autistic individuals. In Connor's case, he was assaulted and placed in physical custody, causing both bodily harm and psychological distress. Indeed, his family is now suing the county for damages. The consequences for Dan were much more benign: the clinician was understanding and patient, and skillfully reengaged him by inviting him to play with toys. However, we know from Dan's medical records and the clinicians' interviews with his mother that he has a history of behavioral problems. His meltdowns at school, in particular, have resulted in police intervention, and on one occasion a security guard had to physically restrain him after he set off a fire alarm and threatened the guard with a two by four.[3] We also know that these episodes tend to be triggered by Dan's resistance to transitioning between activities or being told "no." Thus, it is reasonable to speculate that at least some of these incidents begin in much the same way that Dan's disengagement from Jennifer did, i.e. with Dan refusing to comply with directives. By paying close attention not only to Dan's psychological state, but the interactional environment where his behavior occurs, it may be possible to manage and deescalate troubled *inter*actions before they eventuate in explosive actions. Per the analysis we have presented, this would mean focusing on both the composition *and* sequential position of the actions (Schegloff 1995), treating them as social-interactional phenomena rather than (only) evidence of psychological motivations.

As the population with autism grows and ages into adolescence and early adulthood, we are seeing an increasing number of cases where autistic individuals become entangled in the criminal justice system. We see a similar correlation between age and crime in neurotypical populations (Sampson and Laub 1993). However, the challenges and offending patterns of people with autism are different from their neurotypical peers (King and Murphy 2014), and, for designing effective interventions, it is important to understand these patterns and how they are embedded in social-interactional environments. Such interventions, for purposes of change, should do everything possible to minimize stigma and target these environments and not just the atypical individual.

[3]See Maynard's (2019) discussion of records and record keeping in our two cases with reference to Garfinkel's (1967, Chapter 6) on "Good Organizational Reasons for 'Bad' Record-Keeping." A significant proportion of contact between youth with autism and police is due to school-related incidents. Cheely et al. (2012, p. 1859), for example, report that youth with ASD were significantly more likely than a control group to be charged for "school-based offenses" and "disturbing schools." Thus, Dan's experience fits a larger pattern seen in young autistic offenders, suggesting the importance of focusing on the interactional environment in schools (and similar spaces) and its contributions to offending behavior.

References

American Psychological Association. (2013). *Diagnostic and statistical manual of mental disorders* (5th ed.). Washington, DC: Author.

Baron-Cohen, S. (2003). *The essential difference: Male and female brains and the truth about autism*. New York: Basic Books.

Baron-Cohen, S., Leslie, A. M., & Frith, U. (1985). Does the autistic child have a "theory of mind"? *Cognition, 21*(1), 37–46.

Bolden, G. B. (2006). Little words that matter: Discourse markers "so" and "oh" and the doing of other-attentiveness in social interaction. *Journal of Communication, 56*(4), 661–688.

Bolden, G. B., & Robinson, J. D. (2011). Soliciting accounts with why-interrogatives in conversation. *Journal of Communication, 61*(1), 94–119.

Centers for Disease Control and Prevention (CDC). (2018). *Data and statistics on autism spectrum disorder*. https://www.cdc.gov/ncbddd/autism/data.html. Accessed on 28 June 2019.

Cheely, C. A., Carpenter, L. A., Letourneau, E. J., Nicholas, J. S., Charles, J., & King, L. B. (2012). The prevalence of youth with autism spectrum disorders in the criminal justice system. *Journal of Autism and Developmental Disorders, 42*(9), 1856–1862.

Clayman, S., & Gill, V. T. (2012). Conversation analysis. In M. Hardy & A. Bryman (Eds.), *Handbook of data analysis* (pp. 538–606). London: Sage.

Craven, A., & Potter, J. (2010. Directives: Entitlement and contingency in action. *Discourse Studies, 12*(4), 419–442.

Curl, T. S., & Drew, P. (2008). Contingency and action: A comparison of two forms of requesting. *Research on Language and Social Interaction, 41*(2), 129–153.

Drew, P. (1997). 'Open' class repair initiators in response to sequential sources of troubles in conversation. *Journal of Pragmatics, 28*(1), 69–101.

Durkin, M. S., Maenner, M. J., Newschaffer, C. J., Lee, L. C., Cunniff, C. M., Daniels, J. L., et al. (2008). Advanced parental age and the risk of autism spectrum disorder. *American Journal of Epidemiology, 168*(11), 1268–1276.

Eyal, G. (2013). For a sociology of expertise: The social origins of the autism epidemic. *American Journal of Sociology, 118*(4), 863–907.

Eyal, G., Hart, B., Onculer, E., Oren, N., & Rossi, N. (2010). *The autism matrix: The social origins of the autism epidemic*. Malden, MA: Polity Press.

Fombonne, E. (2018). The rising prevalence of autism. *Journal of Child Psychology and Psychiatry, 59*(7), 717–720.

Frith, U. (2003). *Autism: Explaining the enigma*. London: Blackwell.

Garfinkel, H. (1963). A conception of and experiments with trust as a condition of stable social actions. In O. J. Harvey (Ed.), *Motivation and social interaction: Cognitive determinants* (pp. 187–238). New York: Ronald Press.

Garfinkel, H. (1967). *Studies in ethnomethodology*. Englewood Cliffs, NJ: Prentice-Hall.

Gernsbacher, M. A., Dawson, M., & Goldsmith, H. H. (2005). Three reasons not to believe in an autism epidemic. *Current Directions in Psychological Science, 14*(2), 55–58.

Grandin, T. (2006). *Thinking in pictures and other reports from my life with autism*. New York: Vintage Books.

Grinker, R. R. (2007). *Unstrange minds: Remapping the world of autism*. New York: Basic Books.

Hacking, I. (1999). *The social construction of what?* Cambridge, MA: Harvard University Press.

Heritage, J. (1984a). *Garfinkel and ethnomethodology*. Cambridge, England: Polity Press.

Heritage, J. (1984b). A change-of-state token and aspects of its sequential placement. In J. M. Atkinson & J. Heritage (Eds.), *Structures of Social Action* (pp. 299–345). Cambridge, England: Cambridge University Press.

Heritage, J. (2012). Epistemics in action: Action formation and territories of knowledge. *Research on Language & Social Interaction, 45*(1), 1–29.

Jones, N., & Raymond, G. (2012). "The camera rolls" using third-party video in field research. *The Annals of the American Academy of Political and Social Science, 642*(1), 109–123.

King, C., & Murphy, G. H. (2014). A systematic review of people with autism spectrum disorder and the criminal justice system. *Journal of Autism and Developmental Disorders, 44*(11), 2717–2733.

Liu, K. Y., King, M., & Bearman, P. S. (2010). Social influence and the autism epidemic. *American Journal of Sociology, 115*(5), 1387–1434.

Local, J., & Wootton, T. (1995). Interactional and phonetic aspects of immediate echolalia in autism: A case study. *Clinical Linguistics & Phonetics, 9*(2), 155–184.

Maynard, D. W. (2003). *Bad news, good news: Conversational order in everyday talk and clinical settings*. Chicago: Chicago University Press.

Maynard, D. W. (2005). Social actions, gestalt coherence, and designations of disability: Lessons from and about autism. *Social Problems, 52*(4), 499–524.

Maynard, D. W. (2019). Why social psychology needs autism, and why autism needs social psychology: Forensic and clinical considerations. *Social Psychology Quarterly, 82*(1), 5–30.

Maynard, D. W., & Turowetz, J. (2017). Doing testing: How concrete competence can facilitate or inhibit performances of children with autism spectrum disorder. *Qualitative Sociology, 40*(4), 467–491.

Maynard, D.W., & Turowetz, J. (2019). Doing abstraction: Autism spectrum disorder, the sociology of diagnosis, and social theory. *Sociological Theory, 37*(1), 89–116.

Maynard, D. W., & Turowetz, J. (forthcoming). Commonsense knowledge, disability, and atypical interaction: The case of autism. In D. W. Maynard & J. Heritage (Eds.), *Harold Garfinkel: Praxis, social order, and ethnomethodology's legacies*. New York: Oxford University Press.

Mondada, L. (2009). Emergent focused interactions in public places: A systematic analysis of the multimodal achievement of a common interactional space. *Journal of Pragmatics, 41,* 1977–1997.

Muskett, T., Perkins, M., Clegg, J., & Body, R. (2010). Inflexibility as an interactional phenomenon: Using conversation analysis to re-examine a symptom of autism. *Clinical Linguistics & Phonetics, 24*(1), 1–16.

Nadesan, M. H. (2005). *Constructing autism: Unraveling the "truth" and constructing the social.* London: Routledge.

Potter, J., & Hepburn, A. (2010). Putting aspiration into words: 'Laugh particles,' managing descriptive trouble, and modulating action. *Journal of Pragmatics, 15*(6), 1543–1555.

Rawls, A. W. (1987). The interaction order sui generis: Goffman's contribution to social theory. *Sociological Theory, 5*(2), 136–149.

Rawls, A. W., Duck, W., & Turowetz, J. (2018). Problems establishing identity/residency in a city neighborhood during a black/white police-citizen encounter: Reprising Du Bois' conception of submission as "submissive civility". *City & Community, 17*(4), 1015–1050.

Sacks, H., & Schegloff E. A. (1979). Two preferences in organization of reference to persons in conversation and their interaction. In G. Psathas (Ed.), *Everyday language: Studies in ethnomethodology* (pp. 15–21). New York: Irvington.

Sampson, R. J., & J. H. Laub. (1993). *Crime in the making: Pathways and turning points through life*. Cambridge, MA: Harvard University Press.

Schegloff, E. A. (1995). Discourse as interactional achievement III: The omnirelevance of action. *Research on Language and Social Interaction, 28*(3), 185–211.

Schegloff, E. A. (2007). *Sequence organization in interaction: A primer in conversation analysis*. Cambridge: Cambridge University Press.

Schütz, A. (1962). *Collected papers, volume 1: The problem of social reality*. The Hague: Martinus Nijhoff.

Silberman, S. (2015). *NeuroTribes: The legacy of autism and the future of neurodiversity*. New York, NY: Penguin Books.

Silberman, S. (2017). The police need to understand autism. *The New York Times Online*. September 19. https://www.nytimes.com/2017/09/19/opinion/police-autismunderstanding.html.

Solomon, O. (2015). "But-he'll fall!": Children with autism, interspecies intersubjectivity, and the problem of 'being social'. *Culture, Medicine and Psychiatry, 39*(2), 323–344.

Sterponi, L., & Fasulo, A. (2010). "How to go on": Intersubjectivity and progressivity in the communication of a child with autism. *Ethos, 38*(1), 116–142.

Stribling, P., Rae, J., & Dickerson, P. (2007). Two forms of spoken repetition in a girl with autism. *International Journal of Language & Communication Disorders, 42*(4), 427–444.

Stivers, T. (2004). "No no no" and other types of multiple sayings in social interaction. *Human Communication Research, 30*(2), 260–293.

Turowetz, J. (2015a). The interactional production of a clinical fact in a case of autism. *Qualitative Sociology, 38,* 57–78.

Turowetz, J. (2015b). Citing conduct, individualizing symptoms: Accomplishing autism diagnosis in clinical case conferences. *Social Science and Medicine, 142,* 214–222.

Turowetz, J., & Maynard, D. W. (2017). *The interactional bases of criminaloffending in persons with autism.* Paper presented at the International Institute forEthnomethodology and Conversation Analysis, July, Westerville, OH.

Turowetz, J., & Maynard, D. W. (2019). Documenting diagnosis: Testing, labelling, and the production of medical records in an autism clinic. *Sociology of Health & Illness*. Published online 5 March 2019. https://doi.org/abs/10.1111/1467-9566.12882.

Turowetz, J., & D. W. Maynard. (n.d.). From misalignment to misdemeanor. Unpublished manuscript.

Wing, L. (1981). Asperger's syndrome: A clinical account. *Psychological Medicine, 11*(1), 115–129.

World Health Organization (WHO). 2017. *Autism spectrum disorders*. https://www.who.int/news-room/fact-sheets/detail/autism-spectrum-disorders. Accessed on 28 June 2019.

Wootton, A. (1999). An investigation of delayed echoing in a child with autism. *First Language, 19*(57), 359–381.

[illegible]

3

Making and Taking Opportunities for Co-participation in an Interaction Between a Boy with Autism Spectrum Disorder and His Father

John P. Rae and Monica Ramey

Autism Spectrum Disorder (ASD) is a pervasive developmental condition which is characterised by difficulties in social interaction and communication, and in repetitive interests and behaviour (American Psychiatric Association 2013; World Health Organization 1992, 2018). It is a highly heterogeneous condition and is probably caused by complex genetic factors and possibly environmental triggers. Whilst ASD cannot be cured, the focus of interventions is usually on support for children and their parents, for example involving speech and language therapy, occupational therapy, and educational support. There is evidence for the effectiveness of parent- or carer-mediated interventions for young children (Kasari et al. 2010; Pickles et al. 2016). In their critical review of how language has been researched and understood in relation to autism, Sterponi et al. (2015) distinguish three

J. P. Rae (✉)
University of Roehampton, London, UK

M. Ramey
Formerly of University of Roehampton, London, UK

© The Author(s) 2020

R. Wilkinson et al. (eds.), *Atypical Interaction*,
https://doi.org/10.1007/978-3-030-28799-3_3

perspectives. First, research geared to characterising the distinctive features of the language produced by speakers with autism. For example, based on talk in an informal interview setting, Baltaxe (1977) identified a number of atypical pragmatic practices. Second, research that moved the focus to the functionality of these distinctive features. A notable example is Prizant and Duchan's (1981) demonstration that, in interactions between children with autism and familiar adults, immediate echolia (the uttering of previously heard words or strings of words) can be functional. Third, research that considered how features of the context could impinge on the language use of persons with autism. For example Rydell and Mirenda (1991) showed that in adult-child naturalistic play sessions, when adults' utterances were coded in terms of the level of constraint that they create, differences become apparent in how children respond. For example, high constraint utterances elicited more verbal utterances from the children than low constraint utterances. Whilst the examples just mentioned do not use Conversation Analysis (CA), research using this method can be located in the second and third perspectives (as Sterponi et al. (2015) indicate).

One line of research drawing on CA to examine interactions involving children with ASD has focused on the particular capacities and challenges that they exhibit. For example, the analysis of echolalia in spontaneous interactions, and the identification of its potential interactional relevance, was a focus of pioneering work (Wootton 1999; Local and Wootton 1995; Tarplee and Barrow 1999) and also of more recent work (e.g., Stribling et al. 2007; Sterponi and Shankey 2014). The competences exhibited in a range of other verbal practices have also been examined (for example, Sterponi and Fasulo 2010; Muskett et al. 2010.) Maynard and colleagues have proposed that a careful analysis of actual practices in interactions show that children with ASD have distinctive ways of understanding the world, which they refer to as "concrete competence" and "autistic intelligence". They further propose that clinical testing procedures focus on second-order, abstract competence and thereby systematically exclude certain abilities that children with ASD have (Maynard 2005; Maynard and Turowetz 2017). This latter point is commensurate with another line of research which focuses more on how neurotypical people interact with people with ASD. For example, Maynard and Turowetz (this volume) examine how a police officer interacts with a young person with autism. Another focus has been on delineating the interactional practices used by teachers and learning support assistants in educational settings involving students with autism (Korkiakangas and Rae 2013; Stribling and Rae 2010). In such settings, the professional party might know the child very well, but commonly they do not. One very important class of persons with whom many children with ASD interact is their own family members. Previous studies have drawn on CA in the context of detailed case studies of individual children with autism interacting with a range of familiar adults (mainly family members) at home. For example, Geils and Knoetze (2008) and Sterponi and Fasulo (2010) each examine an individual boy with autism (aged 5:10 years and 8:6 years respectively) engaging in a range of activities. Yet despite the importance of such settings, relatively little is known about the interactional capacities and challenges that children and parents encounter.

Ramey and Rae (2015) draw attention to how domestic interactions between children with ASD and their parents can involve a spectrum of different forms of parental involvement; for example, from the parent being present but otherwise engaged while their child carries out an activity, through to carrying out an activity on behalf of the child. Within developmental psychology, the importance of parental support for children's activity is influentially identified in Vygotsky's idea of the zone of proximal development (ZPD). Briefly, Vygotsky's socio-cultural account of developmental psychology draws attention to the relevance of acting with others. In Vygotsky's account, the ZPD is a metaphorical region into which a child's competence can be extended through interaction with an adult or more able peer (Vygotsky 1978). Vygotsky also proposes that being able to benefit from such interaction is itself an importance competence. A distinct, but related, proposal has been made by Tomasello (1999), who suggests that the capacity of humans to develop technology relies on being able to learn from others which in turn rests on a species-specific human capacity to understand others' intentions. A connected and influential conceptualisation of how a child's capacity can be extended through the support of another is that of "scaffolding"

(Wood et al. 1976). This metaphor draws attention to the idea that through carrying out an activity with parental support, a child might thereafter be able to accomplish it independently. The provision of parental support, and a child's use of it, are deeply interactional matters. Nevertheless, as Wootton (1997/2005) notes, though highlighting the social nature of development, Vygotsky himself did not inaugurate a programme of research into how such interactions actually unfold. (There is, nevertheless a large body of research in developmental psychology that codes selected behaviours in order to consider how certain variables relate to support e.g. Carr and Pike, 2012.) The potential of conversation analysis to examine ZPD interactions was suggested by Jacoby and Ochs (1995). In using CA to examine the work of a learning support assistant (LSA), Stribling and Rae (2010) demonstrate the distinctive practices that she adopts in supporting a girl with autism in a mathematics class. They show how the LSA's supportive actions are contingent upon the girl's progress or the troubles that she encounters; this sensitivity to the local needs of the child (and to other features of the setting) thereby exhibits professional discretion. Ramey and Rae's (2015) analysis of children with ASD interacting with parents at home suggest that in these domestic settings, the parents' support is also deeply contingent and progressive in character. However, they also show that commonly in such settings, one class of situations that parents have to address consists of task-related contingencies which arise from properties of the setting rather than the child's conduct. For example, getting materials or ingredients for an activity at hand might require a change in their involvement with that activity.

Such work intersects with some of the central concerns of interactional analysis in general and conversation analysis in particular. All social interaction involves co-participation to some extent. That is, when one party interacts with another, they are participating in something that is shared. However, in some circumstances the way in which two or more parties co-participate in, or with, something becomes more variegated and nuanced. Goffman (1981) did much to draw our attention to different forms of participation and to delineate and describe them. His notion of *participation framework* refers to the variety of relationships that other parties may have to a speaker's utterance, for example as an addressee, as a hearer, or as an over-hearer. One line of conversation analytic work has concerned the detailed analysis of how different forms of participation come about interactionally, that is, how different forms of participation occur. Across numerous settings, C. Goodwin and M.H. Goodwin have shown how participants recurrently have choices about how to co-participate with unfolding action (e.g. C. Goodwin 2007, 2018; M.H. Goodwin 1997). In the course of an analysis of classroom interaction, and how the teacher's design of questions may turn out to include a child's name and thereby be addressed to that particular child, Lerner (1995) uses the term "participation opportunities" to refer to specific interaction moments where participation may, or may not be, relevant or necessary. (Rae 2001 offers an analysis of the transforming of participation frameworks and a critical discussion of the concept.)

Whilst the situations in which a party might come to be involved with an activity that another party is engaged in are manifold, one situation concerns the provision of assistance. Recently, the concept of *recruitment* has been proposed to describe how one party can become involved with a practical course of action that another party is engaged in, or is attempting to carry out, when the latter encounters a trouble, or is anticipated to encounter a trouble (Kendrick and Drew 2016). Through applying CA to videorecordings of adults interacting in a range of everyday settings, Kendrick and Drew propose that a distinction can be drawn between the method through which a party comes to be recruited on the one hand and how the trouble becomes recognizable on the other. For example, a person who is not visibly encountering a trouble might request assistance. In another situation, a person's trouble might be visibly embodied and thereby display the relevance of assistance. In a further situation, a trouble might be anticipated and the relevance of assistance can be projected. A range of such possibilities is shown in the upper two rows of Table 3.1. Kendrick and Drew further propose that these situations constitute a continuum; who initiates assistance varies from self (the party who might benefit from being assisted) to other (the party giving assistance), and the pressure to assist varies from being an obligation to being an opportunity.

Although Kendrick and Drew's (2016) empirically-based analysis of recruitment was developed in the context of adult interaction, it has relevance for the analysis of assistance in child-parent interaction.

Table 3.1 The recruitment continuum

Method of recruitment				
request	report	alert	display	project
How the trouble becomes recognizable				
implicit	formulated	indexed	embodied	anticipated
Relevance of assisting				
Obligation to assist ←	================	================	================	→ Opportunity to assist
Who initiates assistance				
Self ←	================	================	================	→ Other

Source Adapted from Kendrick and Drew (2016, p. 11)

The nature of troubles that arise, the methods of recruitment, the dimensions concerning who initiates assistance and the relevance of that assistance, are all relevant in the empirical analysis of Vygotskian support in the ZPD, or of scaffolding. However, it should be noted that not all forms of facilitation involve actively providing assistance. For example, Ramey and Rae (2015) show that when addressing task-related contingencies (such as getting relevant materials), a parent might partially withdraw from an activity that a child is engaged in and this can apparently facilitate the child's progression of that activity. The present study aims to extend Ramey and Rae's (2015) analysis of how parents of children with ASD facilitate activities at home by further analysis of how co-participation is managed, and of how this relates to Kendrick and Drew's (2016) recruitment continuum. As such, it aims to complement research in developmental psychology into the play of children with ASD (for example Freeman and Kasari 2013) and to contribute to our understanding of how the participation of children with ASD can be supported and facilitated in everyday, domestic settings.

Method

In order to examine the situated ways in which parents provide support to children with autism, the present study uses conversation analysis to examine a single session of activity in which Ben, a 12-year old boy with autism spectrum disorder, interacts with his father while playing with a construction game at home. This episode (8 minutes 19 seconds duration) was collected as part of set of video recordings, made with consent, of four children interacting at home with relatives, friends and a friend's relative. These data were recorded in the South of England; the participants speak British English. The session was transcribed in full using the standard conventions used in CA to capture talk and visible action (Hepburn and Bolden 2012). Although CA commonly draws on data involving multiple participants in a range of settings, especially when studying neurotypical participants, the analysis of single conversations can be informative. In particular, when studying atypical interaction, the detailed examination of specific participants on specific occasions can be necessary in order to understand the distinctive practices that those participants use. The analysis of multiple instances of interactional practices within single conversations or sessions of activity involving a participant with ASD has been used to identify particular ways in which co-interactants respond in order to propose general challenges encountered by persons with ASD (e.g. Rendle-Short 2002, with respect to Asperger Syndrome) and/or to formulate generalisable competences exhibited by co-interactants (e.g. Stribling and Rae 2010, with respect to learning support assistants).

Unlike some domestic activities which provide opportunities for the child to direct what happens (for example the pottery session described in Ramey and Rae 2015) the construction activity examined here is largely directed by the father. Rather than approaching the data in terms of a theory, the study uses CA in an attempt to understand parts of the session in their own terms. Here, whilst the analysis is informed by an understanding of phenomena that CA has previously identified, as with all CA work, the aim is to understand what these participants are doing rather than to see their conduct as a screen onto which previously identified phenomena can be projected or through which a theory can be tested. A key policy is to think in terms of what Schegloff and Sacks (1973) propose is a pervasive question for participants in interaction: "why that now?"—why did that person do that thing at this time. Furthermore, participants' actions in interaction are understood to be both responsive to what has happened and generative of a new happening; they are "context shaped" and "context renewing" (Heritage 1984, p. 290). As such, analysis requires the examination of stretches of interaction such that actions can be examined in terms of the sequential environment in which they occur. The approach taken here was to examine the data in terms of how the participants create opportunities for each other.

In the session, Ben is seated at a large table, with his father (Dad) to his right. Dad has a construction game in front of him. The game consists of 24 items, each held behind a numbered flap in the box. Each item consists of a small number of plastic components. A pictorial guide on the box shows (in outline) how the pieces should be fitted together to assemble an item. After initially selecting item "number 13" and discovering that they have already completed this item, they move onto "number 14" and proceed to assemble that. In addition to the construction game, a further toy is played with in the session: a sound effects box. This has an array of 16 buttons which, when pressed, produce one of a number of humorous sound effects. Whilst the assembly of "number 14" is a continued focus of the setting, it is important to note that, at one time or another, other activities become the activity of the moment. In particular, there is a bout of father-son physical play; another spate of joint action involves Ben using one of the components as a pretend probe. Then at other times there are activities which Ben engages in more-or-less unilaterally such as sliding a book onto the floor and there are episodes of moving about.

Analysis

The analysis will begin by showing how the father makes use of *multimodal directives* to structure the setting. We then show how these can be designed so as to facilitate responding and how support can be provided if the child encounters trouble in responding to the directive. We then turn to a consideration of the issues raised by the child attending to other matters or engaging in competing courses of action.

Directives

One key resource that occurs in the organisation of the session is Dad's use of instructions that propose that Ben should do something.

Extract 1[1] shows a sequence from early in the session. This sequence is initiated by Dad saying "Can you find number fourteen for me" (line 35). In response, Ben opens the correct box (line 039), and receives a congratulatory response from Dad, "That's right. Well done" (lines 040–041). (This example is also examined in Ramey and Rae 2015.)

Extract 1 [MR2012 Benjamin & Dad Table] Fourteen

Ben and Dad are seated side by side at a table; Dad is to Ben's right and has a Lego box open towards his right-hand side. Dad has moved a sound effects toy to his right-hand side.

```
037 Dad:  Now we need number fourteen

           Ben and Dad are both gazing towards the box
038>Dad:  [Can you find number fourteen] for [me
          [Dad close flap for item14    ]     [Dad gazes at
                                              [Ben and
                                              [adjusts box
                     [Ben reaches towards box
   >                 [     [Ben opens correct flap
039       (----------[1----[-)
                     [Dad looks towards box
040>Dad:  Tha:t's right
041 Dad:  [Well done.
          [Ben gets package and handles it
```

The stretch of action shown in Extract 1 fundamentally consists of a sequence built of out of two actions, an initiating action (the instruction) and the responsive action (complying with the instruction). Such two-part sequences are fundamental to social interaction. Whilst adjacency pairs involve two talk-implemented actions (Schegloff 2007), here the implicated responsive action is not talk but rather visible action. (The circumstance under which recipients of such actions do produce talk has been examined by Stevanovic and Monzoni 2016.) Grammatically, Dad's action is built as a yes/no polar question, using a modal verb ("can you"). However, whilst this is grammatically a question, it is not a request for information but rather an instruction formulated as a request. Such expressions, which

[1]In this chapter, visible conduct, including eye-gaze, is shown in italics. Unless otherwise indicated, annotations above the transcribed talk, or silence, show Ben's conduct; annotations below show Dad's conduct. In some cases time silences are shown as dashes, each dash representing 0.1 seconds, and each whole second shown as a number. E.g. (---------1--) shows a silence of 1.2 seconds.

seek to get another party to do something, have come to be referred to generally as directives (Ervin-Tripp 1976). As such, the term appears to be derived from Searle's (1975) typology of speech acts and should not be understood in the non-technical sense of a "directive" as an authoritative order or ruling. (It was probably precisely to avoid confusions with vernacular terms that led Austin to use invented terms in his original analysis of what he called "illocutionary acts" [Austin 1955/1962]. He placed "order", "command"—along with "warn" and "advise", in a class which he called "exercitives" which he described as "…the giving of a decision in favour of or against a certain course of action, or advocacy of it." [p. 154].) Indeed, the gradation of authority, or lack of it, has been a prominent feature of the recent sustained analysis of directives in talk-in-interaction in recent CA research (e.g. Craven and Potter 2010; Curl and Drew 2008; Drew and Couper-Kuhlen 2014; Kent 2012; Kent and Kendrick 2016; Heinemann 2006); their use in family settings has been specifically examined by Aronsson and Cekaite (2011) and Goodwin and Cekaite (2013, 2014). In their study of how children with autism respond differently to parents' high constraint and low constraint utterances, Rydell and Mirenda (1991) cite directives as one example of high constraint utterances.

The interactional force of sequence-initiating actions is widely exploited in institutional settings such as calls to emergency services (e.g. Zimmerman 1992) and by teachers in classroom interactions. In fact, in Extract 1 the participants' production of an initiating action, a responsive action and a sequence-closing third action shows a structure which is highly ubiquitous in classroom settings and which has been described in terms of initiation-response-evaluation (or feedback) sequence (Sinclair and Coulthard 1975; Mehan 1979). Whilst sequence-initiating actions in general, and directives in particular, might be thought of as having a unilateral character in which an obligation is placed on the recipient, the other side of this coin is that they also thereby provide a structured opportunity for participation (see Lerner 1995 for an analysis of teacher-initiated sequence in classroom settings). In other words, in the midst of Dad's and Ben's other activities, directives provide places which are specifically geared to enabling Ben to co-participate and to thereby create sites for co-operation (C. Goodwin 2018).

The production of Dad's directive contains a number of elements that appear to be geared to supporting Ben in responding. First, the target is produced with deliberate enunciation "number fourteen" (037). Second, in addition to the talk-based features of the directive, Dad also uses multimodal resources. As he produces his turn, he brings his gaze to Ben and simultaneously rotates the box slightly towards him. These two visible actions support the directive in suggesting that a response from Ben is relevant; moreover, the way in which the box is rotated brings the target item closer to Ben. Dad thereby uses multimodal resources to support Ben's responding.

After an item has been selected from the box, the session largely (but by no means entirely) involves assembling the separate pieces. Extract 2 shows one such episode. Having concluded a stretch of pretend fighting, Dad calls Ben a cheeky rascal (235) and, positioning pieces on the table, summons Ben's attention. Ben continues with an activity which apparently relates to the pretend fighting by producing a directive of his own to the effect that his father should pretend to cry (237); Dad obliges (238) and Ben then sits forward and engages with the pieces while producing what appears to be an echolalic utterance. Here Dad uses the directive "Can you put this on top of there" (240).

Extract 2 [MR2012 Benjamin & Dad Table] don't be mean

```
235 Dad:  Cheeky rascal
236 Dad:  [    Look               ]
          [Dad positioning pieces]
237 Ben:  [Crying!        ] =
          [holding pieces]
238 Dad:  =[whoo hoo. Nmmm. ]
           [gaze at Ben     ]
           [pretend sad face]
          [Ben sits forward and reaches towards the pieces
239 Ben:  [(  ) (    ) is ((possibly a person's name))

240 Dad:  [°Can you put this on top of there°]
          [still holding pieces              ]

          [Ben takes piece and pushes it together
241       [(----------)
          [Dad releases pieces
242 Dad:  Tha:t's it well done
```

Dad's use of the indexical expressions, "this" and "there" provide a linkage between his talk and objects in the world, namely the small components that he is handling and presenting to Ben. (The use of indexical expression, or pro-terms, to link talk to objects is a ubiquitous feature of talk in object-related settings, e.g. C. Goodwin 2018.) Thus here, Dad's directive is produced multimodally and brings together talk, bodily orientation and material objects to provide a conspicuous instruction at just this moment. A feature of Dad's embodied display is that the bodily positioning that he adopted when he summoned Ben (line 236) is sustained through the crying game, suggesting that the pretend crying was accommodated within an over-arching activity (compare Schegloff 1998 on sustaining the position of the body during a subsidiary episode of talk.)

We shall now examine two ways in which the basic directive-response-confirmation sequence can be extended. In Extracts 1 and 2, Ben successively responds to Dad's directives and retrieves the correct item from the box within one second. Extract 3 shows another sequence (from earlier in the session) in which Ben less readily addresses the directive. Here, Dad issues the directive "Can you find number thirteen" (09) and after about one second, Ben reaches towards the box, but apparently not towards the correct item (10). Ben subsequently reaches towards the correct item (16) and receives confirmation and congratulations from Dad (17). (This example is also considered in Ramey and Rae 2015.)

Extract 3 [MR2012 Benjamin & Dad Table] Thirteen

```
009>Dad: Can you find number [thirteen

                             [Dad adjusts box

010      (----------1---[-------2)
                        [Ben reaches towards box
011>Dad: [Thirtee:na:
012      (---------) ((Dad looks at Ben))
013 Ben: Thirteen wai[t
014>Dad:             [Whe's- Where's thir[teen
                                         [Ben retracts hand
015 Ben: Way [ weh   (.)   <wait   ] a minute.>
             [Ben rapidly shakes RH]
016      (-----)
017>Dad: Where's [thirt=
                 [Ben reaches towards the box
018>Dad: =Aht's right well done
019      [(-----)
         [Ben retrieves item13 and puts it on the table
```

As in Extract 1, around one second after the completion of Dad's directive, Ben reaches towards the box but on this occasion he evidently has some trouble in locating the correct item. (The nature of the trouble should not be assumed to lie in an inability on Ben's behalf. It subsequently transpires that they have previously completed item 13. It is thus possible that Ben might be performing an operation that relates to this.) Dad seeks to address Ben's apparent trouble by repeating the number of the item, with exaggerated articulation, "Thirtee:na:" (line 011); reformulating the instruction "Where's thirteen" (line 014); and he starts, but curtails, a further repeat (line 016). Dad thereby offers situated support in order to assist Ben, that is, the support that he offers is context dependent, it is contingent upon the course of Ben's actions. (The re-presentation of initiating actions in IRE exchanges has been examined by Zemel and Koschmann 2011. This sequence and other cases are examined and compared to prompts and supportive actions in a therapy session in Rae and Ramey, in preparation.)

In Extract 3 then, we see how, in this setting, a basic directive-response sequence can be expanded by the initiating party to include prompts or pursuits. In terms of the recruitment continuum, Dad's initial involvement with the unfolding course of action can be understood in terms of his addressing a trouble that is *displayed* in Ben's *embodied* response. This extract also shows how the recipient of assistance has resources for resisting the pressure that these prompts can impose.

Selectively Responding to Competing Interests and Activities

Although Ben displays trouble in locating item thirteen in Extract 3, he is nevertheless appropriately oriented to the task that Dad has set him—a point which he makes in his utterance "thirteen wait". (Stribling et al. 2007 suggest that repetitions in the talk of a child with ASD can similarly be used to indicate engagement with a task.) However, on some occasions, Ben shows engagement with concerns that are apparently extraneous to the activities that Dad seeks to engage him in. Extract 4 shows such an example. Just prior to the episode shown in Extract 1, Dad confiscates the sound effects box. As he puts it to one side, Ben produces an utterance involving a proper noun which is apparently unrelated to the current activities “It should be Washington”. (This appears to be an example of delayed echolalia; the production of a previously heard verbal expression.) (This fragment is also considered in Ramey and Rae 2015.)

Extract 4 [MR2012 Benjamin & Dad Table] <Ramey and Rae 2015>

```
007>Dad: Can we put that away for the moment.

   >     [     ((Father removes soundbox)) ]
008 Ben: [It should be [ ( W a s h i ng t ] on )
                       [Ben Gaze at Lego box
                       [Dad Turns Lego box Towards Ben

009>Dad: Can you find number [thirteen

                             [Dad adjusts box
```

On this occasion, Dad does not respond to Ben’s echolalic utterance but proceeds to produce the directive, “Can you find number thirteen” (as examined in Extract 1). However, although Dad does not respond to Ben’s utterance, he does not ignore it because the production of his directive does not overlap with it but is apparently fitted to its completion. Dad might be responding to the fact that, although Ben’s utterance appears to be addressing an extraneous concern, as Ben produces it, he orients his gaze to the Lego box and is thereby appropriately aligned, at least spatially. (It is possible that Ben’s difficulty in locating item 13 involves being distracted by a concern that relates to his utterance in (008)). Yet on other occasions Dad responds to apparently unrelated utterances. For example, in Extract 5, whilst Dad is talking (043) Ben interjects with “Good bye” (044).

Extract 5 [MR2012 Benjamin & Dad Table] Good bye

```
041 Dad:  Well done.
          [Ben gets package and handles it
042       [(-------------------------------------)
043 Dad:  Now let’s have a l[ook at this.
044 Ben:                    [Good bye
045 Dad:  ^Ohoh. (.) I’m not going away?
046 Dad:  ^Do you want me to go away,
047 Ben:  °hrnrnn°
048 Dad:  (°Be careful°) let’s see what’s in the ba:g,
```

In this case, Dad explicitly addresses the concerns that Ben appears to be speaking to. He enacts a disappointed response cry (Goffman 1981; Aarsand and Aronsson 2009) "ohoh" and counters Ben's "Good bye" by saying he is not going away and asking if Ben wants him to go away (046). Dad also occasionally responds to extraneous visible actions. For example in Extract 5, while Dad is fitting pieces together, Ben vigorously propels a spiral-bound book across the table such that it crashes to the floor.

Extract 6 [MR2012 Benjamin & Dad Table] Oops

```
059       (------------------)
060 Dad:  'kay <That goes [there:>
                          [Ben slides book
061 Ben:  (------)
062 Dad:  [Ooops!                        ]
          [Dad gaze towards flying book]
062 Ben:  nnhrnnn nhuhhuhhuh(laughs).
063       (-----)
064 Dad:  Can you work out what we're meant to do [here] cos
                                                  [@Ben]
065       I can't actually understand that pictu[re?
066 Ben:                                        [hnn
```

Dad responds to the book flying off the table with a response cry (line 062), Ben laughs, and Dad resumes his talk figuring out how pieces are to be assembled. Unlike the case in Extract 3, in Extracts 4 and 5, Dad specifically responds to the extraneous activities that Ben is engaged in. Dad's responses are consistent with an analysis of these cases in terms of the extent to which they constitute troubles, or challenges. Namely, in Extract 5, the book flying off the table and crashing to the floor can be understood to be an untoward event, and in Extract 4, the implication that Dad is going away would be a challenge to the progress of working together on the construction activity. Whereas in Extract 3, although Ben's utterance appears to have no relevance for the construction activity, his gazing at the Lego box suggests that it does not challenge working on the construction activity. In Extracts 5 and 6 Ben produces an action which is apparently unrelated to the ongoing construction task, yet Dad responds to it. (A contrast and comparison can be made with side-sequences [Jefferson 1972] in which an activity occurs that whilst not part of an ongoing activity appears to be relevant for it.)

Extract 7 shows another example of co-participation with the sound box. Here, Dad issues an instruction "Now. (.) you put tha piece on top" (206). Following a prompt, "across there" (208), Ben successfully pushes the two pieces together (209) and receives a postitive evaluation "Good boy well done" (210). Having congratulated Ben on this achievement, Dad proceeds to the next subtask "let's see what's next" and starts to talk to it as a next item of business "an' then" (211) (compare Heritage and Sorjonen 1994). However in the meantime, Ben reaches across Dad to the sound effects box and triggers a stock fanfare melody which involves a hiatus and a final pair of beats (213 and 215).

Extract 7 [MR2012 Benjamin & Dad Table] bom bom

```
206 Dad:  Now. (.) you put tha piece on top

          [Ben reaches and touches piece
207       [(---)
208 Dad:  across there
          [Ben pushes pieces together
209       [(--------------------------)]
                                           [Ben moves
                                           [towards
                                           [sound box
210 Dad:  Good boy well done let's see what's [next
211 Dad:  An' then:
212       (------------------)
213       (dad dadada da bam bam) ((fanfare sound effect)
214 Dad:  Yay
215       (ba[m   bam)
216 Dad:     [bom bom
217 Dad:  Yagh huh huh ((slapping dad))
```

Although the fanfare is competing with Dad's proceeding to the next item, Dad shows that he recognises this is a celebration of the recent achievement and produces a celebratory "yay" (214) and co-participates in the production of the final two beats (216). Here then, Ben has produced an action (the celebratory sound effect) which is somewhat misplaced sequentially—Dad has already congratulated Ben and has moved on the next item. Nevertheless, Dad ratifies and co-particpates with this course of action.

Whilst Ben's use of the soundbox in Extract 7 can be understood to be sequentially appropriate—celebrating fitting the pieces together—on some occasions the sound box is less relevantly fitted to the concurrent activities and engagement with it is resisted by Dad. In Extract 8, as Dad says "Then: that piece goes on there?" (127), his gaze and hands indicating the piece and location that he is referring to, Ben reaches over Dad to the sound effects box and sets off a breaking glass sound effect (129–131). Subsequently, Dad re-does the directive (133); after further interaction, Ben apparently fits the pieces together and receives praise from Dad (not shown in the extract).

Extract 8 [MR2012 Benjamin & Dad Table] Crash bang wallop

```
                   [Ben: reaches over dad
127>Dad: Then: [that piece goes on there?
                   [Dad: gaze at pieces
128 Dad: >Here  [here here<
                    [Dad: gaze to sound effects box
                         [Ben gaze at Dad
129          (xxxxxxxxx1x[xxxxxxxx2) ((breaking glass effect))
130 Dad:                 [Ohw:
                         [Dad gaze at Ben

             [Ben gaze at pieces
131          ([xxxxxxxxx3xxxxxx[xxx4)
132  Dad: [                    [Crash bang  wallop]
             [Dad reaches      [Dad gathers pieces]
             [for pieces
                   [Ben reaches
133>Dad: [There [you go (.) put that on there?
             [adjusts pieces
134 Ben: (scuse)
135 Dad: nuh [no nono that goes] next to it (.) on there
              [  hand-over-hand ]
             [Ben handles piece with RH
136          ([---------1---------2---------3)
```

In producing the initial directive in (127), then, Dad is faced with a common enough interactional situation: seeking to interact with a participant who is not properly aligned for his project but is engaged in a competing course of action. Dad's initial response to this state of affairs is to attempt to summon Ben's attention back to the pieces which he is holding on the table. He attempts to do this verbally: "Here here here" (128). Nevertheless Ben proceeds with setting off a breaking glass sound effect (129–131). As this unfolds, Ben and Dad look at each other and Dad makes a disappointed vocalisation, apparently responding theatrically to the calamity represented by the breaking glass (130). Dad then turns his attention back to the pieces (132) and as the sound effect winds down, produces the stock onomatopoeic expression "crash bang wallop", theatrically commentating on the sound effect. He then reproduces a directive, "There you go (.) put that on there?". In this stretch then, two different practices are used in response to Ben's engagement with a competing course of action. First, Dad attempts to redirect Ben's attention back to the task. However, he then co-participates with the competing events. Conspicuously, he does not ignore, or side-step, the intervening course of action, but explicitly acknowledges it. As with the book flying off the table, he responds by displaying an assessment of the course of action that Ben engendered. As such he appears to complete, and thereby bring to an end, the extraneous activity that Ben set in motion.

Ben's production of extraneous activities is an important resource for the creation of new opportunities for participation. In Extract 9, as Dad fiddles with some pieces, Ben slaps him playfully while producing a vocalisation (line 217), then punches him (line 219). Dad continues to speak to concerns relating to his progress with the pieces by saying "Okay" (line 220) but then responds to being hit again (221) with a playful admonishment and a response to yet another blow (line 223). This leads to a round of play fighting (224–226) which Ben terminates with a directive, "Stop it" (line 227).

Extract 9 [MR2012 Benjamin & Dad Table] don't be mean

```
217 Dad:  Yagh huh huh ((slapping dad))
218       Nh nr nr nr
219       ((hits dad))
220 Dad:  Okay
221 Dad:  ^^(oy! yoy yoy yoy)
223 Dad:  ^n don't be mean (that)^oy!
224 Dad:  grrrr! ((play grappling with Ben))
224 Dad:  Grrrr!
225 Ben:  Urgh hah hah
226 Dad:  Grrr[rr
227 Ben:      [Stop it
228       (----)
229 Dad:  Okay okay I'll stop it
230 Ben:  >(I said it-)<
231 Ben:  (--X--) ((Slaps dad on head))
232 Dad:  Oy!
233 Ben:  nhnn nnn
234 Dad:  Cheeky boy! (huh) ((chuckles))
235 Dad:  Cheeky rascal
236 Dad:  Look
237 Ben:  Crying!=
238 Dad:  =whoo hoo. nmmm
239 Ben:  ( ) (   ) is ((possibly a person's name))
```

Having terminated this play fighting, Ben playfully (but quite forcibly) slaps Dad's head (231). Dad responds to this, not by retaliating, but with a verbal characterisation of Ben's wiliness ("Cheeky Boy", "Cheeky Rascal" lines 234, 235) and attempts to get the construction activity back on track. Nevertheless, Ben instructs him to pretend to cry and Dad obliges with a theatrical boo-hoo type expression. As a result of Dad's responsiveness to Ben's extraneous actions (his punches), father and son thereby co-create an opportunity for some physical play in the midst of the construction activity.

Closing Down a Competing Activity

A particular category of activity that warrants parental intervention is where the behaviour is harmful. For example, Extract 10 shows an instance of Ben biting his own hand (line 107).

Extract 10 [MR2012 Benjamin & Dad Table] 02:30 That piece on there

```
                        [Ben looks up
   082  Dad: No:w (.) [what we're [meant to do:
        Ben:            [             [hn
                        [Dad looks up at box
   083       (---------1--)
                         [Ben leans into Dad
   084  Ben: nhn nhn [nhn [unhn.
                       [Dad gazes at pieces ]
                  [Ben straightens and throws hands up
   085  Ben: Hn [Nhn uhn hn uhn.
   086       (-------[--1)
                       [Dad gazes at pieces
   087       [Ben gazes at pieces
   088  Dad: [mOkay:
   089       (---------1)
   090            [Ben starts to gaze away
   091 >Dad: [Loo[k
   092        [   [Dad gazes at Ben's face
   093       [Dad positions two pieces
   094      (------)
   095 >Dad: Can you put-
   096       [Dad taps Ben's arm three times
   097       [(- - -)
   098 >Dad: Listen
   099                               [leans in        ]
   100                               [gaze at piece   ]     [gaze away]
   101 >Dad: Look (.) can you [put tha:t piece] on [there      ]
   102                                [touches piece1]     [ piece2   ]
   103       [gaze at pieces
   104 >Dad: [That piece] on [there for me]?
   105       [touches p1]    [touches p2]
   106 Ben: >ugh! ugh! ugh! ugh! Ugh!<
                        [biting hand
   107 Ben: yowaaaaaa1[aaaaeeeeee2=
   108      =[aaaaaaaaa2aaaaaa[aaa3
   109>Dad:  [n no no n        [Agh agh Agh agh No biting

   110       [please.
   111 Ben:  [°h ughhh
   112 Dad: No:. biting. you don't need to do that?
```

Here Dad makes a number of attempts to engage Ben with the construction activity. He uses a single-word summons "Look" (91), starts to produce and the cut-off a modal verb directive "can you put" (95), and produces another single-word summons "listen" during which he taps Ben's arm. As Dad issues the summons and directive "Look (.) can you put tha:t piece on there" Ben looks at the pieces but then looks away (100). When Dad rephrases the instruction "That piece on there for me?" (104) Ben produces a vocalisation and bites his hand (106). Dad swiftly but calmly intervenes, responding with "n no no n Ah Ah No biting please" (109–110). Given that Ben is biting himself, and given the promptness of Dad's intervention, it is evident that here Dad is under a high obligation to intervene and is acting in accordance with this obligation. However, contra the recruitment continuum (Table 3.1), this high obligation does not relate to a request from Ben but rather it arises from an embodied display.

Concluding Discussion

This study aimed to contribute to our understanding of the competences and challenges involved in parents and children with ASD interacting at home, in particular how co-participation is managed, through the analysis of a session involving one boy and his father. The analysis shows how, in this setting, the father uses directives to organise the session. In addition, a repertoire of interactional skills are drawn on in the deployment and design of these directives and in addressing how the boy responds to them. The father's actions involve "recipient design" (Sacks 1992, p. 438); in several respects, in what he does and in how he does it, the father shows an orientation to the child's concerns of the moment. In particular, in coordinating spoken directives with objects in the material setting, he produces situated configurations of objects for the child to work on.

As noted in previous work on learning support assistants (Stribling and Rae 2010) and in a previous analysis of the activity session examined here (Ramey and Rae 2015), the parent uses interactional resources for supporting children's activities that draw deeply on capacities to address contingencies arising in the child's behaviour. In addition to responding to troubles, some forms of support are proactive and anticipate difficulties. A specific group of forms of support involve managing the child's attention

Table 3.2 Classes of support

Getting the child's attention
Doing initiating actions (e.g. directives)
Designing initiating actions in a facilitative way
Expanding initiating actions
Prompting responsive actions
Re-doing initiating actions
Not responding to child-initiated activities
Engaging with child-initiated activities
Stopping child-initiated activities

or addressing situations when the child becomes involved in extraneous activities (e.g. activating a sound effects box or biting himself). Although the analysis has considered specific individuals in a specific activity session, the participants' conduct can be formulated in a non-case specific way. In the session, the father draws on a range of classes of support to faciliate his son's participation. These are summarised in Table 3.2.

Two groups of resources can be distinguished; first, those concerned with eliciting the child's engagement with an activity and promoting their accomplishment of it; and second, those concerned with orienting to activities that the child initiates. Nevertheless, in practice, these intersect in complex ways; for example getting the child to engage with part of the construction task can involve bringing an action that the child has initiated to a close. On the other hand, an important feature of the character of this session is that on occasion, the father co-participates with activities that the child initiates even though they do not progress the construction game activity. This allows the child some autonomy and creates the scope for playful engagement with each other.

The recruitment continuum (Kendrick and Drew 2016) offers an analytic resource for considering parents' different forms of participation with respect to providing assistance when the child encounters a trouble. The situations examined here differ from those considered by Kendrick and Drew in that the action for which assistance might be relevant relates to responding to a sequence that was initiated by the potential assisting party, here the Dad. Consequently, that party has a particular relationship to troubles that arise in the unfolding course of action. Whilst this might enter into the relevance of offering assistance, such cases can still be located within the recruitment continuum.

The following classes of assistance have not been previously described in terms of the recruitment continuum but could be located within an expanded version of it: (a) designing initiating actions in anticipation of a trouble (b) bringing extraneous activities to completion. Whilst the analysis has examined multiple episodes from a single session, involving one father and son, we anticipate that versions of the practices identified here are likely to be relevant for other children and their parents in other settings. Key capacities are the parent displaying interactional flexibility in creating opportunities for themself and their child to co-participate with each other. On the one hand, structured opportunities are created for the child to engage with the designated activity; on the other hand, opportunities are selectively responded to such that the child can initiate other courses of action. The study used CA, a qualitative inductive methodology, to examine multiple instances of interactional moments where the participants were making opportunities for co-participation. It aimed to examine them in situ, considering their interactional context and examined some of the practices through which they were implemented. Given that this study focused on a single activity session in detail, the limitations arising from the small data base must be acknowledged. Although we have identified actions that are likely to be generic, further investigation is need to confirm this and to explore the range of practices that are used to implement these actions. Future research could consider larger samples of children in multiple settings to better understand the range of ways in which co-participation is managed and the different practices used. There would be practical and theoretical value in establishing what the local consequences of particular practices are in order to identify which ones appear to be most helpful under which conditions.

Acknowledgements We are very grateful to the participants for allowing us to record and study their interactions.

Earlier versions of this work were presented at the following conferences: Atypical Interaction Conference, University of Southern Denmark, Odense,

2016; the International Institute for Ethnomethodology and Conversion Analysis, Otterbein University, Ohio, USA, 2017; and the International Conference for Conversation Analysis, Loughborough, UK, 2018. Aspects of the analysis were also included in departmental seminars at the University of Sheffield and the University of Southern Denmark. We are grateful for critical comments and suggestions made on these occasions. We have also benefitted from anonymous referees' comments on related work. Many thanks to Ray Wilkinson and Gitte Rasmussen.

References

Aarsand, P. A., & Aronsson, K. (2009). Response cries and other gaming moves—Building intersubjectivity in gaming. *Journal of Pragmatics, 41*(8), 1557–1575.

American Psychiatric Association. (2013). *Diagnostic and statistical manual of mental disorders* (5th ed.). Washington, DC: Author.

Aronsson, K., & Cekaite, A. (2011). Activity contracts and directives in everyday family politics. *Discourse & Society, 22*(2), 137–154.

Austin, J. L. (1962). *How to do things with words: The William James lectures delivered at Harvard University in 1955* (J. O. Urmson & M. Sbisà, Eds.). Oxford: Clarendon Press. ISBN 0-674-41152-8.

Baltaxe, C. A. M. (1977). Pragmatic deficits in the language of autistic adolescents. *Journal of Pediatric Psychology, 2*(4), 176–180.

Carr, A., & Pike, A. (2012). Maternal scaffolding behaviour: Links with parenting style and maternal education. *Developmental Psychology, 48*(2), 543–551.

Clayman, S., & Heritage, J. (2014). Benefactors and beneficiaries: Benefactive status and stance in the management of offers and requests. In P. Drew & E. Couper-Kuhlen (Eds.), *Requesting in social interaction* (pp. 55–86). Amsterdam: John Benjamins.

Craven, A., & Potter, J. (2010). Directives: Entitlement and contingency in action. *Discourse Studies, 12*(4), 419–442.

Curl, T. S., & Drew, P. (2008). Contingency and action: A comparison of two forms of requesting. *Research on Language and Socal Interaction, 41*(2), 129–153. https://doi.org/10.1080/08351810802028613.

Drew, P., & Couper-Kuhlen, E. (2014). Requesting—From speech act to recruitment. In P. Drew & E. Couper-Kuhlen (Eds.), *Requesting in social interaction* (pp. 1–34). Amsterdam: John Benjamins.

Ervin-Tripp, S. (1976). Is Sybil there? The structure of some American English directives. *Language in Society, 5*(1), 25–66.

Freeman, S., & Kasari, C. (2013). Parent-child interactions in autism: Characteristics of play. *Autism, 17*(2), 147–161.

Geils, C., & Knoetze, J. (2008). Conversations with Barney: A conversation analysis of interactions with a child with autism. *South African Journal of Psychology, 38*(1), 200–224.

Goffman, E. (1981). *Forms of talk*. Philadelphia: University of Pennsylvania Press.

Goodwin, C. (2007). Participation, stance and affect in the organization of activities. *Discourse Society, 18*(1), 53–73.

Goodwin, C. (2018). *Co-operative action*. Cambridge: Cambridge University Press.

Goodwin, M. H. (1997). Byplay: Negotiating evaluation in storytelling. In G. G. Guy, C. Feagin, D. Schiffrin, & J. Baugh (Eds.), *Towards a social science of language, papers in honor of William Labov, Volume 2: Social interaction and discourse structures* (pp. 77–102). Amsterdam: John Benjamins.

Goodwin, M. H., & Cekaite, A. (2013). Calibration in directive/response sequences in family interaction. *Journal of Pragmatics, 46*(1), 122–138.

Goodwin, M. H., & Cekaite, A. (2014). Orchestrating directive trajectories in communicative projects in family interaction. In P. Drew & E. Couper-Kuhlen (Eds.), *Requesting in social interaction* (pp. 185–214). Amsterdam: John Benjamins.

Heinemann, T. (2006). 'Will you or can't you?': Displaying entitlement in interrogative requests. *Journal of Pragmatics, 38,* 1081–1104.

Hepburn, A., & Bolden, G. B. (2012). The conversation analytic approach to transcription. In J. Sidnell & T. Stivers (Eds.), *The handbook of conversation analysis* (pp. 57–76). Wiley-Blackwell.

Heritage, J. C. (1984). *Garfinkel and ethnomethodology*. Cambridge: Polity Press.

Heritage, J., & Sorjonen, M. L. (1994). Constituting and maintaining activities across sequences: And-prefacing as a feature of question design. *Language in Society, 23*(1), 1–29.

Jacoby, S., & Ochs, E. (1995). Co-construction: An introduction. *Research on Language and Social Interaction, 28*(3), 171–183.

Jefferson, G. (1972). Side sequences. In D. N. Sudnow (Ed.), *Studies in social interaction* (pp. 294–33). New York, NY: Free Press.

Kasari, C., Gulsrud, A. C., Wong, C., Kwon, S., & Locke, J. (2010). Randomized controlled caregiver mediated joint engagement intervention for toddlers with autism. *Journal of Autism and Developmental Disorders, 40*(9), 1045–1056.

Kendrick, K. H., & Drew, P. (2016). Recruitment: Offers, requests, and the organization of assistance in interaction. *Research on Language and Social Interaction, 49*(1), 1–19.

Kent, A. (2012). Compliance, resistance and incipient compliance when responding to directives. *Discourse Studies, 14*(6), 711–730.

Kent, A., & Kendrick, K. H. (2016). Imperative directives: Orientations to accountability. *Research on Language and Social Interaction, 49*(3), 272–288.

Korkiakangas, T. K., & Rae, J. P. (2013). Gearing up to a new activity: How teachers use object adjustments to manage the attention of children with autism. *Augmentative and Alternative Communication, 29*(1), 83–103.

Lerner, G. H. (1995). Turn design and the organization of participation in instructional activities. *Discourse Processes, 19*(1), 111–131.

Local, J., & Wootton, T. (1995). Interactional and phonetic aspects of immediate echolalia in autism: A case study. *Clinical Linguistics & Phonetics, 9*(2), 155–184.

Maynard, D. W. (2005). Social actions, gestalt coherence, and designations of disability: Lessons from and about autism. *Social Problems, 5,* 499–529.

Maynard, D. W., & Turowetz, J. (2017). Doing testing: How concrete competence can facilitate or inhibit performances of children with autism spectrum disorder. *Qualitative Sociology, 40,* 1–25. https://doi.org/10.1007/s11133-017-9368-5.

Mehan, H. (1979). 'What time is it, Denise?': Asking known information questions in classroom discourse. *Theory into Practice, 18*(4), 285–294.

Muskett, T., Perkins, M., Clegg, J., & Body, R. (2010). Inflexibility as an interactional phenomenon: Using conversation analysis to re-examine a symptom of autism. *Clinical Linguistics & Phonetics, 24*(1), 1–16.

Pickles, A., et al. (2016). Parent-mediated social communication therapy for young children with autism (PACT): Long-term follow-up of a randomised controlled trial. *The Lancet, 388*(10059), 2501–2509.

Prizant, B. M., & Duchan, J. F. (1981). The functions of immediate echolalia in autistic children. *Journal of Speech and Hearing Disorders, 46*(3), 241–249.

Rae, J. (2001). Organizing participation in interaction: Doing participation framework. *Research on Language and Social Interaction, 34*(2), 253–278.

Rae, J. P., & Ramey, M. (in preparation). *A comparative analysis of correction, repair and recruitment in a parent and an ABA tutor interactions with a boy with ASD.*

Ramey, M., & Rae, J. (2015). Parents' resources for facilitating the activities of children with autism at home. In J. N. Lester & M. O'Reilly (Eds.),

The Palgrave handbook of child mental health (pp. 459–479). London, UK: Palgrave Macmillan.

Rendle-Short, J. (2002). Managing interaction: A conversation analytic approach to the management of interaction by an 8-year-old girl with Asperger's syndrome. *Issues in Applied Linguistics, 13*(2), 161–186.

Rydell, P. J., & Mirenda, P. (1991). The effects of two levels of linguistic constraint on echolalia and generative language production in children with autism. *Journal of Autism and Developmental Disorders, 21*(2), 131–157.

Sacks, H. (1992). *Lectures on conversation* (G. Jefferson, Ed.). Oxford: Blackwell.

Schegloff, E. A. (1998). Body torque. *Social Research, 65,* 535–596.

Schegloff, E. A. (2007). *Sequence organization in interaction: A primer in conversation analysis* (Vol. 1). Cambridge: Cambridge University Press.

Schegloff, E., & Sacks, H. (1973). Opening up closings. *Semiotica, 8*(4), 289–327.

Searle, J. (1975). A taxonomy of illocutionary acts. In K. Gunderson (Ed.), *Language, mind and knowledge* (pp. 344–369). Minneapolis, MN: University of Minnesota Press.

Sinclair, J. M., & Coulthard, M. (1975). *Towards an analysis of discourse: The English used by teachers and pupils*. Oxford: Oxford University Press.

Sterponi, L., de Kirby, K., & Shankey, J. (2015). Rethinking language in autism. *Autism, 19*(5), 517–526.

Sterponi, L., & Fasulo, A. (2010). "How to go on": Intersubjectivity and progressivity in the communication of a child with autism. *Ethos, 38*(1), 116–142.

Sterponi, L., & Shankey, J. (2014). Rethinking echolalia: Repetition as interactional resource in the communication of a child with autism. *Journal of Child Language, 41*(2), 275–304.

Stevanovic, M., & Monzoni, C. (2016). On the hierarchy of interactional resources: Embodied and verbal behavior in the management of joint activities with material objects. *Journal of Pragmatics, 103,* 15–32.

Stribling, P., & Rae, J. (2010). Interactional analysis of scaffolding in a mathematical task in ASD. In H. Gardner & M. Forrester (Eds.), *Analysing interactions in childhood insights from conversation analysis* (pp. 185–208). New York: Wiley.

Stribling, P., Rae, J., & Dickerson, P. (2007). Two forms of spoken repetition in a girl with autism. *International Journal of Language & Communication Disorders, 42*(4), 427–444.

Tarplee, C., &. Barrow, E. (1999). Delayed echoing as an interactional resource: A case study of a 3-year-old child on the autistic spectrum. *Clinical Linguistics & Phonetics, 13*(6), 449–482.
Tomasello, M. (1999). *The cultural origins of human cognition*. Harvard: Harvard University Press.
Vygotsky, L. S. (1978). *Mind in society: The development of higher psychological processes* (M. Cole, V. John-Steiner, S. Scribner, & E. Souberman, Eds.) (A. R. Luria, M. Lopez-Morillas, & M. Cole [with J. V. Wertsch], Trans.). Cambridge, MA: Harvard University Press. (Original manuscripts [ca. 1930–1934]).
Wood, D., Bruner, J., & Ross, G. (1976). The role of tutoring in problem solving. *Journal of Child Psychology and Child Psychiatry, 17*, 89–100.
Wootton, A. J. (1999). An investigation of delayed echoing in a child with autism. *First Language, 19*(57), 359–381.
Wootton, A. J. (2005). *Interaction and the development of mind*. Cambridge: Cambridge University Press. (Originally published in 1997).
World Health Organization. (1992). *The ICD-10 classification of mental and behavioural disorders: Clinical descriptions and diagnostic guidelines*. Geneva: World Health Organization.
World Health Organization. (2018). *International statistical classification of diseases and related health problems* (11th Revision). Retrieved from https://icd.who.int/browse11/l-m/en.
Zemel, A., & Koschmann, T. (2011). Pursuing a question: Reinitiating IRE sequences as a method of instruction. *Journal of Pragmatics, 43*(2), 475–488.
Zimmerman, D. H. (1992). The interactional organization of calls for emergency assistance. In P. Drew & J. Heritage (Eds.), *Talk at work: Interaction in institutional settings* (pp. 418–469). Cambridge: Cambridge University Press.

4

Difficulties Facing People with Intellectual Disability in Conversation: Initiation, Co-ordination, and the Problem of Asymmetric Competence

Chris Walton, Charles Antaki and W. M. L. Finlay

Introduction

People who have intellectual disabilities (ID) can face great difficulties in communication—both in understanding what is said to them, and making their own ideas and feelings known (Schlosser et al. 2007). Individuals at the more severe or profound end of the spectrum may have very limited vocabularies, impaired attention, and reduced cognitive functioning (Belva et al. 2012). Yet communication with, and by, such individuals is obviously desirable, and certainly possible (Finlay et al. 2008). The possibility of meaningful interaction for even

C. Walton (✉)
University of Lancaster, Lancashire, UK

C. Antaki
Loughborough University, Loughborough, UK

W. M. L. Finlay
Anglia Ruskin University, Cambridge, UK

© The Author(s) 2020

R. Wilkinson et al. (eds.), *Atypical Interaction*,
https://doi.org/10.1007/978-3-030-28799-3_4

the most cognitively and communicatively impaired individual lays bare the fact that the in-practice communicative competence of people with intellectual disabilities can be highly contingent upon the interpretative competence of their interactional partners. Indeed, intellectual disabilities are now understood in terms of a multidimensional model of human functioning that incorporates both individual impairments and the social contexts and systems of support within which the person with ID is situated (Wehmeyer et al. 2008). Further, given the nature of their impairments, people with intellectual disabilities are often located in settings, often social care services, where there are others, members of staff and fellow service users with ID, who have an intimate knowledge of their communicative idiosyncrasies, verbal and non-verbal, their day-to-day activities and interactions, and their personal histories (in Holzner's [1968] terms, such settings may be understood as 'epistemic communities'). As will be demonstrated below, that knowledge is often key to the interpretation of ambiguous utterances, but it can also give rise to interactional practices that are also often sources of trouble.

In this chapter we shall examine some of the difficulties encountered in interactions involving people with ID. We shall do this at three key points in an interaction: the beginning of a particular sequence of interaction, its maintenance, and the negotiation of its successful closure. At all points, we shall see that the interlocutor plays a crucial role in the success or failure of the exchange. We shall demonstrate how, when faced with ill-formatted or otherwise unfamiliar turns from the person with ID, the recipient relies on their knowledge of the individual, their activities, interests and preferences, and, when those resources are inadequate or unavailable, falls back on normative conversational practices. Recourse to such normative practices has, however, the potential to open a gulf between the interlocutor's competences and those of the person with ID, and to set the interaction on a path which may suit the interlocutor more than it does with person with ID. We shall illustrate this unsatisfactory state of affairs with extracts from institutional settings, where care staff objectives can often privilege a typical perspective on atypical communication in the service of getting things done and at the expense of the interactional interests of the person with ID.

The close attention to interactional exchanges offered by Conversation Analysis allows us to develop a highly detailed account of the practices that seem to work well, and those that do not. We shall illustrate these practices with data from three institutional settings: a residential service we call "Comber Hall Way" (CHW), which was home to 5 men all with mild or moderate intellectual disabilities; "Ashgrove", a residential service for 10 adults with more profound disabilities; and "GardenSpace" and "Foxwood Garden Project", two day services offering gardening activities to people with a variety of disabilities, including intellectual disabilities.

We note right at the outset that the overwhelming majority of interactions we recorded were between a service-user and a member of staff or volunteer (and, on occasion, the researcher with the camera). We do not have much data involving interactions between people with IDs and their service-user colleagues, and none with family members or friends. Consequently, it is possible that the practices that members of staff adopt are shaped by some institutional concern or agenda, e.g., promoting choice and independence or some other "instructional" aim. Further, given the previously mentioned high levels of familiarity that often exist between staff and service users (in some cases they have worked alongside each other for many years), we can often also discount mere unfamiliarity as a source of any interactional difficulty. In line with contemporary approaches to ID, when analysing interactions involving people with ID we must be cautious not to assume that any difficulties which arise are necessarily the result of an impairment. We must also be sensitive to the institutional nature of those contexts, as epistemic communities, and the effects that might have on the practices of speakers, both intellectually and non-intellectually disabled. We set out the problems as: trouble in initiating an interaction, troubles in maintaining and progressing exchanges, and troubles in closing.

A. Trouble in Initiating Interaction

Many atypical speakers' interaction-initiating utterances fail to get a timely, or any, response from their apparently intended recipient—almost always, a staff member or other cognitively typical interlocutor.

There were a number of reasons for this, including: the lexical ambiguity of the initiating utterance; poor specification of the intended action, and so deficient projection of the appropriate response; and inauspicious timing. These are of course not exclusive to people with ID, but in their case, cognitive deficits in speech comprehension and production, and pragmatic understanding may have contributed.

Poor Specification of an Appropriate First Pair Part

In Extract 1 "Matthew", who produces vocalisations, some of which are commonly treated as words, e.g., "mummy", seems to attempt to initiate an interaction with "Anna",[1] a support worker. He is seated at a table, along with other residents, whilst Anna stands nearby. Matthew looks up at her across the table and utters a two-syllable sound.[2]

---

[1]All names used the extracts are pseudonyms.

[2]This extract is more fully analysed in Finlay and Antaki (2012).

Extract 1. Ashgrove V26 11.20-11:32 Matthew in park

```
Matt   (nye:hnyeh), ((then drops gaze))
Anna   what darli:ng.
           (1.5)
Anna   >what  d'y want.<
           (1.0)
Anna   hah?
          ((2.0, in which Matt looks up briefly))
Anna   (>havin' a< nice ti:me)?
          ((3.0, in which Matt looks up & raises his right hand))
Anna   >what d'y< want.
          ((10.0, in which Matt looks down & away and returns to habitual hand-wringing gestures))
```

Anna clearly treats Matthew as initiating an interaction. Two possible interpretations exist for her response at line 2. It is hearable as either a response to a summons (Schegloff 2002), or as an open class repair initiator (Drew 1997). Either way, Matthew fails to take up the slot that Anna's response creates. He does not produce any further turn that would function as an elaboration on his summons, having now gained Anna's attention. Nor does he repair any trouble with the intelligibility of his initial utterance, if it was something other than a summons, as would ordinarily be expected in response to an open-class repair initiator. In light of this marked absence and with no further contribution from Matthew, save the two occasions on which he directs his gaze towards her indicating a level of ongoing engagement, Anna resorts to normative practices to progress the interaction by issuing three open-class repair initiators (Drew 1997) "what do you want.", "hah?" and "what do you want". These are interspersed at line 8 with a candidate understanding of Matthew's subjective state "havin' a nice time?", which creates a slot wherein Matthew need only produce a minimal response of agreement or disagreement, which Anna knows he can do both vocally and non-verbally. Despite her repeated attempts to progress the interaction it ultimately breaks down.

This first extract illustrates a number of features that will recur throughout this chapter: a person with ID produces an ambiguous initiating utterance; a non-ID interactional partner attempts to progress the interaction through the use of normative practices; the person with ID does not effectively repair the apparent trouble with their initial turn; and the sequence ends in an unsatisfactory manner for both parties without the need for a closing sequence. A similar sequence can be seen in the Extract 2, except for the fact that the person with ID does effectively repair the trouble with their initial ambiguous utterance. It is important to remember that intellectual disability as a category covers a wide range of cognitive and communicative abilities, and so generalised statements about what people with ID do or not do in interaction may not hold true for all members of the category.

Extract 2. Foxwood 13.50: Casualty

([the sound of an emergency vehicle has just gone by out of shot, possibly an ambulance; Steven has briefly imitated its siren])

```
Steven:    ((looking towards Emma)) (    the cac
           (- ly, cacly,) the cac - ly, cacly,)
           (0.3) (cacly ca'lly).((keeps looking
           at Emma))
           (2.5)
Emma:      sorry?
Steven:    (casualty,) (.5) (cashlty)
           (0.3)
Emma:      oh, Casualty[3].
Steven:    yeah, ((very animated))
```

Given his gaze direction towards Emma, it is clear that she is the intended recipient of Steven's initial utterance. As with Extract 1, it is possible that Steven's initial utterance and gaze direction were designed to secure Emma's attention but were unsuccessful, hence the substantial delay before Emma recognises that she was the intended recipient and that a response is required. Alternatively, the lexical ambiguity of the initial turn is the cause of both the delay in responding and the subsequent open-class repair initiator—"sorry?". On this occasion, Steven demonstrates sufficient speech production ability to repair the pronunciation of his initial utterance (line 7) such that it can now be clearly heard as "casualty". The change of state token "oh" (Heritage 1984) that precedes Emma's repetition of "casualty" suggests that the problem with the initial turn had been in its lexical ambiguity rather than with Emma's failure to appreciate that she was the intended recipient.

Here the use of an open class repair initiator successfully elicits a more intelligible version of the word and in that respect the exchange is successful. However, it might be noted that its success is limited in so far as Steven's competence in connecting the sound of a siren to a television programme about an accident and emergency department is not explicitly recognised and in that sense the interaction is incomplete. Recognition of the competence of people with ID in making apposite comments about and connections between elements in the immediate environment clearly requires an engaged audience.

It is not just lexical unintelligibility that can result in difficulties in getting an interaction off the ground; when the words are clear, they may be unpropitious for a variety of reasons. In Extract 3, resident Dom has support worker Brenda's attention as a previous sequence of interaction closes. Dom then points upwards, and says "new one", not apparently à propos of any previously established topic. Again, the staff member responds with a repair initiator.

Extract 3. CHW04 34:20-34:30 What new one

Dom:	new one
	(0.7)
Brenda:	what new one=
Dom:	=new one
	(0.7)
Brenda:	what new [one
Dom:	[((*raises left hand palm up*
	and shrugs his shoulders))
	(4.4)
Dom:	((*stands looks towards Dave at the other*
	end of the table and makes "swimming"
	gesture))

Dom's opening verbal utterance is clearly marked as a source of trouble for Brenda. The trouble it presents is evident in the significant pause between it and Brenda's repair initiator in line 3 (Schegloff et al. 1977). The pause may, generously, be read as Brenda allowing some time for Dom to engage in self-repair, in light of the lack of an immediate response, and to clarify the referent of his utterance. Dom, however, does not provide a reformulation of his initial utterance and instead only repeats it; at best a minimal form of repair. This elicits another repair initiator from Brenda at line 6. In response, Dom, rather than providing the requested repair, instead shrugs with an upturned left palm. The shrug has been interpreted as constituting a 'compound enactment' expressing obviousness (Jehoul et al. 2017), incapacity, powerlessness and personal disengagement (Debras 2017). These interpretations are consistent with the shrug in this extract as marking Dom's inability to make his meaning any more obvious and to repair Brenda's lack of understanding. Having adopted such a stance, he disengages from Brenda, shifting his gaze and directing his next gesture to a new recipient, Dave, who is seated at the other end of the table, to start a new sequence.

It may be that Brenda, who only occasionally works in the service, lacks the knowledge necessary to render Dom's unelaborated "new one" intelligible. Had Dom directed his initial utterance to Dave, a permanent member of staff and someone much more familiar with Dom's life and activities, it is possible that the progression of the sequence and its outcome would have been quite different. However, given that Dave witnesses Dom and Brenda's interaction but offers no assistance to either party, it may be that on this matter he too lacks the requisite knowledge. As will become apparent in later extracts, shared knowledge is a key resource for staff and residents alike when negotiating interactions. However, that consideration does not obviate the fact that Dom fails to repair the trouble with his initial utterance in response to repeated requests to do so and that consequently the sequence breaks down. It should also be noted that the lack of success results in unilateral abandonment of the interaction without recourse to any formal closing sequence, save Dom's gestural marker of his inability to do anything more to progress the interaction.

Another reason why some initiating practices employed by people with ID may be unpropitious is that they may be dismissed as merely habitual and likely to result in an 'empty' or repetitious interactional sequence. Such sequences were a recurring feature of the data collected at CHW and of Alec's, a man with ID's, talk in particular. In Extract 4, staff and residents are sitting around a table, preparing to plan the next week's meals. To help the residents, the staff have set out images of food to allow residents to point to what they want, in lieu of having to find the appropriate words. We join as Kath is just starting to reply to another staff member; Alec interrupts her by picking up a photograph of something, and holding it up towards her. Twenty seconds prior to this sequence Alec had held up the same image to Chris and asked "what's this called?", to which Chris had replied "chocolate". Whether or not Alec knew the name of the foodstuff in the image prior to that, though he might reasonably be expected to, it is clear from the recording that he ought now to know what the image shows.

Extract 4. CHW12 03:23-03:33. Chocolate

Kath:	take the wh [ole one
Alec:	[who's that
	(1.9)
Kath:	I- I don' know what that [that is,
Alec	[ask Chris
Alec:	*((turning to Chris as he enters the*
	room and holding the image up to
	him))
Kath:	tell me what it is because I haven't
	got a foggiest
Chris:	you tell me
	(1.0)
Alec:	chocolate
	(0.6)
Tim	(s') you know what it is

Alec's putative initiation at line 2 is poorly timed, overlapping Kath's utterance. As later becomes apparent, it is also poorly designed as the referent is an object rather than an individual. Considering the prior exchange with Chris, to which the other speakers were witness, and given any understanding they might hold about Alec's knowledge of food, this question might reasonably be understood as a test or known-answer question (Schegloff 2007). The poor design and the status of the question might account for Kath's delayed response and her demonstrable resistance to offering a substantive answer. It should be noted here that at the beginning and end of Kath's turn (lines 04 and 09–10) she explicitly, if perhaps disingenuously, adopts what Heritage would term a K- epistemic stance (Heritage 2013), i.e., she claims not to possess the requisite knowledge to be able to answer Alec's question, and ascribes to Alec K+ status with the directive "tell me what it is". This presents Alec with two choices, either he makes explicit the known-answer status of the question by answering it himself (adopting a K+ stance), or he continues to pursue a response to an otherwise "authentic" question. He selects the latter option by turning his attention to Chris, repeating the question that he had asked and to which Chris had given a genuine answer 23 seconds earlier. In light of that earlier response, Chris is justified in aligning with Kath in treating Alec as asking a known-answer question and prompting Alec to demonstrate his knowledge of the answer.

In response to these repeated directives, Alec eventually demonstrates his knowledge in line 13 by repeating the answer that Chris had previously given him. This display of knowledge confirms Alec's K+ status and that he had in fact been asking a known-answer question. Tim's declarative comment at line 15, which effectively closes the exchange, can be read as an implicit criticism of Alec and his habit of asking known-answer questions. The ascribed redundancy of this practice, that Alec is not genuinely seeking knowledge or that he has no basis to test the knowledge of his interactional partners, misses one important consideration. As will be demonstrated below, members of staff routinely use known-answer questions to initiate and maintain interactions with people with ID. In those situations, as in other "instructional" contexts, known-answer questions are resources commonly used for eliciting displays of knowledge (e.g., Rusk et al. 2017). That Alec adopts this same strategy is perhaps best understood not as resulting from any cognitive or communicative impairment, so much as it is the result of decades of being asked known-answer questions in social care services. Finally, asking known-answer questions is clearly an effective strategy for engaging others in interaction, and that may well be its primary function for Alec.

The above extracts highlight two features; first that adults with ID may open interactions with utterances that are sources of trouble for their interactional partners, either in terms of the clarity of the speech or the referent of the utterance; and secondly that they may not follow conversational norms, either by failing to repair utterances that recipients clearly mark as sources of trouble or by adopting initiating practices that result in exchanges that the recipients experience as empty or repetitious. On such occasions, the progression of the exchange can break down and the achievement of intersubjectivity, a shared understanding of the meaning of an utterance or exchange, is compromised.

B. Trouble in Maintaining and Progressing Interactions

The following section will examine exchanges that are initiated by a cognitively typical speaker, either a member of staff or volunteer in a service, and the challenges that people with ID can experience in contributing to and maintaining that exchange. Being the recipient of an initiating utterance presents the person with ID with a number of challenges, which will, in part, vary in their difficulty according to the individual's level of cognitive and communicative impairment. At the most basic level, the person with ID must: register that they are the recipient of the previous speaker's turn; understand the second pair part that the initiating utterance projects, e.g., that a question requires an answer; formulate an appropriate response that satisfies the requirements of the initiating turn; and articulate that response clearly and in a timely fashion. As we shall see, any or all of these components can be too demanding for a person with intellectual disabilities, depending on their level of impairment.

B (i) Trouble in Responding to First Pair Parts: Dealing with Questions

The first difficulty that a person with ID faces is understanding what is said to them, and this is more difficult the more pronounced the impairment. Extract 5 involves Oscar, who has severe Down syndrome and very little verbal language (though he does use some signs), and three other speakers: a volunteer, who asks the first question; Jon, Oscar's personal support worker; and Amanda, a horticultural therapist.

Extract 5. GardenSpace Vd00136 What've you been doin'

```
Vol:    Oscar: (2.0) hello:: Oscar (1.5) and
        what have youbeen doin' today my
        friend.
        (2.0)
Jon:    .hh what [( ) (1.0) did we do this
Jon:             [((makes signs))
        morning.
        (3.0) ((in which Oscar looks up at
        Jon))
Jon:    w'd (0.5) [we work on.
Jon:              [((makes signs))
        (1.0)
Jon:    [(you did)
Jon:    [((makes signs))
        (1.0)
Osc:    ((leans onto Jon's shoulder, touches
        his cheek))
Jon:    yeah
Osc:    ((points behind Jon))
Jon:    yeah, over there, [that's right,
Ama:                      [yeh
Jon:    [yeah, well done
Ama:    yep.
```

The people who work with Oscar demonstrate sensitivity to his impairment by providing longer latencies than would be usual in typical conversation (lines 4, 8, 12 and 15), allowing him more time to respond before they self-select to take the next turn. When they take that next turn they use a range of practices including repetition and reformulation (lines 5–7 and 10), provision of candidate answers (lines 13 and 14), and gestures (as opposed to formalized sign language) in lines 6, 11, and 14, in order to scaffold Oscar's answers (lines 16–17 and 19).

It is possible that the volunteer's opening question is a genuine question; they wish to know what Oscar had done during the day. However, it is also clear that Jon's questions at lines 5–7 and 10, with their respecification of the time of day and kind of activities in question, are known-answer questions. As stated above, known-answer questions are a regular practice through which staff in services provide and scaffold opportunities for people with ID, even those with severe or profound impairments, to "speak" about themselves, their activities and interests. Here Oscar's minimal non-verbal contributions are treated as relevant and topicalised to the extent that his reported activities can be celebrated (line 22) and the sequence regarded as complete; with Jon's assistance Oscar apparently answered the volunteer's initial question. The tendency of staff to respond to service-users' inadequate responses with offers of candidate answers (a frequent form of other-initiated repair in ordinary conversation—Kendrick (2015) gives them as about 28% of non-complex cases) to which the person with ID need only provide the simplest indication, vocally or non-verbally, of agreement or disagreement, is an effective strategy for bringing an otherwise troubled exchange to an apparently successful conclusion. Once again, the competence of the person with ID to meaningfully contribute to the maintenance and progression of an exchange is highly contingent on the practices of their interactional partners.

Responding to Questions as Instructions

A great deal of what staff do in services involves getting people with ID to do something. That may be getting someone to have a drink, to make a choice or to speak about their day. All these actions can be performed through practices arrayed along a continuum of deontic authority, from suggesting, through proposing and advising, to outright directive injunction (Stevanovic and Peräkylä 2012). Unless the matter is urgent (see Antaki and Kent 2012 for what happens in such situations), the preferred vehicle for performing such actions seems to be the grammatical question. Though staff usually take care to make their questions, and the actions for which they are vehicles, unambiguous, they nevertheless often fail to elicit a response that is sufficiently clear to signal compliance, and to allow movement to the next phase of the interaction. Where responses are not forthcoming or are ambiguous the initial question will require repair. This is pervasively true when the service user has a profound disability, as has Damien in Extract 6.

Extract 6. Ashgrove 04-9.30-10:13 Toilet

Jill:	Damien[what would you like to do now
Damien:	[*((looks at her with smile))*
Jill:	would you like to go to the toilet?
Damien:	*((appears to make no response))*
Jill:	*((laughs))* Damien (.) would you like
	to go to the toilet?
Damien:	mmn *((turns head away))*
Jill:	huh? (.) yes or no.
Damien:	*((head sways))* mmn *((turns head away)*
Jill:	Tell me (.) coffee's all gone (3.0)
	coming to the toilet?
	(2.0)
Damien:	*((looks at her, then sways head, look*
	ing to left and right))
Jill:	yes?
Damien:	*((looks away, smiles, lets head fall,*
	looking at table)) nnhh *((looks up,*
	then away, then up, then away,
	grinning))
Jill:	shall we go to the toilet Damien?

Following her initial open question, Jill uses the positive polarity question form "would you like to go to the toilet" (line 1–3; repeated verbatim, prefaced by a direct name-address, in line 5), "coming to the toilet" (line 11) and finally "shall we go to the toilet, Damien?" (line 15), one alternative pair (*yes or no*, line 7) and a simple confirmation-projecting *yes*? to propose a next action and to project Damien's agreement with it. To none of these does Damien give an unambiguous answer; if anything, his physical turning away from Jill at line 8 might indicate a refusal. Nevertheless, Jill on the basis of either her familiarity with Damien's physical needs or the informal institutional practices of the service, perseveres in offering him multiple opportunities to understand her question; or, equally, multiple opportunities to comply with what is not a question, but a suggested course of action. When a shared understanding about a next joint action is not achieved, deontic authority may be exercised, assuming at least acquiescence from the person with ID, in projecting and effecting a unilateral aim; Damien went to the toilet.

Responding to Test Questions

In Extract 7, again a resident is asked a series of questions which seem to be soliciting information, but are again, in fact, known-answer questions, apparently designed to get the resident to articulate a lesson he has been taught.[3] Kath and Henry are in the kitchen; Henry is putting things away. Kath has turned the conversation to Henry's activities of the morning, when (it seems) he attended a session that included a role play of what to do were someone to hurt him.

[3]This extract is more fully analysed in Antaki (2013).

Extract 7. CHW18 00:29-01:24 What's it about?

Kath: tell me what happened today at Rose
House then
Henry: ( )
Kath: so who was there, (1.0) what did they
do:, (1.0) what did you lea::rn,
Henry: (stood on a chair)
Kath: so you were stood (in) the chair, an'
what happened, what were they talking
about,
Henry: (what-)
Kath: what were they talking about ( )
Henry: (acting)
Kath: acting, and who was acting, (.8) and
what were they acting.
(1.5)
Kath: what were they acting. (0.2) can you
remember.
Henry: (ner)
Kath: you don't remember >do you remember

	what we were talking to you about the
	other night.
Henry:	([)
Kath:	[with the leaflet
	(1.0)
Kath:	you know the leaflet,
	(0.5)
Henry:	*((turn and points into another room))*
Kath:	yeah=what was it- what's it about.
Henry	err:::
Kath:	>what's it about<
	(.5)
Henry:	(eeyeh) p'li:ce, (0.3) (youh) (an')
	the sta:ff,

The above exchange is best understood as comprised of two parts, distinguished by Kath's epistemic status relative to Henry with regard to the events and activities in question. Lines 1–15 relate to that morning's events at a day care service, about which Kath clearly has some understanding, but at which she was not present. Henry, who clearly was present, therefore occupies a K+ epistemic status relative to Kath. Hence it is uncertain whether Kath's questions in lines 1–15 should be interpreted as genuine or known-answer. That said, Kath is demonstrably concerned to get Henry to articulate what he had learned that morning; clearly marking some level of understanding on Kath's part about that morning's activities, i.e., they were instructional. Her open-ended initial question elicits only a short and unintelligible response (line 2). Ostensibly to help him articulate what he learned, Kath embarks on a series of questions and candidate answers which will gradually build up the account in chronological fashion. Some of these are comparatively successful, in topical relevance if not format (Henry offers "acting" in line 12 to the question "what were they talking about"), but most are not. Possibly (as Antaki 2013, argues) Kath's choice of question form is confusing or too cognitively demanding (her turns at lines 4–5, 7–8 and 13–14 are compound questions requiring the recipient to disentangle separate threads in their answer). In either case, the exchange is not progressing smoothly.

In light of this lack of progress, at lines 19–21 Kath shifts the focus of her questions away from that morning's events at Rose House, a topic on which her epistemic status is uncertain, to the events of the previous evening and an interaction between her, Henry and unspecified others. On these events Kath's epistemic status is at least equal to Henry's and her questions can more readily be interpreted as known-answer questions designed to support Henry in demonstrating his understanding of what he should remember from that interaction, which seems thematically to be linked to the activities at Rose House. In pursuit of Henry demonstrating his knowledge, Kath asks a series of questions moving from a yes/no interrogative (lines 19–21), elaborated with a more specific referent at lines 23 and 25, ending with repeated open known-answer questions in lines 28 and 30. For his part, Henry does attempt to provide the sought-after answer, though his responses are generally verbally and non-verbally ambiguous. Ultimately, Kath's perseverance is rewarded and Henry's knowledge is clearly demonstrated in line 32–33.

Simple repetition of first-pair parts as repair-initiators, of the sort seen in Extract 7, are uncommon in typical conversation; Kendrick (2015) registers none in his corpus of 227 cases in conversational English. Likely this is a consequence of that corpus not including the kind of asymmetric, institutional interactions we see here. The equal epistemic status of residents and staff on matters of resident's daily lives, may contribute to members of staff's use of simple repetition of questions, rather than more complex reformulations, when pursuing displays of knowledge or competence through the use of known-answer questions. It should be noted that Kath's repeated questions at lines 28 and 30 are simply structured, and a concern for simplicity, and by extension comprehensibility, may override reformulations that would increase complexity and potentially be more challenging to the recipient.

As difficult as intersubjectivity can be to achieve in such exchanges as those above, and as inadequate as normative practices can be in effecting intersubjectivity in the face of a range of cognitive and communicative impairments, its pursuit is essential in the accomplishing of joint actions, including the co-production of individual identities. Staff, supporters and families expend interactional effort to co-produce the identities of the people with intellectual disabilities with whom they work.

B (ii) Trouble in Maintaining Interaction: Responding to Less-Constraining First Pair Parts

The forms of question used in the above extracts have the benefit, from the point of view of the recipient with an intellectual disability, of having a constrained class of response as an acceptable second pair part, with, usually, strong indications of what candidate from that class would be appropriate. However, it is true that, as we saw above, those questions could nevertheless be too demanding. Even so, they are formally less problematic than first pair parts which offer less guidance as to what would come next. A good example of a first pair part that does not clearly project what will constitute a sufficient response is the "assessable". With assessables, the recipient is expected to understand the nature of what has been laid out for assessment, and to provide a suitable articulation of it. In Extract 8,[4] staff member Mickie is supervising service-user Douglas in filling a kettle from a large jerrycan.

[4]This extract is analysed more fully in Antaki and Webb (2019).

Extract 8. Foxwood Garden Project 26.01.10 Daffodils
([Douglas is bent down, filling a container from a jerrycan throughout this exchange])

```
Mickie:     I was just looking- d'y see, these
            daffodils are coming up on this one
            ((points to flowerbox))
Douglas:    (      )
Mickie:     but there's nothing coming up in that
            one, so
Douglas:    (yeh)
Mickie:     (I'm sure we put some) in,
            (1.5)
Mickie:     another a dead one (this one) here,
            (3.0)
Mickie:     (      ) a bit (.) cold,
            (5.0)
Mickie:     ((turns to Douglas)) Lena's doing the
            weeding down there,
            ((Douglas carries on filling his con-
            tainer and after c 1. minute moves
            off))
```

At line 1, Mickie directs Douglas's attention to a window box containing daffodils and subsequently (lines 5–6) to a second window box. Mickie's declarative statements at lines 1–2, 5–6, 8, 10 and 12 are eminently assessable, i.e., they provide for agreement, disagreement, qualification or elaboration by Douglas. As assessables, the statements also ascribe at least equal epistemic status to Douglas, i.e., they relate to matters about which Douglas has equal knowledge to Mickie. In the case of those in lines 1–2, 5–6 and 10 they relate to objects in Douglas's immediate environment and in line 6 to some past activity (the planting of the bulbs) in which both Mickie and Douglas participated. Mickie's responses to the statements are minimal at best, despite the longer latencies evident at lines 9, 11 and 13. The only audible response from Douglas is the minimal agreement at line 7. Douglas seems to have difficulty in either registering the requirement to respond, or in generating an appropriate second assessment; hence the absences at lines 9, 11 and 13. Mickie passes over these non-replies without orienting to them as indicating a need to repair any of her preceding utterances in any way.

As should be apparent from the above extracts, many of the difficulties that people with ID face in progressing and maintaining interactions are not wholly attributable to any cognitive or communicative impairment that they may have. Such difficulties also arise by virtue of the forms of practice that their interactional partners adopt. Known-answer questions and assessables ascribe at least equal epistemic status to the person with ID and may reasonably be interpreted as respectful of the individual, their status and competence. However, they also have the potential to present difficulties to the person with ID and to give rise to apparent incompetencies, including failure to demonstrate knowledge of one's activities, learning, immediate environment and even of oneself.

C. Trouble in Closings

Conversational closings generally work to a comparatively elaborate sequence of pre-proposal, proposal and execution, requiring all participants to be alive to what is going on, able to play their part in moving towards disengagement, or ready to delay it by inserting 'unfinished business' into the close-down routine (Schegloff and Sacks 1973;

Button 1990). However, as demonstrated above, interactions involving people with ID may fail to get off the ground, may not progress or be maintained, and may simply end, incomplete and unsatisfactorily for the relevant parties. In such interactions, the slot in which a canonical conversation closing sequence might occur may simply never be reached. There are, however, occasions in our data on which one or other party actively moves to end or to resist the ending of an exchange. Typically, this occurs where there seems to be some obdurate source of trouble that projects an ultimately unsatisfactory outcome, i.e., the prospect of achieving intersubjectivity seems unlikely. In such situations, one party may seek to end a challenging exchange, abandoning the pursuit of intersubjectivity, or to resist the efforts of their interlocutor to end an exchange in the continued pursuit of intersubjectivity.

Initiation of Closure

Perhaps because the majority of interactions in our data are initiated, and largely sustained, by a member of staff it is not surprising that service-users did not often take the lead in initiating closings (they may not feel that they have the 'deontic' authority to do so, in Stevanovic and Peräkylä's [2012] terms). The case below is one of the rare occasions on which a person with ID closes an activity (though see also Dom in Extract 3) and represents the ending of the activity begun in Extract 7.

Extract 9. CHW18 01:18-02:04 What would you do?

Kath:	>what's it about<
	(0.5)
Henry:	(eeyeh) p'li:ce, (0.3) (youh) (an')
	the sta:ff,
Kath:	and wha- what would you tell the
	staff.
Henry:	( ) the p'lice) ( )
Kath:	(would they::?) *((leans towards*
	Henry as if to confirm what she's
	heard))
Henry:	(, yeh)
Kath:	yeh, and what else,
	(0.3)
Kath:	What would you be telling them.
	(1.0)
Henry:	( )
	(0.7)
Kath:	What would you be coming and
	telling me then.
	(0.5)
Kath:	Or what would you be coming and

telling the police.
(2.0)
Henry: (ohm) *((turns away to pick something*
up))
Kath: What would you tell the police.
Henry: *((fixes gaze on Kath))*
Kath: Would you be ha:ppy, would you be
sa:d, would you be angry, would you
be annoy:ed, would you be up [set,
Henry: [ha:ppy,
((points to lips))
happy (0.3) (there:h) [happy
Kath: [you'd be
happy.
Henry: ((*nods*)) yeah ((*walks away*))
Kath: oh you'd ring the police and tell
them that you'd be happy is it?
((swings round to follow Henry))
Henry: (er yeah)
Kath: >no I don't< think so:,
((both go out of shot)

This long exchange may be briefly summarised as a staff member using known-answer questions to scaffold a display of understanding and competence from a person with ID, and that person with ID consistently producing what are clearly receipted as inadequate answers. Kath means to get Henry to articulate the lesson he should have learnt, that if he is harmed he should contact the police. By the time she issues an ironic admonishment (line 66–67) for Henry's incorrect answers he has already unilaterally walked away. By simply physically disengaging from the interaction, Henry does not need to draw upon the kinds of activity closing sequences identified in other institutional settings (e.g., in health care consultations Beach 1995; Robinson and Stivers 2001). Indeed, in this context, Henry may (demonstrably) not be treated as having the deontic right to close an activity that Kath initiated. Consequently, the closing is not jointly accomplished, if it can be considered to be accomplished at all; Kath physically pursues Henry and verbally pursues the activity out of shot. By contrast, Dom's shrug in Extract 3 seems to represent a much more effective non-verbal marker of the unilateral closing of a sequence, and abandonment of the pursuit of intersubjectivity. It must also be noted that, having initiated that sequence, Dom may be regarded as having the deontic authority to unilaterally close it.

Resistance to a Closing Down Sequence

We should end by noting a case where it is a member of staff who attempts to close a particular sequence, one initiated by a person with ID, and those efforts are resisted by that person with ID who is clearly concerned with pursuing a display of understanding from their non-ID interactional partner. It is not, therefore, a deficiency of interactional competence, but rather a determination to get their ideas and feelings acknowledged, to achieve intersubjectivity, that leads to them resisting a closing sequence.

Extract 10. CHW11 09.40-10:53 Lady with glasses.

01 Dom: *((makes circles in front of eyes, then*
02 *"writes" in the air))*
03 Pete: Which one's that one. Talk, I can't
04 under [stand.
05 Alec: [In a skip.
06 Dom: *((gestures to lips, and eyes as be*
07 *fore))*
08 Pete: Lady, with gla:sses, ( )
09 Dom: *((gestures shaking finger "no", points*
10 *upwards))* ( )
11 Alec: In a skip?
12 Pete: *((eyes down to plate, eating))* Dunno
13 which one you're on about, mate.
14 Dom: *((gestures to lips again))*
15 Pete: The girl, (0.5) with glasses

[17 lines of dialogue omitted, in which Dominic continues to use gestures and a few words to express himself]

33 Pete: I don't know which lady.
34 Dom: *((gestures to lips and eyes))* °lady with
35 glasses.°

36	Pete:	Lady with glasses.
37	Dom:	*((writing in the air))*
38	Pete:	Drawing.
39	Dom:	That one.
40		(0.5)
41	Pete:	*((shaking head))* I don't know which
42		one. Eat up then.
43	Dom:	°Write it down°. *((gestures writing))*
44	Pete:	Writing what.
45	Dom:	Lady.
46	Pete:	I know she's a lady, what's she writ-
47		ing.
48	Dom:	*((gestures writing))* (° °).
49	Pete:	Eh?
50	Dom:	(The cloh). (.3) The clock. *((makes*
51		*circular motion with hand))*
52	Pete:	The clock?
53	Dom:	°yeh°
54		(1.0)
55	Pete:	You having a dream again, one of your
56		funny dreams.
57	Dom:	(yeh)

In Extract 10,[5] Dom's utterances (whether as signs or in talk) are hard to decipher individually, and difficult to piece together into a coherent narrative. Notice that the staff member, Pete, does respond with candidate understandings for individual turns (lines 8, 15, 36, 37 and 52), but also explicitly adopts a K- epistemic stance at lines 12–13, 33, and 41–42, wherein he makes explicit his own inability to identify the individual who is the referent of Dom's utterances. Adoption of this epistemic stance may be interpreted as an attempt by Pete to close the sequence, by marking his inadequacy as a recipient, but these displays are not recognised or responded to as such by Dom. Again, a person with ID mirrors the normative practices of staff in services by pursuing intersubjectivity, here a display of shared knowledge, in the face of inadequate responses (see also Extracts 5 and 7). Following his third adopted K– epistemic stance at line 41–42, Pete also explicitly calls for Dom to discontinue this sequence by redirecting him to another task, "Eat up then". Again, this attempt to close the sequence is resisted. Eventually, Pete makes 'sense' of Dom's account by inviting him to agree with a candidate understanding of the referent of Dom's utterances, that the woman in question featured in a dream of Dom's.

The above extract could be interpreted a staff member prioritising an institutional activity (eating lunch) over the possibility of engaging with the resident in such a way as to facilitate a full understanding of the resident's concerns (see also Kristiansen et al. 2019 for how institutional constraints shape the turns of members of staff and their treatment of residents' utterances). But the problem of achieving intersubjectivity in the above sequence is clearly treated as resulting from the epistemic status of the speakers relative to the topic at hand. By locating the referent of Dom's utterances within a domain to which Dom has exclusive epistemic access, Pete also effectively accounts for his own failure to recognise the referent, thereby 'solving' the trouble at hand. The presumption of shared knowledge between speakers and recipients (roughly K= epistemic status) and the pursuit of displays of understanding, whether by or from a member of staff or a person with ID, can, when that activity runs into trouble, give rise to either party attempting to unilaterally

[5] This episode is more fully analysed in Antaki, Finlay and Walton (2007).

close or resist the closing of a sequence. The practices through which either party may attempt to perform either action seem, again, to be the 'normative' practices of a local culture, and the epistemic and deontic statuses of individuals within that community of speakers, more than they seem to be the product of any cognitive or communicative impairments of specific members of that community.

Discussion

As is evident from the above extracts, interactions involving people with intellectual disabilities may be atypical in many respects and at any point, from their initiation, their maintenance and their closing. But their atypicality results from a wide range of reasons. The adults with ID in the above extracts demonstrably produce utterances that are ambiguous, either in terms of their unintelligibility (e.g., Extracts 1 and 2) or in their projection of a next turn (Extracts 3 and 4). Such issues may be the result of problems of speech comprehension and production found within the intellectually disabled population (see Belva et al 2012; Schlosser et al. 2007). Similarly, in the above extracts, adults with ID fail to repair problematic utterances in response to repair initiators (Extracts 1 and 3), compromising the progression of sequences and the achievement of intersubjectivity (Schegloff 1992). It should, however, be noted that, even when they do not repair sources of trouble, speakers with ID clearly demonstrate a concern for the achievement of intersubjectivity through their pursuit of an appropriate response (e.g., Extract 3).

One clear benefit of a Conversation Analytic approach to understanding interactions involving people with ID is that it makes explicit the fact that much of the apparent atypicality of these interactions arises out of the practices of the non-impaired interactional partners. Two potential sources of this atypicality are identifiable in the above extracts: the tendency of staff to rely on ordinary conversational practices to resolve trouble (e.g., Extracts 5, 6, 7, 8 and 9); and their tendency to pursue institutional agendas and instructional concerns over and above more immediate interactional ones (Extracts 6, 7, 8, 9 and 10). Such sequences illustrate how precarious the social functioning of individuals with IDs can be, and how contingent their competence is on the format and design of turns from their interactional partners.

Similarly, staff pursuit of institutional goals and agendas further produces atypicality. The motivation of staff to instruct and to scaffold displays of knowledge, and thereby to demonstrate their own competence and familiarity with the people with ID whom they support, and the perseverance they demonstrate in doing so, are understandable within the institutional context. An understanding of such motivations may not be evident purely on the basis of the Conversation Analysis of interactions but may necessitate an ethnographic understanding of such contexts as social care services, the policies and practices that operate within them and the ways in which these shape staff interactions with residents and service users. Further, the above extracts clearly establish the importance of epistemic and deontic orders as participants' concerns, at least for members of staff. They rely on their knowledge of individuals to interpret ambiguous utterances, to scaffold and pursue social actions (including displays of knowledge and the provision of personal support) and they are clearly concerned to do so in ways that respect and recognise the epistemic and deontic status of people with ID as partners in those social actions.

Given such an understanding of these contexts, staff practices, which can and do result in 'atypical' interactions, must also be appreciated as providing the potential basis for instantiating a fuller and richer identity, and a higher level of functioning, for the person with ID (Wehmeyer et al. 2008). The risk, as is apparent in the above extracts, is that such practices may also produce 'incompetence', which may wrongly be attributed solely to the cognitive or communicative impairment of the person with ID. The atypicality of interactions involving people with ID must be understood as arising out of discrete communities of speakers, both intellectually and non-intellectually disabled, as located in social contexts that constitute particular "epistemic ecologies" (Heritage 2013), and within which individual human functioning must be understood as a distributed accomplishment.

Finally, while familial settings may be marked by the absence of institutional agendas, much the same epistemic and deontic statuses are likely to obtain. There are no a priori reasons to assume that parents and other family members of people with ID are any less likely than are members of staff in social care services to assume knowledge of, or authority over, the activities of their intellectually disabled relatives, to be concerned with instructing them, with eliciting displays of understandings or with pursuing intersubjectivity and joint action. However, these and other social contexts within which people with ID are located, and the epistemic ecologies they contain, remain to be empirically examined.

References

Antaki, C. (2013). Two conversational practices for encouraging adults with intellectual disabilities to reflect on their activities. *Journal of Intellectual Disability Research, 57*(6), 580–588.

Antaki, C., Finlay, W. M. L., & Walton, C. (2007). Conversational shaping: Staff-members' solicitation of talk from people with an intellectual impairment. *Qualitative Heath Research, 17,* 1403–1414.

Antaki, C., & Kent, A. (2012). Telling people what to do (and, sometimes, why): Contingency, entitlement and explanation in staff requests to adults with intellectual impairments. *Journal of Pragmatics, 44,* 876–889.

Antaki, C., & Webb, J. (2019). When the larger objective matters more: Service-providers' epistemic and deontic authority over adult service-users. *Sociology of Health and Illness.* https://doi.org/10.1111/1467-9566.12964.

Beach, W. A. (1995). Conversation analysis: "Okay" as a clue for understanding consequentiality. In S. J. Sigman (Ed.), *The consequentiality of communication* (pp. 121–162). Hillsdale, NJ: Erlbaum.

Belva, B. C., Matson, J. L., Sipes, M., & Bamburg, J. W. (2012). An examination of specific communication deficits in adults with profound intellectual disabilities. *Research in Developmental Disabilities, 33*(2), 525–529.

Button, G. (1990). On varieties of closings. In G. Psathas (Ed.), *Interaction competence* (pp. 93–148). Lanham, MD: University Press of America.

Debras, C. (2017). The shrug: Forms and meanings of a compound enactment. *Gesture, 16*(1), 1–34.
Drew, P. (1997). 'Open' class repair initiators in response to sequential sources of troubles in conversation. *Journal of Pragmatics, 28*(1), 69–101.
Finlay, W. M. L., & Antaki, C. (2012). How staff pursue questions to adults with intellectual disabilities. *Journal of Intellectual Disability Research, 56,* 361–370.
Finlay, W. M. L., Antaki, C., Walton, C., & Stribling, P. (2008). The dilemma for staff in 'playing a game' with a person with profound intellectual disabilities: Empowerment, inclusion and competence in interactional practice. *Sociology of Health & Illness, 30*(4), 531–549.
Heritage, J. (1984). A change-of-state token and aspects of its sequential placement. In J. M. Atkinson & J. Heritage (Eds.), *Structures of social action: Studies in conversation analysis* (pp. 299–345). Cambridge: Cambridge University Press.
Heritage, J. (2013). Epistemics in conversation. In J. Sidnell & T. Stivers (Eds.), *The handbook of conversation analysis* (pp. 370–394). Chichester: Wiley-Blackwell.
Holzner, B. (1968). *Reality construction in society.* Cambridge, MA: Schenkman.
Jehoul, A., Brône, G., & Feyaerts, K. (2017). The shrug as marker of obviousness. *Linguistics Vanguard, 3*(s1). Retrieved June, 11 2019, from https://doi.org/10.1515/lingvan-2016-0082.
Kendrick, K. H. (2015). Other-initiated repair in English. *Open Linguistics, 1*(1), 164–190.
Kristiansen, E. D., Rasmussen, G., & Andersen, E. M. (2019). Practices for making residents' wishes fit institutional constraints: A case of manipulation in dementia care. *Logopedics Phoniatrics Vocology, 44*(1), 7–13.
Robinson, J. D., & Stivers, T. (2001). Achieving activity transitions in physician-patient encounters: From history taking to physical examination. *Human Communication Research, 27*(2), 253–298.
Rusk, F., Sahlström, F., & Pörn, M. (2017). Initiating and carrying out L2 instruction by asking known-answer questions: Incongruent interrogative practices in bi- and multilingual peer interaction. *Linguistics and Education, 38,* 55–67.
Schegloff, E. A. (1992). Repair after next turn: The last structurally provided defense of intersubjectivity in conversation. *American Journal of Sociology, 97*(5), 1295–1345.

Schegloff, E. A. (2002). Opening sequencing. In J. E. Katz & M. Aakhus (Eds.), *Perpetual contact: Mobile communication, private talk, public performance* (pp. 326–385). Cambridge: University Press.

Schegloff, E. A. (2007). *Sequence organization in interaction. A primer in conversation analysis: Volume 1*. Cambridge: University Press.

Schegloff, E., Jefferson, G., & Sacks, H. (1977). The preference for self-correction in the organization of repair in conversation. *Language, 53*(2), 361–382.

Schegloff, E., & Sacks, H. (1973). Opening up closings. *Semiotica, 8*, 289–327.

Schlosser, R. W., Sigafoos, J., Rothschild, N., Burke, M., & Palace, L. M. (2007). Speech and language disorders. In I. Brown & M. Percy (Eds.), *A comprehensive guide to intellectual and developmental disorders* (pp. 383–401). Baltimore, MD: Paul H. Brookes.

Stevanovic, M., & Peräkylä, A. (2012). Deontic authority in interaction: The right to announce, propose, and decide. *Research on Language & Social Interaction, 45*(3), 297–321.

Wehmeyer, M. L., Buntinx, W. H. E., Lachapelle, Y., Luckason, R. A., Schalock, R. L., Verdugo, M. A., et al. (2008). The intellectual disability construct and its relation to human functioning. *Intellectual & Developmental Disabilities, 46*(4), 311–318.

5

Does Atypicality Entail Impairment? Tracing the Use of a Cohesive Marker in the Interactions of an Individual with Schizophrenia

Lisa Mikesell

There has been a fairly long history of examining the speech of individuals diagnosed with schizophrenia (IwS) (Titone 2010), sometimes referred to as "schizophrenic speech" (Docherty 2012; Rutter 1979). Much early research focused on documenting language anomalies from elicited speech samples and/or monologic speech (Pawełczyk et al. 2018; Pienkos and Sass 2017; Rochester and Martin 1979). While this work continues today, recent research highlights the importance of examining communication as it naturally occurs in interaction—that is, the contexts in which language is dynamically and socially used—to more carefully consider what is impaired. Indeed, based on neurobiological and experimental evidence, some now argue that schizophrenia may be best understood as a "disorder of (social) communication" (Niznikiewicz et al. 2013; Pawełczyk et al. 2018; Wible 2012).

This reconceptualization of schizophrenia frames social communication as a core clinical deficit and offers support for the broader claim that the verbal and nonverbal practices normatively required for

L. Mikesell (✉)
Rutgers University, New Brunswick, NJ, USA

© The Author(s) 2020
R. Wilkinson et al. (eds.), *Atypical Interaction*,
https://doi.org/10.1007/978-3-030-28799-3_5

seamless interaction with others are what characterises impairment common to IwS. Impairment is thus not believed to be *linguistic* per se (Niznikiewicz et al. 2013): that is, it is not defined by phonological and morphosyntactic deficits but is thought to impact extralinguistic or paralinguistic aspects of language that are multimodal (Pawełczyk et al. 2018) and most evident across larger units of discourse. The implication is that capturing what is impaired about "schizophrenic speech" requires a more discursive lens than has previously been applied. This chapter considers some of the theoretical and methodological challenges faced in examining the discourse of IwS, focusing on a case of cohesion, and makes a case not only for examining linguistic structures in situated interaction to catalogue what is marked, or atypical, about "schizophrenic speech," but also for considering how such atypicality may be effectively functional for IwS in naturally occurring interactions. This chapter thus cautions against presuming that an atypical discourse practice—one that may verge from normative standards whether in frequency and/or use—is necessarily an *impaired* one.

The speech of IwS has been previously described as disconnected and disjointed, leading scholars to systematically examine cohesion and its role in contributing to such characterizations. Cohesion refers to the range of linguistic elements (e.g. words, phrases) that build connectedness within a 'text,' whether spoken or written. Halliday and Hasan (1976) developed perhaps the most prominent account of cohesion, which they claim "occurs where the interpretation of some element in the discourse is dependent on that of another." They continue, "the one [element] presupposes the other, in the sense that it cannot be effectively decoded except by recourse to it" (p. 4). For example, one common cohesive tie is what they refer to as *reference* which includes demonstrative, comparative, and personal (or pronoun) reference illustrated in *I spoke to Angela recently but I haven't seen <u>her</u> in ages* where the pronoun 'her' serves to develop cohesion by tying back to the proper noun *Angela*. Halliday and Hasan (1976) detail other kinds of cohesive ties in addition to *reference*, namely *substitution, ellipsis, conjunction,* and *lexical*, noting that they are semantic, not merely structural, resources since their interpretation requires reference to some prior 'text.' Shortly following Halliday and Hasan's account of cohesion, Rochester and Martin

(1979), summarizing the literature on impairment in schizophrenic speech, argued that "abnormality appeared to lie in the connection between ideas rather than at the level of individual words and sentences" (as cited in McKenna and Oh 2005, p. 108), thus implicating cohesion as it is situated in disourse as potentially problematic.

To consider the socially situated uses of cohesion in naturalistic interaction, this chapter presents a case study of one IwS with the pseudonym Kevin and analyzes his use of the seemingly high frequency—66 uses in 4 hours of interaction—cohesive marker *like I say* (LIS) that ties back to a prior spate of talk by reformulating it in a new interactional environment. That is, LIS builds connections across conversational turns not only by referencing previous discourse elements, but by introducing reformulations of them. Although such reformulations may allow hearers to engage in some decoding even without reference to the prior element of talk, they nevertheless require reference to that prior talk for their socially situated meaning to be established. Examining a single marker of one individual has obvious limitations for generalizability and realizing broader implications about the nature of "schizophrenic speech." However, the choice of such a focused case study is responsive to criticisms dating back decades (e.g., Dawson et al. 1980), and continuing today (see Cohen et al. 2016), that our understandings of language and communicative impairment have arisen from analysts' third-party determinations of problematic uses of linguistic devices stemming from inappropriate data sources void of real-world purpose and meaning (Alverson and Rosenberg 1990; Harvey 1983). In contrast, this case study relies on 15 hours of video recorded interactions in community settings and is thus more amenable to a deeply contextualised analysis of naturally occurring, interactive discourse as it was produced over an extended period of time (one month). Additionally, while many studies highlight relative frequency of use among IwS as compared to neurotypicals, using a conversation analytic approach prioritises how mutual intelligibility is achieved between Kevin and his interlocutors to accomplish social actions in situ. Thus, while cohesion is fundamentally a linguistic construct, this analysis considers more than whether the semantic and structural connections afforded by LIS are (un)clear to a third-party analyst, as is the case of many cohesion studies. Rather it considers how such connections may establish mutual intelligibility for participants by taking into account what social actions LIS affords the speaker to achieve in particular interactional moments.

The Meaning of Language Anomalies

Early research on schizophrenia discourse described what has been clinically referred to as "formal thought disorder" (TD; Elevåg et al. 2017). While the status of TD has been contested, even falling out of favour (Sass and Parnas 2017), claims that linguistic anomalies in speech production (and comprehension; see Ditman and Kuperberg 2010) reflect disturbances in thought processes, which could not otherwise be empirically investigated, began with Bleuler (1911/1950) and have persisted over time (Pienkos and Sass 2017; see Covington et al. 2005; Elevåg et al. 2017). As Pienkos and Sass (2017) describe, those who view language anomalies as manifestations of underlying thought "suggest that the particular linguistic problems of schizophrenia indicate disturbances in specific cognitive capacities, such as the ability to determine context relevance and inhibit irrelevant thoughts, integrate disparate information, maintain goal directness …" (p. 84). Cohesion is often conceptualised to play a role in transposing how thoughts become meaningfully connected and seamlessly integrated into language and has thus been considered a probable indicator of problematic thought processes.

While most now recognise TD to be merely descriptive of language anomalies associated with schizophrenia rather than an indicator of underlying cognitive deficits (Kuperberg 2010), such "language 'distortion'" is generally understood to be a "sign – in the medical sense – that is potentially measurable" though is "currently without a universally accepted measure" (Elevåg et al. 2017, p. 510). As noted, however, many studies define impairment as a matter of differences in frequency of use as compared to neurotypical controls. Such documented language anomalies include higher rates of overall grammatical deviance in speech (e.g., Hoffman and Sledge 1988), less syntactic complexity (e.g., Fraser et al. 1986), both fewer and more frequent cohesive devices as well as more unclear cohesive references than controls (e.g. Docherty and Gottesman 2000). Conceptualising linguistic anomalies as an indicator of impairment has led scholars to largely ignore what IwS do well, particularly if what they do well may be understood as atypical.

Attending to Situated Discourse: The Status of Cohesion and Coherence

As researchers have become more critical of efforts to catalogue *linguistic* anomalies in contrived speech samples, there has been increased consideration about how to examine linguistic structures in the *situated* discourse of IwS. The importance of coming to terms with how to elicit and examine naturally occurring discourse is important as "schizophrenic speech" has been more recently characterised, not by *language* anomalies, but by "abnormalities at the discourse level" (Ditman and Kuperberg 2010, p. 254). Elevåg (2010), for example, refers to "unconventional discourse" (p. 238) and Marini et al. (2008) describe impairments in "macrolinguistic abilities" relating to "pragmatics and discourse level processing" in contrast to "microlinguistic" abilities such as lexical and morphosyntactic skills. Such efforts to precisely characterise discourse have also been wrought with methodological and theoretical challenges (Alverson and Rosenberg 1990; Cohen et al. 2016), including common orientations to communication as linear, as the "transmission of meaning from speaker to listener" (Docherty 2012, p. 1328), that may mute the interactive and negotiated nature of communication.

Cohesion studies are a case in point. Although even early studies recognised that analyses of cohesive devices must be situated within the sociocultural and interactional contexts in which they are produced (Halliday 1978; Halliday and Hasan 1976), many such studies have adopted coding strategies that neglect such a socially situated orientation (e.g., Rochester and Martin 1979; see Alverson and Rosenberg 1990). Some studies examining cohesion also elicit monologic speech in well-defined tasks and/or speech excerpts too brief to determine how cohesion may facilitate meaning across more than single clauses; indeed, rarely do studies analyzing cohesion among IwS move beyond clause boundaries

(Ditman and Kuperberg 2010). Perhaps contributing to these challenges is Halliday and Hasan's (1976) discussion of how cohesion builds 'texture' across 'texts' which are defined as semantic units. Both of these concepts may seem more elusive in naturally occurring face-to-face interactions than in the selected sets of sentences often used as illustrations: for example, where a 'text' begins and ends in ordinary, multi-party conversation may be hard to delineate since speakers incrementally co-construct sequences of talk that they may close and then revisit.

Fundamental to these potential shortcomings is how cohesion is conceptualised and understood to contribute to coherence. As Carrell (1982) argued years ago, "cohesion is not coherence" and discourse may include few explicit cohesive markers and still be coherent, making cohesion "neither a necessary nor sufficient condition for coherence" (Bublitz 1989, p. 39). Alverson and Rosenberg (1990) provide an illustrative example in which speaker A asks *What time is it?* and speaker B responds *Well, the postman's been already*, which is perfectly coherent but lacks cohesion. They go on to point out that lack of cohesion does not indicate deficit, and as importantly that "there is enormous variation in the level of cohesion exhibited in discourse structures of demonstrable coherence and interpretability" (p. 177). Yet, because cohesion is believed to be "one tool that may help comprehenders establish coherence" (Ditman and Kuperberg 2010, p. 255) and contribute to speakers' illogical discourse trajectories, cohesion has been given a great deal of attention in defining discourse impairments, particularly for IwS identified as presenting with (positive) symptoms of TD (Kuperberg 2010; Martin and Rochester 1979).

There are thus lingering problems with cohesion studies that have yet to be resolved, including presumptions about how to define atypical uses of cohesion and understand what such definitions of atypicality mean for what we can claim about schizophrenia discourse and any associated impairment. These presumptions are bound up in common methodological choices to restrict explorations of "schizophrenic speech" to contrived and well-defined tasks, sometimes written narratives, which poorly represent spoken discourse (Lee et al. 2009, Chapter 3). Consequently, it is not entirely evident how IwS employ such devices in interactive, real-world encounters and what meaningful actions they might achieve beyond the linguistically defined connections they facilitate.

Data and Methods

This case study presents Kevin, who had a SCID-diagnosis [a Structured Clinical Interview for the Diagnostic and Statistical Manual of Mental Disorders (DSM)] of schizophrenia and was 49 years old when he participated in a pilot study (Bromley et al. 2012) that aimed to use a video ethnographic approach to assess the ecological validity of neurocognitive and functional measures of serious mental illness. As part of the original study, Kevin was visited by three field researchers who continuously video recorded daily activities for a total of 15 hours spanning one month (5-3-2009 until 6-5-2009). Regarding formal and clinical assessments, Kevin's composite score on the MATRICS Consensus Cognitive Battery (MCCB) measuring key cognitive domains such as working memory, visual learning and social cognition, was 16 (the MCCB range of the pilot sample was 10–37). On the Brief Psychiatric Rating Scale (BPRS) measuring severity of psychotic symptoms, he scored 57 with two symptom domains—*somatic concern* and *suspiciousness*—scoring as 5 ("moderately severe"), followed by *unusual thought content, depression* and *anxiety*, which were scored as 4 ("moderate"). All other BPRS symptoms scored between 1 ("not present") and 3 ("mild"), and no domains scored as 6 ("severe") or 7 ("extremely severe)" (see also Mikesell 2013; Mikesell and Bromley 2016).

Field researchers, who were blind to Kevin's neurocognitive and clinical assessments (Bromley et al. 2012), described him as "very engaged," "knowledgeable" with "a lot to say." They also noted that Kevin sometimes spoke in "monologues" with one researcher noting that it was often difficult to participate in conversation. In the community (outside of interactions with field researchers), Kevin was observed to frequently engage in brief social interactions and service encounters, averaging 26 seconds in length and ranging between two seconds to say "hello" to an unknown passerby and 76 seconds with a bank teller (Mikesell and Bromley 2016). Thus, while Kevin had many interactions in the community, they were generally quite brief.

In reviewing the video data from the clinical pilot study, Kevin's frequent use of LIS was readily observed, particularly in comparison to the other nine study participants who were not found to use LIS. LIS occurred 66 times in four hours of interaction. Given the number of studies that have focused on the frequency of cohesive devices among IwS, claiming too few or too many devices, it was the apparent frequency of LIS that initially motivated its exploration and questions about what its frequent use might mean: Does its frequency reveal Kevin's *over*reliance on a single cohesive device and therefore suggest some sort of impairment? Or does it suggest some sort of linguistic dexterity, a practice for establishing connections across turns and sequences to establish mutual intelligibility with his interlocutor? To consider these questions, one must examine LIS in situ.

I tracked LIS across four hours of video recorded interactions with Kevin. This included the first two hours from his first visit (recorded on 5-3-2009) and the last two hours recorded from the last visit (6-5-2009) in which the same field researcher (referred to as ETH in the transcripts and subsequent text) visited Kevin. The interactions analyzed take place between Kevin and ETH because it is during these interactions that LIS occurred, likely because these interactions tended to be longer than Kevin's interactions with community members, thus providing the interactional context for Kevin to draw connections to previous talk.

Analysis

This section first provides an overview of the data, summarizing the formal features of LIS that establish connections across turns and sequences. I then discuss those features as they are situated in an interactional sequence in order to highlight not only the formal properties of LIS but also the situated action that LIS affords Kevin in this particular context. In this particular case, LIS works to facilitate sequence closure in the face of minimal uptake from his interlocutor while simultaneously providing a renewed opportunity for his interlocutor to respond, which would in effect prevent sequence closure. Such uses of LIS occur during the first two meetings between Kevin and ETH when they are just getting to know each other, usually during what might be described as 'small talk'. These extracts thus show difficult moments perhaps common to many occasions of small talk when topic talk can be hard to sustain with a stranger; they thus illustrate Kevin's efforts to maintain small talk with ETH who he knows he will see again. I then show how Kevin deploys LIS a month later during their last visit when they are no longer strangers. Having established some rapport, Kevin no longer utilizes LIS to exit challenging topics of small talk but to achieve a range of other social actions reflective of their growing familiarity. Collectively, these uses of LIS show how Kevin is attentive to both the local, immediate context of the talk (when building semantic connections to prior linguistic elements) and to the wider context of his evolving relationship with ETH (by selectively referencing ETH's recently acquired and now shared knowledge).

Summary of LIS and LIS in Action

Fifty-nine viable[1] cases of LIS were identified in four hours of data. All instances of LIS prefaced a reformulation (or second mention) of a prior spate of talk (or first mention). However, there were varying temporal distances between the first and second mentions that LIS connected. The *minimum* distance between the first mention and the second mention introduced by LIS was 9 seconds. The *maximum* distance was 103 minutes, with the average time intervening between first and second mentions being 9.2 minutes. LIS only referred back to first mentions that occurred within the same encounter; that is, they never reached back to build ties to talk that occurred during a previous day.

Extract 1 illustrates a 'short range' connection typical of Kevin and ETH's early interactions shortly after they first met each other. The second mention prefaced by LIS—"like I say it's kind of confu:sing" (line 13)—is a reformulation of the first mention produced 13 seconds earlier: "I don' understa:nd" (lines 3–4).

[1]A total of 66 cases of LIS were identified in the data. However, four of these cases did not have a first mention that could be identified from the data, which may have been because the first mentions were produced off camera or because they were not produced at all. Three cases were abandoned in mid-production.

Extract 1

```
01 KEV:    Alright this is considered Ire:ne.
02         (0.3)
03 KEV:    Which is supposed to be Norman, .hhh which I
04         don' understa:nd .hh it (should) sa[y (.)Norman.
05 ETH:                                       [Oh Irene.
06 KEV:    Ye(h)a(hh).
07         (0.2)
08 KEV:    It's [Norman once you get across Olander, but once
09 ETH:         [Heh.
10 KEV:    you [cross Wilcox, (0.2) it turns back to ↑Nor[man.
11 ETH:        [Oh okay.                                  [Yea::
12         i(t) was_
13 KEV:    And it's- you know like I say it's kind of confu:sing
14         (0.5)
```

Kevin and ETH met about an hour prior to the start of this extract and have just left his apartment to run some errands in his neighbourhood. In line 1, Kevin orients ETH to his neighbourhood streets; he identifies the street they are on by name ("Irene"). Following no uptake (line 2), Kevin continues by declaring that the street should have a different name (line 3: "Norman"), something that he 'doesn't understand' (line 4). He then presents the grounds for his declaration that the street is poorly named: the same street is called Norman elsewhere (lines 8, 10). In line 13, Kevin abandons the beginning of a new turn ("And it's-")[2] to produce "you know like I say," which introduces a reformulation of

[2]Although speculative, this turn may have been on its way to "And it's kind of confusing." In this case, Kevin's repair would been produced specifically to insert "you know like I say," suggesting the interactional importance for making the explicit reference to the first mention in line 4.

the first mention: "I don' understa:nd." This connective feature of LIS that links the first and second mentions was common across all of the cases and can establish connections not only within clause boundaries but across several conversational turns (see Ditman and Kuperberg 2010).

Additionally, the use of LIS does not only achieve these connections between first and second mentions. In Extract 1, for example, LIS occurs in sequence closing position. Indeed, it seems designedly placed to facilitate closing, which may hinge on two features of LIS and the bit of talk it prefaces: First, LIS explicitly marks the upcoming talk—a reformulation of something previously said—as repetitional, which may indicate that there is not much more for Kevin to say on the matter and thus provides a practice to exit the sequence. Second, the reformulation that LIS introduces is an assessment, which is also a regular practice for closing a sequence (Goodwin and Goodwin 1987). We might also consider the nature of the reformulations themselves that LIS introduces and how they contribute to what LIS discursively achieves. Here, the first mention is formulated as "I don' understa:nd." while the second mention is reformulated as "it's kind of confu:sing." While the first mention identifies the problem as one of individual difficulty—it is Kevin who does not understand why the street is called Irene—the reformulation reframes the problem as a more generalised one that may be shared. Positioning the difficulty as one not necessarily unique to him but arising from the situation itself moves the problem from personal to generalizable and thus more accessible to ETH. During the sequence thus far, ETH has either not responded to Kevin's turns (line 2) or offered mere acknowledgements (lines 5, 9, 11). In this context of making small talk with a stranger, Kevin's LIS turn in line 13 may then work to enable ETH to engage with his assessment about the problematic naming of streets in ways that he has yet to do (e.g. offering a confusing experience of his own) while also affording sequence closure in the event that ETH continued to remain unresponsive.

LIS-Prefaced Turns in the Face of Minimal Interlocutor Uptake

The following extract similarly shows an exchange that may also be characterised as 'small talk' between strangers (it occurred about 20 minutes after Kevin and ETH first met) and similarly illustrates how LIS-prefaced reformulations establishing connections across turns may be in the service of sequence closure. In this case, ETH launches a topical discussion about favorite sports—perhaps a canonical 'getting-to-know-you' question—but when Kevin responds, ETH provides minimal uptake and at times no response at all, leaving Kevin to either close the sequence or independently keep the topic alive.

Extract 2

01		(4.0)
02	ETH:	So um- so what's your favorite sport.
03	KEV:	Well I like (0.3) basketball and football, you know
04	ETH:	Nyea.
05	KEV:	I admire baseball,
06		(0.2)
07	KEV:	I admire all athletes you know.
08	ETH:	Uh huh.
09	KEV:	Da (0.9) I would say the work they have to do (0.5) to
10		develop the(y) skills.
11		(0.2)
		((lines omitted))
12	KEV:	I like track and field, uh (0.3) **I was amazed by the**
13		**Olympics**.
14		(0.4)
15	KEV:	You know I was amazed by that an' stuff.
16		(0.5)
17	KEV:	And um (3.2) **like I say it was fascinating the Olympics**.
18		(0.3)
19	KEV:	It was kinda intimidating
20	ETH:	Uh huh
21	KEV:	a little bit you know(0.4)to see a billion people .hhh
22		in synchronization.
23	ETH:	Ye[aheh heh
24	KEV:	[you know at the [(bird's nest).
25	ETH:	[Way- oh yea::, the-
26	KEV:	Yea
27	ETH:	The u:m

```
28  KEV:    At [the opening cerem[ony
29  ETH:       [ (   )           [the opening s- yea: it was-
30  KEV:    You know it was kinda intimidating to me.=And I was
31          kinda (.) mesmerised. I'm like
32  ETH:    Yeah me too. I saw i:t-
```

ETH launches a new sequence (line 2) asking, "So um- so what's your favorite sport." to which Kevin identifies two sports he likes (basketball and football). ETH acknowledges Kevin's turn (line 3) but does not reciprocate with his own preferences or follow-up on Kevin's. Kevin then transitions in stepwise fashion (Jefferson 1984) from sports he likes to a sport he admires (line 5). Again upon receiving no uptake, he continues, noting his admiration for "all athletes" (line 7). ETH produces a continuer, passing up his turn (Schegloff 1982; line 8) and after a bit of a delay, Kevin elaborates on what he finds admirable (lines 9–10).

After identifying additional sports (hockey and soccer) that he does not watch but admires (not shown), Kevin identifies another sport he likes (track and field; line 12), followed by a declaration of amazement for the Olympics (one of the few times perhaps that track and field events are televised). Upon receiving no uptake from ETH (line 14), he reiterates a near identical sentiment about the Olympics prefaced with "you know" (line 15; see Clayman and Raymond, under review), which again receives no uptake (line 16). Kevin continues, appearing to search for more small talk in the face of an unresponsive interlocutor, with an *and*-prefaced turn (line 17; cf. Heritage and Sorjonen 1994) that is suspended for 1.6 seconds. He then articulates for a third time his impressions of the Olympics, this time prefaced with *like I say*, which explicitly references his prior turn, only now reformulated as "it was fascinating the Olympics."

There are notable similarities with this use of LIS and the prior extract. Most evidently, it connects to a linguistic item in a prior turn by reformulating an earlier produced bit of talk. Additionally, the reformulation it introduces is notably similar to the reformulation we saw in Extract 1. While the prior mention ("I was amazed by the Olympics") presents the Olympics as something unique or personal to him, the LIS-prefaced second mention ("it was fascinating the Olympics") is formatted so as to present a more generalizable assessable, that is, not just an event that he was amazed by but that is itself fascinating, which others may also appreciate and more easily comment on. This reformulation of the assessment resembles Extract 1 in reframing an assessment as one that is personal to one that is common. While Kevin's turn in line 17 turns out not to close the sequence as it did in Extract 1, its production nevertheless can provide for this possibility and allow Kevin to exit a sequence of small talk during which his interlocutor is not as readily contributing.[3] At the same time, as an assessment of a world event that ETH likely has access to, reformulating the assessment in more general terms may also work to invite from ETH a second assessment (Pomerantz 1984). However, following a (0.3) second gap where there is still no uptake (line 18), Kevin continues his turn with a new assessment ("It was kinda intimidating"; line 19) to which ETH passes on taking a turn with his production of another continuer (line 20), prompting Kevin to go on to explain what was intimidating (eventually eliciting a more elaborated response from ETH in lines 25, 27, 29).

If one examined Kevin's three consecutive turns (across lines 12–17) in isolation or for only what the cohesive marker achieves referentially, it might be tempting to characterize this bout of talk as repetitive (Kevin produces nearly identical assessments across lines 12–13, again in line 15 prefaced with "you know" similarly displaying Kevin's efforts to facilitate intersubjectivity when faced with 'reception difficulties' (Clayman and Raymond, under review), and a third time in line 17) and consider what it might suggest about impaired integration of ideas or disordered/disorganised thinking. While LIS immediately re-introduces nearly the same turn that was produced only seconds prior, when examined sequentially in the context of getting to know an unfamiliar interlocutor, redoing the turn, explicitly recognizing it as repetitive with the LIS preface, and producing a generalised reformulation may collectively work to elicit a response that has not been forthcoming while also enabling sequence closure in the event that his interlocutor does not readily respond.

Extract 3 similarly highlights an interactional context in which ETH produces little uptake to Kevin's turns or continuers explicitly passing the opportunity to take a turn, again illustrating how reintroducing talk

[3]In that sense, his stepwise topical transitions noted above, while not used to exit the same kind of troubles telling contexts that Jefferson (1984) originally described, may work to exit a different sort of trouble—a sequence of small talk with an unfamiliar interlocutor who is minimally responsive.

with LIS may serve as a practice for navigating a challenging sequence with an unfamiliar, unresponsive interlocutor. This extract also occurs not long after Kevin and ETH meet (just minutes before Extract 1). They have just left Kevin's apartment and as Kevin is locking his door, Kevin shows his prosthetic arm to ETH.

Extract 3

01 KEV: There ya go. I- it can [open an' clo:se.

02 ETH: [Oh wo-

03 (0.2)

04 ETH: That- 's [(ne-)

05 KEV: [But **it's real tight. It's real tight.=**

06 =[Don't put your hand in there.

07 ETH: [So don' put your >hand in there<Okay.

08 KEV: Yea you know cause [it- **it's real crushing.**

09 ETH: [(>°uh<)

10 KEV: It's not [really sensitive,

11 ETH: [Oh:,.

12 (0.2)

13 ETH: °nkay.

14 KEV: y'know [to the touch.

15 ETH: [Can you open it half way? Or does it jus'

16 open or clo:se °er

17 KEV: It jus' open and clo:se.

18 ETH: °Okay.

((lines omitted; 53 seconds))

23 ETH: That's >cool,<=I've always wondered how those things work.

24 KEV: Ah man it- it's fascinating thu-uh (0.3) say the uh

25 industry of it.

26 (.)

27 KEV: Y'know it has came a lo:ng wa:ys.

28 (0.3)

29 KEV: Y'[(know and uh:)

30 ETH: [Yea I guess.

31 (.)

32 KEV: .hh From my understanding y'know it's gonna get better over

33 the yea:rs.
34 ETH: [Yea.
35 KEV: [Y'know they'll make it whe:re (0.2) it's not as sensitive_
36 (.)
37 KEV: [like y'know (.) to the [touch.
38 ETH: [Right. [Nyea.
39 (.)
40 KEV: .hh 'Cause **like I say if you were to pick up a ca::n or a**
41 **(0.2) or a cup or something, like (you-) a cup of coffee**
42 **<y'know<=like a [styrofoam cup with it? .hh it would=**
43 ETH: [Uh huh
44 KEV: **=crush it.**
45 ETH: Uh huh.

In Extract 3, Kevin points out his prosthetic arm to ETH (not shown). He then explains how the prosthetic works (lines 1–2) and subsequently describes it as "real tight" (line 6), which ETH demonstrably understands as a warning to not "put your >hand in there<" (line 7). Shortly after, Kevin reiterates his warning that "it's real crushing" (line 8). After Kevin finishes explaining how the prosthetic works, ETH appreciates his new understanding (line 23), and Kevin transitions to talk about the "industry of it" (line 25). Up until this point the conversation has been about the mechanics of the prosthetic and how it works. However, when the conversation shifts to the future of the industry, ETH provides no immediate uptake (line 26), and Kevin elaborates that the industry has "come a lo:ng wa:ys". After a gap, ETH tentatively responds in overlap with Kevin's continuation (lines 29–30). Kevin then remarks that the industry is "gonna get better over the yea:rs" (lines 32–33) and elaborates on what getting better means (lines 35, 37): the industry will "make it whe:re (0.2) it's not as sensitive" to the touch. Receiving mere acknowledgement tokens, Kevin then references his earlier talk with LIS (that his prosthetic is "real crushing") in lines 40–42, 44, only here it is repackaged in this new sequential environment to illustrate where prosthetics are still lacking: because "if you were to pick up a ca::n or a (0.2) or a cup or something, like (you-) a cup of coffee <y'know<=like a styrofoam cup with it? .hh it would crush it."

The first mention of the sensitivity of the prosthetic (it's real tight; it's real crushing) occurs in the context of showing ETH how the prosthetic functions and discursively serves as a warning to not put his hand in it. In this talk about the here-and-now, ETH readily responds demonstrating understanding of the warning. He also shows appreciation for Kevin's demonstration of how the prosthetic functions. The second mention introduced by LIS and produced 81 seconds later is in the context of discussing the future progress of prosthetics, a topic of talk that ETH less readily responds to, offering continuers and acknowledgment tokens only. Not receiving much uptake to this topical transition of the future of prosthetics, Kevin uses LIS to re-invoke the idea that his prosthetic is real crushing, this time not as a warning, but to identify a current design flaw and thus the kind of progress the industry is likely to make. His LIS-turn, by drawing a connection to the mechanics of his prosthetic that ETH showed enthusiasm for may, similarly to the previous extracts, provide a renewed opportunity for ETH to respond to this related topic.

The prior extracts showed how LIS-prefaced reformulations were employed in the face of ETH's minimal engagement with Kevin's efforts to navigate small talk by, on the one hand, facilitating sequence closure, and on the other, providing a renewed opportunity for ETH to respond. Extracts 1–3 occurred early during the first visit between Kevin and ETH, shortly after they meet and when they are just getting to know each other, also illustrating Kevin's sensitivity to the context of establishing a new relationship. The following extracts show LIS-prefaced reformulations that occur later in Kevin and ETH's relationship and which achieve a range of social actions.

Resuming a Prior Course of Action

The following extract shows how LIS-prefaced reformulations maintained the context-renewing function illustrated in the small talk sequences even after Kevin and ETH had spent some time together. In this case, Kevin deploys LIS, not to provide a renewed opportunity for ETH to respond to a topic he is not readily engaged in, but, quite contrastively, to resume a prior course of action that is in danger of being lost to ETH's intervening turns.

Extract 4

```
01 ETH:   Nor:: y'know I-I: would only get something like that
02        if (1.1) if I was filthy rich [and it was like you know
03 KEV:                                 [Yea.
04 KEV:   Bill Gates or somebo[dy.
05 ETH:                       [nyea: it's like [nothing (to me.)
06 KEV:                                        [ye(h)a(h)huh
07        [some(h)b(h)o(h)dy
08 ETH:   [An' then- and then I'd keep it in a showroom.=Probably(h)
09        Hh: heh
10 KEV:   Yea:(h)
11 ETH:   [heh °heh
12 KEV:   [Y'know then: you know something like that- (0.2) like
13        you say (.) 'cause you never know how (0.6) sa:y the
14        popular demand it might be.
15        (.)
16 KEV:   The economy might cha:nge.
17 ETH:   Yea:[h:.
18 KEV:       [An' the car y'know (.) look at the Hummers.
19 ETH:   Oh yea(h) heh.
20 KEV:   (You pay-) y'know people who own Hummers now are
21        pretty much stuck with 'em.
22 ETH:   Ye(h)a(h) [heh heh heh
23 KEV:             [But see ([0.2) [only- only agencies I can
24 ETH:                      [.hh   [heh
25 KEV:   see buyin' the Hummer is a federal agency:.=
26 ETH:   =Yea where >did I< see- js- jus' the other da:y .hhh (0.3)
27        advertising at a dealer like on the ten somewhere um (.)
28 KEV:   °G[o right here.
29 ETH:     [fifteen- (0.3) fifteen gra:nd off (0.2)
```

30 KEV: ↑Ewh.
31 ETH: on selected [Hummers.
32 KEV: [↑Ehw:.
33 (0.2)
34 ETH: [heh heh
35 KEV: **[Like I sa:y y'know th-the value of 'em, (0.3) the retail**
36 **sale of 'em**
37 (0.5)
38 ETH: [Ye::s.
39 KEV: [Can you resell 'em? [( ) so I can see like the
40 ETH: [Right. ( )
41 KEV: federal government buying 'em.=

In Extract 4, Kevin and ETH are discussing luxury vehicles and ETH has earlier stated his preference for small cars because they use less gas (petrol). He here offers further support for such a practical position (lines 1–2), arguing he would only buy a luxury vehicle "if I was filthy rich." Moments later, Kevin contributes to ETH's line of reasoning, remarking that another reason to avoid luxury cars is that the "popular demand" for them is uncertain (lines 12–13). This becomes the bit of talk he later refers to.

Following Kevin's concern about the fluctuating popular demand, he references Hummers as an illustration. The upshot, according to Kevin, is that owners are "pretty much stuck with 'em" (line 21), and further, they may only be resellable to federal agencies (line 25). At this point, ETH comes in to corroborate Kevin's point about Hummers' loss in value, telling about how he saw Hummers being sold at a considerable discount (lines 26–27, 29, 31). Kevin audibly appreciates ETH's turn (lines 30, 32) and then produces LIS to introduce a reformulation of his earlier point about the uncertain popular demand (i.e., the first mention in lines 13–14), here reformulated as "the value of 'em" or "the retail sale" (lines 35–36).

The reformulation introduced by LIS—similar to the prior extracts—structurally ties back to previous talk, and prefaces a reformulation of a prior mention. It also similarly enables Kevin to, in essence, reproduce or renew an earlier sequential environment. However, in this case, the sequential environment is not renewed to provide ETH another opportunity to respond or for Kevin to close a difficult sequence. Rather, reproducing the prior sequential environment enables Kevin to continue with his prior course of action that was in danger of being lost when ETH came into tell his story about discount Hummers.

Juxtaposing Contrasting Positions

Although less frequent, during the last visit between Kevin and ETH, LIS was also employed to juxtapose two seemingly contrastive positions in a way that was integrative or coherent. In Extract 5, the topic of conversation is notably not a topic perhaps common to small talk between strangers such as neighborhood streets or sports but is a more personal story about Kevin's past. He tells ETH about his time in a detention center when he was young (lines 3–4).

Extract 5

01 KEV: I had a good mouthpiece. My lawyer you kno[w

02 ETH: [Yea [heh

03 h[eh

03 KEV: [and stuff >I mean< 'cause I had went for like a

04 forgery an' a grand theft.

05 (.)

06 ETH: Okay.

((lines omitted))

07 KEV: And- you know if- **I was ashame(d) of it.**

08 (0.2)

09 KEV: and so on and so forth but you know over the yea:rs

10 I look at (.) ma::n these guys that (0.4) rapists and

11 murder[ers and child molesters, they made me look like

12 ETH: [Yea:.

13 KEV: a saint compared to (0.3) what they do:.

14 (0.3)

15 KEV: You know **like I say I kinda regret** because it was more a

16 trust issu:e (0.3) because I tried going to (0.2) like you

17 say (.) the finance wo:rld, (0.2) you know that can come

18 back and haunt you . . .

Kevin remarks that "I was ashame(d) of" his priors (line 7) and mitigates his wrongdoings by presenting them as relative, even saint-like (line 13), when compared to the "rapists and murderers and child molesters" (lines 10–11). Upon no uptake from ETH (line 14), Kevin continues, producing an LIS-prefaced reformulation of his first mention, "I was ashame(d) of it," now formulated as "I kinda regret" followed by the reason for his regret, which is a practical one: his earlier crimes have impeded his efforts to participate in "the finance wo:rld" (lines 15–18), presumably because he is perceived as less trustworthy (line 16).

While Kevin's LIS-prefaced reformulation occurs in the face of no interlocutor uptake, much like Extracts 1–3, in this case, it does not only seem to renew an opportunity for ETH to respond but also seems to resolve a potential challenge that might prevent ETH from easily responding: Across this spate of talk, Kevin presents two positions that may be heard as in opposition to each other. The first position acknowledges being ashamed of his earlier crimes (line 7), which is followed by a second position presenting these same crimes as relatively minor when looked at comparatively (lines 9–11, 13). Structurally, LIS re-introduces his original position (I was ashamed of it) but prefaces a reformulation of it which is presented with some mitigation (I *kinda* regret it) followed by a subordinated *because*-clause explicating the reason for regretting the crimes, a reason that coherently integrates these two contrastive positions. In other words, his regret introduced by LIS is not presented as a moral one but a practical one. Consequently, Kevin is able to present a coherent perspective on his earlier crimes, displaying how one can be ashamed of and regret crimes that one also perceives as relatively 'saint-like.'

Accounting for a Current Action

Only at rather long temporal distances (with significant time intervening between the first and second mentions) was LIS employed to re-introduce a prior bit of talk to account for or justify Kevin's current action that was under scrutiny. These uses of LIS-prefaced reformulations were also only observed during the last visit once Kevin and ETH had a more established relationship.

Extract 6

01 KEV: . . . she used to work with baby doctors.
02 (0.2)
03 KEV: .hh And so you know when I see children, babies especially
04 .hh I'm like okay this is what my mother used to do as a
05 ( ),
06 ETH: Yea.
07 KEV: You know a:n' .hh **she kind of taught me some thi:ngs (.)**
08 **as of (.) emergency (0.3) respo:nse.** (Be)cause you know
09 when you do see-pee-are (CPR) on a baby, you have to be
10 more s:ensitive,
11 ETH: Yeah.
12 KEV: Then you know doing it on an adult.
13 (0.2)
14 KEV: And [stuff so you know I'm like–
15 ETH: [heh.
16 ETH: I- I've never tried. (on a baby) heh heh heh I'm nervous.

49mins, 25secs elapse

17 ETH: Do you have allergies or something?
((lines omitted))
18 ETH: Oh no, but I meant with your- the um- (0.2) tsk with
19 the breathing, the mask.
20 KEV: Oh no [that was y'know (0.3) from the: (0.3) the current
21 ETH: [(with) the mask.
22 KEV: events we see on tee-[vee (TV).
23 ETH: [Oh the swine flu(h)[heh
24 KEV: [Yes the
25 [current events >we see< on tee-vee.

26	ETH:	[Yea so wh(h)en you see somebo(h)dy cou(h)ghin(h)'?
27	KEV:	
28		(0.3)
29	KEV:	Ye[:s.
30	ETH:	[Ny(h)e(hh)a(h) heh heh
31	KEV:	I mean you know it came in [my: first aid kit.
32	ETH:	[heh hm
33	ETH:	[(my caw-)
34	KEV:	[my emergency preparedness kit?
35	ETH:	Oh yea[:.
36	KEV:	[So- (.) they gave us a lot of ma:sks.
37	ETH:	Oh that's what that is.=
38	KEV:	=Yes.
39	ETH:	Oka[y.
40	KEV:	[An' like the American Red Cross, they come to
41		our buildi:ng,
42		(0.2)
43	KEV:	once a year.
44	ETH:	Nyea.
45	KEV:	An' you know they teach us first ai:d and see-pee-
46		are (CPR).
		((lines omitted))
47		(0.2)
48	ETH:	Y[ea.
49	KEV:	[So once you complete y'know you get your certificate,
50		(0.6) you know say first aid you know see-pee-are (CPR)
51		then they give us a ba::g,
52	ETH:	Okay.
53	KEV:	=full of emergency preparedness equipment.
54		(0.3)

55 KEV: Like they call it tria[:ge?
56 ETH: [Yea:
57 KEV: Y'know_
58 (0.2)
59 KEV: So (0.3) **like I say my mother used to be an emergency**
60 **worker.** So I- >y'know< I kinda think like she do.
61 ETH: Nuh hu[h h(he(h) heh heh
62 KEV: [At ti:mes. Y'know what I'm sayin'.<'Cause I seen
63 her (0.2) go into action (.) on the freewa:y,

The first mention comes when Kevin is telling ETH about his mother's profession—she was a pediatric nurse and emergency responder (not shown) who "used to work with baby doctors" (line 1). He then mentions how she "taught me some thi:ngs (.) as of (.) emergency (0.3) respo:nse" (lines 7–8), which is the bit of talk referenced later. They go on to discuss the challenges of responding to emergencies with babies as compared to adults.

About 50 minutes later as they are walking around town, ETH launches a new sequence asking Kevin "Do you have allergies or something?" (line 17). This turns out to be a question referencing a facemask Kevin is wearing around his neck, but Kevin responds to it as a genuine question about allergies (not shown). ETH clarifies his intention that he was asking about the facemask (lines 18–19). Kevin explains that the mask is because of the "current events we see on TV" (line 22), which ETH identifies as the swine flu with laugh tokens (line 23). Kevin confirms this understanding (line 24), and ETH starts to present the upshot "so wh(h)en you see somebo(h)dy cou(h)ghin(h)'?" produced with laugh particles and a tone of skepticism. As Kevin confirms (line 26), ETH continues his laughter, clearly making fun of Kevin's cautious behaviour.

Following ETH's mild ridicule, Kevin explains that the mask came in a first aid kit, providing an account for why he has it (line 31). He then further explains that it was 'they' (line 36)—the American Red Cross (line 40)—that provide the equipment and teach emergency response to the residents in his building, extending his account for why he wears the mask. Receiving only an acknowledgement of understanding from

ETH (line 37) and rather minimal uptake (lines 39, 44, 52, 58) of his accounts for carrying the mask, Kevin produces LIS to re-introduce a fact he mentioned 50 minutes earlier (lines 7–8), that his mother was an emergency worker so he "kinda thinks like she do" (lines 59–60), further justifying why he wears the facemask and framing it as reasonable behaviour—not as overly cautious but as being prepared to help like his mother. Drawing on this much earlier bit of talk may be rather convincing as a justification for a current behaviour under scrutiny because this justification for wearing the mask was already made available to ETH but for a quite different purpose.

Discussion

With increasing recognition that abnormalities characteristic of schizophrenia are most likely to occur at the discourse rather than linguistic level, there is also an increasing awareness that "abnormalities can only be understood within the confines of dyadic" (or multiparty) exchanges (Dombrowski et al. 2014; see Titone 2010) and are "dynamic across time and context" (Cohen et al. 2016). This contextualised examination of LIS, a device employed so frequently it was produced on average every 3.5 minutes, as it is employed in interaction highlights how this single marker can be used to draw connections to prior talk to achieve a variety of real-world social actions, thus cautioning against presuming that abnormalities or atypical discourse practices necessarily entail impairment. It also shows how these uses dynamically evolve across the development of a new and ongoing relationship between Kevin and an unfamiliar interlocutor who he has committed to seeing over multiple occasions, illustrating how Kevin remains sensitive to both the local, interactional sequence of talk and the broader context of his relationship with the researcher. Notably, Kevin's early uses of LIS (i.e. those occurring during the first hours of their first meeting) when Kevin and ETH are engaged in small talk may be easily interpreted to be problematic. For instance, LIS-prefaced reformulations often connect to prior talk that was produced mere seconds earlier and may thus be interpreted as repetitive and not integrating turns to build a coherent sequence of talk. However, one may similarly interpret ETH's lack of responsiveness to Kevin's efforts to engage in small talk as equally problematic. Thus when these early uses of LIS are examined sequentially, it becomes evident that they occurred when Kevin's interlocutor is not forthcoming and the hearable repetitiveness can be understood as a practice for navigating sequences of 'belabored' small talk. Specifically, these early uses constitute a practice for providing Kevin two possible paths for dealing with challenging moments of getting to know someone: first, they provide a renewed context for ETH to respond when he was not immediately forthcoming or responsive to Kevin's attempts to make small talk. Second, they provide Kevin the opportunity to exit from a belabored topic in the event that ETH continues to remain unresponsive. Thus, these early interactions, rather than demonstrating some sort of undisputable impairment integrating turns at talk or sustaining a coherent goal, illustrate Kevin's work to maintain conversation with an unfamiliar interlocutor. Contrastively, during the last visit after Kevin and ETH had spent several hours together and ETH was often more forthcoming, Kevin's uses of LIS to reformulate prior talk were no longer employed to achieve this same function and were produced at 'longer' range distances. Rather, reformulating prior talk during their last visit enabled a range of social actions reflective of a more established relationship such as responding to ETH's critical teasing of Kevin's cautious behaviour.

This study is certainly not without limitations. Schizophrenia is a heterogeneous disorder (Ahmed et al. 2018; Kuperberg 2010; see also Mikesell and Bromley 2016), and not all IwS exhibit language anomalies or communication impairments (Docherty 2012), however those impairments are defined and measured. This case study of a single linguistic structure is thus significantly limited in its ability to generalise across IwS or to make sweeping claims about the status of cohesion and how it is implicated in understandings of language and discourse anomalies. Although small in scope, this work, nevertheless, may serve as an illustration to the ongoing research on investigations into language anomalies in "schizophrenic speech" to help bring it more closely in alignment with current understandings that real-world, dyadic/multiparty interactions are where linguistic structures need to be examined. More importantly, it highlights that although the production of linguistic structures might, on the surface, appear to be atypical (i.e. occurring too frequently or not frequently enough, or determined to establish unclear or inappropriate references), new understandings may arise when they are examined sequentially for what social actions they afford speakers to achieve in interaction. For instance, when Kevin's uses of LIS and the reformulations they introduced were analyzed for how they might achieve mutual intelligibility, it was evident that the actions they afforded were sensitive to a developing and highly unusual (i.e. a long-term researcher-participant) relationship he was attempting to navigate.

Relatedly, this work may offer some real-world insight as to why previous studies find that diagnosed individuals use both fewer and more cohesion markers than neurotypical controls. In four hours of interaction, Kevin employed LIS 66 times or, as noted above, about every 3.5 minutes. Although without a baseline measure for comparison, we cannot know if this is relatively few or many, on the face of it, this seems a rather frequent usage of a single marker. What it means if a speaker uses many or few markers is still not well understood, particularly for what these differences may (or may not) suggest about impairment. While Kevin's high frequency use of LIS may indeed be *atypical*, the prior analysis perhaps more aptly demonstrates that such "vocal abnormalities require grounding within the contextual demands of the conversational partner, and are not abnormal in-and-of themselves" (Cohen et al. 2016, p. 306). This potentially atypical practice then may just as easily be argued to demonstrate Kevin's dexterity in utilizing a single 'ready-made' linguistic device for referencing and reformulating prior talk to serve a range of interactional needs.

References

Ahmed, A. O., Strauss, G. P., Buchanan, R. W., Kirkpatrick, B., & Carpenter, W. T. (2018). Schizophrenia heterogeneity revisited: Clinical, cognitive, and psychosocial correlates of statistically-derived negative symptom subgroups. *Journal of Psychiatric Research, 97,* 8–15. https://doi.org/10.1016/j.jpscyhires.2017.11.004.

Alverson, H., & Rosenberg, S. (1990). Discourse analysis of schizophrenic speech: A critique and proposal. *Applied Psycholinguistics, 11,* 167–184. https://doi.org/10.1017/S0142716400008754.

Andreasen, N. C. (1979). Thought, language and communication disorders: I. Clinical assessment, definition of terms, and evaluation of their reliability. *Archives of General Psychiatry, 36,* 1315–1321. https://doi.org/10.1001/archpsyc.1979.01780120045006.

Bleuler, E. (1911/1950). *Dementia praecox, or the group of schizophrenias.* New York: International University Press.

Bromley, E., Mikesell, L., Mates, A., Smith, M., & Brekke, J. (2012). A video ethnography approach to assessing ecological validity of neurocognitive and functional measures in severe mental illness. *Schizophrenia Bulletin, 38*(5), 981–991. https://doi.org/10.1093/schbul/sbr002.

Bublitz, W. (1989). Topical coherence in spoken discourse. *Studia Anglica Posnaniensia, XXII*(22), 31–51.

Carrell, P. L. (1982). Cohesion is not coherence. *TESOL Quarterly, 16*(4), 479–488. https://doi.org/10.2307/3586466.

Clayman, S. E., & Raymond, C. W. (under review). *You know* as a resource for invoking alignment: The case of speech production and understanding difficulties. *Language.*

Cohen, A. S., Mitchell, K. R., Docherty, N. M., & Horan, W. P. (2016). Vocal expression in schizophrenia: Less than meets the ear. *Journal of Abnormal Psychology, 125*(2), 299–309. https://doi.org/10.1037/abn0000136.

Covington, M. A., He, C., Brown, C., Naçi, L., McClain, J. T., Fjordbak, B. S., et al. (2005). Schizophrenia and the structure of language: The linguist's view. *Schizophrenia Research, 77,* 85–98.

Dawson, D. F., Bartolucci, G., & Blum, H. M. (1980). Language and schizophrenia: Towards a synthesis. *Comprehensive Psychiatry, 21*(1), 81–90.

Ditman, T., & Kuperberg, G. R. (2010). Building coherence: A framework for exploring the breakdown of links across clause boundaries in schizophrenia. *Journal of Neurolinguistics, 23,* 254–269. https://doi.org/10.1093/schbul/sbr048.

Docherty, N. M. (2012). On identifying the processes underlying schizophrenic speech disorder. *Schizophrenia Bulletin, 38*(6), 1327–1335. http://dx.doi.org/10.1037.0021-843X.112.3.469.

Docherty, N. M., & Gottesman, I. I. (2000). A twin study of communication disturbances in schizophrenia. *The Journal of Nervous and Mental Disease, 188*(7), 395–401.

Dombrowski, M., McCleery, A., Gregory, S. W., Jr., & Docherty, N. M. (2014). Stress reactivity of emotional and verbal speech content in schizophrenia. *Journal of Nervous and Mental Disease, 202,* 608–612.

Elevåg, B. (2010). Letter to the editor. *Schizophrenia Research, 120,* 238–239. https://doi.org/10.1016/j.schres.2010.04.006.

Elevåg, B., Folta, P. W., Rosenstein, M., Ferrer-i-Cancho, R., De Deyne, S., Mizraji, E., et al. (2017). Thoughts about disordered thinking: Measuring and quantifying the laws of order and disorder. *Schizophrenia Bulletin, 43*(3), 509–513. https://doi.org/10.1093/schbul/sbx040.

Fraser, W. I., King, K., & Thomas, P. (1986). The diagnosis of schizophrenia by language analysis. *The British Journal of Psychiatry, 148,* 275–278. https://doi.org/10.1192/bjp/48.3.275.

Goodwin, C., & Goodwin, M. H. (1987). Concurrent operations on talk: Notes on the interactive organization of assessments. *IPRA Papers in Pragmatics, 1*(1), 1–54. https://doi.org/10.1075/iprapip.1.1.01goo.

Halliday, M. (1978). *Language and social semiotic: The social interpretation of language and meaning.* London: Edward Arnold.

Halliday, M., & Hasan, R. (1976). *Cohesion in English.* London: Longmans.

Harvey, P. D. (1983). Speech competence in manic and schizophrenic psychoses: The association between clinically related thought disorder and cohesion and reference performance. *Journal of Abnormal Psychology, 92,* 368–377.

Heritage, J., & Sorjonen, M.-L. (1994). Constituting and maintain activities across sequences: And-prefacing as a feature of question design. *Language in Society, 23*(1), 1–29. https://doi.org/10.1017/S0047404500017656.

Hoffman, R. E., & Sledge, W. (1988). An analysis of grammatical deviance occurring in spontaneous schizophrenic speech. *Journal of Neurolinguistics, 3*(1), 89–101. https://doi.org/10.1016/0911-6044(88)90008-5.

Jefferson, G. (1984). On stepwise transition from talk about a trouble to inappropriately next-positioned matters. In J. M. Atkinson & J. Heritage (Eds.), *Structures of social action* (pp. 191–222). New York: Cambridge University Press.

Kuperberg, G. R. (2010). Language in schizophrenia part 1: An introduction. *Language Linguistic Compass, 4*(8), 576–589. https://doi.org/10.1111/j.1749-818X.2010.00216.x.

Lee, N., Mikesell, L., Joaquin, A. D., Mates, A. W., & Schumann, J. H. (2009). *The interactional instinct: The evolution and acquisition of language.* Oxford: Oxford University Press.

Marini, A., Spoletini, I., Rubino, I. A., Ciuffa, M., Bria, P., Martinotti, G., et al. (2008). The language of schizophrenia: An analysis of micro and macrolinguistic abilities and their neuropsychological correlates. *Schizophrenia Research, 105,* 144–155. https://doi.org/10.1016/j.schres.2008.07.011.

Martin, J. R., & Rochester, S. R. (1979). *Crazy talk: A study of the discourse of schizophrenic speakers.* New York: Plenum.

McKenna, P., & Oh, T. (2005). *Schizophrenic speech*. Cambridge: Cambridge University Press.
Mikesell, L. (2013). An impaired interactional instinct: Schizophrenia as a case study. In A. D. L. Joaquin & J. H. Schumann (Eds.), *Exploring the interactional instinct* (pp. 225–255). New York: Oxford University Press.
Mikesell, L., & Bromley, E. (2016). Exploring the heterogeneity of 'schizophrenic speech'. In M. O'Reilly & J. N. Lester (Eds.), *Palgrave handbook of adult mental health: Discourse and conversation studies* (pp. 329–351). Basingstoke: Palgrave Macmillan.
Niznikiewicz, M. A., Kubicki, M., Mulert, C., & Condray, R. (2013). Schizophrenia as a disorder of communication. *Schizophrenia Research and Treatment*. https://doi.org/10.1155/2013/952034.
Pawełczyk, A., Kotlicka-Antczak, M., Łojek, E., Ruszpel, A., & Pawełczyk, T. (2018). Schiozophrenia patients have higher-order language and extralinguistic impairments. *Schizophrenia Research, 192,* 274–280. https://doi.org/10.1016/j.schres.2017.04.030.
Pienkos, E., & Sass, L. (2017). Language: On the phenomenology of linguistic experience in schizophrenia. *Psychopathology, 50,* 83–89. https://doi.org/10.1159.000455195.
Pomerantz, A. (1984). Agreeing and disagreeing with assessments: Some features of preferred/dispreferred turn shapes. In J. M. Atkinson & J. Heritage (Eds.), *Structures of social action: Studies in conversation analysis* (pp. 57–101). Cambridge: Cambridge University Press.
Rochester, S., & Martin, J. R. (1979). *Crazy talk: A study of the discourse of schizophrenic speakers*. New York: Plenum Press.
Rutter, D. R. (1979). The reconstruction of schizophrenic speech. *The British Journal of Psychiatry, 134,* 356–359. https://doi.org/10.1192/bjp.134.4.356.
Sass, L., & Parnas, J. (2017). Thought disorder, subjectivity, and the self. *Schizophrenia Bulletin, 43*(3), 497–502. https://doi.org/10.1093/schbul/sbx032.
Schegloff, E. A. (1982). Discourse as an interactional achievement: Some uses of 'uh huh' and other things that come between sentences. In D. Tannen (Ed.), *Analyzing discourse, text and talk* (pp. 71–93). Washington, DC: Georgetown University Press.
Titone, D. (2010). Language, communication, and schizophrenia. *Journal of Neurolinguistics, 23,* 173–175. https://doi.org/10.1016/j.jneuroling.2010.01.003.
Wible, C. G. (2012). Schizophrenia as a disorder of social communication. *Schizophrenia Research and Treatment*. https://doi.org/10.1155/2012/920485.

6

Singing as a Resource in Conversations Involving Persons with Dementia

Gitte Rasmussen

Introduction

Dementia influences life in many ways. It not only affects cognitive functioning in terms of, for example, memory disorder, inattention, and loss of interest in the surroundings (Shinagawa et al. 2006), it also has effects on communicative functioning (Bayles and Tomoeda 2007), for example, word-finding difficulties (Mok and Müller 2014), perseverations (Lubinski et al. 1995), difficulties in using deictic pronouns, and difficulties in following and maintaining a conversation (Dijkstra et al. 2004; Laine et al. 1998; Macoir and Turgeon 2006). These difficulties may result in a conversational style that differs from the complexity evident in the talk of typical speakers as described in conversation analytic (CA) research (Drew et al. 2006b; Heinemann 2015; Jefferson 1993; Lerner 1995; Schegloff 1982). Such talk is characterised by, for example, extensions of turn-constructional units (Sacks et al. 1974) in terms of add-ons like replacements (Couper-Kuhlen and Ono 2007)

G. Rasmussen (✉)
University of Southern Denmark, Odense, Denmark

© The Author(s) 2020

R. Wilkinson et al. (eds.), *Atypical Interaction*,
https://doi.org/10.1007/978-3-030-28799-3_6

and increments (Schegloff 1996b), delayed turn completions (Lerner 1989; Oloff 2018), collaborative completions (Lerner 2004), and topic initiations and developments (Button and Casey 1984, 1985; Jefferson 1984b).

However, research has documented that people living with Alzheimer's and other dementias still have the ability to sing and to respond to music (Miller et al. 2000; Mithen 2005). Neuroscience explains this by reference to the neurological processes involved in singing which differ fundamentally from those of speaking (Peretz and Coltheart 2003). It has been shown that persons with dementia may also learn to remember a known song better and even learn an unknown one (Bannan and Montgomery-Smith 2008).[1] There are also reports that engagement in music and singing activities contributes to the social and psychological wellbeing of persons with dementia (Aldridge 2000; Brotons and Koger 2000; Camic et al. 2011; Millard and Smith 1989; Prickett and Moore 1991).

Most descriptions in the literature are part of investigations of singing as a social activity which has been initiated and orchestrated by care staff or music therapists for intervention purposes (Aldridge 2000; Kindell et al. 2018; Matthews 2015). Additionally, a few studies analyse caregivers singing and using music e.g. during the course of their caregiving activities, one of which (Götell et al. 2002) addresses the relationship between singing and talk in face-to-face interaction (Drew et al. 2006a) by way of showing that caregiver singing has "a positive influence on verbal communication" (Götell et al. 2002).

This study shares with prior research an interest in the connection between talk and singing in face-to-face interactions involving persons with dementia. It differs though in multiple ways: it investigates how a person with dementia initiates spontaneous singing during the course of a conversation with a visiting researcher and describes and analyses the local interactional environments in which the spontaneous singing emerges. The aim is to study what singing may be a response to and

[1] In patients in late and severe stages of the condition, musical perception may be affected in line with the overall cognitive impairment (Yannou et al. 2003).

what it works to accomplish. In a single case study of the singing behaviour of a client with traumatic brain injury, Azios and Archer (2018) describe how the client sings actions and turns to accomplish itemised news inquiries, answers to questions, and closings of sequences of talk. The current study highlights how the person with dementia starts singing songs when a topic of talk is about to atrophy due to conversational difficulties that research attributes to dementia, as mentioned above. Thus, it shows how singing provides new resources for social interaction (Streeck et al. 2011) which enables the initiator of the singing, the person with dementia, to bring in new perspectives on the atrophying topic of talk.

The Orientation to Sound in Talk

Talk *is* sound (Couper-Kuhlen and Selting 1996). CA research has shown, however, that participants in interaction usually orient to talk as actions (Drew and Heritage 1992) rather than sounds. Still, Jefferson (1996) describes instances in which participants in ordinary conversation do produce talk by reference not only to what the action in a prior turn accomplishes, e.g. asking a question, but also partly to sounds and associations. Speakers may for instance repeat sounds in turns delivered by self or in turns produced by others in what Jefferson calls "cross-speaker poetics" (p. 28). The following two examples illustrate this phenomenon.

```
Ex. A Jefferson (1996: 28) (4.a.1) [GTS:I:1:52:R]d

Roger:    You gotta watch the signs hehhehh 'hehh I
          gotta distinguish myself without (.) u-
          telling people (see)?
Louise:→ °Yah<°u-but I:, I-I
                         (0.7)
Louise:   di[dn't ca]tch the s]i:gns,
Roger: →    [A  y :  :] y  a  i:    ]:
```

In her response to Roger's turn, Louise stammers "I, I-I", which Roger picks up on to turn it into the refrain "Ay, Ay, Ay, Ay" from the Spanish song 'Cielito lindo'.

In the next example, Claire selects Barbara's line "I'm looking for, I'm looking for", which Barbara produces while searching for something in a cupboard. The recipient of Claire's action is Jean with whom Claire has a lunch date. The three of them are sitting in Barbara's kitchen:

```
Ex. B Jefferson (1996: 30)(4.a.6) [GJ:FN]

Claire:    ((To Barbara)) What are you doing.
Barbara:→  I'm looking fo::r, -- I'm looking fo:r,
             ((brief silence))
Claire     ((To Jean, with whom she has a lunch date))
         → I'm looking forward to Saturday. I hope I'm feeling well
           enough.
```

In line with Jefferson's work, Schegloff (2005) describes how sounds in terms of melodies occur as associations. Moreover, he describes how whistling fragments from a melody may be seen as the whistler's response to their environment, which may include not only the social context, but also, for instance, weather conditions. Based on analyses of mostly self-reports, Schegloff finds that the words or phrases in the melodies fit the context in terms of the time and place of the whistle production and that they, though unarticulated, "drive the production" (ibid., p. 29) of the whistling or humming.

In sum, in ordinary (neuro-typical) interaction co-participants may orient towards sounds and associations when responding relevantly to turns at talk and to larger social and environmental contexts. Moreover, ordinary co-participants may do so spontaneously, i.e. without reflecting upon it and without noticing it (Jefferson 1996). The competence in using sounds (and associations) not only for singing activities, but also for engaging relevantly in interaction may, as this paper will show, be preserved while language and communicative functioning has deteriorated due to dementia.

Data and Methods

The data for this study are part of an ongoing research project at the University of Southern Denmark on abilities and possibilities in interaction involving persons with dementia. Data were collected by researchers observing or being involved in the routine activities of persons with dementia in common spaces in a care facility, i.e. through participant observation (Kawulich 2005). The author visited the care facility on a weekly basis for 9 months between 2015 and 2016. Observations were recorded through field notes or through video recordings of naturally occurring interaction with or between persons with dementia. None of the recorded conversations were elicited for the purpose of studying the use of specific practices in them, including, in the case at hand, 'singing'.

The recordings were analysed using the methodology of CA (Drew 2005), which includes a transcription of the micro details of (embodied) actions and turns at talk and an analysis of the ways in which the co-participants orient to and order them. The conversation analyst treats every detail as a possible locus of social order (Sacks 1966/1995).

As the analysis will show, some of the details of the local environment which the person with dementia may orient to when he or she starts to sing, are the pitch characteristics and contours of the co-participants' speech (see also Couper-Kuhlen and Selting 1996; Reed 2011). The Praat acoustic editing software, courtesy of Paul Boersma and David Weenink (www.fon.hum.uva.nl/praat), was used to calculate the vocal pitch and analyse the pitch movement of their relevant speech samples (see Appendix).

A Single Case Study

The analysis is based on a single case study of one person, Nancy, whose practices do not necessarily represent the variation in practices amongst persons with dementia. Neither does her type of dementia, fronto-temporal dementia, represent other types, which, at least in early stages, may alter interactions in specific significant ways. As Oliver Sacks (2011) has pointed out, the use of case histories for research purposes goes back to an ancient tradition in neurology and psychiatry and to Hippocrates. In CA, the emphasis is on the rigorous and detailed analysis of the ways in which the participants order their actions and turns at talk and their features to achieve a common understanding for all practical purposes (Garfinkel 1967). The orderly results that are obtained from these particular participants are treated for what they are: "evidence for an arrangement of the world" (Sacks 1984, p. 23). As indicated through his dictum "Tap into whomsoever, whatsoever, and we get much the same" (ibid., p. 22), Harvey Sacks indicated that research actually might get generalisability from single case studies. Generalisability is otherwise sought in CA studies through building collections of instances of a candidate phenomenon (Schegloff 1996a).

The strength of a detailed examination of interaction with or between persons with dementia is that it increases our understanding of how dementia may recognisably influence the systematic practices involved in how interactions are organised (see also Jones 2013; Jones et al. 2015; Mates et al. 2010; Mikesell 2009). Also, and perhaps more importantly, it may increase our awareness of how individuals like Nancy make use of possible resources and practices that are available for dealing with communicative problems, in spite of whatever difficulties they may have (see also Sacks 2011). As will be shown, Nancy as a matter of fact works to show the co-participating researcher that her singing is triggered by (the sounds of) a single word or phrase and produced as an association.

Nancy's spontaneous singing caught the researcher's interest when she visited the facility after two weeks of leave. Nancy sat at a table in a communal room and the researcher walked up to her and greeted her with '*Hi Nancy*'. Nancy looked at her and started singing a Danish song called Fru Kammerherreinde (*Mrs Chatelaine*). That song had also been produced during the researcher's prior visit two weeks earlier. This greeting caused the researcher to look closer at field notes and recordings of Nancy's spontaneous singing. The paper will analyse two instances, one of which is the instance when the Fru Kammerherreinde song was produced the first time (Ex. 1).

Participants

Nancy is a 90-year-old female resident in a public care facility in Denmark. She suffers from fronto-temporal dementia and has, at the time of the recording, reached a severe stage of loss of episodic memory. She needs help to deal with personal hygiene, dressing and undressing. She cannot walk and uses a wheelchair. She has no problems in producing speech. She still takes part in singing groups that are arranged by relatives or volunteers.

The co-participant, Rita, is a 52-year-old female researcher in social interaction at a Danish University. At the time of the conversation in focus, the researcher had been visiting the care facility on a regular basis, typically 2–3 hours a week for 3 months. The purpose of her visit was to 'hang out' with the residents and staff as part of her research activities. Occasionally, she took part in the singing groups too.

Transcript Conventions

The video recording of the interaction that is used for this study was transcribed using CA conventions as primarily developed by Gail Jefferson (Atkinson and Heritage 1984).

The following non-conventional transcript notations have also been applied:

»	Gaze towards/at
»«	Mutual gaze
//	Co-occurring resources for interaction in building a turn
♫	Singing voice
ξ	creaky voice
Ω	smiling voice

Ethical Considerations

Data for the research project were collected with the informed consent of staff, and relatives who were authorised to give consent on behalf of the residents. Hence, Nancy's daughter gave informed consent to participate in this study on Nancy's behalf. Decisions of this kind are complex and involved the daughter balancing considerations such as: her mother not being able to give the consent herself, her wish to inform dementia care in Danish care facilities based on research of the kind presented in this study, and her wish to work in her mother's best interest. The daughter concluded that the researcher should just go ahead with the project, since "du har ramt en streng hos min mor" (*You touched a string in my Mum*). We were careful not to cause any inconvenience or disturbance for Nancy whether we decided to video record her interacting or not.

The data are managed in accordance with Danish Law and EU regulations as sanctioned and monitored by SDU's Data Protection Office.

Analysis

Nancy and Rita engage in common conversations in a communal room of the care facility that is designed as a one-wall kitchen with a dining table, a lounge section with a couch, chairs and a small table. Nancy and Rita's conversations and the singing are thus often carried out in the presence of other residents and staff.

The conversational environments in which Nancy starts singing, i.e. the organisation and features of the actions and turns that are designed to relate to an initiated topic (Button and Casey 1984, 1985; Schegloff 1990), share certain characteristics (see section below: "'Singing' in Environments of Limited Complexity in Turn-Constructions and Sequential Organisation"). The singing in both cases (Examples 1 and 2) is designed to relate to an atrophying topic and sustains the conversation (see section below: "Orientation Towards Sounds of Talk for Singing Purposes as a Resource to Sustain Conversation"). The topics, though, differ and so do the stances that the co-participants take on them (see section "Topic and Stance in the Interactional Environment of Nancy's Spontaneous Singing"). In Example 1, Nancy and Rita are in disagreement (Pomerantz 1984), whereas they affiliate (Couper-Kuhlen 2012; Stivers 2008) in Example 2.

Topic and Stance in the Interactional Environment of Nancy's Spontaneous Singing

Example 1 takes place at the table in the communal room while other residents are having coffee and/or watching TV in the lounge section. In the background the Danish television news is being broadcast, with the consequences for Denmark of the refugee situation in Europe being debated. One of the staff members is within audible distance in the kitchen section. The staff member is new and is an immigrant to Denmark. Prior to where the fragment starts, Rita has informed Nancy about what is being discussed in the news and explains that "der er krig og uro i verden, så der kommer flygtninge til Europa" (*there is war and unrest in the world, so refugees come to Europe*):

```
#1  [DAP:GR:280116]
1  N →    je synes nu /ik vi har så mange pen:ge,
          I don't think though that we have that much money
                        /nod
          »tw window, R»N

2         (0.3)

3   R     nej
          no
          nods twice
          »the ceiling, N»R

4   N →   synes du
          do you
          »R
```

In her responding turn, line 1, Nancy states her opinion on whether Denmark should receive (more) refugees '*I don't think though that we have that much money*'. After an inter-turn gap (Jefferson 1983a; Sacks et al. 1974) that may indicate upcoming disagreement (Pomerantz 1984), Rita responds with a '*no*' while she gazes towards the ceiling and nods. Through this delayed response, Rita acknowledges having heard what Nancy says, but resists outright affiliation (Couper-Kuhlen 2012; Stivers 2008) with the statement. Nancy treats Rita's '*no*' as insufficient (Heinemann 2003) as she pursues her opinion on the matter. She also, however, orients to Rita's reservations as she downgrades her claim of knowledge about the issue in her turn (*do you?*, line 4) (Heritage and Raymond 2005).

Rita does not respond immediately. Another gap emerges (line 5 below) before she indicates in a pre-beginning (Schegloff 1996b) that a response is on its way. The pre-beginning is accomplished through an open mouth, deep in-breath and gaze towards the ceiling (line 6) and oriented to subsequently by Nancy (line 7):

```
#1 [DAP:GR:200116] continued
5             (0.3)

6  R  →       .hh
      →       opens mouth
      →       »ceiling, N»R

7   N →       det synes de andre jo
              the others think that of course
              head backwards, »«R

8             (0.2)

9   R         j:a (.) tænker du på dem der kommer hertil [syn-]
              yes are you thinking of those who come here do
              smiles, nods, »«N

10 N                                                     [ja  ]
              yes
              head backwards, nods, »window

11            (0.3)
```

In line 6, Rita does not agree; neither does she disagree. Her action, i.e. her explicit delay in initiating the turn, may indicate a concern about how to align with Rita without affiliating with her stance, not the least in the presence of the immigrant worker standing behind the two of them within audible distance.

Nancy responds to the lack of agreement by indicating a rationale behind the reason for why the refugees come anyway, '*the others think that of course*' (line 7). Hence, she pursues agreement on her position, which as we shall see, she does not achieve right away. After the clarification of the '*the others*' category (lines 9, 10), Rita instead pursues her own position:

```
#1 [DAP:GR:200116] continued
12 R      eh ja /ja men det har vi vel os sammenlignet med dem,
          yes yes but we do, don't we, compared to them
               /»ceiling, »N

13        (0.2)

14  R     ↑tror du ik det?
          don't you think so//you agree, right

15 N      jo
          yes
          shakes head; »window


16 R      ξjaξ
          yes

17        (0.4)

18 N →    man ka jo ik sige andet end vi har det jo godt
          you can't say that we're not fine
          »R, »straight forward

19        (0.2)

20 R      nemlig
          right
          »N»ceiling

21        (0.3)
```

Rita exploits the emergent comparison of perspectives of the refugees and the Danes in Nancy's turn (line 7). She initiates her turn (line 12) by agreeing with Nancy concerning what refugees believe and then continues by agreeing with that belief from their perspective (line 12): '*yes yes but we do, don't we, compared to them*'. After a gap, Rita then pursues agreement as already built into her turn in line 12 "det gør vi vel os" (*but we do, don't we*) by adding an increment in the form of a tag question (line 14). Finally, Nancy agrees through a positive response particle (line 15) "jo" (*yes*), which, in contrast to "ja" in Danish, fits the grammatically negatively framed prior action (line 12) (Heinemann 2005), and after a gap through a reformulation (line 18) "man ka jo ik sige andet end vi har det jo godt" (*you can't say that we're not fine*). In line 20 Rita agrees strongly on this reformulation "nemlig" (*right*) and in the subsequent sequence pursues her stance further as she works to try and put herself (and Nancy) in the refugees' shoes (see below). She indicates that from that perspective she would probably have had the same understanding of the world with the implication that she would probably have made the same choice (line 34). In this context Nancy starts singing (line 35):

```
#1 [DAP:GR:200116] continued
22 R      så er det vel ik noget og sige til at
          then it's no wonder that
          »N

23        (0.2)

24 N      »«R

25 R →    dem der ik har det godt fordi der er krig
          the ones that are not fine because of war
          »«N

26 N      nods=

27 R →    =tænker jeg så v- vil de vel os hen et sted
          I think then they would want to go to a place

28 N      nods=

29 R      =hvor de tænker der >har de det godt<
          to where they think that there they are fine

30        (.)

31 N      »window

32 R      °tænker jeg°
          I think
          »N
 33 N      ja
           yes
           nods
           »window

 34 R      det tror jeg os [jeg ville              ]tænke=
           I believe I would think that too
  35N →                    [♫ fru kammerherreinde♫]
           Mrs. Chatelaine
```

Example 2 is an instance of a conversation in which the two co-participants both align and affiliate (Asmuß 2011). Rita also initiates a topic in this example. Prior to where the excerpt starts, she asks Nancy to clarify whether a proper noun 'Trollenborg' refers to a dancing school, which Nancy confirms. Trollenborg emerged in a prior conversation between the two of them. The excerpt starts where, following the confirmation, Nancy makes an assessment of what '*it*' was like then (line 1 below).

#2

1 N det var Ωsjovt dengangΩ
it was fun then
head tw R

2 R→ ja
yes
smiles

3 N→ smiles
leans forward, turns head
»straight forward

4 R ja
yes
smiles
»N

5 (2.0)
N» straight forward

6 N hm (.) vi vah.r johh. ik så
ΩgamleΩ jo deh.ngang he
we weren't that old then you know
»«R

7 R → °ne:j°
no
mutual smiles
»«N

8 (1.5)
→ N» window

9 R sku du så bydes op til
/dans/af en af drengene?
were the boys supposed to invite you to dance
/moves head, body, arm to the right in a jerk/
»N

10 N → »window

11 (1.5)

12 R sku I så sidde på sådn ræ:kke
were you sitting in a row
smiles moves arm straight forward between R and N

13 N→ ja.h
yes
nods
»window, table

14 R jah,
yes
smiles
»N

15 → (6.0)
R»N; N»window

16 N ja det var jo egentlig sjovt
(.) nok (.) ik,
yes it was really fun right
»window

17 (0.7)

18 R ved Trollenborg
at Trollenborg

19 (1.5)

21 R [he he

22 (2.0)

23 R ΩsjoveΩ danse,
fun dances
smiles
»«N

24 N ja
yes

25 R ja,
yes
head backwards, smiles

26 (.)

```
27 R no:gen (0.2) lær- lærte han
     nye danse
     did he teach any new dances
     »N

28 N ja.hh
     yes

     nods

29 R ja,
     yes

30 N ξjaξ
     yes
```

```
31 N ♫danse så (b)øgen  er lyklig det (b)edst♫[1]
     ♫dance till the beech is happy it's best♫
     leans forward tw R
     »«R; mutual smiles
```

In line 2, Rita affiliates with the positive assessment "det var sjovt dengang" (*it was fun then*) with an affiliative "ja" (*yes*) (see Couper-Kuhlen 2012) and an affiliative smile. In this way the turn is redirected to Nancy with the possibility to develop her talk. Nancy however responds with a smile, turns her head, and gazes straight forward (line 3). Nancy then adds that they (*we*) '*weren't that old then*' (line 6), that '*it was really fun right*' (line 16), and that '*he did so many fun things*' (line 20) and Rita aligns and affiliates as she asks questions concerning Nancy's experiences (lines 9, 23, 27) '*were the boys supposed to invite you to dance*'; '*were you sitting in a row*'; ('*did he do*') '*fun dances*' and '*did he teach any new dances*'. Thereby Rita not only positions herself as the party with no, or less, knowledge, with Nancy as the more knowledgeable participant as regards what is being discussed (Drew 2012; Heritage 2012, 2013); the questions for clarification give Nancy the possibility to develop the topic further, whereby the topic remains hers (Rasmussen 2017). In this environment, Nancy starts singing (line 31): ♫ danse så (b)øgen er lyklig det (b)edst♫ (*dance till the beech is happy it's best*).

'Singing' in Environments of Limited Complexity in Turn-Constructions and Sequential Organisation

The actions and turns in the two extended sequences work for different purposes. However, the instances exhibit similarities in turn-construction and sequential organisation, i.e. from the initiation of the topic to the termination of the singing: In both cases, the topic is initiated by Rita and subsequently acknowledged by Nancy through her responses (‘*I don't think though that we have that much money*’ (Ex. 1, line 1); ‘*it was fun then*’ (Ex. 2, line 1)). Rita's subsequent responses are overwhelmingly either minimal or request clarification; moreover they are aligning and work to reallocate the turn to Nancy to develop the topic and points made by reference to it further (e.g. Ex. 1, lines 9, 12 above and Ex. 2, lines 2, 4).

Initially, Nancy's responses carry on the development of the topic (examples of Nancy's talk replicated):

```
#1
1 N       je synes nu /ik vi har så mange pen:ge,
          I don't think though that we have that much money
                  /nod
          »tw window, R»N

7 N       det synes de andre jo
          the others think that of course
          head backwards, »«R

18 N      man ka jo ik sige andet end vi har det jo godt
          you can't say that we're not fine
          »R, »straight forward


#2
1 N       det var Ωsjovt dengangΩ
          it was fun then

6 N       hm (.) vi vah.r johh. ik så ΩgamleΩ jo deh.ngang he
          we weren't that old then you know

16 N      ja det var jo egentlig sjovt (.)  nok (.) ik,
          yes it was really fun right

20 N      han kuhh.ne så /ΩmangeΩ  sjovh.e tih.ng[he he he
          he did so many fun things
                        /nods
```

The first two turns in both examples contribute to developing the initiated topic in terms of assessments that serve as accounts (Ex. 1) and descriptions (Ex. 2). The responses are formatted as sentences with subjects and predicates, as are Nancy's subsequent turns one (Ex. 1, line 7) and two (Ex. 2, lines 6, 16). However, the subsequent turns do not carry the topical talk forward: in Example 1 (line 18) an idiomatic expression makes a closure of the topic relevant and in Example 2 (lines 16, 20) the turns are re-workings of the prior turns or they re-use crucial lexical items in them (Perkins et al. 1998) and may occur after inter-turn gaps (Ex. 2, lines 3, 5). From this stage in the sequential organisation of the topic, Nancy's TCUs often assume the form of minimal though type-conforming (Raymond 2003) responses and then 'fade away', leaving the co-participant with no response. Minimal responses and 'awayness' (Bateson and Mead 1942; Rasmussen et al. 2019) also occur between Nancy's topic-developing contributions in the shape of sentences and may be responses to Rita's pursuit of turn transition (Ford et al. 2002) as in Example 1, line 32, or to her requests for clarification of Nancy's turns which are mostly produced with the use of a deictic expression with no recognisable referent, e.g. '*the others*' (Ex. 1, line 7, above), '*it*', '*we*' and '*he*' (Ex. 2, lines 1, 6, 16, 20, above). This is, as mentioned, a common trait of language use in moderate to severe stages of dementia (Dijkstra et al. 2004; March et al. 2006) (Fig. 6.1).

Previous CA studies of typical forms of conversational organisation have shown that delayed, minimal, or absent responses to prior turns at talk may indicate upcoming problems in terms of disagreement or weak agreement (Pomerantz and Heritage 2013). The format and organisation of turns at talk across speakers in the conversations between Nancy and Rita may however be accounted for by reference to the style in which the conversations are carried out: Rita provides a range of possibilities for Nancy to develop the conversation when she reallocates the turn to her by way of e.g. minimal aligning and affiliating responses with the purpose of topic development, request for knowledge, or clarification of unclear talk. However, rather than building complex actions through e.g. elaborations and connecting them to prior actions of herself or Rita while orienting to their details (Jefferson 1984a, b; Schegloff and Sacks 1973), Nancy limits her contributions

Example	Minimal responses	Lack of responses
#1, lines	15, 17, 21, 33	30, 31
#2, lines	3, 13	8, 10, 11, 15, 19

Fig. 6.1 Overview of minimal responses and lack of responses in the two extended fragments of Ex. 1 and Ex. 2

to one TCU turns, as exemplified in e.g. Ex. 2, line 1 '*it was fun then*' that occurs as a response to the question '*was Trollenborg a place where you learned to dance?*' and line 16 '*yes it was really fun right*' which comes after a confirming '*yes*' (line 13) that served as a (minimal) response to the question '*were you sitting in a row*' (line 12). Alternatively, she often uses minimal responses while she sometimes gazes in other directions or she does not respond at all, which altogether seems to be independent of the degree of affiliation and agreement (see e.g. Ex. 1 lines 15, 31, 33, which are all delivered after the accomplishment of agreement in lines 18–20). This finding is in line with previous research in conversations involving persons with dementia (Bayles 1985; Dijkstra et al. 2004). Also, Rita's responses to Nancy's talk are often minimal and her attempts to invite Nancy to develop an ongoing topic are slightly repetitive in the sense that she, as does Nancy, reemploys words that have been introduced in the prior talk either by herself or by Nancy, e.g. '*(we are) fine*' (Ex. 1, lines 25, 29), '*dance*' (Ex. 2, lines 9, 23, 27), or '*fun*' (Ex. 2, line 23). Hence, she seems also, though maybe for different reasons, to use a limited range of materials, which she employs and reemploys to accomplish actions that work to maintain and keep track of the flow of the conversation that continuously seems to be at risk of atrophying (Jefferson 1983b). While being spontaneous, the accomplishment of turn constructions and the coordination between turns in these conversations seem not to be based on taken-for-granted detailed and dynamic coordination. In these environments Nancy starts singing.

Orientation Towards Sounds of Talk for Singing Purposes as a Resource to Sustain Conversation

When Nancy starts singing, she recognisably orients towards sounds of words in the previous talk. In Example 2, Nancy initiates a song as she picks up "dans(e)", which was repeatedly used by Rita in her previous talk (lines 9, 23, 27):

```
#2 (examples of Rita's turns replicated)

9 R       sku du så bydes op til /dans/af
          en af drengene?
          were the boys supposed to invite
          you to dance

23 R      ΩsjoveΩ danse,
          fun dances
          smiles
          »«N

27 R      no:gen (0.2) lær- lærte han nye danse
          did he teach any new dances
```

The grammatical function of "danse" (*dances*) in lines 23, 27 are identical (objects); they are nucleus in a nominal syntagm (adjective + noun); they occur in final position in the turns that they are part of, and they exhibit similar prosodic contours (see Appendix). Nancy initiates singing as she now (line 31) picks up on "danse" (*dance*) and echoes the prosodic features of "danse" (*dance*) in lines 23, 27 (see Appendix):

```
#2 (replicated)
27  R     no:gen (0.2) lær- lærte han nye danse
          did he teach any new dances
          »N

28    N   ja.hh
          yes
          nods

29    R   ja,
          yes

30   N    ξjaξ
          yes

31   N    ♫ danse så (b)øgen  er lyklig det (b)edst♫
          ♫dance till the beech is happy it's best♫
          leans forward tw R
          »«R; mutual smiles
```

The onset of the singing pivots on the echo of the prosodic features of "danse" and so Nancy retrospectively orients to "danse" (*dance*) in lines 23 and 27 for its sound structures. By initiating a melody, the sound production of '*dance*' is embedded in a context of sounds that have been composed in another time and place in a system of sounds with clear boundaries and thus a clear trajectory, i.e. in a melody. Notice that Nancy leans forward toward Rita, gazes at her, and smiles while starting to sing. This may indicate an invitation to join her in singing and the expectation that Rita recognises what Nancy is doing, i.e. echoing while orienting towards the trajectory of an extra-locally produced melody. The expectation is, in other words, that Rita recognises that the melody is initiated as an association that is triggered by the sound of "danse" (*dance*). Rita responds with a smile.

The same pattern occurs in Example 1. In this example, "har det godt" (*are fine*) is re-instantiated several times (lines 18, 25, 29, below), which Nancy orients toward as she sings (lines 35–43 below). The song is introduced with "fru kammerherreinde" (*Mrs Chatelaine*) which happens to be the title of the song as well. This is a very popular and well-known old Danish song—most of all for its refrain: her går det godt (*here it is fine*). "Har det godt" (*are fine*) is used both by Nancy and Rita in previous talk (lines 18, 25 below), which triggers the initiation of the song:

#1 (examples replicated)

18 N → man ka jo ik sige andet end vi har det jo godt
you can't say that we're not fine

25 R → dem der ik har det godt fordi der er krig
the ones that are not fine because of war

Rita repeats "har det godt" (*are fine*) again in line 29, which is the immediate context of Nancy's initiation of the song

29 R =hvor de tænker der >har de det godt<
to where they think that there they are fine

30 (.)

31 N »window

32 R °tænker jeg°
I think
»N

33 N ja
yes
nods
»window

34 R det tror jeg os [jeg ville]tænke=

```
         I believe I would think that too

35 N →                     [♫ fru kammerherreinde♫]
         Mrs Chatelaine

36 N     =he he
         »«R; mutual smiles

37 R     >hva sig.hh eer du?<
         »«N, mutual smiles

38 N →   .hh ♫ fru kammer[herreinde♫]
         Mrs Chatelaine
         smiles, »«R

39 R →                     [♫herrinde♫]
         laine

         smiles
40  R    ja,
         yes
         »«N, mutual smiles

41       (0.2)

42 N →   ♫ her går det godt her går[det godt ♫]
         here it is fine here it is fine

43 R →                             [♫det godt♫]
         it is fine
         initially R's lips follow N's song without sound
         »«N, mutual smiles

44  N    nods tw table, smiles

45  R    turns head to the right tw other residents, smiles
```

In line 35 Nancy sings "♫ fru kammerherreinde♫" (*Mrs Chatelaine*), stops, smiles and laughs, and achieves mutual gaze with Rita, who she obviously expects to join her in singing and from this hint maybe even to complete the line in the refrain of the song by herself (cf. Lerner 2004). That is, Rita is invited to echo the repeated sound of "går det godt" (*it is fine*), to embed it in and associate it with a melody, and thereby to orient to the phrase for its sound structures and treat it as a refrain. In line 37, Rita initiates repair ('*what did you say*') (Schegloff 1992) while orienting to the laugh (she laughs too, line 37). Nancy repeats the start of the song (line 38) and Rita, finally, joins her in singing as she produces affiliating collaborative completions of the refrain (lines 39, 43) '*Mrs Chatelaine*', '*here it is fine*'.

Of course the sound and melody productions entail items that are recognisable as words that are used to carry out actions and indicate social understandings of the world. By initiating and joining one another in singing, Nancy and Rita work interactionally to embed words that were lodged in previous common talk in lyrics that were, along with the melodies, composed in another time and place and subjected to restrictions in terms of, for example, a predefined trajectory and style. By embedding these words in predefined lyric environments, Nancy and Rita associate them with the songs and give them intensity in ways that one may categorise as poetic—across speakers. A closer look at the songs reveals also that the singing is not only responsive to the prosodic features of previous items but to the interactional work that the words were used to accomplish. In Example 2 the lyrics are abstract and strongly metaphorical (*dance till the beach is happy*) which together with a rather staccato rhythm of the melody provides an atmosphere or a feeling of being in a place and time of learning to dance in a dancing school, i.e. what was '*fun*' about '*dancing*' in Trollenborg. In Example 1 the song turns out to contest Rita's position on the refugee situation in Denmark and the position that "her går det godt" (*here it is fine).* The song is about a Mrs. Chatelaine who calls the servant in her castle to ask how things are. He responds by saying that everything is so fine—"her går det så godt" (*here it is fine*)—apart from the fact that her horse died. She makes further inquiries and is told that the horse died because the barn burned down to its grounds—but apart from that 'her går det godt' (*here it is fine*). As it turns out, the whole thing started because the bank called Mrs. Chatelaine's husband to tell him that he went bankrupt; that he shot himself with a hunting rifle, fell over, hit a candle that put the curtains on fire, which then put the castle on fire which then … and in the end the horse died. But apart from that, Mrs. Chatelaine, *it is fine*, and the song ends. In sum, it is a song that ridicules a tendency to say, when asked, that everything is fine, when in fact everything is as bad as it can be, and a song about how things seem alright at the outset but turn out to be bad and worse than bad.

In sum, the activity of singing a song in the midst of having a conversation is, in the cases shown in this paper, recognisably designed (Drew

2013) to be associated with the prosodic features and use of repeated words, in order to accomplish specific social actions related to prior talk in interaction.

Conclusion

Melodies and songs in the midst of having a conversation seem in our cases to turn on specific repeated words and their prosodic features in previous talk and to be designed to be recognisably relevant as a result of association. In addition to the associative link between specific words with specific prosodic features and their echo in the songs (Jefferson 1996), the songs are associatively responsive to the prior conversational work (cf. Schegloff 2005). In other words, associative singing as responses to talk constitutes new materials (Goodwin 2011) and forms of interaction that move the interaction *beyond* talk, while simultaneously providing the possibility to bring in new perspectives *on* the topics of that talk. In the cases at hand, this form of interaction is initiated by Nancy and acknowledged or joined in by Rita in the context of difficulties in moving beyond a particular point in the conversation through talk.

Talking is making sense by producing sound which is the same resource used for singing. Singing though has been shown to be a different neurological process than talking. Oliver Sacks (2011) suggests that some of the "peculiar" behaviour of people with brain injuries of different kinds is a way of the body (including the brain) to compensate for the disorder:

> But it must be said from the outset that a disease is never a mere loss or excess – that there is always a reaction, on the part of the affected organism or individual, to restore, to replace, to compensate for and to preserve its identity, however strange the means may be. (ibid., p. 6)

Additionally, an increasing body of research shows that persons with dementia *are* able to express themselves when co-participants engage with them in ways which are attentive to the person with dementia's remaining abilities (Eggers et al. 2005; Kindell et al. 2013; Normann et al. 2002).

Singing may be one of these remaining abilities. As such, singing may be used as a means to compensate for decreasing communicative abilities and conversational challenges and may, as shown in Nancy and Rita's conversations, be employed to do various kinds of interactional work.

Acknowledgements I thank Professor Paul Drew for inspiring and fruitful discussions in relation to talks that we presented on the topic of this paper at the Atypical Interaction Conference 2016, University of Southern Denmark, the 3rd International bi-annual conference of Life with Dementia 2016, Linköping University, and the 5th International Conference of Conversation Analysis 2018, Loughborough University.

Appendix

Ex. 1 Nancy 'har det jo godt' (*we're fine*) line 18

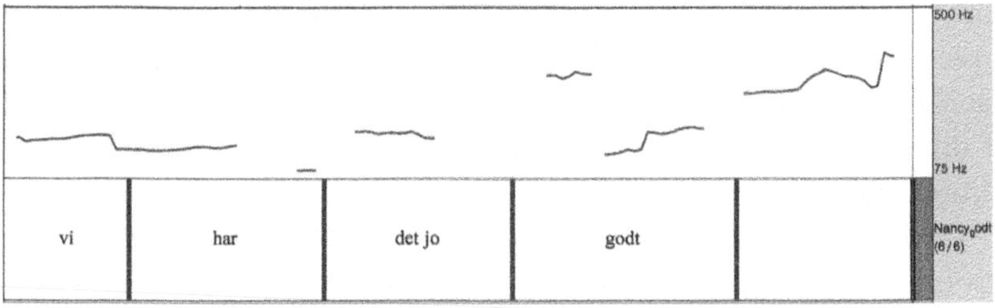

Ex. 1 Rita 'har det godt' (*are fine*), line 25

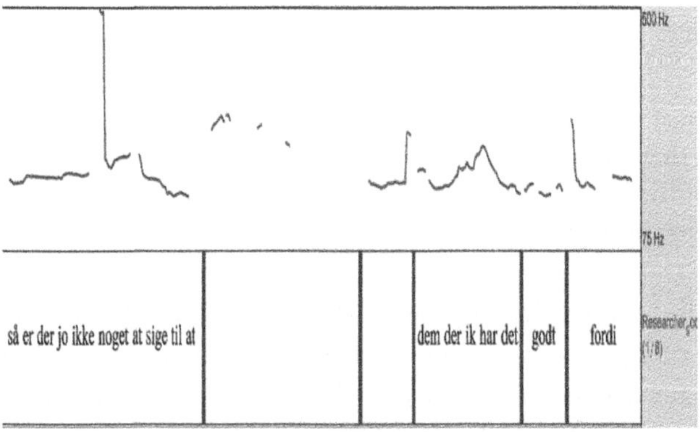

Ex. 1 Rita 'har de det godt' (*they are fine*), line 29

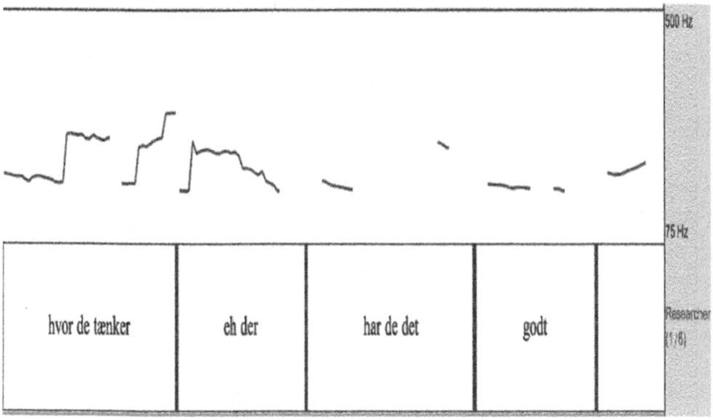

Ex. 1 Nancy 'går det godt' (*it is fine*), line 42

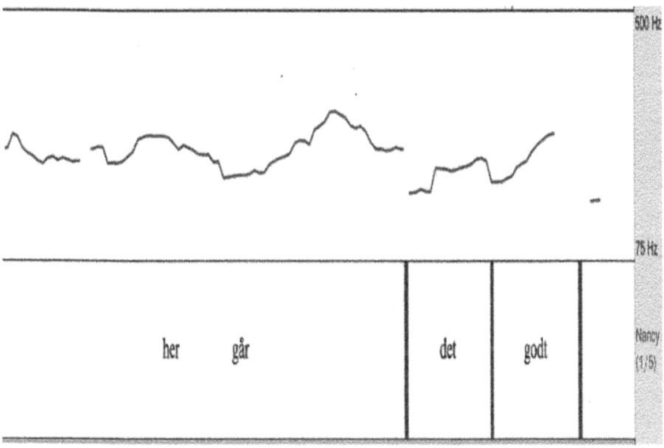

Ex. 1 Nancy and Rita 'det godt' (*it is fine*), lines 42, 43

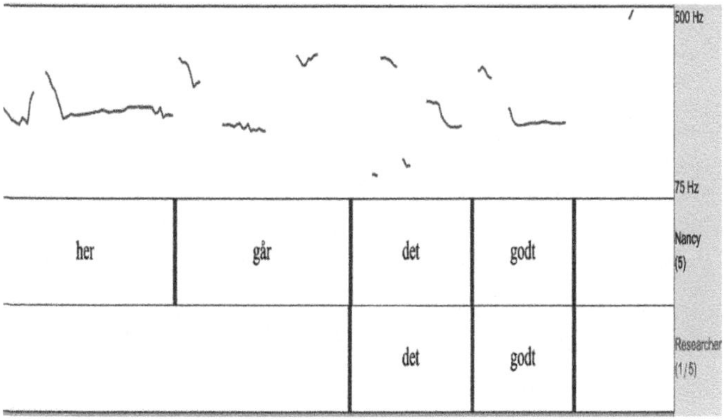

Ex. 2 Rita 'danse' (*dances*), line 23

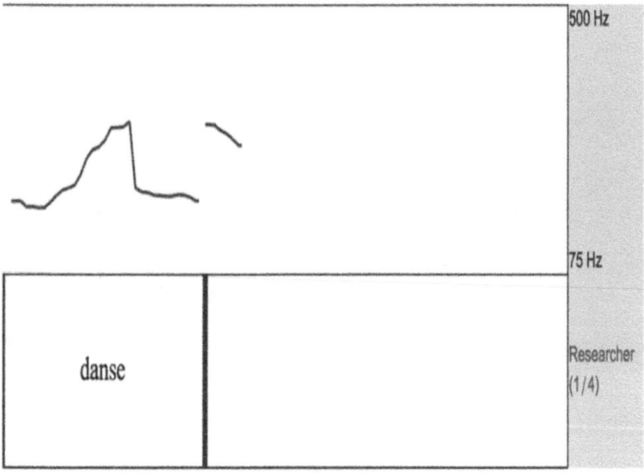

Ex. 2 Rita 'danse' (*dances*), line 27

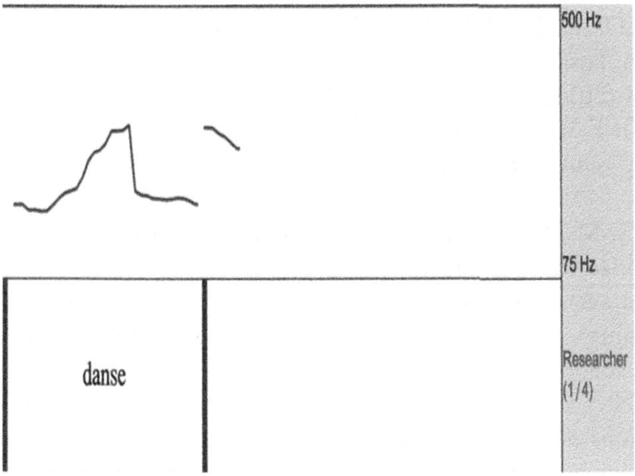

Ex. 2 Nancy 'danse' (*dance*), line 31

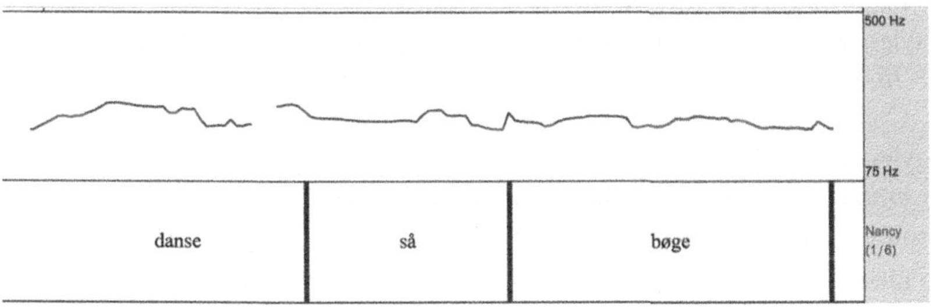

References

Aldridge, D. E. (2000). *Music therapy in dementia care: More new voices.* London: Jessica Kingsley.

Asmuß, B. (2011). Proposing shared knowledge as a means of pursuing agreement. In T. Stivers, L. Mondada, & J. Steensig (Eds.), *The morality of knowledge in conversation* (pp. 207–234). Cambridge: Cambridge University Press.

Atkinson, J. M., & Heritage, J. (1984). *Structures of social action.* Cambridge: Cambridge University Press.

Azios, J. H., & Archer, B. (2018). Singing behavior in a client with traumatic brain injury: A conversation analysis investigation. *Aphasiology.* https://doi.org/10.1080/02687038.2018.1466106.

Bannan, N., & Montgomery-Smith, C. (2008). 'Singing for the Brain': Reflections on the human capacity of music arising from a pilot study of group singing with Alzheimer's patients. *The Journal of the Royal Society for the Promotion of Health, 2,* 73–78.

Bateson, G., & Mead, M. (1942). *Balinese character: A photographic analysis.* New York: New York Academy of Sciences.

Bayles, K. A. (1985). Communication in dementia. In H. Ulatowska (Ed.), *The aging brain: Communication in the elderly* (pp. 210–216). Boston: College Hill Press.

Bayles, K. A., & Tomoeda, C. K. (Eds.). (2007). *Cognitive-communication disorders of dementia.* San Diego: Plural Publishing.

Brotons, M., & Koger, S. M. (2000). The impact of music therapy on language functioning in dementia. *Journal of Music Therapy, 37*(3), 183–195.

Button, G., & Casey, N. (1984). Generating topic: The use of topic initial elicitors. In J. M. Atkinson & J. Heritage (Eds.), *Structures of social action: Studies in conversation analysis* (pp. 167–190). Cambridge: Cambridge University Press.

Button, G., & Casey, N. (1985). Topic nomination and topic pursuit. *Human Studies, 8,* 3–55.

Camic, P. M., Williams, C. M., & Meeten, F. (2011). Does a 'Singing Together Group' improve the quality of life of people with a dementia and their carers? A pilot evaluation study. *Dementia, 12*(2), 157–176.

Couper-Kuhlen, E. (2012). Exploring affiliation in the reception of conversational complaint stories. In A. Peräkylä & M.-L. Sorjonen (Eds.), *Emotion in interaction* (pp. 113–146). Oxford: Oxford University Press.

Couper-Kuhlen, E., & Ono, T. (2007). 'Incrementing' in conversation: A comparison of practices in English, German and Japanese. *Pragmatics, 17*(4), 513–552.

Couper-Kuhlen, E., & Selting, M. (1996). *Prosody in conversation.* Cambridge: Cambridge University Press.

Dijkstra, K., Bourgeois, M. S., Allen, R. S., & Burgio, L. D. (2004). Conversational coherence: Discourse analysis of older adults with and without dementia. *Journal of Neurolinguistics, 17*(4), 263–283. https://doi.org/10.1016/S0911-6044(03)00048-4.

Drew, P. (2005). Conversation analysis. In K. Fitch & R. E. Sanders (Eds.), *Handbook of language and social interaction* (pp. 71–102). Mahwah, NJ and London: Lawrence Erlbaum.

Drew, P. (2012). What drives sequences? *Research on Language & Social Interaction, 45*(1), 61–68.

Drew, P. (2013). Turn design. In J. Sidnell & T. Stivers (Eds.), *The handbook of conversation analysis* (pp. 131–149). Oxford: Blackwell.

Drew, P., & Heritage, J. (1992). Analyzing talk at work: An introduction In P. Drew & J. Heritage (Eds.), *Talk at work* (pp. 3–65). Cambridge: Cambridge University Press.

Drew, P., Raymond, G., & Weinberg, D. (2006a). *Talk and interaction.* London: Sage.

Drew, P., Raymond, G., & Weinberg, D. (2006b). *Talk and interaction in social research methods.* London: Sage.

Eggers, T., Norberg, A., & Ekman, S.-L. (2005). Counteracting fragmentation in the care of people with moderate and severe dementia. *Clinical Nursing Research, 14*(4), 343–369. https://doi.org/10.1177/1054773805277957.

Ford, C. E., Fox, B. A., & Thompson, S. (2002). Constituency and the grammar of turn increments. In C. E. Ford, B. A. Fox, & S. Thompson (Eds.), *The language of turn and sequence.* Oxford: Oxford Studies in Sociolinguistics.

Garfinkel, H. (1967). *Studies in ethnomethodology.* Cambridge: Polity Press.

Goodwin, C. (2011). Contextures of action. In J. Streeck, C. Goodwin, & C. D. LeBaron (Eds.), *Embodied interaction* (pp. 182–193). Cambridge: Cambridge University Press.

Götell, E., Brown, S., & Ekman, S.-L. (2002). Caregiver singing and background music in dementia care. *Western Journal of Nursing Research, 24*(2), 195–216.

Heinemann, T. (2003). *Negation in interaction, in Danish conversation.* Ph.D., University of York, Unpublished.

Heinemann, T. (2005). Where the grammar and interaction meet: The preference for matched polarity in responsive turns in Danish. In A. Hakulinen

& M. Selting (Eds.), *Syntax and Lexis in conversation* (pp. 375–402). Amsterdam: John Benjamins.

Heinemann, T. (2015). Registering revision: The reduplicated Danish change-of-state token nå. *Discourse Studies, 18*(1), 44–63. https://doi.org/10.1177/1461445615614131.

Heritage, J. (2012). The epistemic engine: Sequence organization and territories of knowledge. *Research on Language and Social Interaction, 45*(1), 30–52.

Heritage, J. (2013). Action formation and its epistemic (and other) backgrounds. *Discourse Studies, 15*(5), 551–578.

Heritage, J., & Raymond, G. (2005). The terms of agreement: Indexing epistemic authority and subordination in talk-in-interaction. *Social Psychology Quarterly, 68*(1), 15–38.

Jefferson, G. (1983a). Notes on a possible metric which provides for a 'standard maximum' silence of approximately one second in conversation. *Tilburg papers in language and literature, 42*.

Jefferson, G. (1983b). Notes on a systematic deployment of the acknowledgement tokens "yeah" and "mm hmm". *Papers in Linguistics, 17*(2), 197–216.

Jefferson, G. (1984a). Notes on some orderlinesses of overlap onset. In V. D'Urso & P. Leonardi (Eds.), *Discourse analysis and natural rhetoric*. Cleup Editore: Padua, Italy.

Jefferson, G. (1984b). On stepwise transition from talk about a trouble to inappropriately next matters. In J. M. Atkinson & J. Heritage (Eds.), *Structures of social action: Studies in conversation analysis* (pp. 191–222). Cambridge: Cambridge University Press.

Jefferson, G. (1993). Caveat speaker preliminary notes on recipient topic-shift implicature. *Research in Language and Social Interaction, 26*(1), 1–30.

Jefferson, G. (1996). On the poetics of ordinary talk. *Text and Performance Quarterly, 16*(1), 1–61.

Jones, D. (2013). A family living with Alzheimer's disease: The communicative challenges. *Dementia, 14*(5), 1–19. https://doi.org/10.1177/1471301213502213.

Jones, D., Drew, P., Elsey, C., Blackburn, D., Wakefield, S., Harkness, K., et al. (2015). Conversational assessment in memory clinic encounters: Interactional profiling for differential dementia from functional memory disorders. *Aging & Mental Health, 20*(5), 1–10.

Kawulich, B. B. (2005). Participant observation as data collection method. *Forum: Qualitative Social Research, 6*(2), Art. 43.

Kindell, J., Sage, K., Keady, J., & Wilkinson, R. (2013). Adapting to conversation with semantic dementia: Using enactment as a compensatory strategy in everyday social interaction. *International Journal of Language and Communication Disorders, 48*(5), 497–507.

Kindell, J., Wilkinson, R., Sage, K., & Keady, J. (2018). Combining music and life story work to enhance participation in family interaction in semantic dementia: a longitudinal study of one family's experience. *Arts and Health, 10*(2), 165–180.

Laine, M., Laakso, M., Vuorinen, E., & Rinne, J. (1998). Coherence and informativeness of discourse in two dementia types. *Journal of Neurolinguistics, 11,* 79–87.

Lerner, G. (1989). Notes on overlap management in conversation: The case of delayed completion. *Western Journal of Speech Communication, 53*(2), 167–177.

Lerner, G. (1995). Turn design and the organization of participation in instructional activities. *Discourse Processes, 19,* 111–131.

Lerner, G. (2004). Collaborative turn sequences. In G. Lerner (Ed.), *Conversation analysis: Studies from the first generation* (pp. 225–256). Amsterdam: John Benjamins.

Lubinski, R., Orange, J. B., Henderson, D., & Stecker, N. (Eds.). (1995). *Dementia and communication*. San Diego: Singular Publlshing Group.

Macoir, J., & Turgeon, Y. (2006). Dementia and language. In E. K. Brown & A. Anderson (Eds.), *The encyclopedia of language and linguistics* (2nd ed., pp. 423–430). Boston: Elsevier.

March, E. G., Wales, R., & Pattison, P. (2006). The uses of nouns and deixis in discourse production in Alzheimer's disease. *Journal of Neurolinguistics, 19,* 311–340.

Mates, A. W., Mikesell, L., & Smith, M. S. (2010). *Language, interaction, and frontotemporal dementia: Reverse engineering the social mind.* London: Equinox.

Matthews, S. (2015). Dementia and the power of music therapy. *Bioethics, 29*(8), 573–579.

Mikesell, L. (2009). Conversational practices of a frontotemporal dementia patient and his interlocutors. *Research on Language & Social Interaction, 42,* 135–162.

Millard, K., & Smith, J. (1989). The influence of group singing therapy on the behavior of Alzheimer's disease patients. *Journal of Music Therapy, 26,* 58–70.

Miller, B. L., Boone, K., Cummings, J. L., Read, S. L., & Mishkin, F. (2000). Functional correlates of musical and visual ability in frontotemporal dementia. *British Journal of Psychiatry, 176,* 458–463.

Mithen, S. (2005). *The singing Neanderthals.* London: Weidenfeld and Nicholson.

Mok, Z., & Müller, N. (2014). Staging casual conversations for people with dementia. *Dementia, 13*(6), 834–853.

Normann, H. K., Norberg, A., & Asplund, K. (2002). Confirmation and lucidity during conversations with a woman with severe dementia. *Journal of Advanced Nursing, 39*(4), 370–376. http://dx.doi.org/10.1046/j.1365-2648.2002.02298.x.

Oloff, F. (2018). Revisiting delayed completions: The retrospective management of co-participants action. In A. Deppermann & J. Streeck (Eds.), *Time in embodied interaction: Synchronicity and sequentiality of multimodal resources* (pp. 123–160). Amsterdam/Philadelphia: John Benjamins.

Peretz, I., & Coltheart, M. (2003). Modularity of music processing. *Nature Neuroscience, 6,* 688–691.

Perkins, L., Withworth, A., & Lesser, R. (1998). Conversing in dementia: A conversation analytic approach. *Journal of Neurolinguistics, 11*(1–2), 33–53.

Pomerantz, A. (1984). Agreeing and disagreeing with assessments: Some features of preferred/dispreferred turn shapes. In J. M. Atkinson & J. Heritage (Eds.), *Structures of social action* (pp. 57–101). Cambridge: Cambridge University Press.

Pomerantz, A., & Heritage, J. (2013). Preference. In J. Sidnell & T. Stivers (Eds.), *The handbook of conversation analysis* (pp. 210–228). Malden: Wiley-Blackwell.

Prickett, C., & Moore, R. (1991). The use of music to aid memory of Alzheimer's patients. *Journal of Music Therapy, 28,* 101–110.

Rasmussen, G. (2017). The use of pictures for interactional purposes and the grammar of social interaction. *Journal of Interactional Research in Communication Disorders, 18*(1), 121–145.

Rasmussen, G., Andersen, E. M., & Kristiansen, E. D. (2019). Working out availability, unavailability, and awayness in social face-to-face encounters—The case of dementia. *Discourse Studies, 21,* 258–279.

Raymond, G. (2003). Grammar and social organisation: Yes/no interrogatives and the structure of responding. *American Sociological Review, 68,* 939–967.

Reed, B. S. (2011). *Analysing conversation: An introduction to prosody.* Basingstoke: Palgrave Macmillan.

Sacks, H. (1966/1995). On sampling and subjectivity. In G. Jefferson (Ed.), *Harvey sacks lectures on conversation* (Vol. Part III, pp. 483–488). Oxford, UK and Cambridge, USA: Blackwell.

Sacks, H. (1984). Notes on methodology. In J. M. Atkinson & J. Heritage (Eds.), *Structures of social action* (4th ed., pp. 21–27). Cambridge: Cambridge University Press.

Sacks, O. (2011). *The man who mistook his wife for a hat*. Oxford: Picador.
Sacks, H., Schegloff, E., & Jefferson, G. (1974). A simplest systematics for the organization of turn-taking for conversation. *Language, 50*(4), 696–735. https://doi.org/10.1353/lan.1974.0010.
Schegloff, E. A. (1982). Discourse as an interactional achievement: Some uses of "uh huh" and other things that come between sentences. In D. Tannen (Ed.), *Analyzing discourse: Text and talk* (pp. 71–93). Washington, DC: Georgetown University Press.
Schegloff, E. A. (1990). On the organization of sequences as a source of "coherence" in talk-in-interaction. In B. Dorval (Ed.), *Conversational organization and its development*. Norwood: Ablex Publishing.
Schegloff, E. A. (1992). Repair after next turn: The last structurally provided defense of intersubjectivity in conversation. *American Journal of Sociology, 97*(5), 1295–1345.
Schegloff, E. A. (1996a). Confirming allusions: Toward an empirical account of action. *American Journal of Sociology, 102*(1), 161–216.
Schegloff, E. A. (1996b). Turn organization: One intersection of grammar and interaction. In E. Ochs, E. Schegloff, & S. Thompson (Eds.), *Interaction and grammar* (pp. 52–133). Cambridge: Cambridge University Press.
Schegloff, E. A. (2005). Whistling in the dark: Notes from the other side of liminality. *Texas Linguistic Forum, 48*, 17–30.
Schegloff, E., & Sacks, H. (1973). Opening up closings. *Semiotica, 8*(4), 289–327.
Shinagawa, S., Ikeda, M., Fukuhata, R., & Tanabe, H. (2006). Initial symptoms in frontotemporal dementia and semantic dementia compared with Alzheimer's disease. *Dementia and Geriatric Cognitive Disorders, 21*, 74–80.
Stivers, T. (2008). Stance, alignment, and affiliation during storytelling: When nodding is a token of affiliation. *Research on Language and Social Interaction, 41*(1), 31–57.
Streeck, J., Goodwin, C., & LeBaron, C. D. (Eds.). (2011). *Embodied interaction: Language and body in the material world*. Cambridge: Cambridge University Press.
Yannou, D., Baloyiannis, S., Kostaridou-Eukleides, A., Klonaru, D., Nakopoulou, E., & Tzedaki, K. (2003). *Music perception in patients with dementia due to Alzheimer's disease*. Paper presented at the 5th Triennial ESCOM Conference, 8–13 September 2003.

7

Dementia in Conversation: Observations from Triadic Memory Clinic Interactions

Christopher Elsey

Background

As the global population increases and ages the number of people developing dementia worldwide also increases (Brayne and Miller 2017). The everyday pressures placed upon the person with dementia and those around them can prove to be overwhelming without appropriate healthcare, support and treatment. Early and accurate diagnosis is an important part of improving such provisions (Santacruz and Swagerty 2001). In the UK, for instance, it is estimated that less than 50% of people living with the disease have actually received a complete diagnosis (Alzheimer's Society 2013). This substantial under-diagnosis is known as the 'dementia gap', which the UK Government has attempted to close by establishing targets to increase the number of patient referrals from primary care to specialist neurological services, such as memory clinics (Older People and Dementia Team 2012). However,

C. Elsey (✉)
De Montfort University, Leicester, UK

© The Author(s) 2020
R. Wilkinson et al. (eds.), *Atypical Interaction*,
https://doi.org/10.1007/978-3-030-28799-3_7

providing a diagnosis is only a first step in the process of establishing appropriate care. For example, research from the UK shows that care needs and prognosis are not always adequately covered in these specialist consultations, although the limited *treatment* options available may partly explain this absence (Dooley et al. 2018).

For some family members, friends and carers a diagnosis of neurodegenerative conditions for a loved one (or service user), such as dementia, can be a relief as it provides answers and explanations for the changing behaviours, memory degradation and communication problems encountered (Alzheimer's Society 2015; Jones et al. 2016). Even in the earliest phase of dementia there is a clear link to communicative or linguistic impairments and deficits in spontaneous speech (Forbes-McKay and Venneri 2005). Language impoverishment in dementia can take many forms, including the simplification of grammar, reduced vocabulary, semantic paraphasias (or incorrect word substitution), and overuse of semantically empty words, repetitions, and so on, all which progressively deteriorate over time (Berisha et al. 2015; Jones 2015).

Given the impact that dementia has upon language, communication and interaction conversation analysis (herein CA) is particularly suited to the task of analysing the interactional changes that emerge *between* parties. Since Heidi Hamilton's (1994) ground-breaking study of the changing conversational practices of an individual with Alzheimer's disease, further fine-grained CA research has revealed how dementia can impact many of the constituent features of everyday talk, focusing on the collaborative basis of interaction. The lessons stem from fine-grained analysis of everyday conversation and activities and range from phone calls between relatives and an elderly relative with Alzheimer's (Jones 2015), digital technologies and communication (Ekstrom et al. 2017), cooking together (Majlesi and Ekström 2016), a man with fronto-temporal dementia queuing up and paying in a pharmacy (Mikesell 2016) and storytelling practices (e.g. retelling or repeating) by an individual with fronto-temporal dementia (Joaquin 2014). CA methods have also been used to examine more institutional interactions, particularly within neurological services such as memory clinics, including history-taking (Elsey et al. 2015; Jones et al. 2016), memory testing (Plejert et al. 2015), diagnosis delivery/receipt (Dooley et al. 2018) and patient-centred care (Rasmussen et al. 2019).

Setting

Data for this chapter are drawn from a single Memory Clinic in the North of England in which over 100 patients were recruited in order to obtain sufficient numbers of patients with certain diagnoses (i.e. dementia or functional memory disorders) for comparative purposes following completion of the diagnostic process. For present purposes an important distinction found in the study was that 95% of patients who eventually received a diagnosis of dementia were accompanied during their visit to the clinic (by spouses, family members, friends or carers) compared to only 40% of those who were given a Functional Memory Disorder diagnosis (Elsey et al. 2015). The interactional relevance and consequences of this are discussed in this chapter.

Summary of Original Study Methods and Key Findings

The study design adapted research methods previously used to analyse interactions in seizure clinics (Robson et al. 2012). For the purposes of the memory clinic research project the approach was altered in order to identify candidate interactional features of diagnostic relevance that might help clinicians distinguish between patients presenting with dementia from those with functional memory disorders (FMD) (a benign forgetfulness caused by potentially manageable factors such as stress or sleep problems) (Elsey et al. 2015; Jones et al. 2016; Reuber et al. 2018; Schmidtke et al. 2008).

A fundamental element of the study was that all patients recruited received a 'gold standard' clinical diagnosis, which was based upon interdisciplinary consensus. The 'gold standard' diagnosis was formed of a four-part assessment process:

- An in-depth history-taking with the patient (and any accompanying persons)
- Thorough neuro-psychological testing using standardised measures (including the Addenbrooke's Cognitive Examination [ACE-R] and Mini Mental State Examination)

- Magnetic resonance imaging (MRI) of the brain
- Final diagnosis was delivered to the patient in a separate consultation 1–2 weeks later
  (See Elsey et al. 2015, for full details of tests and procedures).

The conversation analysis focused exclusively on the history-taking phase of the assessment process. Prior to the study the participating neurologists received training designed to help them to encourage patients to talk as much as possible to produce sufficient interactional data to enable the research team to identify any potential memory-related troubles that were manifest in the interactions. For example, patients with dementia routinely struggled to answer questions (e.g. long silences, incomplete utterances, "I don't know" responses) or offered short and unelaborated answers. The neurologists were instructed to ask two specific questions during each history-taking (although the precise wording was not fixed). These questions (or variants of them) included:

1. Can you tell me the last time your memory let you down?
2. Who is most concerned about the memory problems?

Further they were also instructed to ask at least one compound or multi-parted questions, as patients with dementia were known to find it difficult to recall all parts of the original questions (e.g. "why you've come today and what expectations you have about the clinic?"—Jones et al. 2016). However, it is critical to note here that the status and consequences of the history-taking phase within the overall diagnostic assessment process are rather ambiguous and unclear in real-time for the patient and accompanying parties (as well as the conversation analyst).

The studies retrospectively associated several differentiating interactional features with a dementia diagnosis. Within the conversational profiles developed there were a number of clear and unambiguous differences that could be located in the talk that clinicians could readily adopt (e.g. patient responses to questions about who is most concerned or whether they could give detailed examples of recent specific memory problems). In order to corroborate these initial conversational profiles for dementia and FMD a blind test was conducted to see if conversation analysts could predict patients' diagnoses by applying the conversational profiles to video recorded and transcribed memory clinic consultations (Reuber et al. 2018). Some aspects of the profiles proved more difficult to apply reliably or readily to the audio-visual data. In particular this was true of triadic diagnostic features relating to cases in which accompanying persons were present and involved in the interactions, largely due to insufficient data to undertake comparison. One such troublesome feature was the presence of disagreement between the patient diagnosed with dementia and accompanying persons, which was noticeable in the interactions. While requiring further data, on the surface these interactional breakdowns seemed to be significant, especially in terms of the relationship between patients and accompanying persons *outside* of the clinic.

Operationalising and Conceptualising Disagreement in Triadic Memory Clinic Interactions

While the significance and impact of accompanying persons or parties (herein AP) attending neurological appointments has been noticed, exactly what they contribute and their role within the on-going interactions is less well understood. As Karnieli-Miller et al. (2012) express it, the expected role of APs is not always made explicit by clinical staff and therefore it needs careful sign-posting and interactional management so that in the first instance the patient is heard sufficiently. Previous research describes a variety of roles that APs have been found to fulfil. Dooley et al.'s (2018) literature review of observational studies of healthcare encounters involving patients with dementia describe how companions act either as 'patient advocates' or 'professional informants', depending on the levels of concern or a desire to play down certain activities and behaviours. This fits with our own findings in which APs (for those with dementia) frequently acted as spokespersons or advocates and were heavily involved in the on-going history-taking interactions and discussions. This feature of the interaction was rarely found in patients with FMD where APs were generally limited to providing 'confirmation checks' of information just given by the patient or second opinions towards the end of the encounter (Elsey et al. 2015). Essentially the difference is between APs providing facts and monitoring patients' answers or *accompanying* only.

Studies have tried to unpack divergent accounts between carers and persons with dementia. For example, the work of Østbye et al. (1997) examined whether there was agreement and disagreement regarding the perceived level of independence of the person with dementia in terms of routine daily living tasks and activities (e.g. cooking, eating, personal care, shopping, housework etc.). The study found a *reported* difference (i.e. participants separately provided their assessments and the answers were then compared and quantified), rather than demonstrated actual disagreement in real-time interactions. Other more observational and ethnographic studies have noticed a significant number of AP interruptions and interjections that serve to correct inaccuracies in patient utterances (Adams and Gardiner 2005; Karnieli-Miller et al. 2012).

To this end the present chapter highlights how disagreement is delivered and managed in three-party discussions with neurologists. This kind of study requires close analysis of its sequential structure, placement and utterance content. The chapter will unpack why the interactions can be described as disagreements (or agreements) between patients and APs, rather than more emotive or argumentative terms (e.g. a row, fight, dispute, conflict etc.). Given the diagnostic relevance of the interactions we will see how the contradictions or challenges offered by APs regarding facticity or accuracy should not understood as purely oppositional attacks, but as providing a full account of the patients' current competencies, skills and needs (Clayman and Heritage 2002). Crucially the chapter will draw on the classic CA phenomena of AP repair and/or correction of patients as conversational mechanisms for pointing out problems or mistakes in their talk (Jefferson 1987; Schegloff et al. 1977).

Findings

To begin to unpack the notion of disagreement, specifically between a patient with dementia and the accompanying person, it is important to recognise that patients themselves can, and regularly do, seek the assistance of the AP to help answer a neurologist's questions. Below is an example of such a collaboration in which the 61-year old male patient (eventually diagnosed with fronto-temporal dementia) *visibly* defers a question for his spouse (AP1) to answer. His daughter (AP2) is also present.

Extract 1: Head-turning sign ("Last time memory let you down")

033 (dementia, accompanied)

1	Neu	And could you, give me an example of the last time your memory, let you
2		down?
3		(1.5)
4	Pat	Um: ((turns to AP1))
5		(2.8)
6	AP1	In the car you've lost your sense of direction (.) does that count?
7	Pat	Right ((nods head))
8		((Pat and AP1 laugh))

This represents a relatively clear and unambiguous example of a patient who finds himself in a position in which he is unable to answer a question that is posed to him, which is about his memory. The neurologist's question asks the patient about the "last time" his memory failed (lines 1–2), as per the study instructions. The question is seemingly relatively straightforward and under ordinary circumstances the patient (and the AP) would be 'expected' to know and be able to provide an answer. However, the line of questioning around memory failures links back to the reason for the visit to the memory clinic (e.g. signs of problems previously reported by the AP1 and General Practitioner etc.). It is worth noting that given the nature of the question, the neurologist does not have access to the answer, unlike those from the neuropsychological testing phase (on the latter see Maynard (2005) and Mehan (1979) for comparable settings).

The patient's inability to answer is evident in his lengthy 1.5 second pause (line 3) and the resolution begins when he tries to answer ("um") while simultaneous shifting his gaze from the neurologist to his spouse. This classic 'head-turning sign' effectively defers the job of answering the question to the spouse. She provides the answer immediately ("you've lost your sense of direction"), which the patient then subsequently verbally and visually verifies and confirms ("right," combined with a head nod) (lines 6–7) (Elsey et al. 2015; Larner 2012). The important point here is that the patient *visibly* requests help and information from his wife, which contrasts with the examples that follow. Also the patient's inability to answer is also simultaneously exhibiting the latest example of his memory letting him down, there-and-then in the memory clinic, which is diagnostically informative. The simple question from the neurologist creates an interactional space for the patient's difficulties to be made available and identified.

Interactional Dilemmas

Disagreements take many forms that need to be analytically teased apart (Georgakopoulou 2012). For example, for APs in the memory clinic there is an interactional dilemma regarding the accuracy or facticity of a patient's answers to questions:

- Say nothing, thereby maintaining the patient's 'face' as a competent person able to speak for themselves to the neurologist
- Intervene, ensuring that the neurologist is given the 'facts' to adequately reflect the reality of the situation to ensure correct diagnosis

This dilemma permeates the turn-by-turn interactions across the history-taking phase.

Misunderstanding of Questions

One recurrent issue found in the memory clinic interactions is the misunderstanding of questions in which a patient's answers are heard as mismatched to the initial question posed by the neurologist. Without any input being sought by the patient (as in Extract 1) or neurologist, the AP can repair the patient's understanding of the question by rephrasing what they take to be the neurologist's original intent. Below is an example taken from the same consultation as Extract 1.

Extract 2: Misunderstanding questions—"Do you know when your problem started?"

033 (Dementia, accompanied)

1	Neu	Do you know when your problem started?
2		(1.5)
3	Pat	Uh:m (0.9) first of October.
4		(0.8)
5	AP1	You've been off since the first of [October.
6	Pat	[Yeah
7		(1.3)
8	AP1	It's probably about a year ago isn't it?
9		(7.0)
10	Pat	October the- fi:rst.
11		(2.9) ((AP1 turns away from Patient))
12	Neu	Okay
13		(2.9)
14	Neu	((continues))

In this case the disagreement takes the form of a repair and relates specifically to the patient's understanding of the relevancies/parameters of the neurologist's starting question. The neurologist's question is directed towards trying to establish when the patient's *memory* problems *in general* started (line 1), although he does not make the *memory* aspect explicit ("when your problem started") given the preceding conversation has centred on memory issues. After another long pause (1.5 seconds) (line 2) the patient's response orients to when his *work-related difficulties* began (i.e. when he received his sick note from the doctor) (line 3). As such his answer relates to the effects or impact of his problems starting on the "first of October". Recall that the patient is a working-age male and his memory problems were, at least partially, responsible for his enforced long-term sick leave. At this juncture his spouse (AP1) begins to repair the patient's *mis*understanding of the question by stating that the patient's "been off since the first of October", clarifying that he's been off *work* since that date, which the patient agrees with (line 6) (Schegloff et al. 1977). Having provided a more accurate context to his answer AP1 then offers a candidate answer to the original question about when the memory issues started and says "it's probably about a year ago, isn't it?" (line 8). After this contribution there is a long and noticeable silence from the patient (who looks at AP1 and then back to the neurologist) before ignoring or dismissing the repair by repeating and rephrasing his original response ("October the first"). In this instance AP1's attempts to repair the patient's understanding of the question appears to be unsuccessful in that her (other-initiated) repaired version of the question receives the same (i.e. unrepaired) response. AP1's change in posture immediately after signals her dissatisfaction and disagreement with this answer.

A similar problem is demonstrated in the consultation captured below in Extract 3. Here an 83-year-old female patient (who eventually received a dementia diagnosis) is accompanied by her daughter (AP). The neurologist is gathering general background information and is asking about her ex-husband.

Extract 3: Misunderstanding questions—"what did (your husband) do?"

105 (dementia, accompanied)

1	Neu	So (0.3) You married, what, (what's/was) the name of your husband?
2		(0.7)
3	Pat	(Steve) (.) (Steven) (2.6) ((Neu typing))
4	Neu	What did (Steven) do?
5	Pat	He used t' hit me.
6	AP	No-ho (0.2) [For a- <for a living>
7	Pat	[((turns to AP1))
8		(0.5)
9	Pat	Huh ((turns away from AP1))
10		(.)
11	AP	What did he work as moth(h)er? ((laughter))
12	Pat	Oh: he worked in the steel works.
13		(5.9) ((Neu typing))
14	Pat	((turns to AP1)) Well I'm tellin' truth:
15		(0.2)
16	AP	I know:
17	Pat	((turns away from AP1)) O:h
18		((laughing))
19	Neu	So it was an abusive marriage?
20	Pat	Yes.
21		((talk about marriage continues))

Having established the patient's ex-husband's name, anonymised here as "Steve(n)" (lines 1–3), the neurologist continues her line of questioning about the ex-husband by asking what he used to "do" (line 5), where "do" is taken to index employment or work rather than "do to you"/ how he used to treat you. Without hesitation the patient responds that "he used t' hit me" (line 6). Similarly to Extract 2, here the AP first assesses the adequacy of the answer ("no") before repairing the misunderstanding of the question "[what did he do] for a living", which receives a cold response from the patient or a possible hearing problem (line 10) leading to AP re-phrasing the question again ("what did he work as mother?"). The patient then provides the correct or adequate answer ("in the steel works"). However, like with the previous case we find the patient pushing back and re-asserting the accuracy and importance of her original answer. While the neurologist types up some notes the patient turns to her daughter and says "I'm telling the truth", which AP endorses and confirms ("I know") (lines 14–16). This sequence is intriguing in that the patient is sharing what she thinks is the most critical information about her past relationship, as opposed to purely sticking to the relevancies/parameters of the neurologist's starting question. Interestingly in this consultation the upshot of this part of the history-taking is that the issue of the marriage becomes topicalised and discussed in detail.

In short, these two excerpts highlight whether or not the patient has correctly understood a question delivered by the neurologist and how the repair sequence, initiated by an accompanying person, serves to undermine the adequacy of the patient's original answer as properly fitted to a particular question. For the AP and neurologist the focus appears to be upon repairing the understanding of the question, rather than allowing the patient to speak openly and honestly about matters of their own choice. The nature and prevalence of these *repairs* is certainly not an insignificant noticing in that it draws attention to a particular kind of interactional problem exhibited by the patient (i.e. understanding questions and producing relevant and on-topic answers to match). These questioning formats inadvertently reveal a secondary problem in that they highlight difficulties understanding questions, which goes beyond exploring potential memory recall issues that the questions intend. As such these mistakes become exposed and go 'on the record[ing]' in a double-sense (i.e. as clinical evidence and as part of the video recorded session) (Jefferson 1987). Further, it is key that the AP assumes and reasserts the neurologist's 'agenda' (Boyd and Heritage 2006).

Treating the Patient's Answers as Faulty or Incorrect

At other times in history-taking interactions the dementia patient's turn at talk is treated as factually wrong or an incorrect response, at least according to the AP. In such cases, however, the assumption is that the patient understood the focus or parameter of the question based on the form of the response (unlike in Extracts 2 and 3). As mentioned earlier in the chapter neurologists in the memory clinic routinely ask patients questions that they do not know the answers to (i.e. they do not necessarily have access to the information in their medical notes). This is one of the primary reasons that it is recommended that all patients are accompanied to their memory clinic appointments. In part their role is to 'fill in the blanks' and this forms a core part of the responsibilities of APs in this type of setting. An interactional consequence of the presence of accompanying parties is that they can, and do, highlight and provide alternative or contradictory answers to neurologists' questions immediately after patient utterances. One specific kind of sequence in which disagreement and contradict is most exposed is found when polar questions (yes/no) are asked by the neurologist (Raymond 2003).

The excerpts below (Extracts 4 and 5) display how APs interject and correct a patient's prior answers in these types of environments. In Excerpt 4 we return to patient 033 (Extracts 1 and 2) starting from the neurologist's question about when the memory problems started (as analysed above). However, the transcript below captures the discussion that immediately follows it.

Extract 4: AP correction practices—"he can't"/"you do"

033 (Dementia, accompanied)

Neu	Do you know when your problem started?
	(1.5)
Pat	Uh:m (0.9) first of October.
	(0.8)
AP1	You've been off since the first of [October.
Pat	[Yeah
	(1.3)
AP1	It's probably about a year ago isn't it?
	(7.0)
Pat	October the- fi:rst.
	(2.9) ((AP1 turns away from Patient))
Neu	Okay
	(2.9)
Neu	Uh:m (0.3) how is reading and writing
	(1.8)
Pat	Very well
	(4.3)
AP1	((glances AP1 ←→ AP2)) tch He can't be trusted with a credit card.
Pat	((laughing))
AP1	He blew fif-teen (.) (well) fifteen hundred quid?
	(0.4)
AP1	Beginning of October?
	(3.5)
Neu	What happened with the credit card?
	(2.2)
Pat	I:: (.) spent too much.
AP1	.HHHhh That's an understatement. ((turns away from Pat, places head in left-hand))
	(0.6)
(?)	Hhh
	(8.3)
Neu	An:d uh: do you go out by yourself?
	(1.2)
Pat	No
	(0.6)
AP1	°You do go into town, go for a walk around town°
Pat	Yes (1.2) That's true
	(2.1)
AP1	Can't go anywhere new °cos he gets (lost)°
Neu	What?
AP1	Sense of direction's gone.
	(1.4) ((Pat nods head))
Neu	And how do you feel you are when you're out, in town?
	(0.7)
Pat	Um:
	(5.4)
Pat	I can find my way home. ((nods head))
AP1	((looks down))
	((talk moves on to memory problems at home))

Taken together what is most striking about this series of exchanges is how the patient's wife (AP1) orients to the existence of 'problems', whereas the question design of the neurologist displays a 'no-problem' orientation (Boyd and Heritage 2006). For example, the questions posed in line 14 ("how is reading and writing?") and line 32 ("do you go out by yourself?") are not negatively phrased and therefore do not presume inability or incompetence. Having already cast doubt upon the patient's answer in lines 5 and 8 we see another interjection by AP1 here. The clinical significance of the neurologist's question on line 14 ("how is reading and writing") is never fully specified; however, after the patient's response ("very well") is met by a long silence in which the neurologist makes some notes, AP1 (line 18) brings up an issue that the patient has fairly recently started to struggle with, namely, money and profligate spending. AP1's interjection ("he can't be trusted with the credit card") is not fitted to the current line of questioning by the neurologist ("reading and writing?") and her first position assessment in effect by-passes the current neurologist-patient talk and speaks directly to the neurologist ("he can't...he blew") (Heritage and Raymond 2005). Upon receiving no response from either the neurologist or the patient, AP1 extends her account to how much he wasted or "blew" in the music shop ("fifteen hundred quid") (line 20) and to trying to recall when this happened ("beginning of October"). Further, the exact timing of this incident, coinciding with the patient being signed off from work due to his problems, cannot be overlooked here (Extract 2). Finally, the neurologist picks up on this new topic to ask about "what happened" (line 24). When the patient eventually responds after another long pause (2.2 seconds) his version of events (that he "spent too much" money) is immediately undermined by AP1's exasperated exhale and reiterated negative assessment ("That's an understatement") (lines 26–28). Such raw and exposed disagreements by the spouse are designed to emphasise and draw attention to the range of problems that she has noticed in her husband's behaviour over a prolonged period of time. For APs these opportunities represent an opportunity to provide their side of the story and to reveal the extent and range of the problems the patient is experiencing at home.

Having dealt with a problem that AP1 brought up herself we see an example of other-correction shortly after (line 32 onwards). Here we have the neurologist addressing the patient with a simple Yes/No Interrogative ("do you go out by yourself") (Raymond 2003). Again, this is a matter that the neurologist may not necessarily know the answer to, however, given the polar format of the question the patient is expected to be able to answer for himself (responding either "yes" or "no" will be sufficient without further account). After another pause the patient responds with an unequivocal and definitive answer ("no") (lines 33–34). Again, without invitation AP1 corrects the patient's answer ("°You do go into town, go for a walk around town°") (line 37) for the neurologist's benefit, which directly undercuts his original answer (effectively she is saying "[yes] you do…") and she provides some evidence to back up her claim. Note that here the disagreement and correction is directed towards the patient as the person responsible for the faulty response and the action is performed so that the medical record accurately reflects his current level of competence. Following this interjection the patient is forced to reverse his position and confirm that it is "true" that he makes such trips on his own. While this new information indicates some degree of independence for the patient, the carpet is soon pulled from under his feet as AP1 introduces a problem related to journeys that the patient has developed ("[he] can't go anywhere new cos he gets lost") (line 39). The patient's resigned final response in this sequence is aligned with the "new" places being problematic, although it is framed in terms of home representing a familiar and known location that can still be found ("I can find my way home"). In this context it seems that for the APs providing the unvarnished truth is preferred, rather than attempting to gloss over the nature, type and scope of problems that might be diagnostically relevant.

A final example will help to inform our understanding of correction and contradiction in triadic memory clinic interactions. This case has been chosen specifically as it exhibits a qualitatively different kind of interaction, in which the AP often minimises the extent and intensity of the problems being faced by the patient and her descriptions veer towards accounts of coping with and managing the memory changes that her husband is experiencing.

The patient is a 71 year-old man whose neuro-psychological test scores were the third worst overall from the entire cohort of the study. Given this, his wife (AP) answers the majority of the neurologist's questions, after the patient displays problems providing basic personal information right at the start of the interaction (i.e. his age, work history, etc.). This issue is especially relevant here as the neurologists had been instructed to elicit as much patient talk as possible in order to provide sufficient data for the development of conversation analytic informed differential diagnoses.

Extract 5: AP agreement and correction practices—"No, you find that difficult"

Neu	((looks at AP)) So navigating around familiar places is- hasn't been a
	problem.=
AP	=((shakes head)) No. No. That's not a problem at all:.
Pat	The negatives and the positives come in an' [.hhh hhh]
AP	[Yeah. I know.]
Pat	it's hard to say that causes it or: that causes it.
AP	No:: it's difficult.
	(5.5)
Neu	((looks at Pat, briefly to AP)) .h How about people. Have you:, (0.2) been
	forgetting: (1.0) people as well a- as- as: losing thi:ngs.
AP	(0.9) ((shakes head, mouths "no"))
Pat	Not reall[y. No]:.=
Neu	[No,]
AP	=No.
Neu	You recognise:,
	(0.3)
Pat	Yes. The [people (at home).]
Neu	[No problems recog]nising people.
	(1.0)
AP	He's got lots of erm: mates from pub. hu hhh
Neu	Right.
AP	And we always meet them down at the shops.
	(0.2)

```
AP    And he always knows who they are an'(.) (gettin' down to are)
      (3.1)
AP    I don't think he know their names to be honest with £y(h)ou hh huh
Neu   Right.
      (0.8)
Neu   ((looks at AP, briefly to Pat)).hh And remembering events: tha- f-for
      example from the day befo:re:, O[r the week before,]
AP                                    [((shakes head)) No:. (Had that)
Pat   (Didn't)
AP    You fin- No. You find that difficult ((First name)).
      Sometim[es Sometimes you do:.]
Pat          [  (Never beginning)  ]
AP    Yeah.
      (1.7)
Pat   Um but (0.5) Yeah.
      (2.2)
Pat   Usually I can tell ((looks at AP)). But,
AP    Yea:h but you do forget.
      (13.0)
```

An important aspect of these triadic memory clinic interactions is to consider *who* neurologists address their questions to (i.e. patient or the accompanying person), especially as the history-taking phase develops (as opposed to opening exchanges) (Karnieli-Miller et al. 2012; Stivers 2001). Clearly this has implications in that neurologists can, and routinely do, make real-time assessments of a patient's ability and competence to answer. Such assessments present neurologists with another interactional dilemma: the pursuit of answers from patients themselves and/or the pursuit of full and accurate medical records to facilitate the diagnostic process. One way that this dilemma is exhibited can be observed by figuring out who neurologists address each question to (patient or AP) using certain key resources available to the patient and the AP (and by extension the conversation analyst) (Stivers 2001; Stivers and Robinson 2006). Specifically, this includes who the neurologist was looking at during the production of the utterance, who a prior question was addressed to (Heritage and Robinson 2006; Sacks et al. 1978; Stivers and Heritage 2001) and the address terms employed ("[do] you") or their absence. The potential upshot of these types of interactional resources is that the nominated person answers *first* (Sacks et al. 1978). Typically in doctor-patient-accompanying party triadic interactions the preference or expectation is that the patients will speak for themselves, if possible. Evidently there are exceptions to this expectation (Antaki et al. 2007; Stivers 2001, 2007; Stivers and Robinson 2006), such as the long patient pauses found across all the examples in this chapter, in which the preference is for an answer to be delivered. In this excerpt the neurologist continues to try to engage the patient, but when trouble arises the AP 'fills in the blanks', both with and without prompting.

These resources help us look at three key sequences from this excerpt (lines 1–3, 9–14 and 29–41). The neurologist's enquiries follow a sequential mould in which she outlines a series of possible memory-related 'problems' or issues that the patient may be experiencing and seeks yes/no responses that assess the patient's current capabilities (Stivers and Heritage 2001). The initial question of the sequence (lines 1–2) is clearly addressed to the AP as the neurologist gazes exclusively towards her and the question lacks any personal identifiers ("so navigating around familiar places…"). In addition, the question is designed to prefer or minimise problems ("…hasn't been a problem?"). This receives a categorical "no" which is repeated in various forms and is accompanied by a shake of the head, which serves to close down this particular line of enquiry. The next question from the neurologist has a very different shape (lines 9–14). Here the neurologist mainly gazes at the patient during the turn construction with a brief glance towards the AP. However, the focus of the question is made plain by the neurologist as she breaks off the question in motion ("how about people") to single out the patient as the recipient of the question ("have *you* been forgetting people…"). During the 0.9 second pause between the question and the patient's response ("not really no") we *see* the AP shake her head and mouth "no" (lines 11–12). However, she chooses not to vocalise her response immediately and only provides a hearable "no" as a final confirmation (line 14), thereby orienting to the neurologist's designation of the patient as 'next speaker' and allowing the patient to reply for himself, while monitoring the patient's answer for accuracy (Pomerantz and Heritage 2013; Stivers 2001; Stivers and Robinson 2006).

In contrast, the third substantive question in this stretch of talk results in a very different type of interactional organisation. Here it is evident that the question is being directed towards the AP as the neurologist predominantly looks at the AP during its production and also the question lacks a personal identifier ("And remembering events, for example from the day before or the week before" [able to do that?]), as well as AP being the previous speaker (Stivers 2001). While the design of the question is set-up for a "no problem" answer (i.e. "yes" he can do that) here the AP provides the first assessment of the patient's abilities to remember recent life events or activities (i.e. she shakes her head and says "no") (compare this with Excerpt 4 lines 32–37 in which the patient provides the initial assessment and the AP challenges the answer). Here this definitive answer is contradicted by the patient, albeit briefly ("(didn't)") without any explanation or evidence (line 31). As such, the nature of polar questions in this context makes reproach difficult (but not impossible, again see Excerpt 4 lines 32–37) as it requires a 180° reversal of the original answer (can/can't, does/doesn't) and here we see AP repeat and expand her categorical "no", which is then somewhat softened (line 34) to "sometimes, sometimes you do," that prepares the ground for finding a middle way for agreement. Despite this, the patient's suggestion that "usually I can tell, but" (line 40) seeks to maintain his original stance that remembering events is not *normally* an issue for him. Here the AP is therefore placed in a tricky position in which she can either withdraw her initial assessment or, as she in fact does, state what she knows to be true ("Yea, but *you do forget*"—line 41) without contradicting her husband outright (i.e. by partially accepting his response whilst maintaining that he ["you"] does forget things) with what turns out to be the final word on this issue. Examples such as this raise questions about the status of a patient's answers during history-taking interactions at the memory clinic. In particular it draws attention to instances in which APs choose to correct the patient's own characterisation of their health and abilities and the frequency with which neurologists seek a second opinion. That said, this final observation rests on the fact that the patient's *memory* itself is under scrutiny.

Conclusions

Previous observational research within specialist clinics specifically explored the power dynamics found in triadic interactions between physicians, patients with dementia and their companions (Sakai and Carpenter 2011). A key focus of these studies examined the role that third parties (e.g. companions) played in the interactions and how they attempted to become actively involved in the conversation (Karnieli-Miller et al. 2012). The result of the observed *moves* was described as excluding or minimising the input of the patient (Elsey et al. 2017). However, the design and purpose of these studies were not to facilitate or improve the diagnostic process. Critically, the interactional *moves* observed and documented lacked the fine-grained, real-time audio-visual data to fully support the claims made. This chapter offers a corrective of these observations and fleshes out our understanding of the sequential aspects of the triadic interactions.

An initial comment is that there is evidently an 'institutional' character to these memory clinic interactions in that *questions* are almost exclusively led by a neurologist and *answers* provided by the patient and/or any accompanying persons that are present (Heritage 1997). It is the patient's memory and capabilities which are the reason for, and the topic of, the consultation. Clearly what we find is a fundamental 'asymmetric' pattern to these triadic interactions so that during the history-taking phase discussed in this chapter the talk recorded is almost exclusively *about* the patient (and their memory-related problems) compared to more balanced talk that one would expect to see in ordinary conversation (Drew 1991; Maynard 1991). This pattern is also found throughout the memory clinic assessment process (e.g. within neuropsychological testing, brain scans and diagnoses). Therefore, one notable absent feature of these interactions is that the patient does not attempt, or does not feel able, to turn the tables on the neurologist or any accompanying persons to make their issues the subject of the conversation. Furthermore, the interactions documented here cast light upon memory and how the memory functioning is exhibited in real-time interactions.

Triadic interactions such as these bring together institutional and every day considerations in a unique way, whereby features of the home life are brought to the clinic. For example, the analysis presented here does not isolate or focus on the atypical individual only (i.e. a person with dementia and their particular capabilities and weaknesses), but demonstrates how their fellow interlocutors *mark* a patient's utterances as needing supplementation, repair or correction. Significantly, these assessments are most often produced by APs (whether spouses, family members or friends) who have more intimate knowledge of the changes in the patient and superior access to this information than the (previously unfamiliar) neurologist has. This study begins to show *how* interactions between patients and APs are altered or adjusted as neuro-degeneration worsens over time, so that the pursuit of full, appropriate or correct answers becomes necessary and therefore more frequent (Jones 2015). These changes are seen and heard by the need to repair and correct misunderstandings, mistakes and errors in conversation.

However, an important general observation to make is that repair and correction practices proliferate in all interactions, irrespective of the identities of the interlocutors and their medical histories and situations. This ranges from so-called ordinary conversation (Schegloff et al. 1977), all the way through to complex multi-party worksites such as civil aviation (Arminen et al. 2010) or military combat activities (Elsey et al. 2016) where being accurate and correct is critical. A useful comparison is the correction/repair sequences found in educational test contexts (Maynard 2005; Mehan 1979).

In the context of triadic memory clinic interactions, aspects of the encounters have diagnostic relevance (e.g. the presence of repair/correction). These issues are especially relevant in memory clinic history-taking interactions in terms of what is said (or not) by the patient and how it is produced, which can be taken to be consequential in the diagnostic process. Omitted, delayed or challenged responses can be seen as 'signs' of underlying issues (Lynch 1984). On a fundamental level turn-taking (specifically the allocation of turns to AP's instead of patients themselves) means that patients do not always get to speak for themselves. Patient's own accounts of their memory and related problems can be further undermined by the repair and correction procedures, which serve to highlight problems and furnish different answers. The prevalence of *other*-initiated repair/correction and *other*-correction is particularly telling in this context (Schegloff et al. 1977). Correcting patients can serve to undermine the patient's perceived competence and ability to answer accurately and fully on their own (for comparison see Rasmussen 2016, on repeated use of requests for confirmation). For APs (and neurologists) this is, in part, a practical issue as they must continually decide if they want to address any perceived faulty or inaccurate answers (and in so doing halting progress to other matters). Evidently in memory clinic consultations priority is given to providing the right or correct answer.

Ultimately the practical constraints of the visit and the diagnostic purpose of the encounter represent an intractable dilemma. Diagnostically-speaking these history-taking interactions are particularly informative. For the neurologist to do their job properly and accurately they need to be given a full and honest account of a patient's memory problems. The data included in this chapter reveal how APs sometimes deem a patient's responses as faulty or incomplete and in need of attention (i.e. things are worse than the patient is describing). However, the dilemma for AP's is how to provide this complete picture without side-lining or challenging the patient's views and opinions. Furthermore, the interactions raise important questions about subjective/objective or authorised accounts of an individual's *current* health and how this can be identified, observed or measured (e.g. memory tests). It is interesting to note in closing that in the cases included in this chapter we see some evidence of patients pushing back and resisting the contradictory version offered to the neurologist by those closest to them.

References

Adams, T., & Gardiner, P. (2005). Communication and interaction within dementia care triads: Developing a theory for relationship-centred care. *Dementia, 4*(2), 185–205. https://doi.org/10.1177/1471301205051092.

Alzheimer's Society. (2013). *Dementia diagnosis rates*. Alzheimer's society. http://www.alzheimers.org.uk/site/scripts/documents_info.php?documentID=2165. Accessed 27 Aug 2014.

Alzheimer's Society. (2015). *Understanding and supporting a person with dementia* [online]. Available https://www.alzheimers.org.uk/get-support/help-dementia-care/understanding-supporting-person-dementia. Accessed 7 June 2019.

Antaki, C., Finlay, W. M. L., & Walton, C. (2007). Conversational shaping: Staff members' solicitation of talk from people with an intellectual impairment. *Qualitative Health Research, 17*(10), 1403–1414. https://doi.org/10.1177/1049732307308950.

Arminen, I., Auvinen, P., & Koskela, H. P. (2010). Repairs as the last orderly provided defense of safety in aviation. *Journal of Pragmatics, 42*(2), 443–465.

Berisha, V., Wang, S., LaCross, A., & Liss, J. (2015). Tracking discourse complexity preceding Alzheimer's disease diagnosis: A case study comparing the press conferences of Presidents Ronald Reagan and George Herbert Walker Bush. *Journal of Alzheimer's Disease, 45*(3), 959–963. https://doi.org/10.3233/jad-142763.

Boyd, E., & Heritage, J. (2006). Taking the history: Questioning during comprehensive history-taking. In J. Heritage & D. W. Maynard (Eds.), *Communication in medical care: Interaction between primary care physicians and patients* (pp. 151–184). Cambridge: Cambridge University Press.

Brayne, C., & Miller, B. (2017). Dementia and aging populations—A global priority for contextualized research and health policy. *PLoS Medicine, 14*(3), e1002275. https://doi.org/10.1371/journal.pmed.1002275.

Clayman, S. E., & Heritage, J. (2002). Questioning Presidents: Journalistic deference and adversarialness in the press conferences of U.S. Presidents Eisenhower and Reagan. *Journal of Communication, 52*(4), 749–775. https://doi.org/10.1111/j.1460-2466.2002.tb02572.x.

Dooley, J., Bass, N., & McCabe, R. (2018). How do doctors deliver a diagnosis of dementia in memory clinics? *British Journal of Psychiatry, 212*(4), 239–245. https://doi.org/10.1192/bjp.2017.64.

Drew, P. (1991). Asymmetries of knowledge in conversational interactions. In I. Markovà & K. Foppa (Eds.), *Asymmetries in dialogue* (pp. 29–48). Hemel Hempstead: Harvester Wheatsheaf.

Ekstrom, A., Ferm, U., & Samuelsson, C. (2017). Digital communication support and Alzheimer's disease. *Dementia (London), 16*(6), 711–731. https://doi.org/10.1177/1471301215615456.

Elsey, C., Challinor, A., & Monrouxe, L. V. (2017). Patients embodied and as-a-body within bedside teaching encounters: A video ethnographic study. *Advances in Health Sciences Education, 22*(1), 123–146. https://doi.org/10.1007/s10459-016-9688-3.

Elsey, C., Drew, P., Jones, D., Blackburn, D., Wakefield, S., Harkness, K., et al. (2015). Towards diagnostic conversational profiles of patients presenting with dementia or functional memory disorders to memory clinics. *Patient Education and Counseling, 98*(9), 1071–1077. https://doi.org/10.1016/j.pec.2015.05.021.

Elsey, C., Mair, M., Smith, P. V., & Watson, P. G. (2016). Ethnomethodology, conversation analysis and the study of action-in-interaction in military settings. In A. J. Williams, N. Jenkings, R. Woodward, & M. F. Rech (Eds.), *The Routledge companion to military research methods* (pp. 180–195). Abingdon: Routledge.

Forbes-McKay, K. E., & Venneri, A. (2005). Detecting subtle spontaneous language decline in early Alzheimer's disease with a picture description task. *Neurological Sciences, 26*(4), 243–254. https://doi.org/10.1007/s10072-005-0467-9.

Georgakopoulou, A. (2012). 'A simple disagreement? A row? Or a massive fall out?': On the challenges of an analytical task. *Journal of Pragmatics, 44*(12), 1623–1625. https://doi.org/10.1016/j.pragma.2012.07.004.

Hamilton, H. E. (1994). *Conversations with an Alzheimer's patient: An interactional sociolinguistic study*. Cambridge: Cambridge University Press.

Heritage, J. (1997). Conversation analysis and institutional talk: Analyzing data. In D. Silverman (Ed.), *Qualitative research: Theory, method and practice* (pp. 222–245). London: Sage.

Heritage, J., & Raymond, G. (2005). The terms of agreement: Indexing epistemic authority and subordination in talk-in-interaction. *Social Psychology Quarterly, 68*(1), 15–38. https://doi.org/10.1177/019027250506800103.

Heritage, J., & Robinson, J. (2006). Accounting for the visit: Giving reasons for seeking medical care. In J. Heritage & D. W. Maynard (Eds.), *Communication in medical care: Interaction between primary care physicians and patients* (pp. 48–85). Cambridge: Cambridge University Press.

Jefferson, G. (1987). On exposed and embedded correction in conversation. In G. Button & J. Lee (Eds.), *Talk and social organisation* (pp. 86–100). Clevedon: Multilingual Matters.

Joaquin, A. D. L. (2014). Participation, pragmatics, and the prefrontal cortex: storytelling strategies of an individual with frontotemporal dementia. In C. Box, C. M. Jacknick, & H. Z. Waring (Eds.), *Talk in institutions: A LANSI volume* (pp. 127–148). Newcastle upon Tyne: Cambridge Scholars Publishing.

Jones, D. (2015). A family living with Alzheimer's disease: The communicative challenges. *Dementia, 14*(5), 555–573. https://doi.org/10.1177/1471301213502213.

Jones, D., Drew, P., Elsey, C., Blackburn, D., Wakefield, S., Harkness, K., et al. (2016). Conversational assessment in memory clinic encounters: Interactional profiling for differentiating dementia from functional memory disorders. *Aging & Mental Health, 20*(5), 500–509. https://doi.org/10.1080/13607863.2015.1021753.

Karnieli-Miller, O., Werner, P., Neufeld-Kroszynski, G., & Eidelman, S. (2012). Are you talking to me?! An exploration of the triadic physician-patient-companion communication within memory clinics encounters. *Patient Education and Counseling, 88*(3), 381–390. http://linkinghub.elsevier.com/retrieve/pii/S0738399112002443?showall=true.

Larner, A. J. (2012). Head turning sign: Pragmatic utility in clinical diagnosis of cognitive impairment. *Journal of Neurology, Neurosurgery and Psychiatry, 83*(8), 852–853. https://doi.org/10.1136/jnnp-2011-301804.

Lynch, M. (1984). "Turning up signs" in neurobehavioral diagnosis. *Symbolic Interaction, 7*(1), 67–86. https://doi.org/10.1525/si.1984.7.1.67.

Majlesi, A. R., & Ekström, A. (2016). Baking together—The coordination of actions in activities involving people with dementia. *Journal of Aging Studies, 38,* 37–46. https://doi.org/10.1016/j.jaging.2016.04.004.

Maynard, D. (1991). Interaction and asymmetry in clinical discourse. *American Journal of Sociology, 97*(2), 448–495.

Maynard, D. (2005). Social actions, gestalt coherence, and designations of disability: Lessons from and about autism. *Social Problems, 52*(4), 499–524.

Mehan, H. (1979). *Learning lessons: Social organisation in the classroom.* Cambridge, MA: Harvard University Press.

Mikesell, L. (2016). The use of directives to repair embodied (mis)understandings in interactions with individuals diagnosed with frontotemporal dementia. *Research on Language and Social Interaction, 49*(3), 201–219. https://doi.org/10.1080/08351813.2016.1196550.

Older People and Dementia Team. (2012). *Prime Minister's challenge on dementia: Delivering major improvements in dementia care and research by 2015.* London: Department of Health. https://assets.publishing.service.gov.uk/government/uploads/system/uploads/attachment_data/file/215101/dh_133176.pdf. Accessed 2 July 2014.

Østbye, T., Tyas, S., McDowell, I., & Koval, J. (1997). Reported activities of daily living: Agreement between elderly subjects with and without dementia and their caregivers. *Age and Ageing, 26*(2), 99–106. https://doi.org/10.1093/ageing/26.2.99.

Plejert, C., Antelius, E., Yazdanpanah, M., & Nielsen, T. R. (2015). 'There's a letter called ef' on challenges and repair in interpreter-mediated tests of cognitive functioning in dementia evaluations: A case study. *Journal of Cross-Cultural Gerontology, 30*(2), 163–187. https://doi.org/10.1007/s10823-015-9262-0.

Pomerantz, A., & Heritage, J. (2013). Preference. In J. Sidnell & T. Stivers (Eds.), *The handbook of conversation analysis* (pp. 210–228). Cambridge: Cambridge University Press.

Rasmussen, G. (2016). Repeated use of request for confirmation in atypical interaction. *Clinical Linguistics & Phonetics, 30,* 849–870.

Rasmussen, G., Andersen, E. M., & Kristiansen, E. D. (2019). Professional interactional practices in dementia care. *Special Issue of Logopedics Phoniatrics Vocology, 44*(1), 1–6.

Raymond, G. (2003). Grammar and social organization: Yes/No interrogatives and the structure of responding. *American Sociological Review, 68*(6), 939–967. http://www.jstor.org/stable/1519752.

Reuber, M., Blackburn, D. J., Elsey, C., Wakefield, S., Ardern, K. A., Harkness, K., et al. (2018). An interactional profile to assist the differential diagnosis of neurodegenerative and functional memory disorders. *Alzheimer Disease and Associated Disorders.* https://doi.org/10.1097/wad.0000000000000231.

Robson, C., Drew, P., Walker, T., & Reuber, M. (2012). Catastrophising and normalising in patient's accounts of their seizure experiences. *Seizure, 21*(10), 795–801. https://doi.org/10.1016/j.seizure.2012.09.007.

Sacks, H., Schegloff, E., & Jefferson, G. (1978). A simplistic systematics for the organisation of turn-taking for conversation. In J. Schenkein (Ed.), *Studies in the organisation of conversational interaction* (pp. 7–55). New York: Academic Press.

Sakai, E. Y., & Carpenter, B. D. (2011). Linguistic features of power dynamics in triadic dementia diagnostic conversations. *Patient Education and Counseling, 85*(2), 295–298.

Santacruz, K. S., & Swagerty, D. (2001). Early diagnosis of dementia. *American Family Physician, 63*(4), 703–713.

Schegloff, E. A., Jefferson, G., & Sacks, H. (1977). The preference for self-correction in the organisation of repair in conversation. *Language, 53*(2), 361–382.

Schmidtke, K., Pohlmann, S., & Metternich, B. (2008). The syndrome of functional memory disorder: Definition, etiology, and natural course. *The American Journal of Geriatric Psychiatry, 16*(12), 981–988. https://doi.org/10.1097/JGP.0b013e318187ddf9.

Stivers, T. (2001). Negotiating who presents the problem: Next speaker selection in pediatric encounters. *Journal of Communication, 51*(2), 252–282.

Stivers, T. (2007). *Prescribing under pressure: Parent-physician conversations and antibiotics*. Oxford: Oxford UniversityPress.

Stivers, T., & Heritage, J. (2001). Breaking the sequential mold: Answering 'more than the question' during comprehensive history taking. *Text, 21*(1–2), 151–185.

Stivers, T., & Robinson, J. D. (2006). A preference for progressivity in interaction. *Language in Society, 35*(3), 367–392.

Part II

The Impact of Language Impairments Within Social Interaction

8

Shifting Granularity: The Case of Correction and Aphasia

Scott Barnes and Francesco Possemato

Introduction

Aphasia is a language disorder caused by acquired brain damage, and it can differentially impair semantic, phonological, and syntactic processing. These language impairments and their symptoms have provided a basis for defining aphasia as a unique diagnostic condition, and for delineating profiles of processing deficit (e.g., Berthier 2005). By contrast, the specific consequences of aphasia for everyday communication are much less well established, and theoretical frameworks for exploring them are few (see Barnes and Bloch 2019).

The turn-constructional unit (TCU) is an empirically-grounded concept that holds much potential for specifying how aphasia affects communication. The language processing deficits associated with aphasia

S. Barnes (✉) · F. Possemato
Macquarie University, Sydney, NSW, Australia

© The Author(s) 2020

R. Wilkinson et al. (eds.), *Atypical Interaction*,
https://doi.org/10.1007/978-3-030-28799-3_8

cause a variety of disruptions to TCU efficacy. For example, aphasia affects the *sequential progressivity* of TCUs, i.e., their normatively accountable sound-by-sound, word-by-word, and phrase-by-phrase development. This chapter addresses the TCU as a locus for focused collaboration between people with aphasia and their familiar conversation partners. We will explore actions and practices that thematize components of TCUs for production. We will also examine the moral implications of these actions and practices, and discuss how they, ultimately, shape the agency of people with aphasia.

Turn Construction and Aphasia

Single parties typically regulate the internal organization of TCUs.[1] The turn-taking system for conversation grants a current speaker exclusive rights to produce one TCU prior to the transfer of speakership becoming relevant (Sacks et al. 1978). Sequential progressivity in a TCU is achieved via the predictable addition of successive sounds, syllables, words, and phrases (Lerner 1996; Schegloff 1979, 2013). This provides a transparent trajectory for its progress toward possible completion, and the prospect of turn recipients making an unproblematic bid for the floor (see Couper-Kuhlen and Selting 2018).

A current speaker may manipulate sequential progressivity in order to forestall points of possible completion (see Schegloff 1996, pp. 93–94, on “maximum grammatical control”). For instance, they can initiate repair and variously halt, alter, or reset the syntactic trajectory of a TCU-in-progress (see Schegloff 2013). Adjustments to sequential progressivity can be initiated at various levels of “granularity” (Schegloff 2000a). Speakers may arrest the development of a syllable, or a word, or a phrase (Lerner 1996; Schegloff 1979, 2013). The strong normative expectations relating to the internal organization of TCUs make these

[1]This is not to say that TCUs are the sole achievement of *single interactants*. At a very basic level, when one party is speaking, others are electing not to, thereby tacitly supporting the current speaker. Of course, there are also forms of (particularly embodied) conduct that recipients of a turn may engage into support TCU and turn development (see Couper-Kuhlen and Selting 2018, for an extensive introduction to TCUs).

kinds of interruptions and adjustments salient; both for analysts and recipients (Lerner 1996). However, the precise communicative actions that self-initiated same-TCU self-repair operations accomplish are not well understood (Schegloff 2013; Wilkinson and Weatherall 2011).[2] Schegloff (2000b) demonstrated that speakers may use these practices to resolve periods of overlapping talk. As well, Wilkinson and Weatherall (2011) found that a particular kind of same-TCU self-repair—insertion repair—often serves to "specify" or "intensify" a selected TCU component in service of a wide variety of context-specific interactional objectives. The regulation of syllables, words, and phrases is, therefore, a highly consequential locus of activity for turn-taking organization and action formation, and is closely monitored by speakers and recipients.

Turn construction is challenging for people with aphasia. Their lexical and syntactic processing impairments can preclude efficient access to, and control of, the linguistic resources that underwrite TCUs.[3] This inhibits the development of speaking turns that conform with the normative expectation for sequential progressivity and heightens the likelihood of problems with intersubjectivity. An example of this is provided in Extract 1. Here, a speaker with aphasia occupies the conversational floor at 5–8, but he makes little transparent syntactic progress, and his conversation partner other-initiates repair.

---

[2]Actions and practices do not stand in a one-to-one relationship (Enfield and Sidnell 2017). The same repair practice/operation may therefore accomplish different actions across different contexts. As well, same-TCU self-repair operations tend to target rather fine issues of action calibration and recipient design, and are sensitive to the particulars of the interactional moments in which they are employed (Wilkinson and Weatherall 2011, p. 88). Together, this means they can be resistant to analytic inquiry, and to the development of aggregate characterizations of their functions.

[3]TCUs are (1) talk-based; and (2) projectable, i.e., signal when they are likely to be complete. People with severe aphasia may not be able to produce talk that is projectable in this sense. So, some of their contributions through talk might not effectively constitute a TCU. See Pilesjö and Rasmussen (2011) for further discussion on this point.

Extract 1

```
      C  'ts a bit h[ard in a] wheelchair *when it's raining.*
      R             [°( )°    ]
      R  °u- u- r-r:ight;°
         (0.2)
->    R  °right, .hh° (0.2) (y:our:(h)) (2.4) message (.) ( )
->       (0.5) °( ) .hhh (roogut)° THE: (1.7) (en or: your)
->       (1.9) pf::(for) (0.9) (uh n(h)o-) .hhh your (1.2)
->       >(y' v- d-)< (0.7) °eh° (dammit) hh .hhh (0.5) °um°
=>    C  >what you< talking about the rain: at the last concert?
```

People with aphasia may compensate for their language processing impairments by arranging TCU components in strategic ways (e.g., Beeke et al. 2007; Helasvuo et al. 2004; Wilkinson et al. 2003). They may also creatively combine talk with non-talk semiotic resources while holding the floor (e.g., Wilkinson et al. 2010; Goodwin 2003). Neither of these adaptations, however, is likely to completely and persistently address problems with sequential progressivity in their TCUs.

Another, rather different solution involves turn recipients participating in the production of turn elements; typically, via other-initiations of repair (Aaltonen and Laakso 2010; Barnes 2016; Goodwin 2003; Helasvuo et al. 2004; see also in regards to AAC interaction Pilesjö and Rasmussen 2011). That is, the conversation partners of people with aphasia may take the floor and produce talk that conforms to normative expectations for TCU design (as projected by the person with aphasia's talk). The gross effect of this collaboration is that the incremental production of sequentially progressive TCU components—an activity that is usually accomplished within a TCU, by a single interactant—becomes distributed across a sequence of turns, and multiple interactants (Barnes 2016; Helasvuo et al. 2004; see also Lerner 1996, on typical interactions). However, there is no guarantee that this process will be efficient or successful. Other-initiations of repair targeting the turns of people with aphasia tend to require multiple attempts at a repair solution (e.g., Laakso and Klippi 1999) and may not be resolved at all (e.g., Barnes and Ferguson 2015). This means that, in addition to violating normative expectations relating to TCU design, turns that lack sequential progressivity may fail to adequately implement the *actions* they convey.

In summary, the normative internal organization of TCUs involves predictable succession between adjacent syllables, words, and phrases, culminating in possible TCU (and turn) completion. Aphasia disrupts the arrangement of TCU components, resulting in turns relying on atypical configurations of talk, and/or TCU components being produced by multiple interactants.

Soliciting Talk from People with Aphasia in Conversation

Correction, as it relates to repair organization for conversation, is a set of practices dedicated to identifying and solving problems with speaking in the turn of another party.[4] In everyday conversations involving typical speakers, correction is usually infrequent and short (Jefferson 1987; see also Kurhila 2001). By contrast, empirical studies of aphasia and everyday conversation have documented long periods focused explicitly on encouraging and shaping the production of talk. In particular, it has demonstrated that family members direct test questions (i.e., known-answer questions) to people with aphasia, and solicit the production of selected words with various correcting practices (e.g., Aaltonen and Laakso 2010; Bauer and Kulke 2004; Beeke et al. 2013; Lindsay and Wilkinson 1999). Given the degree of difficulty aphasia implicates for speaking, it may seem curious for people with aphasia and their conversation partners to focus on the production of talk in this way. Both Bauer and Kulke (2004) and Beeke et al. (2013) associate test questioning with scaffolding the participation of people with aphasia. As Beeke et al. (2013) argue, test questions can prospectively address problems with turn construction, and the probability that they will disrupt intersubjectivity. Bauer and Kulke (2004) also argue that these actions and practices—which they collectively refer to as "language exercises"—are designedly paedagogical.[5] In particular, Bauer and Kulke (2004) suggest that they:

[4]The definition of "correction" has often been a point of debate, particularly in contexts where it has more technical senses (see, e.g., Possemato 2018, for an up to date overview in the context of classroom interaction).

[5]This is also how they are characterised in many conversation-focused interventions for aphasia.

> ...import an institutional interactive format into informal contexts of domestic everyday life to which this format is otherwise alien. ... Exercising is thus not about transfer of knowledge, exchange of information, or mutual understanding, but about the processes of lexical retrieval, articulation, or the formulation of a correct sentence. The central element of this activity is *learning by repeating*, for example, the processes of lexical retrieval or articulation. Repetition takes place as often as necessary to achieve an accurate realisation, or until breaking off the attempt signals that a correct utterance cannot be achieved. (Bauer and Kulke 2004, pp. 1155–1156; emphasis added)

All of these studies offer empirical evidence of familiar conversation partners uttering partial syllables, words, and phrases to solicit the production of talk. That is, conversation partners of people with aphasia alter and halt the sequential progressivity of their own TCUs in order to solicit talk from people with aphasia. The organization of these particular techniques has yet to be systematically explored in everyday conversations involving people with aphasia, but there is some evidence for their operation in other contexts.

Test Questions and Designedly Incomplete Utterances in Institutional Talk

Test questions are prominent in institutional interactions; particularly, classroom interactions. A considerable portion of the teaching-learning process in instructed contexts is carried out via questioning activities (e.g., Lee 2008; Margutti 2010), and test questions are often the first turn in an Initiation-Response-Evaluation (IRE) sequence (Mehan 1979). In IRE sequences, teachers solicit information from students and then adopt a stance towards their response(s). Teachers ask these (and other) questions to make students publicly exhibit their knowledge, and to control the participation framework of the ongoing interaction (Margutti 2006, 2010). Moreover, given that questions generically entail distributions of entitlements, responsibilities, and knowledge among interactants (e.g., Levinson 2012), questioning practices inevitably embody the institutional character of classroom interactions;

particularly, the deontic and epistemic imbalance between teachers and students.

Another questioning-like practice that teachers employ has been termed a "Designedly Incomplete Utterance" (DIU) (Koshik 2002). With these turns, teachers offer (sometimes a large) part of an utterance, but also encode an expectation that students will take the floor and produce its outstanding components (see, e.g., Koshik 2002; Margutti 2010; Netz 2016). Margutti (2010) explores the use of DIUs in primary school classrooms during whole-class instruction. She demonstrates that teachers render their turns incomplete—and solicit student completion—by means of syntax, prosody, and silence. That is, teachers halt the syntactic development of a phrase, word, or syllable, produce try-marked intonation and stretched sounds, and allow silences to emerge at points of TCU incompletion. On a turn incorporating this sort of silence, she writes:

> In fact, it is designed as an intra-TCU silence (that is, deployed in non-transition space) precisely in order to make recipients hear that the utterance is not finished and, thereby, elicit completion. The sense of incompleteness provides for turn transition by way of TCU completion, which, subsequently, makes the pause into an *interturn pause* (however, for clarity they will be referred to as *intra-TCU pauses* in the article). (Margutti 2010, p. 322; emphasis added)

The upshot of this discussion is that, although DIUs implicate *sequences of turns*, they trade on practices that are typically employed for composing *individual TCUs*. Margutti (2010) highlights a number of functions for DIUs in this context. She argues that DIUs are employed to crystalize a line of argumentation that has been developing through the prior discussion. That is, they target matters that should already be available to students and offer an opportunity for them to display their knowledge/learning. Margutti (2010) also compares DIUs to syntactically formatted questions (i.e., test questions). She suggests that DIUs offer a way to maximally structure student participation; particularly for those targeting the co-production of a single word. At the same time, DIUs provide teachers with the flexibility to deliver the projected component themselves with minimal disruption to the ongoing course of action.

There are a small number of studies that evidence test questioning and DIUs in institutional interactions involving people with aphasia (e.g., Horton 2008; Merlino 2018; Wilkinson 2013). Wilkinson (2013) and Merlino (2018) describe DIUs as a form of "cueing" in aphasia assessment and aphasia intervention respectively. Like Margutti (2010), both studies provide examples of DIUs that present incomplete phrases (Wilkinson 2013, p. 816) and words (Merlino 2018, pp. 343–344) for the person with aphasia to complete. Interestingly, Wilkinson (2013) and Merlino (2018) also demonstrate that clinicians employ other, more meaning-oriented ways of soliciting the production of words (i.e., what might be conventionally labelled "semantic cueing"). Again, like in the classroom, these practices are dedicated to professional speech pathology tasks, and their underlying objectives of diagnosis and rehabilitation. The question remains, however, as to how closely such techniques resemble the talk-soliciting actions and practices attested in everyday conversations involving people with aphasia. Are familiar conversation partners, as Bauer and Kulke (2004) suggest, "importing" them from institutional talk to effect "learning by repetition"? And, if so, how does their organization reflect this objective? We will begin to consider these matters by examining the organization of talk soliciting actions and practices by the spouses of people with aphasia in conversation, focusing on the use of DIUs.

Data and Method

The data supporting the present analyses were collected with three men who have aphasia and their respective female spouses (i.e., 6 participants). Data were gathered in the course of two separate research projects.[6] The participants will be referred to using the pseudonyms

[6]Both projects received ethical approval from the Macquarie University Human Research Ethics Committee and were conducted in accordance with these approvals (Refs: HE26SEP2008-D06134; 5201400899).

Table 8.1 Summary characteristics of participants with aphasia

Participant	Age	Years post-onset	Co-morbidities	Previous occupation	WAB-R AQ[a]
David	74	4	Right-sided hemiparesis	Human resources manager	81.2
Hilton	66	3	Right-sided hemiparesis; Apraxia of speech	Builder	62.6
Russell	72	1	Right-sided hemiparesis	Solicitor	59.2

[a]WAB-R AQ, Western Aphasia Battery (Revised) Aphasia Quotient (Kertesz 2007)

"David and Carmen", "Hilton and Gail", and "Russell and Carol". Summary information about the participants with aphasia is presented in Table 8.1. Participants were provided with a video camera and asked to make recordings of their conversation in their own homes. No topics or activities were suggested for discussion. 1 hour and 13 minutes of participant recordings were transcribed. Transcripts were then inspected for candidate instances of talk-soliciting actions and practices targeting a turn produced by a participant with aphasia. In this process, 124 individual DIU segments were collated. These DIUs were analysed using "single episode" conversation-analytic methods (see Schegloff 1987). The analyses to follow will focus on the recurrent features of the sequential organization of these DIUs, and the action sequences they engender.

Analysis 1: The "Technology" of Correction

In this section, we will explore the technical accomplishment of correction in conversations involving people with aphasia and their spouses. First, we will examine how conversation partners generate a "correctable" item, i.e., an aspect of a turn for correction. We will focus on instances generated via test questioning. Second, we will describe how conversation partners use DIUs to isolate the correctable item; that is, frame and pursue its production in talk. Finally in this section, we will outline how conversation partners respond to the accurate production of the target correctable.

Generating Correctables

Solicitation of talk from people with aphasia arises in a number of different ways. In some instances, as in Extract 2, it is tied to the production of an erroneous word by the person with aphasia in an adjacent turn (see Jefferson 1987, p. 88, on this three-part "series"; see also Lindsay and Wilkinson 1999, pp. 311–315). In these cases, the correctable item emerges *retrospectively*, as is typical for other-initiated other-repair (i.e., correction) sequences. In Extract 2, Carol twice corrects Russell in this way; at line 5, she adds a plural morpheme to the word *customer*, and at line 10 she replaces the word *play* with the more topically apposite word *business*.

Extract 2

```
    001  C  yeah:¿ en we were their first cus(t)-
    002     (0.3)
->  003  R  customer.
    004     (.)
=>  005  C  customers. yep,
    006  R  ₒc'st'ₒmers, [en]
    007  C               [ye]ah:.
->  008  R  p- (en the) (0.4) ( ) (0.5) °.hh e- eh-° (0.4) °.hh
->  009     just ( )° s:tart of play:.
=>  010  C  start ev business;
    011     (0.2)
    012  R  yuh.=
    013  C  =*yeah:.*
```

More commonly in the present data, a correctable is *prospectively* foreshadowed via an initiating turn from a conversation partner;

overwhelmingly, a test question.[7] Test questions are usually specifying *wh* questions (see Fox and Thompson 2010) and *yes/no* interrogatives soliciting the production of noun phrases (see, e.g., Extract 3(a), line 4). With these test questions, conversation partners tacitly identify a target noun phrase for production via talk. Once foreshadowed, people with aphasia and conversation partners work towards saying the correctable.[8] People with aphasia demonstrate their progress by producing, for example, pre-TCU elements and TCU beginnings (see Schegloff 1996), and offering candidate versions of the targeted word(s). Conversation partners re-issue test questions specifying the correctable, respond to candidate versions of the correctable produced by the person with aphasia (often with further corrections, as in Extract 2), employ DIUs, and, in some cases, produce the correctable item themselves.[9] An instance involving a number of these patterns is presented in Extract 3(a). Here, Carmen focuses her test questioning to David on the names of their grandchildren, who had visited them the day before.

---

[7]Syntactically imperative turns and other deontically-strong actions are also used to commence periods in which talk is solicited from people with aphasia.

[8]A reviewer noted that correction is inherently retrospective, which may make problematic the prospective sense of "correctable" we are proposing here. We appreciate this point, and a more apt description might be "sayable" given that the production of talk is ultimately the outcome sought from test questions, DIUs, and conventional correction. However, we have chosen to retain "correctable". This is because "sayable" fails to convey the strong tacit orientation to the production of particular words by both parties, and the asymmetries—particularly, deontic ones—realised via test questions and DIUs. For some similar arguments on tacitness in repair, see Clift (2016, pp. 264–270) on implicit other-initiations of repair.

[9]As we shall see, there are also various "attendant activities" (Jefferson 1987, p. 90) in the period after the correctable has been foreshadowed.

Extract 3(a)[10]

```
001   C  two of taryn's gi:[rls ca]me¿
002   D                     [yeah, ]
003      (0.6)
004   C  d'you remember what their names ↑are?
005      (0.9)
006   C  >what's the< youngest one;
007      (1.6)
008   D  .hh hh
009   C  ↑j'st take y'r time,=i'm sure you can get (it out:);
010      (0.6)
011   C  taryn's youngest daughter.
012      (0.5)
013   D  hhh (0.5)
014   C  she's blonde¿ long hair:,
015      (0.6)
016   D  yeah: i c'n see 'er,
017      (.)
018   D  but (.) (i j'st) can't get the words out.
019   C  a-
020      (0.9)
021   C  a(p)-
022      (0.7)
023   D  ap- (0.4) .h a april.
024      (0.2)
025   C  april.
026   D  *yeh.*=
027   C  =an what about the other one that's=f- quite tall now:¿
028      (0.4)
029   D  yeah- hh (1.1) *(m)ah::*
030      (0.2)
031   C  j'st take y'r time;=↑can y' think?
032      (0.9)
033   C  e-
034      (0.9)
035   C  e-
036      (1.3)
037   C  eb-
038      (1.2)
039   D  °*e*° (0.4)
040   C  eb,
041      (0.3)
042   D  h. e- (0.2) eb (0.2)
043   C  ebony,
044      (0.3)
045   D  ebony.
```

[10]Following Margutti (2010), any silence following a DIU turn will be presented on the line below the DIU, reflecting the relevance of speakership transfer at that moment.

```
046       (0.3)
047   C   ↓ebony.
048       (0.4)
049   D   °°yeah.°°=
050   C   =°°yeh.°°
051       (0.8)
```

Carmen replaces her *yes/no* interrogative at line 3 with a *wh* question at line 6. This narrows the correctable to one of the two names she initially foreshadowed for production. After a long silence, David produces some audible breaths, and Carmen directs him to *take his time* with an imperatively formatted turn before asserting that she is sure he *can get it out*. Carmen purses production of the correctable with her turns at 11 and 14, and David accounts for his failure to say the name at 18. At 19 and 21, Carmen changes tack, and offers two DIUs. She first conveys the initial syllable of the correctable, and then the initial syllable and the onset of its second syllable. David steadily progresses towards saying the correctable, producing it in full at the end of 23. Carmen's next test question returns to the other name foreshadowed. David commences a response at 29 but makes little progress. This, again, spurs an imperative from Carmen, and similar DIUs at 33, 35, 37, and 40. David does not assemble a relevant TCU beyond the syllable and onset provide by Carmen. She relents at 43, supplying the correctable, which both she and David subsequently repeat.

In Extract 3(a), Carmen prospectively indexes the production of two proper nouns using test questions at 4 and 27. In doing so, she relies on sequence organization to solicit talk from David. We have also seen that Carmen and David both employed a variety of actions and practices to manage the delays following her production of test questions. This includes Carmen's revision of her test questions, her directions, and her assertions, and David's account and possible turn beginnings. The pursuit of each correctable also resulted in Carmen employing DIUs and, in one case, producing the correctable herself. Carmen and David then both repeated the correctable item. We will now explore these patterns in more detail, focusing on the organization of DIUs.

Isolating Correctables with DIUs

DIUs provide a mechanism for isolating correctable items foreshadowed via test questions. More abstractly, DIUs also represent a subtle change in method for soliciting talk; from a sequence-based strategy via test questioning to a repair-based (i.e., correction-based) strategy.[11] Two aspects of DIUs were apparent across the instances examined in the present data. First, DIUs were delivered with and without dedicated syntactic frames. That is, some DIUs—as in Extract 3—relied on the shape of the test question(s), and parts of the word form delivered via the DIU for their connection to the talk in progress. Other DIUs employed syntactic frames additional to the test question (see Margutti 2010, on "main-clause" DIUs). Second, some DIUs were constructed to realize the entirety of the correctable, whereas others were designed to realize part of it. These features are variously present in Extracts 4, 5, and 6.

Extract 4 commences with Carol asking Russell a topic-initiating test question about where they will soon be *off to*. Russell steadily develops a TCU in response, but it culminates in a semantically anomalous word—*system*—that Carol corrects to *aphasia group*. Russell adjusts his position at 9, asserting that they will *go here*, which Carol hears as referring to their current activity, i.e., *doing this*. She then begins a multi-unit turn that reimplements the constraints of the test question, while also delivering a DIU.

[11]To be clear, sequence organization is still relevant for DIUs. They have their own sequential organization and they are designed in ways that are sensitive to the sequence-based pressures implemented through test questions. It is also worth noting that DIUs represent an interesting middle ground between test questions and conventional retrospective correction in terms of the way it renders the correctable item.

Extract 4

```
     C  .hh ↑and uh- dy' know where we're going: (0.7) now:=
        =af[ter we] fi:nish our coffee=where we're off [to¿
     R     [KGM    ]                                    [°w-°
        we're g- (0.3) going t' the a- (0.8) (m- a-) (0.3) th-
        that, (0.3) °.hhh° °°eh°° system? (.) f'r a .hh °k- k-°
        (fu- for-) .hh (0.8)
     C  no we're going to the (0.3) <aphasia group.>
        (0.3)
     R  aw yes, b't the g- (0.7) going to (0.2) go here;
        (0.6)
     R  the:n °the ( ).°
     C  aw yeah=we're doing this, [en then] we're going to=
     R                            [yes,    ]
     C  =the- (0.2)
     R  ye[(ah)_ ]
     C    [°the-°] the: w- >watta-< ↑where 're we going,=>wh't
->      're< we going t' [do there,]=we're having a:, °.hhh°
     R                   [°( )°     ]
        (0.7)
->   C  chr[::
     R     [tr- chr-=christmas:
->   C  christmas,=
     R  =s:- (0.4) cheer.
        (0.5)
     C  yeah¿ christmas party;
        (0.8)
=>   C  christmas lunch.
=>   R  ehlunch. °lunch.°
     C  (↓right:.)
        (0.2)
     C  °.hh° so y' c'n c:atch up on all your, (0.7)
     R  ((sniffs))
        (0.5)
     R  °( [ )° (people et [all  th]e) (0.4) [( )
     C     [people et      [(yeah.)]         [<royal: sydney.>
        (0.3)
     R  sydney, en
     C  yeah:;
```

Carol interrupts the progressivity of her TCU at 14 and 16, cutting off the word *the* twice, before producing it with a sound stretch. It is somewhat unclear as to whether these constitute DIU segments, or whether they are differently motivated. Russell's *yeah* is, perhaps, indicative of hearing the first *the* as a DIU, but the lack of sound stretching and rising intonation on this and the next *the* at 16 is not typical of this practice. Moreover, Carol's reshaping of the syntax of her TCU into a *wh* interrogative—which she quickly replaces with another TCU conveying a *wh* interrogative—is suggestive of some problems deciding how to format her turn to support Russell's production of the correctable.[12] She returns to the test question of *where are we going*, replaces it with *what are we going to do there*, and follows both with the DIU *we're having a*. That is, she halts the progression of this final TCU when (the head of) a noun phrase should properly follow, inviting Russell to take the floor and produce it; however, he does not. Carol then moves forward this TCU (and DIU) at a finer level of granularity, realising the onset of the first syllable of the correctable. This secures a response from Russell, who eventually produces the word *Christmas* in full. Carol's framing of the noun phrase with the determiner *a* (along with the framing of the *do* test question) prevents *Christmas* from being heard as the terminal item in this TCU, and hence the entirety of the correctable. She relaxes the granularity of her subsequent DIU segment, repeating *Christmas*, and projecting the production of another noun. Russell produces the word *cheer*, which is topically and syntactically fitted to Christmas, but not apposite for the progressivity of Carol's original TCU/DIU. She then receipts his response at 19, and (retrospectively) corrects the noun phrase to *Christmas party*, before self-correcting to *Christmas lunch*.

In Extract 5(a), Gail has been test questioning Hilton about where they had been during the day, focusing on its location. He had been unsuccessful with providing an answer in prior talk, resulting in Gail reissuing the test question at line 2. A long silence follows at 4, which encourages Gail to supply (what turns out to be) part of the correctable. She does so in an extremely minimal way, delivering the name *Pendle Hill* in a very quiet voice and with little movement of her mouth and face. Hilton responds by producing a more elaborate (and perhaps more accurate) version of the correctable; *Pendle Hill RSL* (i.e., a "Returned & Services League" club in the suburb *Pendle Hill*). This sets off a series

---

[12]It is the next item due after *the*, so the pressure to settle on a way forward is acute at 14 and 16.

of DIUs from Gail focusing on the individual syllables in *RSL*. She then builds on this noun phrase, adding a prepositional phrase that delivers another DIU.

Extract 5(a)

```
     001  G  .TK (0.3) you tal:ked about wh't y' did es a job- (0.3)
     002     t'da↑y? [b't where d'd we go.
     003  H          [↓yeah
     004     (2.0)
     005  G  °°pendle hi(ll)°°
     006     (0.2)
     007  H  hu- (.) ha-=ehm (0.2) pendle hill .hh ar (.) eh(s) (.)
     008     (el)
     009     (0.8)
->   010  G  ar:_
     011     (0.3)
=>   012  H  (ay),
     013     (.)
->   014  G  es:,=
=>   015  H  =es:,
     016     (2.1)
->   017  G  e-
     018     (0.3)
     019  H  a(y)=
->   020  G  =el:.=
=>   021  H  =el:.
     022     (0.5)
     023  H  el:.
     024     (0.4)
->   025  G  to our speech,
     026     (0.4)
     027  H  °eh°=.hh uhm. (0.8)
->   028  G  °s::(p[h)°
     029  H        [ehhh
     030     (1.5)
->   031  G  ↓peec[h,
=>   032  H       [°( )° (0.8) °(eh=.h)° peesh:,
     033     (4.1)
     034  G  speech what;
     035     (2.7)
     036  H  °.hhh° kg:m:::=
     037  G  =°↓group.↓°
```

Gail's initial DIUs are somewhat unusual in that she employs them for retrospective correction (cf. Extract 2), rather than to prospectively move towards production of the correctable. This is also evidenced through how Hilton responds to these DIUs, in that he repeats each component produced by Gail, rather than producing the relevant *successive* (i.e., sequentially progressive) components.[13] The form of correction pursued via the DIUs between 10 and 20 likely also shaped how Hilton came to address the subsequent DIU at 25. Gail builds this DIU as an increment (see Couper-Kuhlen and Selting 2018, pp. 94–96) to the first correctable, projecting the production of a noun. Hilton does not make substantial syntactic progress at 27, and Gail begins to operate at a finer level of granularity. However, rather than offering the beginning of the syllable of the correctable item—as we have seen in Extracts 2, 3(a), and 4—she decomposes the onset of the most proximal word of the DIU, which she produces in full at 31. As he did between 10 and 20, Hilton responds by repeating the DIU. Gail, however, orients to the absence of a sequentially progressive contribution from Hilton, moving her open hand in front of her around the middle of the long silence at line 33, and highlighting the gap with a *wh* word, i.e., *speech what*. This part of the sequence concludes with Gail quietly supplying the correctable in full.

Extract 6 captures a lengthy and complicated period of test questioning between Carol and Russell. Carol persistently attempts to have Russell produce the correctable item in the syntactic frame provided by her DIU, which itself was generated from one of Russell's turns. Her persistence is particularly marked given that Russell in fact produces the correctable item accurately on a number of occasions in response to the repeated test questioning.[14] Prior to Extract 6, Carol asked Russell whether he remembers what he had done that morning, and his answer is presented in line 1.

[13]Gail might have been seeking a "successive" contribution from Hilton at 17 with her partial production of the syllable. When it was not forthcoming, she returned to producing the entire syllable at 20.

[14]The portion of the transcript omitted has further, similar test questioning. It is omitted simply with a view to brevity.

Extract 6

```
    001  R  i had eh (1.0) firstly i (0.3) went to (0.7) uh=the
    002     (0.8) neh- (1.1) hh shop.
    003  C  ↑mm:,
    004     (0.3)
    005  R  to (0.9) use the (3.4) eh (.) ∘( )∘=gift- gift=
->  006  C  =to [bu↑y:¿     ]
    007  R      [(voucher.)]
    008     (0.8)
    009  C  the gift vouch[er.
    010  R                [no not [vo- ∘(voucher.)∘
    011  C                        [no.
    012     (0.4)
->  013  C  to: bu[↑y:,]
    014  R        [ehh ] t' bu:y (.) my: (1.0) ne:w (1.4) (f-) leg.
    015     (0.3)
    016  R  .hhh=
    017  C  =whaty' wear on y' leg,=[on the bottom ev y' leg.=
    018  R                          [(oh)
    019  R  =$(i [c(h)-)$
    020  C       [huh heh hah hah [.hhh [wha-  ]
    021  R                        [$i   [don't] ↑kno[w (do] i;)$=
    022  C                                          [hhih  ]
    023  C  =what dy' wear on y' feet_
     .   .
     .   .  ((19 lines omitted))
     .   .
    043  C  so wha- what's 'is¿ wha- what've y' got on y'r feet
    044     no:w;
    045     (1.4)
    046  R  (i) (.) sho:es.=
    047  C  =shoe.=
    048  R  =shoes n' socks.
    049  C  sho:es n' soc[ks.   ok[ay, ] .hh so t'day you went to=
    050  R               [°(socks [n')°]
    051  C  =the shop,=
    052  R  =shop (a[nd,)
->  053  C          [t' bu:y some,
    054     (1.9)
    055  R  hh (1.6) uhn- (1.5) t- tie (0.7) °tie°-=.hh (2.9) =
    056     (buy;-) no. (1.4) eh (blue bottle.) n(h)o. .hh
    057  C  b't y' j'st said it a [moment ago.   ]
    058  R                        [°(i- i don't)°] know.
    059     (0.6)
    060  C  y'know, we- what'che put on in the morning when y'
    061     get up¿ n' go f'r a wa↑lk?
    062     (1.0)
    063  R  walking sho:e.
    064     (.)
->  065  C  <sho:es:=so:>[ y'] went t' the s[hop   ]t' bu:y som[e¿
```

```
      066   R              [( )]              [(shop)]            [( )
      067      (0.3)
=>    068   R  sho:es.
=>    069   C  sho:es.
      070      (.)
      071   R  some sho[e:s.
      072   C          [shoes.
      073      (.)
      074   C  okay:.
      075      (0.6)
      076   R  then (i-)=a:fter that i we- after the- .hhh °(     )° sh-
```

Russell adds an increment to his answer at 3, but experiences difficulty developing it promptly. His production of the phrase *gift voucher* proves troublesome for Carol, who other-initiates repair at 9. Carol produces her first DIU at 6, which corrects and replaces the verb *use* in Russell's turn with the verb *buy*, and again projects the production of a noun phrase. Once the erroneous *gift voucher* has been dealt with, Carol reproduces the same DIU. This time Russell repeats the DIU frame, and then steadily develops a sequentially progressive TCU, i.e., *my new leg*. Although grammatical, and broadly on topic, it is not the correctable Carol is seeking, which she describes as *what you wear on your leg*. At 43, Carol employs a test question to solicit the correctable, and Russell successfully produces *shoes* at 46. However, instead of closing this period of correction, Carol works towards reissuing her previous DIU, reassembling Russell's and her own prior talk at 49 and 51, which culminates in another version of the DIU.[15] Russell is unable to reproduce the correctable in response, and encounters severe difficulty developing a lexically and grammatically transparent turn. Carol gears up yet another test question at 60–61, and Russell again produces the word *shoe* in response at 63, but in the phrase *walking shoe*. She then produces a very similar frame to the one at 49/51, culminating in another DIU at the end of 65. This time Russell is successful at producing the correctable in a way that conforms with the sequential progressivity of the DIU/TCU, and the period of correction is closed.

[15]The addition of *some* narrows the scope of the DIU further, and reduces the number of words Russell is expected to say.

Confirming Correctables and Moving on After DIUs

The regularity of repetition is a striking feature of the turns following the production of correctables. In particular, for correctables solicited using a DIU, there are very few instances in which conversation partners do not repeat the correctable item (cf. Extracts, 2, 3(a), 4, and 6). We might speculate that this reflects the tacit availability of the correctable, and conversation partners' epistemic and deontic primacy on its precise form (see Margutti 2010, p. 319, for a similar argument on classroom DIUs; see also Heritage and Raymond 2012).[16] Like other repair practices, corrections and DIUs suspend the line of talk in progress to address a trouble source; in this case, a problem with speaking. These repetitions, therefore, also work to confirm the repair solution, and provide for (possible) resumption of the disrupted course of action. There are also commonly minimal expansions following repetition of the correctable; particularly acknowledgement tokens (e.g., *yeah*, *mm*) and change of activity tokens (e.g., *okay*) (cf. Extracts, 2, 3(a), 4, and 6). However, in some cases, the problematicity of test questioning and correcting encourages its topicalisation.

Analysis 2: The "Morality" of Correction

In this section, we will briefly explore the moral dimensions of sustained orientation to correction and the co-production of TCU internal components. We will do this by continuing with Extracts 3 and 5. Collectively, the extracts presented so far have demonstrated that test questions and DIUs create a highly constrained sequential environment for people with aphasia. In a sense, this is highly supportive, in that it affords a maximal set of resources for designing a TCU. However, it also means that failures to produce a fitted TCU will be salient, and interactants will search for, and give, reasons for not doing so. The accounts

[16]In the present data, it is more common that people with aphasia repeat the correctable when it is retrospectively targeted by conversation partners, as per Extracts 2, 4, and 5.

(cf. Barnes 2019; Robinson 2006) that are used in these environments in the present data tend to focus on the capability of people with aphasia and interactants' responsibility for problems with talk.

Extract 3(b) follows 3(a). As it begins, Carmen mentions another of their grandchildren; a sibling of the two who had previously been named. After the test question at 55–56, Carmen does not produce any DIUs, and simply provides the correctable item at line 61, which David receipts with *okay*.

Extract 3(b)

```
055   C   °°eh-°°=d'you- d'you: know the name e' the one th't
056       ↑wasn't ↓there;
057       (1.5)
058   D   *eh:m_*
059       (1.5)
060   D   °(mt)hh .hh (.) hhhh[h
061   C                         [o:kay. that one w's <kara.>
062       (0.2)
063   D   aw *okay.*
064       (0.6)
065   C   so:, (0.4) you know we've gotta practice (0.3) the
066       names of your grandchildren.=don't we.
067       (0.2)
068   D   °yes we ↓do.°
069   C   °°yeah°°=because you know their ↑face,
070       (0.2)
071   D   yeah,
072       (0.3)
073   C   j'st can't get their >na↑mes ↓out.<
074       (0.4)
075   D   yeap_
076       (0.3)
077   D   °(yeah) it's:° p(h)art e' the aphasia.
078   C   °°↓mm.°°
079       (0.4)
080   C   ↑so=d'you remember the name:s of uhm (.) jim's two
081       children?
```

David's difficulty responding to Carmen's test questions is topicalized at 65. She asserts that *we've gotta practice the names of your grandchildren*, and David agrees. That is, she chooses to account for David's failures to produce TCUs as a matter of *practis[ing]*, and she further distinguishes

David's knowledge from his ability to *get their names out* at 69 and 73.[17] David then invokes *aphasia* as a reason for his difficulty naming.

Extract 5(b) picks up immediately after Gail has uttered the correctable item *group*. Ordinarily, one would expect the person with aphasia to repeat the correctable in the moments after, but a silence emerges at 38, and Hilton produces a minimal acknowledgement token at 39, signalling his disalignment with the sequence.[18] Hilton's next contribution is an apparently non-lexical vocalisation. At the same time, he leans back, lifts up his arm, and moves it towards his mouth. Intuitively, he appears frustrated, and perhaps distressed.

Extract 5(b)

```
038        (0.5)
039   H    mm:.
040        (1.4)
041   H    °hhm::° (aw des)
042   G    ↑well[:-
043   H         [.nhhh nhh[h
044   G                   [you k↑eep looking t' me f'r every
045        wor:d; y' don't- (°y-°) y'know? y' gotta l↑ook f'r the
046        word y'rself_
047        (4.9)
```

Gail responds immediately, beginning a turn with a high pitched *well.* Hilton closes his eyes, places his hand in front of his mouth, and draws a long breath in and out through his nose. Gail organizes her response as a rebuttal of sorts, suggesting that she has taken Hilton's conduct at 39 and 41 as indicating that she is responsible for his disalignment. Specifically, she asserts that Hilton is *looking to [her] for every word* and that he should instead *look for the word [himself]*. With this account, Gail constructs an asymmetry in their efforts, and casts Hilton as not independently contributing to the development of talk.[19]

---

[17] Through these responses, Carol also orients to the degree of problematicity caused by her test questioning and DIUs, and explicitly indicates the fact that they were dedicated to pursuing the production of talk.

[18] In fact, Hilton's disalignment is already palpable much earlier.

[19] As an aside, it is also worth noting Carol's turn at line 57 in Extract 3. She orients to Russell's severe difficulty reaching the correctable as inexplicable given his production of it *a moment ago*.

Discussion

With DIUs, interactants construct sequences of talk from practices that are conventionally used to compose individual TCUs. This provides a basis for collaboration at a finer level of granularity across turns, which may be rendered even finer depending on how minutely the DIU speaker chooses to decompose their talk. DIUs impose strong expectations on the production of talk that are aligned with the normative expectations for sequential progressivity of TCUs, i.e., the normative expectations for well-formed TCUs at various levels of granularity. People with aphasia often fail to meet these expectations in their TCUs more generally. DIUs solicit their participation in the production of talk in a way that is consistent with typical sequential progressivity (cf. Beeke et al. 2013, on the participation opportunities provided by test questions).

The DIUs in the present data bear strong resemblances to those studied in institutional contexts. There is also some evidence that the conversation partners of people with aphasia account for them in apparently paedagogical terms. However, the kind of "learning" that conversation partners might be targeting via correction is often opaque. For instance, it is unclear what sort of learning Carol was targeting via her multiple DIUs in Extract 6. Even if we take this as a coarse "learning by repetition" as per Bauer and Kulke (2004), there is little evidence in the data that Carol was treating the word *shoe(s)*, in particular, as relevant for Russell to "learn". The same could be said of *customer*, *speech group*, *Christmas party*, etc.[20] Our point here is not to dismiss "learning" as an ideological or pragmatic motivation for sustained correction; in many cases, we expect this is present in some form.[21] Instead, we will argue that viewing them through a singularly paedagogical lens underestimates how these moments are influenced by generic expectations for speaking and interacting.

[20]It is certainly the case that some words subject to test questioning—particularly proper nouns—are likely of personal importance.

[21]Framed more interactionally, we are sure that it may be invoked as an account for correcting.

Organizations of practice for speaking—like turn-taking organization, repair organization, and sequence organization—involve sets of normative expectations for designing and interpreting talk (see Schegloff 2006). By talking in turns, initiating repair, and developing sequences in certain ways, interactants are reproducing these normative expectations, and offering their practices for evaluation by others. Through test questions and DIUs, the conversation partners of people with aphasia evidence their orientation to these pressures. That is, the normative expectations associated with talking in turns are pervasively relevant for test questions and DIUs, alongside any other, more local motivations specific to the interactional scene. For example, returning again to Extract 6, Carol's persistence with having Russell respond to her DIU can be parsimoniously—but perhaps only partially—explained with reference to maintaining sequential progressivity, i.e., addressing the outstanding incompleteness of her DIU. Similarly, and more generally, test questions are first pair parts of adjacency pairs, which implicate a responsive action accomplished through a *turn-at-talk*. So, extended pursuit of a response to a test question—and, arguably, a DIU[22]—is tied to maintenance of the normative expectation for second pair parts to be carried out through speaking.[23]

It is not, however, coincidental that test questions and DIUs are common to institutional interactions and the present conversations. Rather than paedagogy, we will suggest that the concept of "agency" offers a more generic way of conceptualizing their use in both contexts. Enfield (2017) defines agency as a function of *flexibility* and *accountability*. Flexibility concerns agents' capacity for *controlling* behaviour and *composing* behaviour, while *subprehending* (i.e., anticipating) its consequences. Accountability concerns the standards by which agents' behaviour may be evaluated by others, and agents' *entitlements* and *obligations*

[22]At a number of points in the chapter, we have referred to DIUs as involving a sequence of turns. We are mindful that others might be warier about describing them in this way; hence, the "arguably" above. Our position is that the normative sequential pressure that DIUs impart is, at the very least, highly akin to conditional relevance in adjacency pairs. See Iwasaki (2008) on similar kinds of sequential pressure within a TCU.

[23]This also explains why conversation partners utter the solicited correctables when people with aphasia fail to.

to act in certain ways. Test questions and DIUs have distinctive effects on agency, in the sense that they dramatically restrict an agent's flexibility (i.e., they pre-determine the composition of talk) while acutely heightening their accountability (i.e., they impose strong normative constraints on the production of talk, *there and then*). Framed in these terms, there is nothing essentially paedagogical about these actions and practices.[24] They are instead rendered paedagogical by the ways that agents are made accountable in and through them. This means that claims about their paedagogical status in conversations involving people with aphasia should be minimally grounded in close analyses of the design of test questions and DIUs, and how interactants account for their use.[25]

There are a number of potential practical applications for understanding talk solicitation and correction in everyday conversations involving people with aphasia. As we have discussed, these actions and practices form important parts of the technical expertise of speech pathologists diagnosing and treating aphasia. With this chapter, we have begun to sketch their recurrent features, including how conversation partners solicit and receipt correctables. This can provide a reference point for exploring these practices in professional contexts—as per Merlino (2018) and Wilkinson (2013)—and discovering the ways that the technology of correction is adapted for professional tasks. It may turn out that some differences between clinicians and everyday conversation partners are quantitative rather than qualitative. In addition, repetition—as implied by Bauer and Kulke (2004)—has a large role in naming intervention for aphasia, as well as psycholinguistic studies of language processing (see, e.g., Soni et al. 2012). Describing how repetition arises organically and recurrently in courses of action

[24]A polar question from a judge to a witness is broadly consistent with this configuration of agency, yet it would be difficult to view it as, in any sense, paedagogical.

[25]It would be interesting to compare the ways people account for their use in conversation with the ways they explain their use when asked after the fact. See Barnes (2019) for related observations on the former in some of the present data.

in interaction—such as during periods of repair and correction—may contribute to characterizing the communicative conditions under which lexical retrieval and production is optimized for people with aphasia. This may then be useful for designing intervention regimes that leverage the normative infrastructure of conversation to elicit targeted word production in salient, communicatively meaningful environments.[26]

The combination of reduced flexibility and heightened accountability realized via test questions and DIUs is also interesting for considering the effects of aphasia on participation in everyday life. As we have seen, people with aphasia are still likely to experience difficulty controlling and composing their linguistic behaviour, creating moments in which they may be taken as *less agentive*, i.e., disabled. Empirical description of interaction has been underutilized for capturing the lived experience of the disability of aphasia and is likely to be valuable alongside more conventional research methods and measurement practices (e.g., Hilari et al. 2015).

Finally, it is worth considering how TCUs might contribute to conceptualizing the communicative consequences of aphasia. As we outlined previously, the direct effects of aphasia on TCUs and turn construction are beginning to be established. Delineating how the language processing impairments associated with aphasia interact with the real-time, practical and moral constraints of TCU composition holds substantial potential for novel theoretical and empirical approaches to communication and aphasia (see Beeke et al. 2007; Laakso 1997; Wilkinson et al. 2003). The data we have explored in the present chapter provide a different, but complementary source of evidence for the relevance of the TCU. By shifting granularity with DIUs, and tuning it to the internal organization of TCUs, conversation partners display their in situ understanding of the TCU as an important locus for addressing the communicative consequences of aphasia, and one way of dealing with the erosion of TCU efficacy it causes. Put another way, conversation partners' use of test questions and DIUs is indicative of the

---

[26]This is a core premise of what is usually known as Constraint Induced Aphasia Therapy (see Difrancesco et al. 2012). Barrier games are currently the standard communicative activity that is employed.

pervasive implications of aphasia for the organization of TCUs. Perhaps, then, it may be useful to consider the specific communicative effects of aphasia as, first and foremost, a *disruption to the sequential progressivity of TCUs*, which may then propagate through interactional organizations with more expansive temporalities and dependent normative expectations.

References

Aaltonen, T., & Laakso, M. (2010). Halting aphasic interaction: Creation of intersubjectivity and spousal relationship in situ. *Communication & Medicine, 7*(2), 95–106.

Barnes, S. (2016). Aphasia and open format other-initiation of repair: Solving complex trouble in conversation. *Research on Language and Social Interaction, 49*(2), 111–127.

Barnes, S. (2019). "Accountability" in interaction-focused intervention: A conversation-analytic study of therapeutic effects. *Aphasiology, 33*(2), 163–186.

Barnes, S., & Bloch, S. (2019). Why is measuring communication difficult? A critical review of current speech pathology concepts and measures. *Clinical Linguistics & Phonetics, 33*(3), 219–236.

Barnes, S., & Ferguson, A. (2015). Conversation partner responses to problematic talk produced by people with aphasia: Some alternatives to initiating, completing, or pursuing repair. *Aphasiology, 29*(3), 315–336.

Bauer, A., & Kulke, F. (2004). Language exercises for dinner: Aspects of aphasia management in family settings. *Aphasiology, 18*(12), 1135–1160.

Beeke, S., Beckley, F., Best, W., Johnson, F., Edwards, S., & Maxim, J. (2013). Extended turn construction and test question sequences in the conversations of three speakers with agrammatic aphasia. *Clinical Linguistics and Phonetics, 27*(10–11), 784–804.

Beeke, S., Wilkinson, R., & Maxim, J. (2007). Grammar without sentence structure: A conversation analytic investigation of agrammatism. *Aphasiology, 21*(3–4), 256–282.

Berthier, M. L. (2005). Poststroke aphasia: Epidemiology, pathophysiology and treatment. *Drugs and Aging, 22*(2), 163–182.

Clift, R. (2016). *Conversation analysis.* Cambridge, UK: Cambridge University Press.

Couper-Kuhlen, E., & Selting, M. (2018). *Interactional linguistics: Studying language in social interaction*. Cambridge, UK: Cambridge University Press.
Difrancesco, S., Pulvermüller, F., & Mohr, B. (2012). Intensive language-action therapy (ILAT): The methods. *Aphasiology, 26*(11), 1317–1351.
Enfield, N. J. (2017). Elements of agency. In N. J. Enfield & P. Kockelman (Eds.), *Distributed agency* (pp. 1–8). New York, US: Oxford University Press.
Enfield, N. J., & Sidnell, J. (2017). *The concept of action*. Cambridge: Cambridge University Press.
Fox, B. A., & Thompson, S. A. (2010). Responses to *wh*-questions in English conversation. *Research on Language and Social Interaction, 43*(2), 133–156.
Goodwin, C. (2003). Conversational frameworks for the accomplishment of meaning in aphasia. In C. Goodwin (Ed.), *Conversation and brain damage* (pp. 90–116). New York: Oxford University Press.
Helasvuo, M., Laakso, M., & Sorjonen, M. (2004). Searching for words: Syntactic and sequential construction of word search in conversations of Finnish speakers with aphasia. *Research on Language & Social Interaction, 37*(1), 1–37.
Heritage, J., & Raymond, G. (2012). Navigating epistemic landscapes: Acquiescence, agency and resistance in responses to polar questions. In J. P. De Rutier (Ed.), *Questions: Formal, functional and interactional perspectives* (pp. 179–192). Cambridge, UK: Cambridge University Press.
Hilari, K., Cruice, M., Sorin-Peters, R., & Worrall, L. (2015). Quality of life in aphasia: State of the art. *Folia Phoniatrica et Logopaedica, 67*(3), 114–118.
Horton, S. (2008). Learning-in-interaction: Resourceful work by people with aphasia and therapists in the course of language impairment therapy. *Aphasiology, 22*(9), 985–1014.
Iwasaki, S. (2008). *Collaborative construction of talk in Japanese conversation*. Unpublished dissertation, University of California, Los Angeles, CA.
Jefferson, G. (1987). On exposed and embedded correction in conversation. In G. Button & J. R. E. Lee (Eds.), *Talk and social organization* (pp. 86–100). Clevedon: Multilingual Matters.
Kertesz, A. (2007). *The Western aphasia battery—Revised (WAB-R)*. San Antonio, TX: PsychCorp.
Koshik, I. (2002). Designedly incomplete utterances: A pedagogical practice for eliciting knowledge displays in error correction sequences. *Research on Language and Social Interaction, 35*(3), 277–309.
Kurhila, S. (2001). Correction in talk between nature and non-native speakers. *Journal of Pragmatics, 33,* 1083–1110.

Laakso, M. (1997). *Self-initiated repair by fluent aphasic speakers in conversation*. Helsinki: Finnish Literature Society.

Laakso, M., & Klippi, A. (1999). A closer look at the 'hint and guess' sequences in aphasic conversation. *Aphasiology, 13*(4/5), 345–363.

Lee, Y.-A. (2008). Yes-no questions in the third-turn position: Pedagogical discourse processes. *Discourse Processes, 45*(3), 237–262.

Lerner, G. H. (1996). On the "semi-permeable" character of grammatical units in conversation: Conditional entry into the turn space of another speaker. In E. Ochs, E. A. Schegloff, & S. A. Thompson (Eds.), *Interaction and grammar* (pp. 238–276). Cambridge: Cambridge University Press.

Levinson, S. C. (2012). Interrogative intimations: On a possible social economics of interrogatives. In J. P. De Ruiter (Ed.), *Questions: Formal, functional and interactional perspectives* (pp. 11–32). Cambridge: Cambridge University Press.

Lindsay, J., & Wilkinson, R. (1999). Repair sequences in aphasic talk: A comparison of aphasic-speech and language therapist and aphasic-spouse conversations. *Aphasiology, 13*(4–5), 305–325.

Margutti, P. (2006). Are you human beings? Order and knowledge construction through questioning in primary classroom interaction. *Linguistics and Education, 17*(4), 313–346.

Margutti, P. (2010). On designedly incomplete utterances: What counts as learning for teachers and students in primary classroom interaction. *Research on Language and Social Interaction, 43*(4), 315–345.

Mehan, H. (1979). *Learning lessons: Social organization in the classroom*. Cambridge, MA: Harvard University Press.

Merlino, S. (2018). Assisting the client with aphasia in speech therapy: A sequential and multimodal analysis of cueing practices. *Hacettepe University Journal of Education (HUJE), 33*, 334–357.

Netz, H. (2016). Designedly incomplete utterances and student participation. *Linguistics and Education, 33*, 56–73.

Pilesjö, M. S., & Rasmussen, G. (2011). Exploring interaction between a non-speaking boy using aided augmentative and alternative communication and his everyday communication partners: Features of turn organization and turn design. *Journal of Interactional Research in Communication Disorders, 2*(2), 183–213.

Possemato, F. (2018). *Creating pre-evaluation opportunity spaces in IRE sequences: Evidence from Italian L2 classrooms in a university context*. Unpublished dissertation, University of Sydney, Sydney.

Robinson, J. D. (2006). Managing trouble responsibility and relationships during conversational repair. *Communication Monographs, 73*(2), 137–161.

Sacks, H. H., Schegloff, E. A., & Jefferson, G. (1978). A simplest systematics for the organization of turn-taking for conversation. In J. Schenkein (Ed.), *Studies in the organization of conversational interaction* (pp. 7–57). New York: Academic Press.

Schegloff, E. A. (1979). The relevance of repair to syntax-for-conversation. In T. Givon (Ed.), *Discourse and syntax* (Vol. 12, pp. 261–286). New York: Academic Press.

Schegloff, E. A. (1987). Analyzing single episodes of interaction: An exercise in conversation analysis. *Social Psychology Quarterly, 50*(2), 101–114.

Schegloff, E. A. (1996). Turn organization: One intersection of grammar and interaction. In E. Ochs, E. A. Schegloff, & S. A. Thompson (Eds.), *Interaction and grammar* (pp. 52–133). Cambridge: Cambridge University Press.

Schegloff, E. A. (2000a). On granularity. *Annual Review of Sociology, 26,* 715–720.

Schegloff, E. A. (2000b). Overlapping talk and the organization of turn-taking for conversation. *Language in Society, 29,* 1–63.

Schegloff, E. A. (2006). Interaction: The infrastructure for social institutions, the natural ecological niche for language and the arena in which culture is enacted. In N. J. Enfield & S. C. Levinson (Eds.), *Roots of human sociality: Culture, cognition and interaction* (pp. 70–96). London: Berg.

Schegloff, E. A. (2013). Ten operations in self-initiated, same-turn repair. In M. Hayashi, G. Raymond, & J. Sidnell (Eds.), *Conversational repair and human understanding* (pp. 41–70). Cambridge, UK: Cambridge University Press.

Soni, M., Lambon Ralph, M., & Woollams, A. (2012). Repetition priming of picture naming in semantic aphasia: The impact of intervening items. *Aphasiology, 26*(1), 44–63.

Wilkinson, R. (2013). The interactional organization of aphasia naming testing. *Clinical Linguistics and Phonetics, 27*(10–11), 805–822.

Wilkinson, R., Beeke, S., & Maxim, J. (2003). Adapting to conversation: On the use of linguistic resources by speakers with fluent aphasia in the construction of turns at talk. In C. Goodwin (Ed.), *Conversation and brain damage* (pp. 59–89). New York: Oxford University Press.

Wilkinson, R., Beeke, S., & Maxim, J. (2010). Formulating actions and events with limited linguistic resources: Enactment and iconicity in agrammatic aphasic talk. *Research on Language & Social Interaction, 43*(1), 57–84.

Wilkinson, S., & Weatherall, A. (2011). Insertion repair. *Research on Language and Social Interaction, 44*(1), 65–91.

9

Repair Organization in Linguistically Asymmetric Interaction: Comparing Child-Parent Conversations and Conversations Involving Speakers with Aphasia

Minna Laakso

Introduction

This study examines repair organization in linguistically asymmetric interactions which involve participants with limited competencies in producing language. Two kinds of linguistically asymmetric interactions are analyzed: (1) the interactions of 0 to 3-year-old children, and (2) the conversations of participants with aphasia, a linguistic disorder caused by brain damage. The children are in the process of learning language, whereas the adults with aphasia have lost some of their prior linguistic skills due to a stroke or a brain haemorrhage. The conversational repair organization in these two kinds of linguistically asymmetric interactions, developing and challenged, is analyzed with a specific focus on problems of speaking and how they are handled by the speakers themselves and their linguistically more competent interlocutors. The main motivation for the study is that the examination of repair organization

---

M. Laakso (✉)
University of Helsinki, Helsinki, Finland

© The Author(s) 2020
R. Wilkinson et al. (eds.), *Atypical Interaction*,
https://doi.org/10.1007/978-3-030-28799-3_9

can increase our understanding of how the problems of speaking are handled, and what kind of consequences different kinds of actions may have on linguistically asymmetric interactions.

As a "self-righting mechanism for language use in social interaction" (Schegloff et al. 1977, p. 381), repair organization handles problems in hearing, speaking and understanding language. It ensures that the participants can understand each other and that the on-going conversational activity can proceed. In ordinary conversation, repair operations are short and transient side events in which the repair operation is over within one or two speaking turns. For example, speakers reformulate their speech, or the recipients ask for clarification. Repair can thus be self- or other-initiated, but if the recipients initiate repair they leave it to the speakers to do the actual repair, i.e., self-repair is preferred over other-repair. The following examples present the four types of repair sequences typical of ordinary conversation, self-initiated self-repair, other-initiated self-repair, self-initiated other-repair, and other-initiated other-repair. Note that in the examples S refers to Self, i.e. the speaker of the problem turn, and O to Other, the recipient of the problem turn (Table 9.1).

First, self-corrections completed within the speaker's own turn or in its transition space are the most common and social-organizationally preferred type of repair in ordinary conversation (Schegloff et al. 1977). There are several kinds of self-corrections: the speaker can replace or add something or complete a word search (1 a, b, and c) (Schegloff 1979). Second, in self-initiated other-corrections the speaker of a problem turn interrupts speaking and the recipient other-completes the turn (2). This happens especially if the speaker is looking at the recipient as if seeking for assistance (Goodwin and Goodwin 1986). These repair sequences are constituted by two different speakers, Self and Other, but the end product is one syntactic construction produced by two speakers (Lerner 1996). Third, in other-initiated self-repairs the recipient requests for clarification from the prior speaker but leaves it to the speaker to do the actual repair (Dingemanse et al. 2015). Other-initiations can be open, addressing the whole prior turn, in which cases the speaker usually responds by repeating the prior turn (3a). If the problem concerns some

Table 9.1 Four trajectories of repair organization in ordinary conversation according to Schegloff et al. (1977)

1. *Self-initiated self-repair*, i.e., *self-correction*, initiated and completed by the speakers themselves (Schegloff et al. 1977, p. 363; Schegloff 1979)

a. Replacement

=>S: She was giving me a:ll the people that were go:ne **this yea:r I mean this quarter**.

b. Addition

=>S: Sure enough ten minutes later the **bell r- the doorbell rang**.

c. Word search

=>S: Yihknow Mary **uh:::: (0.3) oh:: what was it. Uh:: Tho:mpson**.

2. *Self-initiated other-repair*, e.g. word search completed by the other (Goodwin and Goodwin 1986)

→S: Her dress was white**, (0.7) uh**

=>O: **Eye let**.

3. *Other-initiated self-repair* (Schegloff et al. 1977, pp. 367–368)

a. Open-class other-initiation

S: Have you ever tried a clinic?

→O: **What**?

=>S: **Have you ever tried a clinic**?

b. Clarification request

S: Oh Sibbie's sistuh had a ba:by bo:y.

→O: **Who?**

=>S: **Sibbie's sister**.

O: Oh really?

c. Offer of candidate understanding

S: Why did I turn out this way

→O: **You mean homosexual**?

=>S: **Yes**.

4. *Other-initiated other-repair*, i.e. *other-correction* (Schegloff et al. 1977, p. 378)

a. Other-correction

S: They're going to drive ba:ck Wednesday.

=>O: **Tomorrow**.

S: Tomorrow. Right.

b. Modulated other-correction

S: Lissena pigeons.

=>O: **Quail, I think**.

part of the prior turn, the recipient can ask for clarification of that part with more specified question words (e.g., *who*, *where* etc.) and the original speaker responds only to that (3b). If the recipients have come up with some understanding but are not sure whether it is accurate, they can ask for confirmation by offering their current understanding as a candidate, which the speaker can accept or reject (3b). Other-initiated self-repairs consist of a sequence of two turns by different speakers, Other and Self. The fourth, less common and dispreferred, option is other-correction in which the recipient directly corrects the prior talk of the other speaker (4a). Being dispreferred actions, other-corrections can be "modulated", i.e., marked as uncertain (4b). Other-corrections are made within one turn (4b) but sometimes receive a confirming response from the original corrected speaker (4a). It is of interest for the current study that according to Schegloff et al. (1977) "*one exception to the highly constrained occurrence of other-correction*" is adult-child interaction *w*here other-corrections are a means to socialize children to the norms of language and social interaction. They also noted that other-corrections may occur in conversations involving not-yet-competent speakers regardless of age. But do other-corrections similarly occur in other linguistically asymmetric interactions, e.g. in conversations involving speakers with aphasia, and generally, what happens to the organization of repair in linguistically asymmetric interactions?

According to Schegloff et al. (1977, p. 381) other-correction is "*one vehicle for socialization*", a device for dealing with those "*who are still learning to become adequate self-monitors and self-correctors*" of their own talk. Based on limited data, Schegloff et al. (1977) also hypothesized that adults' other-correction of children's speech is only transitional, and, as the children's linguistic competence grows, self-repair supersedes other-correction. The hypothesis of adults other-correcting children has been confirmed in some later studies that have shown that adults' other-corrections are more numerous than children's self-repairs in child-adult interactions at least in the early phases of language acquisition and when error corrections are considered (Norrick 1991; Chouinard and Clark 2003; Laakso 2010; Morgenstern et al. 2013). If researchers also consider types of self-repairs other than error correction, e.g., reformulations and additions, child self-repairs have been found to be more common than adult other-corrections by the time the child produces multi-word utterances (e.g., Forrester 2008; Morgenstern et al. 2013). Children can also attempt to self-repair in longer sequences if the adult does not understand their talk (Forrester 2008; Laakso et al. 2010).

Problems of speaking and subsequent breakdowns in the progressivity of interaction are frequent in conversations involving participants with aphasia (PWA) (e.g., Lubinski et al. 1980). As a linguistic deficit, aphasia hampers efficient self-repairing of language problems (Laakso 1997; Wan and Liao 2018). Studying conversations in speech-language therapy, Laakso (2003) found that when aphasic speakers get into trouble in conversation, the interlocutors could either join in the repair activity or withdraw from working with the difficulty. If the interlocutors did not take part in repairing the problems, but only gave minimal follow-up responses, the PWAs had to repair the problems by themselves with their limited linguistic resources. This often leads to long sequences of self-repair efforts. Prolonged attempts at self-repair can lead to delicate and potentially embarrassing displays of linguistic incompetence (Wilkinson 2007) or increased affect displays (Laakso 2014). In particular, difficulty in lexical retrieval may lead to lengthy repair sequences in which both the speakers with aphasia and the interlocutors try to repair the problems collaboratively (Milroy and Perkins 1992; Laakso and Klippi 1999). The recipients try to co-construct the problematic utterance and offer the strongest possible interpretation that requires least collaborative effort from the speaker with aphasia (Milroy and Perkins 1992; Goodwin 1995; Heeschen and Schegloff 1999). In interpreting problematic utterances, inferences from background information and context play a much more important role than in most other interactions (Ahlsén 1993). In a case study, Oelschlaeger and Damico (2000) found a wife of a PWA used four strategies to repair problems of lexical retrieval: guess, alternative guess, completion, and closing. In another case, Lindsay and Wilkinson (1999) found a husband to frequently revise and correct the speech production errors of his wife with aphasia. Thus it seems that the type of problem may have an effect on the repair trajectories: with difficulties of lexical retrieval interlocutors offer words to complete the search and with sound errors even other-corrections are used in conversations involving participants with aphasia.

The aim of this article is to describe the organization of repair in linguistically developing vs. challenged conversation. This will be done by inspecting how the problematic speaking turns of young children and speakers with aphasia are handled by the speakers themselves and their interlocutors. The focus of the analysis is on the structure of repair sequences, and all four trajectories of repair organization are inspected. A question addressed will be: are the trajectories similar to the overall organization of repair described by Schegloff et al. (1977) or are there differences in the occurrence of self-repair vs. other-correction and even in the preference for self-correction in these linguistically asymmetric interactions?

Data

Children's interaction data discussed in this chapter come from The Helsinki Longitudinal Child Language Corpus (HLC) in which five children were followed longitudinally from 10 months to 5 years of age (see Table 9.2). Here the data from the children at between 1 and 3 years of age are analyzed as the children were still in early stages of their language development at this point. Children's everyday interactions with parents were video recorded at their homes. The data consist of mainly two-party interactions and activities such as playing with toys, reading picture books, card games, feeding etc. Videotaped interactions of speakers with aphasia were collected in the project *Managing problems of speaking and understanding in conversations of speakers with aphasia* and consisted of 10 home recordings and 10 clinical recordings in speech-language therapy sessions (Table 9.2). Home interactions took place with family members or friends in activities such as drinking coffee, talking at the kitchen table or in the living room. These were mainly two-party interactions except for two cases. In the speech-language therapy data the discussions took place in the beginning of a therapy session and dealt with therapy issues and recent life activities of the client. These were mainly two-party interactions except for one case where the spouse of the PWA was also present.

Table 9.2 Information about the data analyzed

Situation	Child-Parent	PWA-Interlocutor	
Data Source	The Helsinki Longitudinal Child Language Corpus (HLC)	The project Managing the problems of speaking and understanding in conversations of speakers with aphasia	
Setting	Home	Home	Speech-language therapy
Number of participants	Five children	10 adults with aphasia	10 adults with aphasia
Chronological Details	Longitudinal follow-up from 1 to 3 years of age	Cross-sectional	Cross-sectional and longitudinal
Co-interactants	Parents	Family members (friends)	Speech-language therapists (spouse)
Kind of data	Video recorded	Video recorded	Video recorded
Participation framework	Mainly two-party interactions	Mainly two-party interactions	Mainly two-party interactions
Activities	*Playing with toys, reading* picture books, card games, feeding	*Drinking coffee, talking at* the kitchen table or in the living room	*Discussions in the beginning* of sessions on recent life activities of the client

The data were transcribed and analyzed according to the conventions of conversation analysis (e.g., Schegloff 2007). Both speech and relevant gestures were included in the transcript. All names are pseudonyms. The activities in different data sets are somewhat different but the phenomena studied are similar to a great extent: we collected instances where the speaker, either a child or an adult with aphasia, encountered some difficulty in speaking. The difficulty could be manifested as overt phonological or lexical errors or as cutting-off and pausing the on-going speech. In the following, all four repair trajectories, self-initiated self-repair, self-initiated other-repair, other-initiated self-repair, and other-correction, are inspected in both data sets.

Self-Initiated Self-Repair

Self-initiated self-repairs were common in both data sets. Children produced their first self-repairs before two years of age when they started to produce single words. The following extracts present self-initiated self-repairs by children at the age of one year and 8 months (see Example 1). The extracts from Juha's and Nuppu's conversations show self-repairs focusing on phonological (1) and lexical (2) aspects of a single word.

Example 1. Early self-initiated self-repairs by children at the age of one year and 8 months.

(1) Nuppu 1;8 and her mother are picking up plastic toys and inspecting them.

```
01 Nuppu:     Manen- (.) banaanni.
              manen-     banana
              ((Nuppu searches for a toy banana from a bag of toys))
```

(2) Juha 1;8 and her mother are playing with cardboard pictures of different everyday items.

```
01 Juha:      Mum-  äiti? ((Juha turns towards the mother))
              Gran- mother

02 Mother:    Mmmh?
              ((Juha shows his mother what he is doing with a toy spoon))
```

In (1) Nuppu is searching a bag filled with plastic toys with her mother watching her do it. Her turn in line 1 can be understood as a request to mother to help in looking for a toy banana she is trying to find. In her turn Nuppu cuts of the word, *manen-*, and replaces it with a more adult-like form *banaanni* of the word *banaani* 'banana'. Nuppu thus self-repairs the phonological form of a word. In (2) Juha addresses his mother first with the word that seems to be emerging as *mummi* 'grandmother' but he cuts it off and replaces it with the word *äiti* 'mother'. Juha thus self-repairs the lexical choice he has made. Both repaired words are effectively monitored and immediately self-corrected by the children whose speech is developing in a regular way.

Participants with aphasia also produced self-initiated self-repairs in their conversations. Due to their challenges with speaking, self-repair attempts were often prolonged consisting of several attempts to accomplish a self-repair. In Example 2 there are three extracts of self-repairs by different aphasic speakers. In the first one, Kalevi, a 63-year-old man with chronic non-fluent agrammatic aphasia, is self-repairing his utterance when explaining to his wife what he is going to do in the evening. In the second one, Hannu, a 33-year-old man with acute fluent neologistic aphasia, is trying to name the company he worked in before his illness. In the third one, Niina, a 55-year-old woman with difficulties in lexical retrieval, is explaining what she has been doing at home.

Example 2. Self-initiated self-repairs by three different speakers with aphasia.

(1) Kalevi with non-fluent aphasia and his wife Eliisa are drinking afternoon coffee.

01 Kalevi:	Minä toi khhh	kauppa	toi (.)	**leh-**	**toi lehti**?	
	I that	store	that	{magazine}	that magazine	
	I that khhh	shop	that(.)	mag-	that magazine?	
02 Eliisa:	*Nii?*					
	Yes?					
03 Kalevi:	Ja ((coughs))	**kir-**	**kirje (.)**	**kirja.**		
	and	{letter}	letter	book		
	And ((coughs))	let-	letter (.)	book.		

(2) Hannu is talking with his speech-language therapist (SLT) in the beginning of a therapy session.

```
01 SLT:      Ei pankki ollu.
             It wasn't a bank?

02 Hannu:    Ei (.) kun (.) se on (0.6) PESAppi (0.8) setappi, jees. he he
             No (.) but (.) it is (0.6) PEsappi (0.8) setappi, yes. he he

03 SLT:      Etappi, [e:i?
             Etappi, [no::?
04 Hannu:            [Se-tamp- (0.6) pes- (0.2) peramppi.
                     ((neologistic non-words: not translated))
05           (1.0)

06 Hannu:    Semmonen on (.) tuola.
             Such     is (.) there.

07 SLT:      Semmone firma.
             Such a company.
```

(3) Niina is talking with her speech-language therapist (SLT) in the beginning of a therapy session.

```
01  SLT:     no  mitäs    sä  oot nyt kotona puuhaillu.hh
             well what have you been doing at home now

02 Niina:    .mt  no< (0.2) #ää# (0.8)  hh .mt
             .tch well      #er#        hh .tch
                                  ((Niina shakes her head))

03           la- lii- ö noita< (0.8).mt
             la- li- uh those  (0.8) .tch
                           ((Niina looks and grabs her sleeve))

04           mm [pes/sy<(.) asti- aas- >ei astioit<
                [wash-PCP   dish  dish NEG dish-PL-PAR
             mm [washed dish- diis- not dishes
05  SLT:        [((SLT leans forward, opens mouth))

06  Niina:   >no astioit     tietysti $ainahan    niitä
             PRT dish-PL-PAR of.course always-CLI they-PAR
             well dishes of course sure there are always

07           [tulee< (h), no  m(h)utta$ joo he he
             [come-3      PRT but       yeah
             [dishes          but yeah he he
08  SLT:     [$nii:h  hi hi niitä  joutuu  aina(h) pe(h)seen$..hh
             [$yeah:h he he those one must always  wash$. .hh
```

In (1) Kalevi first cut-offs the word *leh-* and then produces *lehti* 'magazine/newspaper' (line 1) when describing what he is going to buy from a shop (line 2). As he first says *kirje* 'a letter', he immediately self-corrects and replaces it with *kirja* 'a book'. There is thus a sound error that he self-corrects. Kalevi's self-repair is an immediate phonemic replacement showing effective monitoring of his own speech production.

In (2) Hannu is trying to say the name of the company where he has worked, but the sound form of the company name is neologistic and unrecognizable (line 2). He tries to self-repair the word in several subsequent attempts but ends up producing more distorted versions of it (line 4) and the self-repair is not successful. He solves the problem with a general explanation *sellanen on tuolla* 'such is there' and the SLT receives this by offering her candidate understanding *sellanen firma* 'such a company' (lines 6–7).

In (3) Niina first pauses and searches for a word (line 2), then cut-offs some attempts at a word (line 3), then again searches and finds the verb form *pessy* 'washed' (line 4), and finally produces cut-off attempts at the word *astioita* 'dishes' which she immediately rejects as not what she was meaning to produce. Thus the self-repair is not fully successful here either. The problem is solved by a humorous comment from Niina that there are always dishes to wash, to which the SLT joins with an affiliating utterance which displays understanding: she too recognizes a similar experience. It can be seen from Extracts 2 and 3 that if self-repairs are less successful they nevertheless tend to become dealt with using some kind of compromise resolutions or humorous noticings.

In the extracts above we can see how participants with aphasia are aware of their phonological and lexical challenges in producing speech. They self-initiate self-repair but self-repairing may take several attempts and even lead to phonologically more distorted words (2) or lexical items the speaker was not meaning to produce (1 and 3). When comparing self-initiated self-repairs by children and by the participants with aphasia it can be noticed that children's self-corrections are more immediate and effortless. Participants with aphasia self-initiate self-repair but their ability to complete the repair by themselves varies with regard to the linguistic challenges they have. One notable difference is also that in children's early interactions the repairables are usually simple noun phrases with visibly present referents, whereas in the case of adults with aphasia the referents are parts of an emerging utterance in which the referents are not necessarily visible or known to the co-participants.

Self-Initiated Other-Completed Repair Sequences

When the problematic turns by young children and adults with aphasia were examined, it was found that recipients were active in both settings. With children, parents completed preverbal children's very early expressions, whereas in the case of aphasia, recipients offered candidate completions when the PWAs were searching for words. These are collaborative and sequentially composed repairs.

When children's early expressions were not recognizable as normative words of a language, the parents offered candidate understandings, which were often interpretations of the child's multi-modally produced expressions. In Example 3, the parent interprets the one-year-old child's gesturing and word-like vocalization, a proto-word, which does not yet have any referential meaning. Proto-words consist of one articulatory movement during phonation, such as the closure of the airway with the tongue (Menn 1983). The child, Nuppu, is here 1;0 and is only able to use proto-word vocalizations and pointing gestures to express herself (c.f. Goodwin 1995, for the treatment of similar kinds of multimodal expressions by a person with severe aphasia).

Example 3. Nuppu, 1;0, is sitting in her high chair and her mother is feeding her porridge.

```
01 Mother:   ((mother is feeding Nuppu)) (5.0)

02 Nuppu:    ↑ÄT:TI, ((Nuppu looks and points at the camera))

03           (2.0) ((N continues pointing and looks at the mother))

04 Mother:   Nii.  (1.0) Siel  on tä↑ti,
             PRT         there is auntie
             Right.(1.0) It is auntie there.

05           (0.8)((N continues to look at the camera, M feeds her))
```

With her pointing gesture and proto-word *ätti*, Nuppu is able to label a referent, that is, the researcher and/or the camera (line 2). The repair sequence is not self-initiated by the child pausing or interrupting her talk. She just freezes her pointing gesture and looks at her mother, which may be interpreted as a non-verbal request. Her mother first recognizes her action with *nii* (right) and then offers a more precise candidate label to the referent, i.e., *täti*, an auntie (line 4). Parents' reformulations or candidate offers for unclear referents enable the children's learning of words (Chouinard and Clark 2003; Laakso et al. 2010). Little by little children become more aware of the qualities of words as they engage in recurrent sequential routines of the following sort:

1. Child: produces a problematic utterance and displays embodied orientation towards a referent
2. Parent: completes child's action with a candidate referent
3. Child: moves on or rejects the candidate

Children at this early age do not usually confirm parents' candidate offers but just move on. Children may, however, reject parents' candidates when they, for example, request an object and are not given one (Laakso et al. 2010). Then they try to reformulate their expressions to be more understandable, thus making their first attempts at self-repair sequentially, i.e., not within the same turn.

Similarly, family members may offer candidate completions to the utterances of adult speakers with aphasia. These candidates are based on their shared knowledge and the emerging linguistic construction of the PWA's turn. In Example 4, Armi, an elderly lady with aphasia is talking in her living room with her visiting middle-aged daughter, Oili, about the TV programmes they have recently been watching. Armi has difficulty constructing her turn due to problems of lexical retrieval (lines 1–2) and Oili completes her word searching with a candidate indicating that Armi had been watching the TV debate of the presidential candidates (line 3). Note that Oili completes the turn when Armi starts to look at her (line 2; cf. Goodwin and Goodwin 1986).

Example 4. Armi, a woman with non-fluent aphasia and Oili, Armi's daughter

```
01 Armi:     Niin (.) tota Ajan ko(t)taanen kakkonen   ja  ja tota(.)↑uutiset
              So    (.) er   Current.affairs channel.two and and er (.)↑news

                                                                      O_______
02           ja tuota(0.5)ja sitten (0.8) öö tuli tuota öö ↑eilen (0.6) tota
             and er (0.5) and then (0.8) uh came er  uh ↑yesterday (0.6) er

03 Oili:     Niin presidentti[ehokkaat.
             Right the presidential candidates
04 Armi:                     [Niin.
                             [Right.
05 Oili:     Kattoik[ko sen.
             Did.you.watch that.
```

In Example 4, when the frequent conversational partner (FCP) completes the PWA's turn by offering a candidate, the interactive sequence is structurally quite similar to Example 3, that is:

1. PWA: produces problematic utterance projecting a potential referent
2. FCP: completes PWA's action with a candidate referent
3. PWA: confirms the candidate.

The candidate completion is designed linguistically in the same manner as in Example 3: the recipient first uses the particle *niin* (right) which shows that she mutually recognizes the referent projected in the PWA's turn. In Finnish, *niin* (appr. 'right') is a particle that clearly recognizes and affiliates with the previous speaker, whereas *joo* 'yes' is more neutral and factual (Sorjonen 2001). It is noteworthy that as soon as Armi has recognized the word 'presidential' she confirms the offered completion by also using *niin*. By beginning with *niin* Armi gives an affiliative recognition to her daughter's assisting completion. As compared to children, people with aphasia more explicitly confirm or reject the candidates offered to them. By confirming the accuracy of other-completions, PWAs display their epistemic authority regarding their own speech. Through their confirmations the PWAs display that they know what they want to say, but they just cannot successfully produce it. As a contrast to the PWA's clear actions of self-initiation of repair and confirmation of the recipient's other-completion, children in their earliest interactions with parents do not explicitly self-initiate repair or confirm the candidates their parents offer.

It is noteworthy that gazing at the recipient is used to seek assistance in completing the utterance. Armi's word searching makes her speaking turn progress slowly and her daughter's candidate completion comes when Armi looks at her. Searching and gaze behaviors show that Extract 4 is a self-initiated other-completed repair sequence, in which an other-completion efficiently solves the problem of progressivity in the conversation.

Other-Initiated Self-Repair

Parents of children older than two years of age tend to other-initiate repair by asking questions. This regularly occurs when the children already use multi-word utterances and have a larger vocabulary, and when unclear referents may also not be present (see Example 5.2) or the meanings have to be inferred (Example 5.4).

Example 5. Types of parental clarification requests.
(1) Juha (3;0) and his mother are playing with cars on the traffic carpet.

```
01 Juha:      Tossa, ((points at a place in the traffic carpet))
              There,

02            (0.7)

03 Mother:    £M(h)itäh,£
               What

04 Juha:      Tossa se voi olla,
              There  it  can be
```

(2) Liisa (3;0) and her mother are talking about Liisa's father and big sister Hilma.

```
01 Liisa:     Mut isi   voi hakea suoraan  sieltä     Hilman?
              but Daddy can fetch directly there-ELA Hilma-ACC
              But Daddy can pick up Hilma from there directly?

02 Mother:    Mistä,
              where-ELA
              From where

03 Liisa:     Päiväkodista,
              daycare.centre-ELA
              From the daycare centre
```

(3) Nuppu (3;0) and her mother are playing a fishing game with pictures of animals

```
01 Nuppu:     Sitten <poss:u>?
              then    pig
              Then    a pig?

02            (2.0) ((Nuppu lifts up the picture of a cow))

03 Nuppu:     Pos:[°su°. ((Nuppu gives the picture to her mother))
              A pig.
04 Mother:        [Onko se possu,
                  [Is   it a pig,

05 Nuppu:     ↑On,
              It is,
```

(4) Liisa (3;0) and her mother are negotiating their play with small toy animals.

```
01 Liisa:    Mut nää-   mut nää   tiput      nyt kelää, (.)
             But these- but collect now these chicken

02           mut .hh mut nää   tiput      on    vielä munia?
             but     but these chicken are  still  eggs
             ((Liisa collects chicken into a basket))

03 Mother:   Ai ne    on  niinku    leikisti   munia    vai,
             oh they are like.that as.in.play eggs-PAR or
             Oh you like pretend they are eggs or what,

04 Liisa:    Mm-m.
```

As we can see in the four extracts in Example 5, the parents no longer collaboratively construct their 3-year-old children's speech. Instead, they challenge their children by asking questions that other-initiate repair and promote the children's self-repair of their own utterances. This is understandable as 3-year-old children are already competent language users and can clarify their own intentions. In extract (1), after the mother's open-class other-initiation, Juha is able to repeat and specify his prior expression regarding a place-referent *tossa* 'there' (lines 3–4). Similarly, in (2), after her mother's question, Liisa specifies that she meant a day care centre when she used the expression *sieltä* 'from there' in her problematic utterance (lines 2–3). In (3), instead of directly correcting, the mother asks a challenging question 'Is it a pig' when Nuppu names a picture of a cow as a pig (lines 3–4). Interestingly, Nuppu displays her epistemic authority on the matter by claiming that she thinks that the picture represents a pig (line 5). In extract (4) the mother offers her candidate understanding in which she inquires what the child means. It is also noteworthy that the sequences now consist of three parts: (1) the child's problem turn, (2) the parent's other-initiation, and (3) the child's self-repair (Extracts 1–3) or confirmation of the candidate understanding (4). At the age of three children are thus already treated similarly to adults, i.e., as independent actors having epistemic authority regarding their own speech.

In connection with aphasia, other-initiations with questions are more frequent in speech-language therapy sessions than in home conversations (cf. Laakso 2015). In speech-language therapy sessions SLTs tend to ask question to solve the problems of speaking (see Example 6).

Example 6. Niina and her SLT are talking about Niina's recent home activities.

```
01 SLT:     $nii:h hi hi niitä joutuu  aina(h) pe(h)seen$..hh
            yea:h he he those one must always wash

02 Niina:   JOO,
            yeah

03 Niina:   mut vähä: tämmösiä:        ee
            but a little these kinds of er

04          pu↑seroa oli o-   laitettu ja (0.2)ja [k- ka-
            shirt    had been put       and       and
           ((Niina grabs her left sleeve))((Niina nods))
05 SLT:                                           [>ook   sä  pessy<
                                                  [have you been washing

06          TALvivaatteita      pois vai,
            winter-cloth-PL-PAR away or
            winter clothes (to put them) away or what,

07 Niina:   e::i ku ihan [ihan tavallista
            no::    just [just ordinary
08 SLT:                  [i/han ihan tavallista pyykkiä.
                         [just  just ordinary   laundry.

09 Niina:   iha tavallista pyykkiä, montaa sorttia.
            just ordinary laundry, many sorts.

10 SLT:     nii.
            right.
```

Here the SLT has listened to Niina's explanation of what she recently has been doing at home (lines 3–4, see also Extract 3 in Example 2). In lines 5–6 the SLT then makes an other-initiation of repair, a candidate understanding that Niina has been washing winter clothes to put them away as it is spring time and summer is approaching. In forming her candidate understanding she makes use both of the current time of the year and Niina's words and gesturing. Niina however rejects the candidate understanding and specifies that she has just been washing ordinary laundry. It is noteworthy that the difficult word, laundry, that Niina has not been able to find, is here first produced by the SLT but the correction is embedded in a repetition (cf. Jefferson 1987). As with the interactions involving children, the repair sequence here consists of three turns: the PWA's problem turn, the SLT's other-initiation, and the PWA's self-repair/confirmation. However, with adult speakers with aphasia the recipients' other-initiations tend to be offers of candidate understandings, rather than the challenging questions directed towards the 3-year old children.

Other-Correcting the Linguistically Less Competent Speaker

Parental other-corrections focusing on the children's pronunciation and lexical choices were quite common when the children were approaching two years and were already producing one-word utterances (c.f. Laakso 2010). In the following two extracts (1 and 2 in Example 7) the parent other-corrects the phonemic structure of the word the child has produced. In (3) the parent other-corrects the child's lexical selection.

Example 7. Nuppu 1;10; and her mother are looking at a picture book (1) Mother points at the picture of a frog.

```
01 Mother:   Entäs täällä?
             And here?
             ((mother points to a picture of a frog in a book))

02           (0.8)

03 Nuppu:    Ampuuko.

04 Mother:   Sammakko.
             a frog

05 Nuppu:    (H)ammakko.
```

(2) Nuppu points at the picture of a rake.

```
01 Nuppu:     mm hevava
              ((Nuppu points at the picture of a rake))

02 Mother:    harava
              a rake

03 Nuppu:     havava

04 Mother:    joo:o
              ye:ah
```

(3) Nuppu points at the picture of a wasp.

```
01 Nuppu:     Mmm (kh)aapanen.
              Mmm  a fly
              ((Nuppu points at the picture of a wasp))

02 Mother:    Se on ↑ampiainen,
              It is a wasp,

03 Nuppu:     Ampinen↑
              a wasp

04            (1.6)
```

All these cases can be considered as other-corrections. The target of the child's expression is clearly visible in the picture book at which the mother and the child are looking and pointing, and the parent immediately other-corrects the name of the referent. In (1) and (2) the parent repeats the word the child has produced using correct adult-equivalent pronunciation (lines 4 and 2, respectively). It is noteworthy that the child also immediately repeats the mother's correction and in doing so is able to approach the adult-like production (Extract 1, line 5; Extract 2, line 3). This sequential practice clearly enhances the child's learning of the phonemic word forms. In extract (3) the parent other-corrects the child's lexical selection and child also again repeats the corrected word thus learning new words and more precise meanings (Extract 3, lines 2 and 3). The other-corrections are produced in a manner of embedding them into the labelling of pictures in a book and are not treated as dispreferred in any way. On the contrary, children happily repeat the parental corrections in learning the names of the different referents displayed in the picture book.

To conclude; in 2-year-old children's conversations with parents, other-corrections form a recurrent sequence of three turns as follows:

1. Child: problematic word
2. Parent: other-correction
3. Child: repetition of the corrected item.

As the children grow a little older, the parents no longer use these kinds of immediate corrective repetitions, or they use them only occasionally, when there is, for example, a specific proper name that the child tries to pronounce (see Example 8). In this example, three-year-old Juha is playing with cars with his mother on a traffic carpet on the floor. As Juha tries to say the brand name of a car, his mother other-corrects the phonemic form of the word (line 3). The pausing before the problematic word may display searching or other efforts at self-initiating repair by Juha.

Example 8. Juha's (3;0) and his mother are playing on the traffic carpet

```
01 Juha:      Tässäpä (se) on (h)eeppo käyä tankkaamassa?
              It is so easy to fill up the tank here
              ((Juha plays in front of a plastic petrol station))

02 Juha:      Siitä se lähtee se Fiiat (0.3) Phlavo (make of a car)
              From there it goes this Fiat (0.3) Phlavo

03 Mother:    Bravo

04            (1.9)

05 Juha:      Plavo
```

After the mother's other-correction Juha does not repeat the corrected form immediately but produces the imitated phonemic form of the brand name after quite a long pause. The length of the pause after the mother's correction may reflect the fact that direct other-corrections are already treated as a less preferred option in the interaction of three-year-old children. By three-years-old these kinds of other-corrections are also very rare (cf. Laakso 2010).

Similarly, family members may other-correct the phonemic form of a word produced by a speaker with aphasia. In Example 9, Lauri, a 79-year-old man with conduction aphasia is talking in his living room with his two teenaged grandsons, twins, who are currently preparing for the final school ending matriculation exams. Lauri runs into trouble when he is commenting on these preparations (line 1).

Example 9. Lauri is discussing in his living room with his young grandsons Aku and Tommi.

```
01 Lauri:    Teidän pitää (1.1) nyt sitte (.) preta- peretal eng[lang-
             So you need to(1.1)now then  (.) preta- peretal Englis-
02 Aku:                                                        [Prepata.
                                                               [prepare

03 Lauri:    Nii.
             Right.

04 Aku:      Joo.
             Yes.

05 Tommi:    Ni:i.
             That's ri:ght.
```

Aku other-corrects Lauri's hesitant and self-repairing expression *preta-peretal with* the word *prepata* 'prepare' (line 2). Lauri confirms this with *Nii* 'right' thus confirming the assistance offered (line 3), and both boys then answer Lauri's original comment about having to prepare for the exams (lines 4 and 5). Here the other-correction immediately produces the problematic word and is thus orienting to promote the progressivity of the interaction. The correction is confirmed by the aphasic speaker. As in Example 4, here the confirmation is also produced with the affiliating particle *nii.* Other-correction is thus not treated as dispreferred or problematic. This may reflect the fact that the other-correction solves the problem efficiently and enhances the progressivity of conversation when speech problems emerge. As with the other-corrections in child-parent conversations, the repair sequence is structured in three turns:

1. PWA: problematic word
2. FCP: other-correction
3. PWA: confirmation with *nii* (or sometimes repetition of the corrected item).

However, unlike the children, the PWAs do not usually repeat the correction. They just confirm the correction displaying a stronger epistemic authority on their speech production. The PWAs do not place themselves in the position of a learner of language in the same manner as children do. Furthermore, in comparison with the children's data, where parental other-corrections were regularly used with children who were approaching two years of age, in the aphasia data other-corrections were rare and focused almost solely on phonemic errors in which the word was immediately recognizable in its local context.

Conclusion of the Findings

It can be concluded that in the children conversations, parents elaborate on their 0 to 3-year-old children's utterances by first completing their early multimodal expressions (1-year-olds), then other-correcting phonemic and lexical errors (2-year-olds), and finally by other-initiating repair with questions (3-year-olds). The parents thus change their way of dealing with their children's utterances as their children's language develops. As a whole, the parents' other-contributions are adjusted to the child's stage of language development and can be seen to enhance it. First, the parents co-construct their children's early vocalizations and gesturing, introducing the world of language and the relationship between words and their referents to the children. Later, when the children are approaching two years of age and already producing single words, the parents other-correct the children's lexical selection and the phonemic realization of those words, and children imitate their parents' corrections. Simultaneously, when approaching two years of age, children start to monitor their own speech and produce their first self-initiated self-repairs, which become more and more common when the children approach the age of 2;6 (Laakso 2010). With three-year-olds, the parents use multiple ways to other-initiate repair with questions that enhance their children's own efforts to self-repair. In parent-child interaction there is thus a developmental continuum from co-construction of meaning to other-initiation of repair. It is noteworthy that other-corrections are not treated as dispreferred actions and self-initiated self-repairs become more common as the children grow older. Also, the structure of parent-initiated repair sequences gradually develops from a two-part to a three-part structure: in the two-part structure the child's turn is treated as a repairable by the parent and in the three–part structure children start to act in a third position. In the third position of the repair sequence the children first repeat parental other-corrections and then, at three years of age, already self-repair after the parents' other-initiation, thus displaying their emerging epistemic authority on their own speech.

Considering interactions involving participants with aphasia, co-constructive elaborations are also common, especially in home interactions with familiar conversational partners. At the same time, PWAs regularly show awareness of their problems and self-initiate repair but are not very efficient in self-completing the repair. Family members tend to align to ordinary conversational practices to enhance the progressivity of the interaction: they complete PWAs' word searches and offer their candidate understandings of problematic expressions. Occasionally, FCPs may even other-correct PWAs' phonemic errors. FCPs' other-contributions appear to be somewhat dependent on the type and severity of the PWA's aphasia: if the PWA can construct sentences the partners offer one-word completions to match the sentence, whereas the more problematic expressions are managed with candidate understandings. Questions offering candidate understandings are used more often by speech-language therapists.

As compared to children, there were differences in the construction of repair sequences. In conversations involving speakers with aphasia, repair sequences always consisted of (at least) three turns. First, the sequences were clearly self-initiated by the PWAs, and followed by FCPs' other-contributions in the second position. After the FCPs' other-contributions the PWAs confirmed or rejected them in the third position. In sum, in connection with aphasia repair organization seems to be skewed towards self-initiated other-completed repair and repairs were done collaboratively with distributed speakership. Although the speakership may have been distributed, the participants with aphasia displayed their epistemic authority on their own speech production and the repair activities concerning it by confirming the FCPs' other-contributions. This reflects the underlying preference for self-repair although it cannot be realized due to the challenges brought by aphasia. Furthermore, the non-aphasic conversational partners regularly provided other-contributions as a response to the PWAs gestures (e.g. gazing and pointing at their recipients to invite them to participate in repair) which displays their orientation to the preference for self-repair.

Discussion

In this study, both children acquiring language and adults with aphasia were found to initiate self-repair on their own speech. In the case of children the first self-initiated self-repairs emerged before two years of age, whereas adults with aphasia regularly self-initiated but could not always self-complete the repair. This early emergence of the preference for self-correction in parent-child interaction is in line with the findings of the case study by Forrester (2008). Adults with aphasia were seldom directly corrected and they were given time to self-repair and find their words, which they often could not do by themselves, as several previous studies have noted (e.g., Laakso 1997, 2003; Wilkinson 2007). When the children were under two years of age, the parents also corrected their children's speech directly. This finding is in line with earlier observations that children learning language are more readily other-corrected by adults (e.g., Schegloff et al. 1977; Morgenstern et al. 2013). However, parents did not other-correct children over two years of age but a preference for self-correction was already evident: children produced self-initiated self-repair and parents other-initiated by asking questions. In connection with aphasia, familiar conversational partners often other-completed their utterances. Despite this, participants with aphasia retained their epistemic authority by confirming or rejecting the other-contributions of their conversational partners.

What Happens to the Organization of Repair in Linguistically Asymmetric Interactions?

As compared to ordinary conversation, the intersubjective organization of repair can be seen as somewhat altered in linguistically asymmetric interactions. This alteration is reflected in the fact that other-contributions, such as other-completions and other-corrections by the linguistically more competent participants, are pronounced in both linguistically developing and challenged interactions. In children's developing interactions other-correction is a transient phenomena concerning mainly children in their early phases of linguistic development, whereas in interactions involving aphasic speakers self-initiated other-completion may be a more permanent feature. Inevitably, linguistic competence, shared knowledge/epistemic access, and the transparency of on-going action (i.e. the emerging turn and its sequential context) affect the construction of repair sequences. Data from asymmetric interactions suggests that in them the organization of repair may not be as inclined towards self-correction as Schegloff et al. (1977) originally proposed, but due to the linguistic challenges, the talk of less competent speakers may become other-completed or even other-corrected.

When repair organization in the linguistically developing and challenged interactions are compared, there are clear differences between child-parent interactions and conversations between participants with aphasia and their interlocutors. In child-parent conversation there are asymmetries of language, world knowledge and social participatory roles. Parents co-construct their children's emerging utterances from early on which promotes learning of more advanced linguistic skills and world knowledge. Parents' participation changes from co-construction of meaning and other-correction to other-initiating self-repair as the children develop more advanced language skills. The preference for self-repair fully emerges when the children become two to three years of age. On the other hand, in home conversations of people with aphasia there is asymmetry of language, but not necessarily in world knowledge or participatory roles. Using their shared background knowledge and contextual support, familiar conversational partners co-construct PWAs' emerging utterances by completing them and offering candidate understandings. FCPs' participation changes depending on PWAs' linguistic challenges and the transparency of referents and is often negotiated using bodily orientation. In sum there seems to be a preference for progressivity of interaction.

One obvious reason for the observed difference is that adults with aphasia have permanent language disorders but children are rapidly learning language during their early years. Children learning language are easily offered help and even corrected, whereas adults with aphasia are considered as having the knowledge of the language and as not needing socialization into the use of the linguistic system. The similarities in repair behaviors point in the direction that the organization of repair is reflective of the linguistic competencies of the participants in a way that the more competent participants may take a stronger role in accomplishing the repair activities. To explore this in more detail, more comparative research on repair organization across different linguistically asymmetric interactional contexts is needed.

Clinical Implications for Speech-Language Therapy and Future Directions of Research

This study points out, as several previous ones have already done, that the organization of repair sequences should be investigated as part of the assessment of the everyday life consequences of aphasia (see, e.g., Whitworth et al. 1997; Lock et al. 2001). The repair behaviors used by the person with aphasia and/or the conversational partner show clearly how they deal with the impact of linguistic impairments on conversation. This information is clinically relevant for the planning of therapeutic interventions. Somewhat similarly to parent-child interactions, changes in repair organization may reflect recovery of linguistic abilities in participants with aphasia. Clinical assessment could include systematic study of repair practices and the distribution of repair contributions of all of the participants. Besides assessment, conversation-based speech-language therapies should be developed to include guidance and instruction to use collaborative other-contributions in a more systematic way.

The preliminary comparison of the linguistically developing and challenged interactions made in this chapter raises the question of whether the interlocutors' other-contributions could enhance the recovery of language abilities in adults with aphasia in somewhat the same manner that parental other-contributions develop children's language. As with children's language, similar embedded corrective practices might promote recovery from aphasia in conversation-based speech-language therapy. This aspect could be explored in further studies of conversational interventions with carefully designed individually relevant follow-up measures. Furthermore, more research is still needed to explore features of the organization of repair in other communication disorders in both children and adults, and potential changes over time during speech-language therapy.

References

Ahlsén, E. (1993). Conversational principles and aphasic communication. *Journal of Pragmatics, 19*(1), 57–70.

Chouinard, M. M., & Clark, E. V. (2003). Adult reformulations of child errors as negative evidence. *Journal of Child Language, 30*(3), 637–669.

Dingemanse, M., Roberts, S. G., Baranova, J., Blythe, J., Drew, P., Floyd, S. Gisladottir, R. S., Kendrick, K. H., Levinson, S. H., Manrique, E., Rossi, G. & Enfield, N. J. (2015, September 16). *Universal principles in the repair of communication problems.* Open Linguistics. Published.

Forrester, M. (2008). The emergence of self-repair: A case study of one child during the early preschool years. *Research on Language and Social Interaction, 41*, 99–128.
Goodwin, C. (1995). Co-constructing meaning in conversations with an aphasic man. *Research on Language and Social Interaction, 28*, 233–260.
Goodwin, M. H., & Goodwin, C. (1986). Gesture and co-participation in the activity of searching for a word. *Semiotica, 62*, 51–75.
Heeschen, C., & Schegloff, E. A. (1999). Agrammatism, adaptation theory, conversation analysis: On the role of so-called telegraphic style in talk-in-interaction. *Aphasiology, 13*, 365–405.
Jefferson, G. (1987). On exposed and embedded correction in conversation. In G. Button & J. R. E. Lee (Eds.), *Talk and social organisation* (pp. 86–100). Clevedon, UK: Multilingual Matters.
Laakso, M. (1997). *Self-initiated repair by fluent aphasic speakers in conversation*. Helsinki: Finnish Literature Society.
Laakso, M. (2003). Collaborative construction of repair in aphasic conversation: An interactive view on the extended speaking turns of persons with Wernicke's aphasia. In C. Goodwin (Ed.), *Conversation and brain damage* (pp. 163–188). New York, NY: Oxford University Press.
Laakso, M. (2010). Children's emerging and developing self-repair practices. In H. Gardner & M. Forrester (Eds.), *Analyzing interactions in childhood: Insights from conversation analysis* (pp. 74–99). Oxford: Wiley-Blackwell.
Laakso, M. (2014). Aphasia sufferers' displays of affect in conversation. *Research on Language and Social Interaction,* 47(4), s. 404–425.
Laakso, M. (2015). Collaborative participation in aphasic word searching: Comparison between significant others and speech and language therapists. *Aphasiology, 29*(3), 269–290.
Laakso, M., & Klippi, A. (1999). A closer look at the "hint and guess" sequences in aphasic conversation. *Aphasiology, 2*(4/5), 345–363.
Laakso, M., Helasvuo, M.-L., & Savinainen-Makkonen, T. (2010). Children's early actions in learning language: A study of proto-words and pointing gestures in interaction between one-year-old child and parent. *SKY Journal of Linguistics, 23*, 199–226.
Lerner, G. (1996). On the "semi-permeable" character of grammatical units in conversation: Conditional entry into the turn space of another speaker. In E. Ochs, E. Schegloff, & S. Thompson (Eds.), *Interaction and Grammar* (Studies in Interactional Sociolinguistics, pp. 238–276). Cambridge: Cambridge University Press.

Lindsay, J., & Wilkinson, R. (1999). Repair sequences in aphasia talk: A comparison of aphasic—Speech and language therapist and aphasic—Spouse conversations. *Aphasiology, 13*(4/5), 305–325.

Lock, S., Wilkinson, R., & Bryan, K. (2001). *SPPARC: Supporting partners of people with aphasia in relationships and conversation*. Abingdon: Routledge.

Lubinski, R., Duchan, J., & Weitzner-Lin, B. (1980). Analysis of breakdowns and repairs in aphasic adult communication. In T. R. Brookshire (toim.), *Clinical aphasiology conference proceedings* (s. 111–116). Minnesota: BRK Publishers.

Menn, L. (1983). Development of articulatory, phonetic, and phonological capabilities. In B. Butterworth (Ed.), *Language production. Volume 2: Development, writing and other language processes* (pp. 3–50). London: Academic Press.

Milroy, L., & Perkins, L. (1992). Repair strategies in aphasic discourse; towards a collaborative model. *Clinical Linguistics & Phonetics, 6*(1 and 2), 27–40.

Morgenstern, A., Leroy-Collombel, M., & Caët, S. (2013). Self- and other-repairs in child–adult interaction at the intersection of pragmatic abilities and language acquisition. *Journal of Pragmatics, 56*, 151–167.

Norrick, N. R. (1991). On the organization of corrective exchanges in conversation. *Journal of Pragmatics, 16*, 59–83.

Oelschlaeger, M., & Damico, J. S. (2000). Partnership in conversation: A study of word search strategies. *Journal of Communication Disorders, 33*, 205–225.

Schegloff, E. A. (1979). The relevance of repair to syntax-for-conversation. In T. T. Givón (toim.), *Syntax and semantics 12: Discourse and syntax* (s. 261–286). New York: Academic Press.

Schegloff, E. A. (2007). *Sequence organization in interaction*. Cambridge: Cambridge University Press.

Schegloff, E. A., Jefferson, G., & Sacks, H. (1977). The preference for self-correction in the organization of repair in conversation. *Language, 53*, 361–382.

Sorjonen, M.-L. (2001). *Responding in conversation: A study of response particles in Finnish*. Amsterdam: John Benjamins.

Whitworth, A., Perkins, L., & Lesser, R. (1997). *CAPPA. Conversation analysis profile for people with aphasia*. Hoboken: Wiley-Blackwell.

Wilkinson, R. (2007). Managing linguistic incompetence as a delicate issue in aphasic talk-in-interaction: On the use of laughter in prolonged repair sequences. *Journal of Pragmatics, 39*(3), 542–569.
Wan, I.-P. & Liao, L. (2018). Self-repair patterns in conversational speech of Mandarin aphasics. *Archives of Psychology, 2*(2).

10

Increasing Learner Authority in the Classrooms of Children with Speech, Language and Communication Needs

Julie Radford

Introduction

Speech, language and communication needs (SLCN) is an umbrella term which, in the UK, refers to children who have problems with understanding and/or using spoken language (DfE 2015). This area of need is common: 10% of children are estimated to have SLCN which means potentially two or three in every classroom (Norbury et al. 2017). The categories used by the American Psychiatric Association (2013) help distinguish between three areas of language difficulty. First, difficulties associated with speech sound production affect children's intelligibility. Second, children may have a general language difficulty owing to problems with comprehension or production and this can affect various modalities (spoken, written and sign language). Comprehension problems have an impact on how children understand words and sentences and also the ability to follow verbal instructions.

J. Radford (✉)
University College London, London, UK

© The Author(s) 2020

R. Wilkinson et al. (eds.), *Atypical Interaction*,
https://doi.org/10.1007/978-3-030-28799-3_10

Expressive difficulties, by contrast, are visible through grammatical errors or the choice of words. A third key area affects children's social and pragmatic communication; these skills influence how communication is used for social purposes, how the young person follows the rules of conversation and also how they adapt communication to match the needs of the listener.

Since children with SLCN have a wide range of needs, the classroom implications are complex. The language used by adults is key to effective learning but may present challenges for such children if they are not enabled to be active participants. Teachers' questions, for example, are abundant in the classroom although the default is use of 'test' questions rather than questions which are 'real' or authentic (Cazden and Beck 2003). The problem is that such questions lead to epistemic asymmetry which means that epistemic authority rests with the teacher (Rusk et al. 2017). Such lack of involvement in the talk could have a negative impact on the child's learning of both language and the curriculum. Sidnell (2012) talks of 'epistemic gradients' where some practices are stronger or weaker according to who has the greater knowledge in the talk (speaker or recipient) and depending on the design of the turns. In order to understand the different kinds of question formats that teachers use and how children respond to them, it is necessary to examine stretches of actual classroom interaction in detail. By using conversation analysis (CA), this chapter aims to show ways in which questions and other 'initiating' turns (such as sequence and topic-initiating turns) have different implications for the child's contributions. Earlier research using CA showed that questions such as 'can you tell me about..?, open up the talk by generating topic ideas from the child (Radford et al. 2006). As such, using CA allows us to analyse how topic is constructed over a series of turns and to capture how the child interprets and responds to the different turn designs that teachers use.

Button and Casey (1984, 1985), using CA, describe three types of topic generation in mundane talk that have different implications for the involvement of the recipient. A topic initial elicitor takes the form of an open enquiry directed at the possible activities of the conversational partner (Button and Casey 1984). A noteworthy feature of this initiator is that it carries no topical material itself, but invites the recipient in the next turn to provide a report of events which are newsworthy (e.g. 'what's new?' or 'what's this all about?'). Radford and Tarplee (2000) found a similar practice in the classrooms of children who have SLCN (e.g. a teacher asking a child 'what did you do at the week-end?'). In this way there is orientation to the epistemic authority of the recipient.

An itemised news enquiry differs from a topic initial elicitor because the speaker elects to nominate topical material (Button and Casey 1985). Radford and Tarplee (2000) found that children with SLCN used this type of query to elicit information from another child. A third way of initiating novel topical material is by making a news announcement (Button and Casey 1984). These statements function as a sort of headline news (e.g. 'I got hurt'), projecting more to be told in further turns. Radford and Tarplee (2000) found examples of this type of opener by children with SLCN. In this case, it falls to the recipient to topicalise the news in the second turn by providing the sequential opportunity for its elaboration. Prototypical examples are 'yes?' or 'did you?' which invite elaboration of the news by the first speaker, and so implicate extended talk on the topical material in third turn. A second turn response which fails to do this may lead to topic curtailment, as it may be construed as displaying unwillingness on the part of the second speaker to continue on this topic.

Children with SLCN commonly make many linguistic errors, both grammatical and lexical, during their classroom interactions. In addition, their turns frequently lack clarity, especially when complex curriculum concepts are being discussed. There are two ways of interpreting this: on the one hand, their use of language presents a challenge to staff and peers who have difficulty understanding them; on the other hand, their errors and misunderstandings could provide valuable opportunities for language learning. The reason that problem talk is valuable is because the turn following the child's 'error' or 'trouble source' provides a contingent opportunity for the adult to supply a repair or correction that the child may notice. How the repair or correction is initiated and/or carried out is important to explore in detail because there may be different interactional implications for the learner's involvement following the adult's turn.

Conversation analysts use the term 'repair' for sequences of talk that deal with any type of problem with hearing, speaking or understanding of talk within an interaction (Schegloff 2007). There are different types of repair trajectories, depending on (a) who initiates the repair and

(b) who carries out the repair (Schegloff et al. 1977). For the purpose of supporting language learning, there are two notable types of repair sequences: (a) other-initiated other-repairs (OIOR), where the adult carries out the repair or correction, and (b) other-initiated repairs (OIR) where the adult highlights the trouble source and prompts the child to self-repair it. However, the implications for learning are very different because when adults use OIORs, for example, they retain a high level of control which means that they are not transferring responsibility to the child for thinking about how to reformulate their language (Radford et al. 2012). By contrast, in using other-initiation of repair the adult is not carrying out the repair themselves and the child is thus prompted to consider how to reformulate the grammar and/or semantics of their talk.

Owing to the instructional nature of the classroom, it can be the case that correction of what the child has said is more common in this environment than repairs of hearing or understanding. The reason that corrections are frequent is because of the recurrent sequential structure whereby teachers initiate with a question, particularly a 'known information' (or 'test') question (Mehan 1979) (I), children respond (R) and in the third turn teachers provide an evaluation (E) of whether the answer was correct or not i.e. Initiation-Reply-Evaluation sequences (Mehan 1979). Since the third turn offers a place in which repair or correction can occur, there can also be a more extended sequence: for example, Initiation-Reply-Evaluation-Correction (McHoul 1990). A high percentage (74%) of McHoul's correction sequences involve teacher-initiations and he reports that these happen immediately after the trouble source. Macbeth (2004), by contrast, argues that repair and correction are distinct phenomena. His data show that repair and repair initiation may occur within correction sequences, owing to the need of speakers and hearers to reach a common understanding. In other words, problems of common understanding need to be resolved before correction can happen.

Using CA, Radford (2010a) found that in the classrooms of children with SLCN, specialist language teachers employed a range of practices to highlight an error or trouble but withhold correction (e.g. clueing). Another case study showed that the teacher used a range of devices to withhold correction from a child during word searches (for example, prompting, hinting and supplying a model) and that these operated on a scale where they offered least to most assistance (Radford 2010b).

In both of these studies, the teachers set a trajectory where the children were assumed to be able to self-correct. In terms of issues such as children's displays of epistemics and their language production, withholding correction is obviously important for maximising children's active participation in classroom activities.

The chapter will address the following questions:

1. What practices afford teachers the opportunity to increase learner authority through turns which initiate or develop topics within classroom activities?
2. What practices afford teachers the opportunity to increase learner authority during episodes of repair and correction?

Video recordings were made during a project that took place in the London region. Three specialist language teachers were recruited because they had an advanced qualification in the field of speech, language and communication and had extensive experience of specialised language teaching. Six children with SLCN were chosen who ranged in age from 4;4 to 8;7 years old. The children had primary expressive and/or receptive language difficulties. Information about their language difficulties was obtained via a questionnaire that was completed by the teacher and the speech and language therapists that were based at each of the three schools. Table 10.1 sets out this information, based on the speech and language therapists' test data and their reports of informal assessments.

The teachers were asked by the researcher to select activities for video-recording that they used explicitly to teach language skills in small groups or one-to-one contexts. Six activities were videoed over four consecutive weeks, totalling 24 language activities. These lasted between 7 and 25 minutes, giving a total recording time of 265 minutes. There were two main types of activity: book-sharing or group story writing. During book-sharing, the talk concerned picture books; the younger children talked about a standard children's book, whilst the older pairs had exercise books in which pictures of personal interest, such as photographs, had been placed. In the story writing activity, small groups of 5–6 children sat close to the teacher. The younger group was required to write a story together and the teacher recorded their ideas onto a flipchart whereas the older children used picture boards to help them create individual stories.

Table 10.1 Children's speech, language and communication difficulties

Child	Age	Gender	Receptive	Expressive syntax	Phonology	Naming	Word meaning	Pragmatics
Ali	8y 7m	F	3	2	0	1	2	1
Beth	8y 3m	F	2	2	0	2	2	1
Chip	4y 4m	M	2	2	1	2	2	1
Dina	4y 8m	F	3	3	2	3	3	0
Ele	5y 10m	F	3	3	1	2	2	1
Fay	5y 5m	F	3	3	1	3	3	3

Key: 0 = none, 1 = mild, 2 = moderate, 3 = severe

Informed, written consent was obtained to undertake video-recording from each participant and from their parents. Since the research involved video-recordings, the opportunity to withdraw their participation was offered at any point. A researcher was present during the recordings and took field-notes. Observer effects were minimised by the researcher sitting at the back of the classroom and not interacting with the participants. Rigour in the data collection was obtained by sampling over four consecutive weeks. Detailed transcriptions were made of the entire dataset, using CA conventions. In terms of the analysis, the video-recordings were viewed repeatedly to observe patterns in the data. The patterns emerged inductively from the dataset and were not pre-determined by the researcher before the analysis.

Initiation and Development of Topic in the Classroom

The first examples (Extracts 1–6) are relevant for answering research question one about practices involved in the initiation of sequences and, in particular, the initiation and development of topic as part of classroom activities. Extract 1 begins with the child (Chip) turning over a page of her speaking book, so there has been no prior talk about this topic. The teacher (T), in the first turn, produces a question about the picture which aims to elicit talk on this topic (the picture) from the child. In the next turn, Chip produces an answer through which he develops the topic of what is in the picture.

Extract 1

→ 1. T: right oh! I haven't seen this picture, what's this all about
2. Chip: scissors=a pencil sharpener (.) a clip

In this example, although the domain of talk is bounded (by relating to the picture), the teacher is allowing the child to select what to talk about within that domain.

The teacher's turn bears some similarity to the topic initial elicitors of Button and Casey (1985) although the teacher is talking about the joint focus of a picture rather than newsworthy events.

Many teacher turns that initiate topic in the dataset are designed as 'wh' type questions (such as 'what' or 'where') that orient to the child as knowing something about the picture and being in a position to inform the teacher. However, there are alternative designs to questions that perform the same kind of work. 'Tell me about ...' in the next extract serves to generate talk about a different picture in the child's 'speaking book'. Beth treats the teacher's turn as requiring her to select something about one of the pictures that the teacher has indicated and to talk about it.

Extract 2

→1. T: I haven't seen these pictures either (.) tell me about tho:se

2. Beth: uhh:: there's a kitten an she's looking for mice

3. T: mm hh

4. (0.5)

5. Beth: an when he eat the mice he gonna die

In Extracts 1 and 2 the teacher, through her acknowledgement that she has not seen the pictures before, is suggesting that the child is in a position to inform her about the topic. In this way, she is signalling that the child has authority to choose what to say about the picture (Heritage and Raymond 2005).

Extract 3

→1. T: tell me about this one

2. Beth: uhh:: there's a girl (.) an she's crying (.) cos (0.2) her brother is killed

3. T: can you tell me about the girl?

The teacher's third turn in Extract 2 is a minimal phatic response 'mm hh'. This turn works as a continuer which signals that Beth should expand on what she has said. This is one practice by which teachers can elicit further talk on the topic from the child, and indeed in Extract 2 following this turn the child proceeds to produce further relevant topical material in the next turn. By contrast, the teacher's third turn in Extract 3 (line 3), elicits further development of the topic using another method of developing talk on a topic i.e. by selecting part of the child's answer and requesting further talk on part of it ('can you tell me about the girl?').

So far the analysis has examined a recurrent method of initiating sequences and topics within classroom activities used by teachers. This can now briefly be contrased with some sequence/topic initiating turns by the children in the classroom. In Extract 4 (from Radford and Tarplee 2000), an itemised news enquiry by one child, Tim, targets a specific item of information ('who was your first teacher here?') from another child, Ele. In the next turn, Ele provides this information. In the third turn of the children's conversation, Tim produces a clarification request about Ele's answer which is responded to affirmatively with 'yeah', and this is then followed (in line 5) with a further elicitation of a specific item of information. In terms of epistemics, Tim is treating Ele as possessing knowledge that he (Tim) does not have, but the form of elicitation here results in contributions from the recipient which, compared to those seen in Extracts 1–3, are more minimal and contribute less to the development of the topic.

Extract 4

→ 1. Tim: who was your fi<u>r</u>st teacher here

2. Ele : Mrs Healey

3. Tim: Mrs Healey in rec<u>ep</u>tion?

4. Ele : yeah

5. Tim: an=then who.

Extract 5 provides another example from conversations between children in the classroom where a topic is initiated by one of the children (Radford and Tarplee 2000; Radford et al. 2006). Here, Ali presents a report of news about her holidays in Tanzania. By initiating topic in the form of a news announcement, it projects more to be told in further turns. In this example, another child, Tim, topicalises the news in the second turn ('did you') thus providing the sequential opportunity for its elaboration. Indeed, Ali treats the topicaliser as an opportunity to continue her talk about her holiday in the third turn. In terms of epistemics, the topic initiator is providing information to the recipient, rather than eliciting it as in Extract 1–4.

Extract 5

→ 1. Ali : I went to Tanzani:a in the holidays,

2. Tim: di̲d you?

3. Ali : yeah and I saw.....*(continues on topic)*

Finally in this section, an example will be examined where the teacher invites the children to contribute topical material to the group activity underway. Extract 6 provides an example of a form of 'topic invitation' sequence and shows how this type of elicitation by the teacher encourages the children's participation and involvement in decisions about topical content. Literacy lessons potentially lend themselves to collaborative topic generation and could be helpful for language learning. In the activity discussed in Extract 6 there are eight children, aged 5–6 years old, who mainly have expressive language difficulties. In this activity, the teacher skilfully elicits the children's own ideas though 'invitations'. The key point is that she is asking the children to make all of the decisions, including how to open the story, the types of characters, the setting, the plot, the ending and the title e.g. 'What should we call our story?'. She draws each of their ideas onto a flipchart, thus demonstrating the collective principle of generating a story together.

In Extract 6, the group has already responded to the question 'who should be in our story?' by offering the idea of a 'cheetah', thus deciding on the key character. In line 1, the teacher asks the question 'where does it live?'. The response from one of the children, Fay, is a proposal that the setting of the story is a 'house'. It is also notable that Fay volunteers further information at line 6 regarding the number of the house ('forty four'). Volunteering of ideas by children in classrooms is rare in the dataset but is worthy of mention because it allows then to display their epistemic competencies and achieve different types of participation within the activity. The extract also illustrates how the teacher accepts the children's ideas by reformulating them as part of a narrative and drawing them onto the flipchart.

Extract 6: Topic invitation

→1	T	one day (.) there was a cheetah. whe::re does it live?
2	Fay	in=a house
3	Adult	in=a house?
4	Fay	*(nods)*
5	T	cheetah lives in a house?
6	Fay	forty four
7	T	A house called forty four. Okay, here comes the house. One day
8		*(draws the house*
9		there was a cheetah, lived in a house, number, forty four
		(draws roof and door) *(writes 44)*

Notable features of these types of elicitations by the teacher include the fact that they are often wh-type questions, and they commonly emphasize the collective nature of the task (for example, through the use of the pronoun 'we'), highlighting that it is the joint responsibility of the group to generate the ideas needed for the story. Extract 6 is impressive given that these children are as young as five and have speech and language difficulties. This example demonstrates how the epistemic authority of the children can be augmented through encouraging them to contribute story content based on their own imagination and ideas, and through the teacher incorporating these ideas and contributions to achieve a collaborative production of the story.

Repair and Correction: The Issue of 'Exposure'

The next examples are relevant to answering research question two about repair and correction. Extracts 7 and 8 show sequences of talk where there is a linguistic error that is corrected by the teacher (see the turns indicated with →). In Extract 7, the teacher and Beth are looking at a picture in Beth's speaking book.

Extract 7: Correction

	1. Beth:	that's her gi̲rlfriend,
	2.	*(points at picture of girl)*
→	3. T:	that's his gi̲:rlfriend ye̲::ah.
	4.	so what are they going to do̲:? (.)
	5.	tell me about the a̲eroplane.
	6. Beth:	they fly o̲ff,

In line 1 Beth introduces a tangential topic about her picture, whilst pointing to a picture of a girl. She gives a description that includes a noun (*gi̲rlfriend*) with the female determiner (*her*). In the second turn, the teacher's repeat is modified in so far as she changes the determiner to *his*, treating *her* as an error. This correction of form is embedded since there is no marking of the contrast; in fact, the teacher's stress is placed on the following noun, *gi̲:rlfriend*. The teacher also attends to meaning in the second turn: her use of a positive receipt (*ye̲::ah*) displays acceptance of the content of the child's utterance. Furthermore, rather than pausing to allow Beth an opportunity to acknowledge or otherwise orient to the correction, the teacher makes a topic continuing move, signalled by the topic marker *so*.

Extract 8: Correction

	1. T:	(turns over page) so they go and have a look at their cha̲:̲:̲irs,
	2.	(.)
	3. T:	oh de̲:ar.
	4.	(2.6)
	5. Dina:	[dog,
	6.	[*(points at picture of bear)*
→	7. T:	you think that looks like a do̲g?
	8. Dina:	*(nods)*
	9. T:	yeah it does a bi:t,(.) but do you think it i:s a dog? (.) or
	10.	[do you think it's baby be::ar
	11.	[*(points at bear)*

In Extract 8, Dina is looking at a picture of 'Goldilocks and the Three Bears' with her teacher. In line 5, whilst pointing to a picture of a bear, Dina says *dog*, without a determiner such as 'the' or 'a'. The teacher's expansion of the single noun to a noun phrase (*a do̲g*) is produced in the subsequent turn. The contrast between the adult and child versions of the noun phrase is in a sense marked because the teacher adds loudness but notably the teacher stresses only the noun and not the determiner, making the latter less salient in the steam of speech. Also, line 7 simultaneously performs other important work in terms of meaning. One interpretation could be that the teacher is simply displaying a candidate understanding of the semantic content of the child's *dog* turn. Yet, the pitch rise suggests that the turn initiates a sequence that concerns the child's meaning, given that the picture was of a bear rather than a dog. The child's confirmation (via a nod of the head in line 8) that she believes the picture resembles a dog displays that she is not yet orienting to the teacher's question as highlighting 'dog' as a possible trouble source. The teacher responds with weak agreement (*Yeah it does a bi:t,)*, which is followed by a disagreement component that is introduced by the conjunction *but*. The teacher's priority is with the accuracy of the label, to get Dina to recognise that the picture is of a bear, not a dog. As such, even though there is an expanded version of the noun phrase in line 7, the determiner is not proffered by the teacher for repetition by Dina, and thus the correction of the determiner remains embedded.

Another type of correction sequence takes the form of a grammatical reformulation. The next example contrasts with the earlier examples because the trouble source turn does not contain any hearable instance of linguistic error or omission. Rather, the teacher modifies the grammatical structure of the child's previous turn. In Extract 9 the teacher is working in a small group and asking for ideas to write a story.

Extract 9

```
  1.  T:    [what's yo:ur idea?
  2.          [(points at child)
  3. Ele:   the boy is sad,
→4.  T:     the boy who was sad?
  5. Ele:   [(2.0)
  6.        [(nods)
  7.  T:    okay.
```

In response to the teacher's question, Ele offers a candidate idea about a character (line 3). In the next turn, line 4, the teacher offers a version of the child's turn. This turn by the teacher alters the syntax of the child's turn by modelling a more complex syntactic structure, a relative clause, to create a potential 'title format' for the story that they are creating. The teacher's phrase (*who was sad)* does not include stress on the copula and thus there is no intonational contrast between Ele's 'is' and the teacher's 'was'. Ele, by nodding at line 6, agrees with the teacher's suggestion, rather than orienting to the grammatical reformulation (by, for example, producing a repeat of any of the reformulated turn).

Although also dealing with correction, the next examples differ from those above in two key respects. First of all, the corrections are 'exposed' since the teacher's turn is concerned with addressing the child's turn as in some way problematic or limited (with these corrections also often marked prosodically). Next, there are different sequential implications following the correction: the child orients to the exposed correction by the teacher through practices such as repeating the teacher's correction. While such examples differ from instances of self-correction by the child, there is still a potentially positive pedagogic impact of these teacher corrections for the child's language learning. Since the child 'notices' the repair, and hence the trouble source in their own talk that the repair is targeting, the child has the potential to work on this trouble, including producing a corrected version of the trouble source item.

In Extract 10, Chip is talking about a book into which he has put personal photographs. The picture being discussed below is of a model that he has made out of lego. In this extract it will be shown how the correction is 'exposed', following a more implicit prompt which might elicit a self-correction by Chip.

Extract 10

1. Chip: leg
2. T: *(mouths 'le - go')*
3. T: lego [lego
4. Chip: [lego

On hearing a single syllable version of *lego*, the teacher first (line 2) provides a mouthing of the correct form which could elicit a self-correction from Chip. This prompt does not, however, lead to an attempt by Chip and the teacher then provides an audible model which she repeats (line 3). These two other-corrections are 'exposed' and there is stress on both of the first syllables. Chip orients to this repair and repeats the teacher's version, including the stress.

Extract 11 features Fay writing a story together with the teacher in a small group of six children. Fay is searching for the name of a building and makes a partial attempt (line 1). The adult orients to this struggle by producing the correct version (line 2), which Fay then repeats (line 3). In Extract 12, whilst sharing a picture book, Dina responds to the teacher's incomplete utterance with a possible lexical completion (line 2) which is not accepted by the teacher (line 3). The teacher supplies a correction (from 'snow' to 'ski'), and Fay orients to this correction by repeating it (line 4).

Extract 11

1. Fay: uhhm (.) the (.) mo=modern ate,
2. T: Tate Modern=
3. Fay: =Tate Modern=
4. T: =ye:s the Tate Modern. you went there.

Extract 12

1. T: here is a mountain see me ss::,
2. Dina: (0.4) uhhm sno:w
3. T: good try. see me ↑ski
4. Dina ski,

In Extracts 10, 11, and 12, therefore, an error by the child has been followed by a correction of that error by the teacher. In response, the child produces a repeat of the correction.

In some instances, however, the trouble source is not evidently an error. In Extract 13, for instance, Chip is talking about a favourite photograph in his speaking book where he is featured doing painting of monsters with his mum at home.

Extract 13

1. T: you and mum are doing=what are you doing?
2. Chip: we're doing monsters like this,
3. T: that's ri:ght (.) you're pa:inting the monsters
4. Chip: painting.

The teacher asks Chip what he is doing in the photo and he responds by saying 'doing monsters'. The teacher accepts this answer positively with 'that's right'. The teacher then continues the turn by offering a lexical alternative ('painting') to the child's verb. This re-doing provides a semantic upgrade in the sense that the child's version is semantically vague whereas the adult's alternative is more precise about the nature of the activity. Chip's repeat of the teacher's verb in line 4 suggests that he is orienting to it as an other-correction. A pedagogic purpose of these exposed corrections by the teacher, therefore, can be that the child will produce the correct form in the future, or in the event of an error, will be able to produce a self-correction.

Teacher Initiation of Repair and Correction

A key feature of correction in response to troubles related to linguistic form and meaning is that the adult retains a high level of epistemic authority over the interaction in terms of supplying vocabulary or correct grammar. For the purposes of language learning opportunities this can be unhelpful because it potentially reduces children's involvement and responsibility for finding the word or phrase on their own. Other-initiated repair and other-initiated correction, by contrast, are better for increasing children's authority because there is withholding by the teacher.

The following extracts explore in detail the design of the teachers' repair initiators (RIs) and the actions accomplished by them. The analysis will highlight the relative strength of the repair initiator to locate the problem with hearing/speaking/understanding (Schegloff 1997).

Turns that provide the least help in locating the trouble, such as open-class repair initiators (e.g. 'pardon') (Drew 1997) will be contrasted with those that locate the repairable more specifically and/or supply a candidate offer to the child.

First, there are examples of repairs that are 'non-specific' in the sense that they have open designs that orient to the adults' problems with hearing or understanding the child's turns. In most cases in my data they are treated by the child as prompts to repeat (see Radford 2010a, for further examples). What is distinctive about non-specific repair initiation is that when teachers signal trouble with the child's response turn, they do not in any way locate a specific item to be repaired. As such, they target potentially any aspect of the child's prior utterance. Children have different options in response: they can either repeat or reformulate their own previous material in the following turn or turns. Extract 14 illustrates three examples of 'general' RIs: a repetition request at line 3 and two statements of uncertainty (lines 5 and 7). The context of the extract is story writing with a small group of six children. The teacher (T) has already written and drawn several of the children's ideas onto a flipchart regarding the characters and story-line and now asks the children a question.

Extract 14: Non-specific repair initiation

```
   1.     T: can you think of=a na:me for the story
   2.  Fay: (        )
→ 3.      T: say that again.
   4.  Fay: (        )
→ 5.      T: ooh I'm not sure what you're saying
   6.  Fay: ee:::
→ 7.      T: ee: I don't know what that means
   8.           (0.2)
   9.     T: so I think something about chee:tahs
  10.           (0.2)
  11.     T: Dina and the two cheetahs?
  12.  Fay: yeah.
```

Given other examples in the dataset (Radford et al. 2006), the teacher's question (line 1) could be heard by the child as a request for an idea concerning the story's title. As Fay offers a verbal contribution at line 2, the teacher's relevant next turn would be to accept the idea (often in the form of a repeat). Instead, an insertion sequence suspends production of the acceptance in order to deal with a trouble. T's use of 'say that again' gives the child an unambiguous message that a repeat is needed. In fact, line 3 has the appearance of an instruction, given the absence of lexical or syntactic markers of politeness. Although Fay offers a response in line 4, the teacher indicates continued trouble with a further non-specific marker of uncertainty (line 5). Fay next produces a non-lexical item ('ee::'), so the adult responds with a third repair initiator, this time clearly displaying her difficulty with understanding. This also fails to solve the problem so it is left to the teacher to suggest a story name idea. The teacher's repair initiators target the whole of the child's prior turn as opposed to marking out specific elements for Fay's attention.

The previous extract showed three examples of non-specific RIs: a statement that a repeat is needed, and two statements that display general trouble with hearing or understanding. The next examples will be referred to as 'specific' correction initiations because the teacher pinpoints, in various ways, the location of the trouble. In Example (15), the teacher uses a non-completed utterance 'a:::' which elicits a repeat from the child in the next turn. Extract 16 takes place during the early phase of a group story-writing session where the characters are being decided. In line 1 the teacher asks Ele to select a character, prompting him with an incomplete utterance 'one day there was a:::'. In response, Ele begins to repeat the teacher's story starter. Prolongation of the vowel sound, constructed with continuing intonation, as well as the brief silence, suggests that he is searching for an idea to offer the teacher.

Extract 15: Specific correction initiation

1. T: Ele you ready? one day there was a:::,

2. Ele: there was a:::, (0.2) ch<u>ee</u>tah.

→3. T: a::, *(shakes head, leans forward)*

4. Ele: a ch<u>ee</u>tah.

5. T: a ch<u>EE</u>tah?

6. Ele: yeah

7. T: what's a ch<u>ee</u>tah?

8. Ele: it's (.) it's a (0.8) bit like a tiger.

9. T: it's like a t<u>i:</u>ger (.) mhm. (.) that's helpful. (.) mhm like a tiger (.)

10. do [<u>you</u> know what a cheetah is.

[*(points at another child)*

Although Ele offers the name of an animal (cheetah), the teacher withholds acceptance of this idea. Instead, in line 3 she other-initiates a self-correction (line 4) with 'a:::'. The teacher's turn is a single word that is formed in a similar fashion to her earlier version and the child's production: it repeats the element that preceded 'cheetah', preserving the lengthening of the vowel and continuing intonation. The teacher's trouble could have entailed hearing and is confirmed by her body language: a shake of the head and leaning posture. Ele repeats the noun phrase (line 4), rather than reformulating the turn. Although the hearing is confirmed by the child (line 6), the teacher pursues a definition to find out if the child knows what a cheetah is. One notable feature of such a minimal correction initiation is that it targets the trouble source very precisely by leading the child, at least syntactically, up to the location of the trouble. Furthermore, the turn has pedagogical value in so far as it leads to both confirmation and definition sequences that afford further opportunities for language learning.

In the next example, the correction initiation is similar in so far as it is initiated by an incomplete utterance but the sequential implications are different because the child hears it as a request for revision rather than repetition. The example takes place during a speaking book activity.

Extract 16: Specific correction initiation

1. T: what can you tell me about th<u>is</u> one

2. Ali: uh: she has (hair) (0.2)

   (T and Ali look at the picture)

→3. T: she has,

   (T turns eye gaze to Ali)

4. Ali: long

5. T: l<u>o</u>ng hair. yes.

6. Ali: and she has a (.) (large) dress

Ali responds to the teacher's question with a description of a girl (line 2). That Ali's gaze remains on the picture suggests that she is engaged in solitary searching during the silence. At line 3 the teacher withholds topicalisation and, instead, partially repeats Ali's phrase, thus other-initiating a self-correction from Ali. Line 3 is formed by using two words of Ali's turn up to the point at which there was potentially a missing adjective, as seen in the subsequent turn (line 4). It is notable that there is continuing intonation and gaze directed at the child, rather than at the picture. Ali hears the turn as a prompt, presumably owing to the syntactic incompleteness of 'she has'. She does not produce the noun but a relevant next adjective 'long'. The teacher displays acceptance of Ali's idea with a repeat of the child's adjective, adding the noun from line 2.

In Extract 15 a minimal incomplete item ('a::') led the child to self-correct her noun and therefore complete the noun phrase. In Extract 16 by contrast, a phrase was not only interpreted as an invitation to complete the sentence, but also taken as an opportunity by the child to revise the next item of her original phrase. The teacher's correction initiations are prosodically marked by sound stretches and by continuing intonation which position the child to continue the phrase or sentence. They thus target, very precisely, the location of a trouble. Yet, even when they are heard as invitations to self-correct, they do not give the child semantic information that could be used to inform the subsequent correction. Both examples have pedagogical value in so far as the teacher indicates the trouble source very specifically but affords responsibility for the correction to the child. Furthermore, by generating further information from the child, the correction sequence creates an opportunity for the teacher to expand the child's ideas and supply further contingent models of language.

The next type of specific OIR sequences involve RIs that are formed as 'wh' questions. The analysis will show how this design pinpoints not the *location* of the item to be repaired (as in Extracts 15 and 16) but the *nature* of the repairable. As such they are not heard as requests for repetition, but are interpreted either as a request to provide specific information or to give a word definition. In Extract 17 Beth and the teacher are talking about a photograph of her dog, Penny. The sequence begins with Beth offering a news account of taking Penny for a walk.

Extract 17: Specific correction initiation (wh-question)

1. Beth: and we took Penny for a walk.

2. T: whe:re did you ta:ke her?

3. Beth: (1.0) uh::m

4. T: outside the house you mean

5. Beth: no we went a:ll the way down (.) we did.

→6. T: down whe:re.

(puzzled look)

7. Beth: uh:m (.) to see the sea

8. T: oh ri:ght? it's near the sea is it.

9. Beth: yeah

The teacher responds to Beth by enquiring about the walk with the dog. The enquiry is itemised in so far as she targets the location of the walk as a topic for further talk. Beth's pause and hesitation ('uh::m') show that a response is being searched for. To assist Beth's search, the teacher offers a candidate location in line 4. However, as the reported event is Beth's experience, she holds the expert knowledge about what happened and rejects the teacher's version with 'no'. Following the rejection, Beth does supply some information that answers the teacher's enquiry ('we went all the way down'). At line 6, given the puzzled look, the teacher treats this turn as providing partial information regarding the location of the walk. The request uses just one lexical item of the child's turn ('down') but adds a wh-type question. There are two important dimensions to the word: lexically, 'whe:re' indicates that a location is the source of trouble; prosodically, the stress on 'whe:re' marks out the specific item that lacks clarity. In response (line 7) Beth answers the question by supplying potentially clarifying information. The teacher next displays an understanding which is confirmed by Beth. The correction initiation at line 6, then, is heard by the child as an invitation to offer further information which has the additional effect of clarifying her news report.

The final example displays a definition-type request that has a grammatical format 'what's X?'. In this way, the teacher initiates correction on a lexical item used by the child in that context. The child hears the teacher's initiation as a request to provide a partial definition regarding the trouble source. The example takes place during a story writing activity where ideas about the story's plot are being discussed.

Extract 18: Specific correction initiation (wh-question)

1. T: what did they do:

2. Fay: ge (0.2) get a sh<u>e</u>d

3. T: a SHED?

4. Fay: *(nods)*

→5. T: what's a sh<u>e</u>d.

(shakes head)

6. Fay: when it's <u>rai</u>ning when it's <u>rai</u>ning

7. T: you've got an idea that a shed is for when it's <u>rai</u>ning?

8. (0.3)

9. T: is that right?

10. Fay: yeah

The teacher is asking about what the characters of the story might do next. Fay offers a candidate idea about getting a 'shed'. The teacher then repeats the last two words that the child said with additional loudness on 'SHED' and rising intonation. The child treats this as a confirmation check and nods. The teacher's question at line 5 signals her ongoing trouble with Fay's idea, also confirmed by the shaking of her head. The question has the appearance of a request for definition. Perhaps owing to her language difficulty, Fay is unable to supply a standard definition (e.g. a small wooden building). Interestingly, Fay instead supplies a novel idea that is relevant to the story-line. The teacher's subsequent reformulation (line 7) incorporates the ideas from line 2 as well as the new material from line 6. Important sequential work has been done by the correction initiation: it achieves a definition by the child which contributes to the on-going story-line; it also creates a sequential opportunity for the teacher (line 7) to supply an expanded re-formulation of the child's ideas.

Conclusion

This chapter has shown how children with SLCN can be active and competent participants during classroom interactions despite their language difficulties. The chapter has illustrated a range of teacher practices that facilitate this participation. In terms of topic initiation, 'wh-type' questions, and initiations such as 'tell me about…' have been shown to signal that the child has authority for talking about the topic at hand. 'Topic invitations' during story writing are strongly suited to the children's involvement in decisions about topical content (e.g. story beginnings, characters, setting and plot).

The chapter has shown how children's errors and omissions can be harnessed as language learning opportunities by the teacher. In the examples here where the teachers corrected the children's grammar or phonology, the children did not orient to the correction when it was 'embedded' in the teacher's turn. By contrast, when the teachers 'exposed' the correction with prosodic features such as loudness or final turn placement, the children did self-correct. The conclusion is that the teacher is increasing the children's authority through the use of 'exposed' correction of form. It is important to note that the exposed/embedded distinction used in this chapter is related to, but slightly different from, Jefferson's (1987) usage.

The analysis also examined repairs and corrections that are located in sequences following the teachers' initiating questions and the learners' problematic responses. In Extract 14, the teacher signalled problems with hearing or understanding of the child's responses in three ways during the episode. However, the teacher did not help the child by locating the item to be repaired. Instead, the repair initiators targeted the whole of the child's prior turn. The final extracts (Extracts 15–18), demonstrated ways in which the teacher provided more assistance to the learner with SLCN. These examples are termed here 'specific correction initiations' because the teachers targeted either the location or the nature of the troublesome turn. By indicating the location, further information was generated from the child and the learner's authority was increased.

This chapter has theoretical significance because it is the first to address the issue of how teachers can downgrade their authority and increase the participation of children with SLCN. The oral intervention examples from the chapter will therefore be helpful for those who work with children with SLCN in classrooms: for example, speech and language therapists, teachers and teaching assistants.

References

American Psychiatric Association. (2013). *Diagnostic and statistical manual of mental disorders* (5th ed.). Washington, DC: Author.

Button, G., & Casey, N. (1984). Generating topic: The use of topic initial elicitors. In *Structures of social action*. Cambridge: Cambridge University Press.

Button, G., & Casey, N. (1985). Topic nomination and topic pursuit. *Human Studies, 8,* 3–55.

Cazden, C. B., & Beck, S. W. (2003). Classroom discourse. In A. Graesser, M. Gersbacher, & S. Goldman (Eds.), *Handbook of discourse processes* (pp. 165–198). Linden, NJ: LEA.

Department for Education. (2015). *Special educational needs and disability code of practice 0 to 25 years*. London: DfE.

Drew, P. (1997). Open class repair initiators in response to sequential sources of trouble in conversation. *Journal of Pragmatics, 28,* 69–101. https://doi.org/10.1016/s0378-2166(97)89759-7.

Heritage, J., & Raymond, G. (2005). The terms of agreement: Indexing epistemic authority and subordination through talk in interaction. *Social Psychology Quarterly, 68,* 15–38. https://doi.org/10.1177/019027250506800103.

Jefferson, G. (1987). On exposed and embedded correction in conversation. In G. Button & J. Lee (Eds.), *Talk and social organization* (pp. 86–100). Clevedon: Multilingual Matters.

Macbeth, D. (2004). The relevance of repair for classroom correction. *Language in Society, 33,* 703–736. https://doi.org/10.1017/S0047404504045038.

McHoul, A. (1990). The organization of repair in classroom talk. *Language in Society, 19*(3), 349–377. https://doi.org/10.1017/S004740450001455X.

Mehan, H. (1979). *Learning lessons: Social organization in the classroom.* Cambridge, MA and London: Harvard University Press.

Norbury, C., Vamvakas, G., Gooch, D., Baird, G., Charman, T., Simonoff, E., et al. (2017). Language growth in children with heterogeneous language disorders: A population study. *Journal of Child Psychology and Psychiatry, 58,* 1092–1105. https://doi.org/10.1111/jcpp.12793.

Radford, J. (2010a). Practices of other-initiated repair and correction in SSLD classroom discourse. *Applied Linguistics, 31,* 25–44. https://doi.org/10.1093/applin/amn046.

Radford, J. (2010b). Adult participation in children's word searches: On the use of prompting, hinting and supplying a model. *Clinical Linguistics and Phonetics*, 83–100. https://doi.org/10.3109/02699200903407149.

Radford, J., Ireson, J., & Mahon, M. (2006). Triadic dialogue in oral communication tasks: What are the implications for language learning? *Language and Education, 20,* 191–210. https://doi.org/10.1080/09500780608668723.

Radford, J., Ireson, J., & Mahon, M. (2012). The organisation of repair in SSLD classroom discourse: How to expose the trouble source. *Journal of Interactional Research in Communication Disorders, 3,* 143–165. https://doi.org/10.1558/jircd.v3i2.171.

Radford, J., & Tarplee, C. (2000). The management of conversational topic by a ten-year-old child with pragmatic difficulties. *Clinical Linguistics and Phonetics, 14,* 387–403. https://doi.org/10.1080/02699200050051092.

Rusk, F., Sahlstrom, F., & Porn, M. (2017). Initiating and carrying out L2 instruction by asking known answer questions. *Linguistics and Education, 38,* 55–67.

Schegloff, E. A. (1997). Practices and actions: Boundary cases of other-initiated repair. *Discourse Processes, 23,* 499–545. https://doi.org/10.1080/01638539709545001.

Schegloff, E. A. (2007). *Sequence organisation in interaction: A primer in conversation analysis*. Cambridge: Cambridge University Press.

Schegloff, E. A., Jefferson, G., & Sacks, H. (1977). The preference for self-correction in the organization of repair in conversation. *Language, 53*, 361–382.

Sidnell, J. (2012). Who knows best? Evidentiality and epistemic asymmetry in conversation. *Pragmatics and Society, 3*, 294–320.

Part III

The Impact of Fluency Impairments Within Social Interaction

11

'My Own Space in This World': Stammering, Telephone Calls, and the Progressivity and Permeability of Turns-at-Talk

Ray Wilkinson and Sarah Morris

While there is some disagreement surrounding the definition of stammering,[1] most studies describe similar forms of stammering behaviours. The disruption in the rhythmic flow of speech can be characterised by repetition (of sounds, syllables or words), sound prolongations, and blocking on sounds (Bloodstein and Bernstein Ratner 2008). These features can also be accompanied by 'secondary behaviours', which include facial grimaces, eye blinking and loss of eye contact (Blomgren 2013). The person who stammers (PWS) may also display avoidance and

[1]'Stammering' and 'stuttering' are synonyms. The former is commonly used in the UK (and will be used in this chapter), while the latter is more commonly used in, for example, the USA, where many of the videorecordings we discuss in this chapter appear to have been made.

R. Wilkinson (✉)
Department of Human Communication Sciences,
University of Sheffield, Sheffield, UK

S. Morris
Worcestershire Health and Care NHS Trust, Worcestershire, UK

© The Author(s) 2020
R. Wilkinson et al. (eds.), *Atypical Interaction*,
https://doi.org/10.1007/978-3-030-28799-3_11

compensatory behaviours such as circumlocutions, substitutions and manual gestures (Guitar 2013). Psychosocial and emotional issues such as social anxiety are commonly associated with stammering (Bricker-Katz et al. 2010). The causes of stammering are not well understood but the condition typically develops in children between the ages of two and five (Guitar 2013). The prevalence of stammering in the general population is currently believed to be around one per cent, with many children recovering spontaneously before adulthood (Yairi and Ambrose 1999), and boys five to six times more likely than girls to stammer at the age of ten (Bloodstein and Bernstein Ratner 2008).

In this chapter we use Conversation Analysis (CA) to investigate dyadic interactions between people who stammer and non-stammering interlocutors. Compared to other forms of communicative impairment, there has been relatively little research using CA to investigate naturally-occurring interactions involving people who stammer (with some exceptions being, for example, Tetnowski and Damico 2001, Acton 2004, and Lind and Sønsterud 2014).

The data we analyse here consists of the PWS in a particular context: talking to another person on the telephone. The telephone is notoriously a mode of communication which many people who stammer find difficult; one survey found, for example, that 63% of people who stammer surveyed experienced it as more difficult than having a face-to-face conversation (James et al. 1999). James et al. (1999, p. 301) summarise some of the likely reasons for this difficulty:

> The combination of the highly defined beginnings of telephone calls, their generally dyadic nature and often specific content, anticipation as the telephone rings and the need to start speaking at the moment the call is answered contrive to make using the telephone a potentially hazardous task for those with stuttering impairment, and one exacerbated by the fact that, should blocking difficulties arise, their interlocutor may be unclear as to what is happening.

They also note that for people who stammer, the phone removes the use of non-vocal resources, with the speaker having to rely on the vocal modality alone.

The data for the analysis comes primarily from *YouTube* and consists of video-recordings of phone calls where the PWS makes a call to an institutional setting such as a doctor's surgery, restaurant, shop or other business. We found around 400 of these video-recordings on *YouTube* and examined around 30 of these in some detail, from which the extracts analysed here are chosen. The recordings appear to have been uploaded most commonly by the PWS who is in the recording, and many include the PWS addressing the camera before and/or after the telephone call, often discussing the call they are about to make or have just made. Some of these addresses to camera are clearly directed primarily at an audience of other people who stammer, and most of the people who stammer in our data set have uploaded more than one video, with several providing a name (either verbally or visibly on the screen) and/or a twitter handle. Where the PWS provides a name, we use a pseudonym in the transcript; otherwise we use the generic 'PWS'.

While the focus of our analysis here is on the telephone calls in the recordings, in the concluding section of the chapter we will also present and discuss a quote from one of these addresses to camera in the context of highlighting some possible links between the interactional issues examined in the analysis and some of the more psychosocial issues highlighted in this address to camera.

The transcriptions of the extracts make use of the usual CA transcription symbols. One symbol we make use of here which is perhaps less commonly used is an italicized letter within brackets—e.g. (*d*)—which can be used to indicate an 'incipient sound' (Jefferson 2004). It is used here to capture some instances where the PWS is forming a particular phoneme but is not at that moment actually fully producing it.

Analysis

In analyzing these interactions between people who stammer and service providers (such as people who work in a shop, restaurant or doctor's surgery) we will focus on three main questions.

The first is: how does a stammer manifest itself within talk-in-interaction? In other words, how is the talk within interaction of people who stammer systematically different to that of typical speakers (i.e. here, people who do not have, or appear to have, a stammer or other communicative impairment).

The second is: in what way can stammering be seen to have an interactional impact, including an impact on the interactional contribution of the other person in the interaction? Another way of considering this question is in terms of how stammering may be seen to have interactional consequences for the participants and whether, and how, these consequences may be seen to be potentially problematic or troublesome, in particular for the PWS.

The third is: in relation to features of stammering interaction which may indeed prove problematic for the PWS, what type of resources or practices might people who stammer use to push back against, or mitigate, this problematicity?

Stammering and Disrupted TCU Progressivity

We will consider the first question first. In examining these interactions, it is clear that a systematic way in which stammering becomes manifest within talk is through disruption to the progressivity of the PWS's turn-constructional units (TCUs), and hence his/her turns-at-talk.

In explaining what we mean by this, it is necessary to provide some information on what CA research has uncovered about the nature of turns and TCUs. Turns (or 'turns-at-talk') are made up of one or more TCUs i.e. a sentence, clause, phrase or word which can, within the context in which it is produced, constitute a complete turn by the speaker (Sacks et al. 1974). When a participant begins to produce a TCU and successfully takes the floor (for example, they are the only person speaking), then the TCU they are producing is their 'turn space' (Lerner 1996). The speaker has a right to keep possession of this turn space (and hence the conversational floor) until their talk reaches a transition-relevance place (TRP) i.e. a possible end of the turn. At a TRP another participant can take over the floor without being seen to be 'interrupting', or otherwise be entering the turn space of, the current speaker. However, as well as having a right to maintain possession of the turn space, the speaker with the floor also has obligations, including an obligation to continue the TCU until it reaches a TRP, and to do so in a manner which displays (relatively) smooth progressivity (Lerner 1996). TCU progressivity here refers to the forward movement of the TCU towards completion such that 'each element – each word, for example – should come next after the one before; in fact, at a smaller level of granularity, each syllable – indeed, each sound – should come next after the one before it' (Schegloff 2007, p. 14).

It is this expected smooth progress of the TCU, word-by-word and sound-by-sound, towards its possible completion that stammering disrupts. Indeed, to consider it another way, it is this disruption which makes the speaker hearable to other participants *as* a stammerer (or at least, as someone who is systematically having difficulty in 'getting their words out'). This is because while undisrupted TCU progressivity is the preferred, 'unmarked' state of affairs which renders the process of producing talk something which is un-noticed and taken for granted (Garfinkel 1967), disrupted progressivity is a 'marked' and noticeable phenomenon which can lead to listeners examining the talk and the speaker for possible reasons for this particular form of disrupted progressivity (Schegloff 1979, 2007).

The delayed progressivity evident in stammering talk regularly takes a particular form whereby it is at the level of progression to the next sound or syllable that delay is evident.[2] Consider Extract 1 for instance. Here Tabitha, a young woman who stammers, has called a restaurant to see if they take reservations:

[2]This is different to, for example, anomia in the talk of people with aphasia where it is commonly at the level of progressing to the next *word* that delayed progressivity is evident (Wilkinson 2019). That form of delayed progressivity may be marked by signs of searching for a word or phrase, including production of the word search token 'uhm', and utterances such as 'what's the word?'.

Extract 1

```
01              ((Tabitha dials a number; phone rings))
02     Rest:    (name of restaurant) this is Martin can I help you?
03  →  Tab:     hi uhm, n-n-n-n->du-du-< n-n- do- do- (.) do- do-
04  →           do- do you guys take re- re- re- re- reservations?
05     Rest:    yes! (.) for when?
06  →  Tab:     uhm for (.) t- t- (.) t- t- t- (4.5) t- t- t-
07              tomorrow night?
08     Rest:    yuh perfect. how many?
```

After a restaurant employee ('Rest' in the transcript) answers the phone (line 02) Tabitha (in lines 03 and 04) produces a greeting and a question which constitutes her reason for the call (to see if she can make a reservation). The greeting ('hi') is produced unproblematically, but the TCU within which Tabitha is attempting to produce her question displays markedly delayed progressivity. For example, there is a delay which takes the form of repeated sounds before the first word of the TCU, 'do', is produced. A further delay in progressivity is caused by that word then being repeated several times before the next words in the unfolding TCU are produced fluently i.e. 'you guys take'. The next word, 'reservations', is started but the first syllable is repeated four times. This again delays the progress of the TCU before the word is then produced as a whole (line 04). On the completed production of 'reservations', Tabitha has produced a TCU which can be heard as syntactically, intonationally and pragmatically complete, and at this point the other participant can (and does) start a TCU without this talk being heard as invasive of Tabitha's turn space. Similarly, when Tabitha responds concerning when she wants the reservation for (lines 06–07), she is able to produce the first phoneme of the word 'tomorrow' but repeats it several times, halting the progressivity of the TCU, before she is then able to produce the words 'tomorrow night'. The progressivity of this utterance is also significantly delayed by a 4.5 second silence (line 06) when Tabitha appears to block. This length of intra-TCU silence is noticeably long compared to silences in typical interaction, where the standard maximum length is around 1 second (Jefferson 1989).

Another Speaker Entering the Turn Space of the Person Who Stammers

The phenomenon of delayed TCU progressivity that was evident in Extract 1 will be seen to a greater or lesser extent in all of the other extracts in this chapter. In this section, however, we wish to focus predominantly on our second question, concerning the interactional consequences of this delayed progressivity and how it may prove potentially troublesome or problematic, in particular for the PWS. One recurrent consequence of delayed progressivity in the turn of the PWS in our data is that another participant enters the turn space of the PWS. We will examine three forms that this type of incursion takes: (1) TCU completion; (2) incursive other-initiation of repair; and (3) checking on the availability or presence of the PWS in the phone call. While such incursion does not, of course, invariably occur in the environment of stammering dysfluencies (as seen from Extract 1)[3] the turns of people who stammer do appear to be recurrently vulnerable to such incursion in certain systematic ways as will be discussed in this section.

This vulnerability to turn incursion by another participant when a speaker's turn displays dysfluencies and other forms of TCU delays to progressivity is also present in the talk of typical speakers. Discussing these progressivity delays, or 'hitches' as she sometimes calls them, Jefferson (1983, p. 27) notes that "'hitches' generate recipient activities. And not infrequently the activity engendered by a 'hitch' is the starting up of a recipient's talk, regardless of the (in)auspiciousness or interactional (im)propriety of starting at such a place". In this situation, if the first speaker continues to talk then this can be a site for overlapping talk, here in the form of what Jefferson (1983) calls 'progressional' (or 'hitch') overlap onset. As such, what we can see in this section is a phenomenon (turn incursion) that is present in the social interactions

---

[3]It is notable, however, that in her address to the camera after the call Tabitha explicitly comments on how good the restaurant employee was as a call recipient of a person who stammers, and how this kind of response is unusual. She says, for example: 'That was a really awesome reaction… That guy was super patient and understanding. He didn't really do anything wrong, which is – sadly – not that common'.

of typical speakers at points of dysfluency or delay, but which people who stammer may be particularly vulnerable to given the regularly dysfluent nature of their talk.

TCU Completion

Lerner (1996) discusses one particular form of turn incursion by another participant that recurrently occurs when a speaker's talk displays delayed progressivity: that of TCU/turn completion when another participant enters the speaker's turn space and completes the TCU, building on the TCU from the point it has reached at that time.

Two examples of this type of turn incursion in stammering interaction will be discussed here (cf. Lind and Sønsterud 2014). In Extract 2, Mick, a PWS, is calling a doctor's surgery to make an appointment.

Extract 2

01			((*Mick dials a number; phone rings*))
02		Rec:	good morning the surgery good morning?
03	→	Mick:	uh-uhm h-h-h-h-hi uhm
04	→		a-a-a-a-I-a-a-a-a-a-I-I would like to book
05	→		ay-ay-ay-ay-ay-ay-ay uhm (0.5) uhm uhm uhm
06	→	Rec:	appointment yes?=
07		Mick:	=yes

After Mick produces a greeting, he attempts to provide the reason for his call, but this utterance (lines 04–05) is markedly delayed and gets a candidate completion by the surgery receptionist ('Rec') in line 06.

Similarly, in Extract 3 the PWS phones with an enquiry about how far the service being contacted makes deliveries. After the greeting by the PWS, the question which constitutes the reason for the call displays delayed progressivity (lines 04–05) and the service provider (SP) produces a candidate completion of that question (lines 06–07):

Extract 3

```
        ((phone rings))
SP:     (     ) what can I do for ya?
PWS:    uh h- h- h- h- h: °(gh gh)° (1.0) hi,
        I- I was wondering:, how fa:r you all d- d- >d-
        d- d-< d- > d- d- d-< d- d- (0.6) [>d- d- d-<
SP:                                       [how far we
        deliver?
PWS:    Yes
SP:     uh:m, eh its just kind of more, its not really a
        distance thing, its like a ti:me thing
```

In both of these cases the candidate completion is produced at a point in the talk where the significant delay in progressivity highlights the noticeable difficulty the PWS is having in producing the next due items. In Extract 2, the completion occurs following several repeated 'ay's and then four 'uhm's with a silence (an intra-turn pause of 0.5 seconds) within them. In Extract 3, it occurs in the environment of a 0.6 second pause which follows 11 repeats of the first phoneme ('d') of the target word 'deliver'. In both cases the co-participant does not simply complete the TCU but rather presents the completion as tentative and something to be confirmed by the PWS, and in each case the PWS provides such a confirmation.

Incursive Other-Initiations of Repair

In our data it is not uncommon for a recipient of the PWS' talk to produce an other-initiation of repair (OIR) (Schegloff 2000) following dysfluent talk. The OIRs in these interactions generally function to indicate that the recipient is having a problem in understanding the talk of the PWS at this point.

In Extract 4, for instance, the PWS is phoning an organization that runs swimming pools in order to try to choose which of two swimming pools ('Gamforth' or 'Gampark') run by the organization he might send his children to for lessons. Three times within this short extract the service provider (SP) who answers the call responds to the PWS' dysfluent turn with an other-initiation of repair (lines 07, 15 and 18).[4]

Extract 4

((*phone rings*))
PWS: hi (.) uhm uhm uhm I eh I- I was w- w- w- w- w-
w-wo:ndering wha- wh:at makes G- G- G- G- G- G-
G-Gamforth better (.) than ehm G- G- G- >G-_G-
G- Gam (.) p- p- >p- p- p-< park.
(1.3)
→ SP: what makes Gamforth better than Gampark?
PWS: y- y- y:es.
(0.9)
SP: uhm well we do a high dive and Gampark doesn't.
(1.2)
PWS: i- i- i- i- i- i- i- (.) i- is z- z- z- is:::::
th- th::at the only th:::::ing?
(1.4)
→ SP: sorry, what?
PWS: is th:::::::::::::: that the only
th:::::::::::::ing?
→ SP: is that the only thing?
PWS: y:::: y:es.
(0.5)
SP: well I mean both pools are goo:d.

[4]It should be noted that the reasons why the talk of people who stammer can regularly be treated by another participant as a trouble source may be more complex than simply the fact that the turn is produced dysfluently. Informal observation of the data (which we are not in a position to expand on here more systematically) suggests that on some occasions a PWS may produce talk which is more 'compacted' than might generally be the case in typical speakers. The compactness may be at the level of social action and its position within the conversation (e.g. an action is produced in an earlier 'slot' than might be expected in the conversation) or of form (e.g. the lexical and grammatical construction of the turn may be different/more compacted compared to that commonly used by typical speakers). In Extract 4, for instance, the PWS' question in lines 02–05 may be slightly unexpected to the call receiver who may instead be expecting a more explicit 'reason for call' in this slot (e.g. 'I'm phoning to enquire about swimming lessons you offer for children').

A feature of these three OIRs is that, in comparison to the pattern we will show in the following extracts in this section (Extracts 5–7), they are produced in the manner generally observed in typical interaction (Schegloff et al. 1977); that is, the OIR is not produced until the other participant's turn is hearably complete, and indeed is often only produced after a gap following that turn (as in lines 06–07 and 14–15).

While it is evident that some of the OIRs in stammering interaction are produced in this 'typical' manner, a recurrent feature of OIRs by recipients of the talk of speakers who stammer is that their OIRs are 'incursive', that is, they are produced prior to the PWS's turn reaching a TRP and being hearably complete and, as such, they occur within the turn space of the PWS.

Three examples of this phenomenon are presented here. In each case, because the PWS continues to speak as the other participant starts talking, overlap occurs. As such, these examples are similar to those described by Jefferson (1983) as 'progressional' (or 'hitch') overlap onset, although in the examples here the delays to progressivity are generally more significant than in Jefferson's (1983) examples.

Extract 5 (continuation of Extract 2)

```
08      Rest:  yuh perfect. how many?
09      Tab:   uhm just (1.4) >t- t- t- t- [t-<
10  →   Rest:                              [how many?
11      Tab:   uhm just (.) t- t- t- t- two
12      Rest:  two? what time?
```

In response to the restaurant employee's question about how many people the reservation is for (line 08), Tabitha is able to produce the word 'just' but then the production of the next word ('two') is significantly delayed, first by a long silence (cf. Jefferson 1989) and then by repeats of the first phoneme of the target word (line 09). While Tabitha is continuing to try to produce the word 'two', the restaurant employee enters her turn space and produces an OIR[5] which overlaps with Tabitha's continued attempt (line 10).

Incursive OIRs such as that seen in Extract 5 can be heard as highlighting the problematicity of the PWS's talk in two ways. First, they can mark that the recipient is having trouble understanding the PWS's talk and this can make salient the issue of whose responsibility (the speaker's or the recipient's) it may be that communication here was not successful (Robinson 2006). As such, attention can be drawn to the dysfluent talk of the PWS as a possible factor in the repair being produced. Second, the OIR here is 'marked' and noticeable in that its positioning is different to that generally observed in typical interaction (i.e. it is produced early and incursively). Again, this can make inferable possible reasons for this marked occurrence, such as the fact that the progressivity of the PWS's TCU towards completion was significantly delayed.

In Extract 6, Janice has phoned a cafeteria to ask about their opening times. However, after her greeting and before the reason for the call, she produces another action: an announcement that she stammers and that it therefore can take longer for her to get her utterances out (lines 03 and 05–06). Later in the chapter we will look in more detail at this practice of a PWS mentioning (typically near the beginning of the phone call) that they stammer; here, our interest is in the fact that this utterance, which displays delayed progressivity, particularly in the form of two long intra-TCU silences, is the target of an incursive OIR (line 07). In this case it is an 'open class' OIR (Drew 1997), which may signal to the PWS that is something about the turn as a whole (rather than one or more particular words) that is proving troublesome for the recipient to understand.

[5]While the words are a repeat of his original question (in line 08), the prosodic features, including a stress on 'how' (marked in the transcript with underlining) make this hearable as an OIR in response to Tabitha's ongoing turn and not simply a repeat of the question as if Tabitha had not spoken.

Extract 6

01		Café:	(name of cafeteria) this is Cameron how may I
02			help you
03		Jan:	hi, (.) I stu-
04		Café:	hi ⌈:,
05		Jan:	⌊stu- (.) stutter and so s-s-sometimes uhm
06			(1.5) (I) (1.6) (i⌈ts)
07	→	Café:	⌊I'm sorry what?
08			(0.3)
09		Jan:	I stutter and so- so- so it takes t:ime
10			for me to (.) talk s-s-sometimes okay?
11		Café:	okay.
12		Jan:	thank you. uhm I was tr- tr- trying to figure out

Extract 7 (which is a continuation of Extract 3) provides another example where a PWS' turn which is displaying delayed progressivity (lines 13–14) is responded to with an incursive OIR (line 15), again in the form of an open-class repair initiation.

Extract 7

09		SP:	uh:m, eh its just kind of more, its not really a
10			distance thing, its like a ti:me thing=well, where
11			you located at?
12			(1.1)
13		PWS:	the th- th- th- th- th- th- th- th- th- (.)>lu-
14			lu-< (1.1) lu- the lan⌈dings.
15	→	SP:	⌊I'm sorry what was that?
16			(0.6)
17		PWS:	l- the lu- lan (.) gh (.) l:andings.

This extract displays a further feature of incursive OIRs; namely, that by being produced while the other speaker is still speaking they risk overlapping a key word that may in fact have made the turn understandable and not in need of repair. Here, for example, the SP's OIR is produced just at the point when the PWS is starting to produce a key word that will provide an answer to the service provider's question about her location (lines 14–15).

Checking on the Availability/Presence of the PWS Within the Phone Call

A third recurrent practice of the co-participant which involves entering the turn space of the PWS is when the co-participant checks that the PWS is still available/on the line. In Extracts 8 and 9 this takes the form of 'hello?', used here not as a greeting but as akin to a summons (Schegloff 2002), eliciting a response from the PWS as a means of checking that the PWS is still on the line and that the phone connection is still working.

In both extracts here it can be seen how the dysfluency of the PWS can lead to the co-participant being unsure if the PWS is still available on the phone and thus needing to check.[6] In Extract 8, for instance, Tabitha is phoning a restaurant (a different one to that in Extract 1), but after her greeting she has difficulty in producing even the first phoneme of the next word clearly (lines 02 and 03). After some time has passed without a clear phoneme being produced, the restaurant employee produces a 'hello?', apparently to check that Tabitha is still on the line (line 04). At this point, therefore, the co-participant is entering the turn space of the PWS, albeit for a different type of reason to those seen above in this section.

[6]Extracts 8 and 9 can be seen as empirical instances of the risk for people who stammer talking on the telephone which was highlighted as a hypothetical possibility by James et al (1999, p. 301) in the quote above i.e. that 'should blocking difficulties arise, their interlocutor may be unclear as to what is happening'.

Extract 8

```
01        Rest:   (         )
02        Tab:    hi:, uhm (d) (d) (d) (d) (d) (.) (d) (d)
03                (d) ⌈(d)
04   →    Rest:       ⌊hello?
05                (0.4)
06        Tab:    uhm do- do- do- do- do- >do you guys< take ru-
07                ru- ru- reservations?
08                (0.3)
09        Rest:   we eh do in our dining room,
```

In Extract 9 (later in the same call that was seen in Extract 6), the co-participant's checking of availability occurs as the call is heading towards its closing. Janice has called a restaurant and has enquired what time they stop serving breakfast. The answer is given as five pm (line 15). Janice then indicates that that was all she wanted to ask and thanks the restaurant employee (lines 16–17), who receipts this with 'yeah. no problem' (line 19). After a brief silence, Janice produces an 'alright' (line 21). All the indications are that the business of the call is now completed and both speakers are moving to close the call (Schegloff and Sacks 1973). It might be expected that since Janice was the person who made the call, she will also be first to move into the closing proper with a token such as 'bye'. While this is indeed the case, Janice's 'bye' is delayed in its production, with a long 1.5 second silence occurring at this point. This delay is what appears to trigger the checking of the PWS's availability by the restaurant employee, which occurs just after Janice eventually produces her first 'bye' (lines 21 and 22).

Extract 9

```
15        Rest:    (        ) five pm
16        Jan:     okay. (0.3) uh well that's all s-so th-th-
17                 th-thank you.
18                 (0.3)
19        Rest:    yeah. no problem
20                 (0.8)
21        Jan:     alright (1.5) bye b[ye
22     → Rest:                        [hello?
23                 (uh) (.) have a good one. take care
24        Jan:     [same] th-thank you.
```

In both extracts, therefore, the checking of availability has occurred where the recipient is by rights expecting the PWS to produce a next due item (for example, a reason for calling in Extract 8, and a closing token in Extract 9). The delay in that next due item being produced (apparently linked to dysfluencies in both cases) is what leads the co-participant to check availability/presence and thus (since in both cases the PWS is indeed still on the line and is trying to continue the turn) entering the turn space of the PWS.

Presenting Oneself on the Phone as Someone Who Stammers

So far in this chapter we have focused on two main phenomena within interactions involving a PWS. One is that stammering disrupts TCU progressivity. The other is that this delayed/disrupted TCU progressivity constitutes a site within the TCU where another participant may – and in our dataset regularly does – enter the turn space of the PWS. We examined three forms which such turn incursion recurrently takes in our dataset: TCU/turn completions, incursive OIRs, and availability/presence checks. As such, our findings suggest that the dysfluencies associated with stammering may make the turn space of the PWS particularly vulnerable and 'permeable' (Lerner 1996) to other speakers. Since one's turn space is typically seen as one's own preserve, with incursions into it by others potentially perceivable as interruptive,[7] these incursive practices by other speakers run the risk of challenging the interactional autonomy of the PWS and highlighting their inability to patrol the borders of, and maintain, their own interactional space i.e. their turn space.[8]

These observations bring us to the third question we posed above, i.e. whether people who stammer may display some practices in their talk which can be seen as working to mitigate some of the interactional difficulties stammering may engender for them. Here we focus on what appears to be one such practice, namely presenting oneself on the phone as someone who stammers (a practice referred to by people who stammer as 'advertising'). This practice typically appears at or near the start of the phone call in our dataset. We will discuss three examples of the phenomenon here.

In Extract 10, Amanda is phoning a store to enquire about returning an item. The store employee (SE) answers the phone and says something which is not intelligible on the recording, but is likely to be an institutional self-identification, including the name of the company/store that the caller has got through to. At this point, Amanda as the caller would be expected to produce a greeting and a reason for her call (as in, for example, Extracts 1–4 above). Before she does this however, she produces two other TCUs. The first (lines 03–06) is an announcement and self-presentation of herself as someone who stammers ('actually first let me tell you that I'm a person who stutters') and,

[7]Not all incursions into another's turn space are necessarily perceivable as interruptive or invasive. See, for example, Lerner (1996) for speaker practices which allow another participant to enter the speaker's turn space in ways which are not necessarily treated as interruptive.

[8]This is not to suggest that every incursion into the turn space of people who stammer will necessarily be perceived by them to be unwelcome or unhelpful; such issues of what is deemed to be helpful or unhelpful in particular circumstances await further research. Rather, the more general point is perhaps that people who stammer are more vulnerable than typical speakers to others entering their turn space, whether or not on that particular occasion they facilitate this happening.

immediately following that (as shown by means of the 'latching' symbol) the second presents a consequence of that fact ('so I'm gonna need you to be a little patient'). It is only after this (line 11) that she then does a greeting (which sounds like it is done as a response to a greeting by the store employee) and the reason for her call.

Extract 10

01		SE:	*((store employee answers the phone; sound of*
02			*talk but not intelligible on the recording))*
03	→	Aman:	uhm, a- actually uhm >f- f- f-< f:irst le- le-
04	→		let me tell you tha- >th- th- th-< that I'm a
05	→		pu- pu- person who (.) s::(*t*) s::(*t*) s::(*t*)
06	→		stutters=so I'm go::nna need you to be a little
07	→		pu- pu- patient,
08		?SE:	⌈*((?store employee response, including*
09			*greeting?; no talk audible in recording))*
10		Aman:	⌊.hhh uhm
11			hi! uhm, I'm uh ca- ca- calling uh because

Interactionally, what might the PWS gain through presenting themselves as a stammerer in this way and at this point in the phone call? Saying that she needs the recipient to be patient can be heard as the PWS highlighting the fact that her talk may not be as fluent as a typical speaker and that the recipient will need to give her more time to get her utterances produced. In the terms we have been using in this chapter, Amanda's turn in lines 03–07 is, in effect, providing a reason for the dysfluencies which may occur in her talk and, in this way, possibly lessening the chance at these junctures of the recipient entering her turn space in ways such as we have seen above.

Of course, a possible risk of such a strategy is that self-identifying as a stammerer itself necessitates talk, the very form of communication which is vulnerable to dysfluencies in its production and hence vulnerable to possible incursion by another participant. Another possible source of problems is that in the interactional 'slot' where the self-identification is produced (for example in Extract 10) the recipient is likely to be expecting a different kind of action or actions (for example, a greeting and a reason for the call) and this may make the self-identification as a stammerer vulnerable to not being properly grasped at that point. These risks are not simply hypothethical as can be seen in Extract 11 (which was presented earlier as Extract 6). Here the eventual utterance that Janice produces is 'I stutter and so it takes time for me to talk sometimes okay?' (lines 09–10). But Janice's first attempt at such an utterance is interrupted by the café employee with an incursive OIR (line 07).

Extract 11

```
01        Café:  (name of cafeteria) this is Cameron how may I
02               help you
03  →     Jan:   hi, (.) I stu-
04        Café:  hi⌈:,
05  →     Jan:     ⌊stu-  (.)  stutter  and  so  s-s-sometimes  uhm
                 (1.5)
06  →            (I) (1.6) (i⌈ts)
07        Café:                ⌊I'm sorry what?
08               (0.3)
09  →     Jan:   I stutter and so- so- so it takes t:ime
10  →            for me to (.) talk s-s-sometimes okay?
11        Café:  okay.
12        Jan:   thank you. uhm I was tr- tr- trying to figure out
```

Here, therefore, the attempt to mitigate the possible effects of stammering on the phone call has itself become a trouble source in the interaction, with the café employee apparently not following what Janice is saying here, perhaps because he was not expecting this type of action at this point at the start of the call.

There are, however, ways to present oneself as a stammerer towards the start of a phone call which can reduce the risk of the type of problems occurring which were evident in Extract 11. See, for example, Extract 12, where a PWS is calling an airline company with some questions about booking a ticket, and speaks to service provider (SP) from the sales section of the company.

Extract 12

01			((*phone rings*))
02		SP:	thanks for calling, this is general
03			sales. this is Mary how may I assist you?
04			(0.3)
05	→	PWS:	hu-hi. I actually was hu:-ha:ving a lo:t
06	→		lot of trouble with your au: au: automated
07	→		system, cos I s::: stutter, so it kept=
08		SP:	=uhuh
09	→	PWS:	m:i misunderstanding me.
10			(0.3)
11		SP:	oh no problem. i-it misunderstands a lot
12			of people
13		PWS:	yeah, ⌈I (.) ( )
14		SP:	⌊(so whats your) a:ccount number?

Here when the PWS starts to talk (lines 05–09) he produces the expected actions in this opening slot: a greeting and a reason for the call (i.e. he is calling the sales number after having trouble with the automated system). His presentation as a stammerer (line 07) is *embedded within* the reason for the call. This format means that the presentation as a stammerer does not itself take the form of a separate action, such as an announcement (as in Extract 10) produced within a turn which risks displaying delayed progressivity and possibly being the target of incursive talk by the co-participant. Also, by avoiding an action such as an announcement in the opening slot where the recipient will be expecting other actions from the caller (a greeting and/or reason for the call), he avoids producing a turn which leads to understanding problems for the recipient and the production by that recipient of a (possibly incursive) OIR.

Conclusion

Talking with others involves packaging one's talk within turns-at-talk (Sacks et al. 1974) and hence being subject to the social conventions (including the associated rights and obligations) involved in how turns-at-talk should be produced. Turns-at-talk are inherently *temporal* in that they unfold bit-by-bit over time as each item (sound, word, phrase etc.) is produced. But the nature of their temporality also includes some particular properties (Lerner 1996). For example, turns and the TCUs that constitute them are also *directional* in that they are hearable not just as emerging over time but also as heading towards a possible end point, a TRP. And this unfolding towards completion is expected to display smooth *progressivity*, with each next due item in the TCU being produced in the slot, and within the timeframe, as projected by the TCU produced thus far.

As has been highlighted in this chapter, these temporal features of turns-at-talk can be a source of difficulties for people who stammer. The dysfluencies associated with stammering disrupt the progressivity of the TCU towards completion and a regular consequence at this point is that another participant starts to talk, entering the turn space of the PWS.

One aspect of these temporal issues is that in interactions where a PWS talks with a person who does not stammer each may be on a rather different 'timeline' in regard to the production of their respective turns-at-talk (cf. Engelke and Higginbotham 2013). For example, each may be producing TCUs which advance towards completion with different 'styles' of progressivity (i.e. the non-stammering speaker may progress quicker towards completion and with less delays such as those in the form of repetitions or silences). Also, as suggested by the data analysed in this chapter, it is likely to be the case that these two 'styles' of progressivity are different in their interactional consequences; for example, the disruptions to progressivity in the talk of the PWS means that the turn space of the PWS is more likely to be entered by the non-stammering speaker than vice versa. And all of this, of course, occurs against a background where these two 'styles' may be judged by interactional participants quite differently; while a non-stammering speaker is producing talk in a manner where the progressivity of that talk is relatively smooth and thus 'unmarked' and generally 'normal' and un-noticed, dysfluencies in the talk of the PWS make that style of talking 'marked', noticeable and 'not normal'.

These issues may possibly be mitigated to some extent when the PWS is talking with an interlocutor who knows the speaker and has some knowledge of, and experience with, stammering.[9] However, they are likely to be particularly relevant in the type of situation analysed in this chapter, where the PWS is making a phone call to a setting where the institutional representative who answers the phone will not know the caller, will not know (at first) that they are a stammerer, and may have little knowledge or experience of stammering and what it entails within interaction.

In this context of talking to a stranger, then, we can see the act of verbally presenting oneself towards the start of the call as someone who stammers (as in Extracts 10–12), and perhaps making explicit the need therefore for the recipient to be patient (Extract 10) or to allow more time (Extract 11), as an attempt to subvert the usual tacit practices around turns and their timelines that would otherwise be implicitly adhered to by the call taker. As such, in Extracts 10 and 11 particularly, the PWS can be viewed as attempting to set particular 'ground rules' for the conversation which is about to take place, with the interlocutor being in effect requested to respect, and (to some extent at least) adapt their interactional conduct so as not to impede, the 'marked' form of TCU production which is likely to be displayed by the PWS.[10]

---

[9]In his discussion of 'stigma', Goffman (1963, p. 41) terms such people who are 'in the know' the 'wise'.

[10]In the sense used by Wilkinson (2019) the presentation of oneself towards the start of the call as a stammerer (for instance, in the form of an announcement) and the request for the interlocutor to be patient/allow more time (Extracts 10 and 11) can be seen as an example of an interactional adaptation. Adaptations can function as means of dealing with possible negative consequences of the communicative impairment, and a property of this particular type of adaptation by the PWS is that it can be seen to be designed to put some interactional pressure on the interlocutor to also adapt *their* usual conduct.

Thus, while the norms of typical interaction can create difficulties for people who stammer and highlight their hearable 'difference', people who stammer can, at least in individual conversations, push back against these norms of 'typical' society and attempt to influence the interlocutor to adopt interactional practices which are more facilitative for the person who stammers.

We conclude with some considerations concerning possible links between (1) the *interactional* issues that we have observed and analysed in the participants' conduct within these conversations, and (2) what the PWS who made the phone call says about their experience of it in the address to camera following the call, with particular regard to the *psychosocial* issues that the speaker raises. Immediately following the call that we have examined the start of in Extract 10 where Amanda presents herself to the store employee as a stammerer, she addresses the camera and discusses this practice and why she thinks it is a useful one:

'So there we go. No apologies, no asking them to excuse us. I simply told her a simple truth, that I am a person who stutters. And in doing that I made my own space in this world. And the walls that maybe could have seemed like they were closing in on me, I spread 'em open, I created a space where I could authentically be who I am, and keep the dignity intact. I simply told her what is going to happen and told her I need her to be patient. No 'bear[ing] with me', no shame. You and I are not something that needs to be dealt with'.[11]

These words appear to be addressed in particular to an audience of other people who stammer and while there are many interesting issues here, we wish to focus only on some features of Amanda's use of spatial descriptions.

She talks of how announcing herself to be a stammerer at the start of the call meant that 'I made my own space in this world' and how in this way 'I created a space where I could authentically be who I am'. She also talks of how this practice allowed her to spread open the walls that otherwise could have seemed like they were closing in on her. Amanda's

[11]Since our interest in this quote concerns its content rather than how it is produced, the transcription is a simple orthographic one which does not include the speaker's dysfluencies.

reflections here in relation to space appear to be focused primarily at a psychosocial level (for example, her right to authentically be herself in the world without any sense of inferiority or shame). There are also, however, interesting echoes of another—interactional—form of space i.e. the turn space. As we have described above, the turn space of people who stammer may be particularly vulnerable to incursion by others, whereas a practice such as presenting oneself as a stammerer and requesting time or patience from the interlocutor may be one way of attempting to maintain the boundaries of one's turn space and make it less permeable and liable to incursion. While we are not suggesting that Amanda here is necessarily consciously aware of notions such as 'turn space', her comments point to possible links between interactional and psychosocial issues that could be further explored. Such an exploration may be useful since for people who stammer, problems and the strategies they employ to combat those problems at the interactional level may have important resonances at the psychosocial level.

References

Acton, C. (2004). A conversation analytic perspective on stammering: Some reflections and observations. *Stammering Research, 1*(3), 249–70.

Bricker-Katz, G., Lincoln, M., & McCabe, P. (2010). Older people who stutter: Barriers to communication and perceptions of treatment needs. *International Journal of Language & Communication Disorders, 45*(1), 15–30.

Blomgren, M. (2013). Behavioral treatments for children and adults who stutter: A review. *Psychology Research and Behavior Management, 6,* 9–19.

Bloodstein, O., & Bernstein-Ratner, N. (2008). *A handbook on stuttering* (6th ed.). New York: Thomson-Delmar.

Drew, P. (1997). 'Open' class repair initiators in response to sequential sources of trouble in conversation. *Journal of Pragmatics, 28,* 69–101.

Engelke, C. R., & Higginbotham, D. J. (2013). Looking to speak: On the temporality of misalignment in interaction involving an augmented communicator using eye-gaze technology. *Journal of Interactional Research in Communication Disorders, 4*(1), 95–122.

Garfinkel, H. (1967). *Studies in ethnomethodology*. Englewood Cliffs, NJ: Prentice Hall.
Goffman, E. (1963). *Stigma*. Englewood Cliffs, NJ: Prentice-Hall.
Guitar, B. (2013). *Stuttering: An integrated approach to its nature and treatment* (4th ed.). Baltimore: Lippincott Williams & Wilkins.
James, S., Brumfitt, S., & Cudd, P. (1999). Communicating by telephone: Views of people with a stuttering impairment. *Journal of Fluency Disorders, 22*, 232–326.
Jefferson, G. (1983). Notes on some orderliness of overlap onset. *Tilburg Papers in Language and Literature, 28*(1), 1–28.
Jefferson, G. (1989). Preliminary notes on a possible metric which provides for a "standard maximum" silence of approximately one second in conversation. In D. Roger & P. Bull (Eds.), *Conversation: An interdisciplinary perspective* (pp. 166–196). Clevedon: Multilingual Matters.
Jefferson, G. (2004). Glossary of transcript symbols with an introduction. In G. Lerner (Ed.), *Conversation analysis: Studies from the first generation* (pp. 13–31). Amsterdam: John Benjamins.
Lerner, G. (1996). On the 'semi-permeable' character of grammatical units in conversation: conditional entry into the turn space of another speaker. In E. Ochs, E. A. Schegloff, & S. A. Thompson (Eds.), *Interaction and grammar* (pp. 238–276). Cambridge: Cambridge University Press.
Lind, M., & Sønsterud, H. (2014). Co-construction of turns at talk: Active listening or disruptions in conversation with persons who stutter? *Journal of Interactional Research in Communication Disorders, 5*(2), 141–166.
Robinson, J. D. (2006). Managing trouble responsibility and relationships during conversational repair. *Communication Monographs, 73*, 137–161.
Sacks, H., Schegloff, E. A., & Jefferson, G. (1974). A simplest systematics for the organization of turn-taking in conversation. *Language, 50*(4), 696–735.
Schegloff, E. A. (1979). The relevance of repair to syntax-for-conversation. In T. Givon (Ed.), *Syntax and semantics 12: discourse and syntax* (pp. 261–288). New York: Academic Press.
Schegloff, E. A. (2000). When 'others' initiate repair. *Applied Linguistics, 21*, 205–243.
Schegloff, E. A. (2002). Opening sequences. In J. E. Katz & M. A. Aakhus (Eds.), *Perpetual contact: Mobile communication, private talk, public performance* (pp. 326–385). Cambridge: Cambridge University Press.
Schegloff, E. A. (2007). *Sequence organization in interaction*. Cambridge: Cambridge University Press.

Schegloff, E. A., Jefferson, G., & Sacks, H. (1977). The preference for self-correction in the organization of repair for conversation. *Language, 53*, 361–382.

Schegloff, E. A., & Sacks, H. (1973). Opening up closings. *Semiotica, 8*, 289–327.

Tetnowski, J. A., & Damico, J. S. (2001). A demonstration of the advantages of qualitative methodologies in stuttering research. *Journal of Fluency Disorders, 26*, 1–26.

Wilkinson, R. (2019). Atypical interaction: Conversation analysis and communicative impairments. *Research on Language and Social Interaction, 52*, 281–299.

Yairi, E., & Ambrose, N. (1999). Early childhood stuttering I: Persistency and recovery rates. *Journal of Speech, Language and Hearing Research, 42*, 1097–1112.

Part IV

The Impact of Speech Impairments and Hearing Impairments Within Social Interaction

12

Person Reference as a Trouble Source in Dysarthric Talk-in-Interaction

Steven Bloch and Charlotta Saldert

Introduction

This chapter provides an analysis of talk between people with acquired motor speech disorders (dysarthria) and family members. Using conversation analytical principles it focuses on how *person references* are treated as trouble sources in everyday interaction, and how such troubles arise and are collaboratively managed. Following a review of relevant literature we present a detailed examination of person references produced by people with dysarthria in conversation with family members. We will show that person references are vulnerable to becoming trouble sources given their potential ambiguity or relatively weak relationship

S. Bloch (✉)
University College London, London, UK

C. Saldert
University of Gothenburg, Gothenburg, Sweden

© The Author(s) 2020
R. Wilkinson et al. (eds.), *Atypical Interaction*,
https://doi.org/10.1007/978-3-030-28799-3_12

to immediately prior talk. We will then discuss some of the reasons why names might be prone to difficulties in conversation. Finally, we consider the potential implications of this work.

Amyotrophic lateral sclerosis (ALS) is an acquired progressive neurological disorder, and is the most common form of what is often referred to as motor neurone disease (MND). People with ALS, typically between the ages of 40 and 70, develop weakness and spasticity of muscles and, over time, become increasingly paralysed. The majority report initial symptoms in their limbs but approximately 30% experience initial changes in the bulbar region, resulting in speech deterioration (dysarthria). Regardless of the initial location of symptoms, over time all areas of the body are affected. Overall, it is reported that dysarthria occurs in 80–95% of people with ALS (Tomik and Guiloff 2010), with speech remaining adequate on average for 18-months from the first bulbar symptoms (Makkonen et al. 2018). Speech symptoms are typically a mixed spastic-flaccid dysarthria characterised by reduced articulatory range, phonatory-weakness, hypernasality and slow speech (Tomik et al. 2015; Lee and Bell 2018).

Repair in Conversation

Repair refers to practices used by participants to manage troubles in talk (Schegloff et al. 1977; Schegloff 2000). The term *trouble source* describes what participants themselves identify as problematic during their own conversation. These troubles are typically the types of problems encountered in everyday conversation through unclear speech sounds, misunderstandings etc. Repair takes place in two stages: initiation (i.e. displaying something in the prior talk as a trouble source), and outcome (most commonly, the repair itself). In two-party conversation, the participants involved in repair may be just the speaker of a trouble source (e.g. altering a word in progress), the recipient of the trouble source turn, or both.

Of interest here is the practice of other-initiated self-repair (Schegloff et al. 1977) where both participants are involved. One participant (person B) treats something in another participant's (person A's) turn as a trouble source by other-initiating repair on it. Regularly, though not always, the other-initiation of repair (OIR) functions to highlight some difficulty participant B is having in understanding participant A's turn (Schegloff 2000). There are a number of forms this repair initiation might take, including an *open class* repair initiator such as 'huh?' (Drew 1997), or a repair initiator which displays which part of the prior turn is the trouble source (e.g. 'you told him when?'). Participant A then carries out a repair on their prior talk which has been highlighted as problematic. The success of participant A's self-repair attempt will be seen in the fact that on its completion participant B produces no further other-initiations of repair but rather produces a turn in which s/he explicitly or implicitly displays an understanding of the previously problematic turn.

Schegloff (1979) notes that in normal conversation, the practice of repair is designed for success and usually, although not invariably, a single repair effort resolves the trouble it addresses. Thus, repair is an essential, and often collaborative, practice which disrupts the progressivity of talk but at the same time is usually done in a way which minimises that disruption.

Troubles and Repair in Dysarthria-in-Interaction

The functional consequence of dysarthric speech is reduced intelligibility. This equates to a potential increased incidence in troubles and repair sequences relating to speech sound production (Rutter 2009), some of which prove to be extended (Bloch and Wilkinson 2013; Griffiths et al. 2015). Trouble sources identified by a recipient using other-initiation of repair are a regular feature of conversations involving speakers with dysarthria (Bloch et al. 2015; Bloch and Wilkinson 2004, 2009, 2011). It has been established that whilst dysarthric troubles in conversation are typically linked to unintelligible speech, the problems that recipients experience in these conversations can be described more generally as problems with *understandability* (Bloch and Wilkinson 2004). This refers to difficulties in perceiving how a turn is constructed in relation to the previous talk and points to an important distinction between treating a prior turn, or element within that turn, as intelligible and treating it as understandable. For example, an important issue in a listener understanding a turn is that s/he grasps the sequential relationship between that turn and the turns immediately preceding it (Drew 1997). This can be a problem for speakers with dysarthria and their recipients, even when utterances are produced using assistive communication systems such as SGDs (speech generating devices). In these cases, recipients may have difficulty understanding an SGD-produced utterance due to the fact that, even when each of the words is intelligible, slow production means they cannot understand the sequential relationship between that utterance and what has preceded it (Bloch and Wilkinson 2004, 2013). Further problems relating to the understandability of the speaker with dysarthria's turn can arise if the recipient fails to grasp what it is about the speaker's turn which is making it difficult to understand (Bloch and Wilkinson 2009). This can lead to additional problems in completing the repair, with these problems intensified if in turn the speaker with dysarthria does not perceive that the recipient is having difficulty in understanding what the exact nature of the trouble is (Bloch and Wilkinson 2009, 2013).

With reference to trouble resolution, many problems can be resolved promptly, particularly in cases where the recipient finds one particular word of the speaker with dysarthria's turn to be unintelligible. The speaker with dysarthria can then focus their efforts on making phonetic adjustments to the word(s) highlighted by the recipient as problematic (Rutter 2009; Bloch and Wilkinson 2011). In other cases the nature of the trouble source may be more global, potentially comprising several words but also revealing a wider difficulty with understanding the action which is being produced by the talk (Bloch and Wilkinson 2011, 2013). In such cases the repair resolution can extend over several turns, addressing different elements of the problematic talk. Put together, the combined difficulties associated with intelligibility and understandability can create significant problems leading to lengthy sequences of talk that halt the conversation's progressivity.

Person Reference in Conversation

Person reference in conversation can be accomplished through a variety of means. For co-present participants it may be enough to indicate 'I' and 'you' through eye-gaze or gesture, but there are a variety of forms used to identify non-present persons. These might be characterised, amongst others, as a person's name, a pronominal form, or a role (e.g. family or work relationship) (Schegloff 1996). Two key principles of person reference have been identified: (1) a preference for minimisation and (2) a preference, wherever possible, for using a recognitional reference form (Sacks and Schegloff 1979). Minimisation states that person reference should be done using a single reference form (e.g., one name or one role rather than a name and a role). Recognitional reference forms are those that convey to the recipient that they ought to know, or know of, a particular person. Recognitional reference forms include names (such as first names and/or surnames) and recognitional descriptors (e.g., 'the man living opposite'). Referring to people using a first name alone (e.g., 'Simon') simultaneously satisfies the principles of recipient design and minimisation by making a known individual recognisable via a single word. In her collection of 219 instances of initial singular recognitional references to third persons, Stivers (2007) contends that if a name were possible it was used 93% of the time. Non-recognitional reference forms can be used by a speaker to convey to the recipient that the person being referred to is someone the recipient does *not* know, with forms including, for example, 'someone' or 'a woman I once worked with'.

In sum, we have a wide variety of person reference forms at our disposal, but there are organisational principles that reveal a preference for a recipient-designed form using a recognitional reference wherever possible.

Person Reference in Atypical Interaction

The impact of communicative impairments on person reference in interaction has received relatively little attention. In the field of aphasia, isolated proper name anomias and problems with proper names within a wider aphasic language disorder have been documented (Geukes and Muller 2015) but a focused examination of problems with proper nouns, more specifically person reference, as they play out in conversation, is relatively rare.

Wilkinson (2009) was the first to investigate aphasia and proper noun production during everyday conversation from a CA perspective. Through his investigation of how a man with fluent aphasia (Derek) constructs person-referencing turns Wilkinson suggests that certain practices may have provided Derek with more time to access and successfully produce the desired proper nouns. The analysis highlights how features of language, such as the production of a name, can be an outcome of interactional practices, as well as of neuropsychological processes. Further work by Barnes (2013) presents a single case study of a speaker who recurrently utilises common noun phrases (e.g., 'that young bloke') as reference forms in place of proper nouns. The conclusion drawn is that such turn construction practices represent adaptations to proper noun anomia in conversation.

Penn et al. (2015) address mentions of persons by a person with aphasia which are shown to prove problematic by the (non-aphasic) recipient. Using one case (JD in conversation with a speech and language therapist) four instances of other-initiated repair are presented—all of which feature troubles with person reference. The difficulties experienced are varied, including person recognition ('who is X?'), relational components ('what is the relationship between X and Y?' and phonemic paraphasias ('scanner girl' instead of 'spanner girl' used as a colloquial term for 'mechanic'). It is important to note that at least one of the troubles is also characterised by difficulties in recognising the turn's action: 'scanner girl' for example, turns out to be a self-reference by the person with aphasia, something that proves particularly problematic for the recipient. The instances examined all show how vulnerable references to persons by speakers with aphasia are to not being correctly understood.

In the field of dysarthria, reference to persons as a specific area of enquiry is even less common. An episode of talk between a woman with acquired dysarthric speech and her partner (Extract 4: Wilkinson et al. 2011) features a problem with two names within one turn construction unit (TCU) resulting in an extended repair sequence beginning with natural speech but then utilising a speech generating device to pursue a self-repair. In this case, the difficulties encountered by the recipient relate initially to the (un)intelligibility of the naturally spoken trouble source turn but then to additional SGD output that compounds the problem by adding further, non-repair related, information.

Subsequent work by Bloch and Wilkinson (2013) specifically addresses reference to persons in dysarthric talk. The name 'Gladys' proves to be particularly challenging for the participants given its placement within the SGD -produced utterance 'and we have a new lady, Gladys' (referring to a new person at a day centre). The ensuing talk is characterised by a series of SGD- and natural-speech-mediated repair sequences lasting over three minutes. Once the name has, eventually, been made intelligible, the recipient has trouble in understanding what the name Gladys is being used to do in the talk. Ultimately these troubles are resolved through natural speech and the use of shared referential knowledge (see also Penn et al. 2015). The most significant feature within this sequence is how repair attempts by the speaker with dysarthria can become new trouble sources in their own right. This has a significant impact on the recipient's ability to understand what is being said and to recognise the relationship between an immediately prior turn at talk and whatever has come earlier.

Methods and Participants

The data were collected as part of a study into interaction between people with progressive dysarthria and family members. UK National Health Service (NHS) research ethics approval was granted prior to data collection. Each family was loaned video camera equipment. They were then asked to record themselves, with no researcher present, for approximately 30 minutes. It was requested that the recording take place during a regular opportunity for everyday conversation. This process was repeated at three-monthly intervals over an 18-month period. Each video recording was then examined for potentially interesting interactional phenomena.

It was noted throughout that references to people's names made by speakers with dysarthria were being treated by recipients as problematic.

In some instances this resulted in extended repair sequences. A series of extracts featuring problems with references to people was then identified and the talk transcribed using CA conventions (Jefferson 1984). A closer analysis of repair followed with ongoing refinement of the transcripts. Each sequence was then subjected to an in-depth analysis, which focused on explicating the sequential context in which the phenomenon was occurring, the interactional work that was being achieved and the orientation of the participants towards the phenomenon.

Data from four different dyads are presented below. In each dyad one person has a diagnosis of ALS with an associated dysarthria. Each person's speech profile varies depending on the speech-subsystems affected. Alex, for example, has significantly reduced breath support, whilst for Brenda, the difficulties are related to hypernasality. Rose has predominantly articulatory problems whilst Jean is *anarthric* with no ability to produce meaningful speech for communication, just some residual gross vocalisations. For all of the participants with ALS, articulation, particularly tongue function, is problematic. In terms of intelligibility their conversation intelligibility ratings on the Frenchay Dysarthria Assessment (Enderby and Palmer 2007) vary from grade 'b' ('speech abnormal but intelligible: patient occasionally has to repeat') to grade 'e' ('Patient totally unintelligible').

In the following analysis it is noted that reference to persons is clearly part of the everyday talk of people with dysarthria but that such references are one type of action that appear to be treated as problematic by recipients. There is, therefore, value in examining how troubles with person reference arise, and how they are manged. The analysis is presented through six extracts across three sections.

Section 1: The first two extracts feature talk in which a person's name is treated as problematic, largely in terms of intelligibility. These troubles are resolved promptly enabling talk to progress.

Section 2: In this section there is some degree of ambiguity or uncertainly regarding the person reference. The nature of the problems is still rooted in intelligibility but the recipient displays at least some degree of difficulty in establishing the person to whom the speaker is referring.

Section 3: Here, the speakers with dysarthria have more significant intelligibility problems. This is qualified both through speech sound/ intelligibility measures but also through how their contributions in interaction are designed. Both dyads employ augmentative strategies that alter turn design and turn receipt practices. For these final two extracts the problems experienced relate to action as much as (un) intelligibility, with the recipients displaying uncertainty as to what is being attempted by the speakers' turns.

Analysis

Section 1

Prior to the following extract Pete and his mother Brenda have been talking about neighbourhood friends and acquaintances with young children.

Extract 1

```
01   P   they >the-it's just a< whole stream of (0.4) either boys or [girls!   ]
02   B                                                                [((nods))]
03       (1.0)
04   P   but-er when you think there's a fifty fifty chu-hance so=
05   B    =yes (0.3) wi-(0.2) [with Vhikey.        ]
06                            [((points to Pete))  ]
07       (1.0)
08   P   Vicky? ye [ah         ]
09   B             [ ((nods))  ]
10   P   yeah yes they still haven't decided on a name
```

Pete's talk about boys and girls (line 01) makes relevant the potential for person reference although at this point there has been no mention of any particular name. It is then Brenda who produces the name 'Vicky' (line 05). This reference is accompanied by a pointing gesture towards Pete. This gesture may display an expectation of that Pete will recognize the name or have knowledge of the person named.

Whilst there is no significant trouble here, the fact that there is a one-second silence followed by Pete's hearing display (line 08) with rising intonation provides evidence that 'Vicky' is not totally unproblematic. It is at least an item that demands some attention by Pete in offering it as a *candidate understanding* for confirmation (Heritage 1984). The progression here is prompt. Brenda confirms via a head nod and Pete reveals his understanding of the reference with agreement and what appears to be an update on Vicky, and potentially her partner's, decision regarding their baby's name. The nature of the trouble in this extract may relate to (un)intelligibility, to person recognition, or potentially, to a combination of both.

Extract 2

Prior to the talk in this extract Tom has been reporting how two, unnamed, people have queried whether Rose has had a stroke.

```
01  T   an they went for the x-rays and brain scan I said the um I told em the
02       brain scan was perfect perfectly clear
03  R   ((nods))
04  T   and er nothing to do with [er ] stroke at all
05  R                             [mm ]
06  R   ((coughs))
07      (4.0)
08  T   °er:°
09  R   (2 syllables) (0.3) (3 syllables) Jan-(1 syllable) (4 syllables)=
10  T   =yo [u what ]
11  R       [(Janet)]
12      (0.5)
13  T   Janet asked?=
14  R   =(Brenda) (.) (Brenda)
15  T   oh that's the first time she's spoken to you >when you went to have
16      yer hair done<
```

The extract begins with Tom's reference to 'perfectly clear' scans and his report that there is no link to a stroke at all (line 04). There is then a lapse in the talk before Tom minimally initiates talk, followed by a more substantive utterance by Rose (line 09). The turn comprises a series of syllables which are shown subsequently to be unintelligible. Tom follows this immediately with an other-initiation of repair. This action treats Rose's prior turn as problematic although the exact nature of the trouble source is not specified. Tom's 'you what' (line 10) performs an open-class repair initiation indicating the need for a full repeat of the prior turn.

Rose provides an overlapping repair attempt (line 11). This repair treats, in the first instance, the name 'Janet' as the trouble source. There is then a pause before Tom displays both a hearing of the repair with his repeat of 'Janet' together with his understanding that it is Janet who has asked something. Tom's utterance in line 13 may have a double function here; both to receipt/display what he has heard, but also, in the form of an incomplete utterance, to do a further other-initiation of repair on Rose's talk. Tom is in effect saying, 'I now know the first part of the utterance in line 09 was "Janet asked" but I don't know what the next word(s) was- please supply it' (which Rose then does). In retrospect we can see that the whole phrase 'Janet asked Brenda' is in fact treated as a repairable as the sequence proceeds.

Section 2

In Extract 3 Brenda enquires whether Pete has had contact from someone called John. Having established a name reference, further repair work is required to identify the exact person to whom Brenda is referring.

Extract 3

```
01   P   °yeah°
02       (4.0)
03   P   °but er: °
04   B   °ha- haf (0.2) you (heard) (.) frum (.) ↓Jhohn lhhately
05   P   have I heard from (.) John?
06   B   ((nods)) (1 syllable)
07       (1.0)
08   P   John?
09       (3.0)
10   P   John-John LaMette?=
11   B   =yeah
12   P   ((shakes head)) NO
13       (0.4)
14   P   >I think-I think< we had a card but I'm not sure
```

Brenda initiates a new topic (line 04) with a first pair part enquiry about John. Given her use of this person reference we may assume that John is a person with whom both Brenda and Pete are familiar. In next turn position Pete produces an other-initiated repair with a recast of her talk placing a stress emphasis on the person reference together with a slight pause prior to its production. At minimum, Pete displays his awareness that Brenda is making an enquiry about another person. Through this turn Pete offers an understanding check for Brenda to accept or refute. Through her subsequent head nod Brenda attempts to show that John's hearing of her talk is correct. She also expands the meaning with further specificity, possibly through the production of his surname, although this proves unclear to us as well as to Pete.

Whatever Brenda is attempting through her talk in line 06 is again treated as problematic by Pete with a second other-initiated repair. He repeats 'John' despite Brenda's prior affirmation. With no uptake by Brenda, John now self-selects (line 10) and reveals the potential nature of his difficulty. His production of John + surname, a third other-initiated repair, provides evidence that 'John' in isolation is not enough. It may be the case that given its commonality the name John, in isolation, is too ambiguous for confident recognition. In adding a surname Pete is attempting to establish the exact person to whom Breda is referring. Pete's candidate surname is then confirmed by Brenda in line 11 enabling Pete in next turn to respond to the original first pair part enquiry. The nature of the trouble in this extract is again potentially related to (un)intelligibility but with additional ambiguity as to which John Brenda is referring. With three other-initiated repair turns addressing the same trouble source we begin to see how each of these actions structurally delays the ongoing progressivity of the sequence and therefore the conversation (Bloch and Wilkinson 2013; Griffiths et al. 2015).

Extract 4 is taken from a conversation between Rose and Tom. The main feature is one of other-initiated self-repair. The talk follows a natural break in the conversation.

```
R    oh, [Jean were surprise]-ta °aver° frum Kay?
         [((looks to Tom))  ]
     (0.5)
R    weren't  sh[e.                                   ]
T               [((begins to shift gaze to Rose))] who?
     (0.2)
R    Jean were surprise-ta-averfrom Kay:.
     (1.1)
T    [OH: Jean Jean       ] yeah
R    [Kay: (phoned) yeah  ]
R    [m:    ]
T    [Jean  ] knew that er:
R    °yeah°
     (0.4)
T    °sh°(.) °k° she was pleased that er (0.3) Kay had rung us=
R    =yeah [m:   ]
T          [yeah ]
```

Rose initiates this sequence with news about two people, Jean and Kay (line 01). The turn beginning 'oh' indicates a possible departure from the prior topic and that what follows should treated as newsworthy by Tom. There is no immediate uptake by Tom (line 03), and, following a 0.5 sec silence, Rose self-selects to add an increment (Ford et al. 2002) to her first utterance, in the form of a tag question, marking it as an explicit question action, thus implicating an answer response by Tom. It is possible that Rose is expecting an uptake after her first turn, but when this does not occur she adds further talk making a next turn uptake by Tom more accountable.

Tom then displays a trouble with the prior talk (line 05). By saying 'who?' he is locating a person reference in Rose's prior talk as problematic. This reveals some level of hearing on the part of Tom, that is, he is showing that he has heard enough of Rose's talk to know that she has made reference to a person or people, but he does not know, at the point, the actual name(s).

Given that the trouble source turn makes reference to two people, Rose now repeats the full turn, dispensing (Schegloff 2004) with the initial 'oh' and the follow up increment from line 04, as both named people are potential candidates for the target of Tom's other-initiation of repair. The notable change in the attempted repair completion turn from the original trouble source turn is a stress on the two name forms:

Jean and Kay. Following a silence at line 08, Tom produces his hearing of Rose's attempted self-repair completion. Then through a repetition of 'Jean' he makes public the specific name reference he found problematic. As well as repeating the repaired item Tom also adds an acknowledgement—'yeah' (line 09). Through saying 'yeah' Tom may be acknowledging a hearing, but he may also be doing an agreement with the action of the trouble source turn, in this case an agreement with Jean's surprise 'to have heard from Kay'. The agreement would be relevant here given that Rose is not offering this as news but rather as something to be agreed on, as demonstrated through her question action in line 04. At this point, it is only clear that Tom has now heard the prior trouble name 'Jean'. However, subsequent talk by Tom at line 15 does show that he has now heard and understood the full trouble source turn.

In both prior extracts the recipients have encountered a trouble with the dysarthric speakers' talk. A repair has been initiated by the recipient of the trouble source turn. This initiation has signalled, to some degree, the nature of the trouble, enabling an attempted repair completion. Neither extract shows immediate resolution. There are a series of OIRs in Extract 3 as the reference to John unfolds, and in Extract 4 the OIR is ambiguous given the presence of two names in the trouble source turn itself.

Section 3

Extract 5 is taken from a conversation between Alex and Molly. Whilst still using speech as the primary modality, the participants have developed a highly collaborative turn exchange system featuring the production of single words or letter names by Alex in the first turn position followed by a redoing of the same turn item(s) in the next turn position by Molly. This dyad's system has been described previously (Bloch 2005; Bloch and Beeke 2008). Immediately prior to this sequence Alex and Molly have been discussing Alex's move to a new room, on a new floor, in the nursing home in which he lives. Molly has drawn attention to the fact that he will be living amongst new people. Alex's utterance: 'I will hear Anne' is subsequently treated by Molly as a third party tease, making reference to Anne as someone who, presumably, is known for being loud. The issue here is the accomplishment and recognition of Anne as a person reference.

Extract 5

```
01   A    (I:e::)
02        (0.3)
03   M    eye
04        (0.5)
05   A    (wull heyar)
06        (0.4)
07   M    will
08        (0.4)
09   A    (hear)
10        (0.8)
11   M    I will:
12        (0.5)
13   A    (hear)
14        (0.3)
15   M    hear?
16        (0.6)
17   A    (ay en)
18        (0.4)
19   M    ay:
20        (0.6)
21   A    (en en)
22        (0.3)
23   M    en en
24        (0.6)
25   Al   (e:)
26        (1.0)
27   M    ay en en?
28        (0.5)
29   A    (°he:)
30        (0.3)
31   M    E
32        (1.8)
33   M    ⌈ay en en ee?     ⌉
34        ⌊((puzzled look))⌋
35        (0.3)
36   A    ((moves lower lip))
37        (0.7)
38   Mo   °what's that°.
39        (2.5)
40   M    £ay en en ee£ I c(h)an't ⌈work that out!⌉
41   A                             ⌊((smiles))    ⌋
42        (0.4)
43   M    huh-ha-ha-HUH  it's not >another one of my<
44        ⌈spelling     ⌉ but er:
45   A    ⌊(1 syllable)⌋
46        (1.2)
47   A    (er:na:me)
48        (1.0)
49   M    I (.) will?
50        (0.3)
51   A    (her name)
52        (0.4)
53   M    her name
54        (0.2)
55   A    ((moves lower lip))
56        (0.2)
57   M    whose name?
```

```
58          (2.0)
59    M     OH [SO-HAHA-HAHA-↑HA] (0.4) ha-ha (.) ↓ha=
60    A        [ ((smiles))     ]
61    M     =(0.4) °ha ha-ha  ha-ha (0.3) [°ah ha.  ]
62    A                                   [(1 syll)]=
63          =[(1 syll)    ]
64    M       [£it w(h)as ] another one of my spelling  (.)
65          [things wasn't it£] (.) ay en en ee (.) Anne
66    A     [(ay en  en  ee)  ]
67          (0.4)
68    M     oh is ↑Anne [ on that ] floor?
69    A                 [uh-huh:  ]
70          (0.2)
71    A     °huh
72          (0.3)
73    M     y(h)es!=
74    A     =[((smiles))]
75    M      [ ha       ] oh huh-huh °ha right.
```

Alex initiates this sequence with a one syllable utterance which is collaboratively constructed between lines 01–13 to produce what appears to be an utterance in progress: 'I will hear'. Molly's redoing of 'hear' at line 15 features a questioning intonation. The tentative treatment of 'hear' in this turn may be attributable to intelligibility or it may relate to the ambiguity of the word as either the verb form 'hear' (as in 'to hear something') or a prepositional 'here' (as in 'this place here'). It is not possible, at this point, to know the nature of this uncertainty in repeat turn status.

Alex's next action continues the utterance in progress and so displays an acceptance of Molly's prior turn hearing. By line 31, Alex and Molly have jointly spelt four letter names 'a – n – n – e'. Following Molly's production of 'e' at line 31, there is a 1.8 second silence. The absence of Alex as next speaker here is potentially indicative of end of spelling or utterance completion work. In fact it is Molly who takes next turn following this silence. She offers a repeat of the prior letter names 'ay en en ee?' (line 33). Her questioning intonation and puzzled look implies further uncertainly as to the hearing and/or meaning of this construction. Alex now takes next turn to produce a characteristic lower lip movement, offering confirmation of the prior talk repeat. The evidence available to Molly at this point is that 'a-n-n-e' is a correct hearing and production of the utterance construction.

Molly now displays an indication of the nature of the trouble (line 38). She has provided a repeat of the prior spelling turn talk and Alex has confirmed this as correct, but she now asks 'what's that'. Through this turn she is displaying an inability to understand the meaning of utterance in progress. The individual grapheme names are intelligible but what they mean in combination is not understandable. Molly is neither able to construct a meaningful unit from the individual letters, nor recognise the action that the unit might play (i.e., that these letter forms might represent what she later realises is a person reference in the form of a female name). There is then a 2.5 second silence, providing Alex with an opportunity to self-repair, before Molly repeats the individual parts again and then saying 'I can't work that out!' (line 40). It is here that the full impact of the trouble is made explicit. In the same turn, Molly is showing her hearing of the utterance, but also displaying her trouble in establishing its meaning. It is the inability to make sense of collated individual letter names that is so problematic here. Alex begins to smile in overlap with Molly's talk at line 41 and this is followed by Molly's laughter (line 43). She now makes reference to her spelling competency before Alex talks in overlap.

Through the next series of turns Alex says 'her name', repeated by Molly at line 53 and confirmed by Alex with a lower lip movement in line 55. Molly then initiates a further repair by asking 'whose name?'. There is then a two second silence which is perhaps notable given that there is no attempt by Alex to repair the trouble indicated by Molly in the prior turn. It is after this silence that recognition and understanding are displayed. At line 59 Molly begins her turn with 'OH' before starting to say a word beginning with 'so' (possibly 'sorry') and then continuing with extensive laughter. Molly then takes ownership of the prior trouble by referring to her spelling and then repeating 'a-n-n-e' and saying the sum of the parts 'Anne'.

Having established the prior talk as making reference to a person called 'Anne', Molly now responds to the whole utterance 'I will hear Anne' with a question—'oh is Anne on that floor' (line 68). Molly is thus treating Alex's utterance as news about the location of someone with whom she is already familiar.

This extract reveals, very clearly, an explicit sense-making process. The fundamental work of intelligibility is achieved through repeats and clarifications of hearings, but the accomplishment of understanding and appropriate next turn action is not simultaneous, requiring repair initiation and the provision of additional referential information. Even with the addition of 'her name', Molly does not immediately understand Alex's reference. One possible reason for this difficulty is the relationship that 'A-n-n-e' has to the larger utterance in progress. It is unclear whether Molly has fully understood the meaning of 'hear' and so may have difficulties in establishing the relationship between 'A-n-n-e' and what has come prior.

In the final extract Jean produces the utterance 'Mike's coming on Friday'. This appears to be a new topic initiation, following Ali's topic closing talk about one of Jean's friends. The fact that Jean is unable to produce any intelligible speech means that she must utilise non-verbal modalities such as finger spelling, hand gestures etc.

Extract 6

```
A  I'll give her a call (0.4) and tell her ta give you the right number
   (.) make sure she sends it to the right phone °h okay I'll give
   her ring >in a minute< then we cun-when finished
J  uh: uh [              uh: uh                        ]
          [((finger spells 'W' and holds looking at A))]
A  Wednesday=
J  = ((shakes head)) [               uh uh:        ]
                     [((raises & shakes hands))]
   ((looks at A, finger spells 'M'- 'I'- 'K' - 'E'))
   (1.6)
A  um=
J  = ((finger spells 'M,' holds position and looks at A))
A  Em
J  ((finger spells 'I' then looks at A))=
A  Eye
J  [((finger spells 'K' then looks at A)]
A  [             Mike.                  ]
J  ((points to A with R index-finger and nods))uh: h:urm:
   (shifts finger from A, across room, towards self))
A  okay ((nods head))
J  ur:: (1.0)  ur [                         ur: ur        ]
                  [((looks at A and finger spells 'F'))]
A  Friday.
J  [                ur:           ] ((moves hand towards self)) ur ur:=
   [((nods head with R thumbs up))]
A  °okay°
   [give me a clue before you start spelling willya then I got an idea]=
   [ ((signs 'clue' and gesture action of signing))                   ]
J  =((laughs and slaps R hand on lap))
A  [It's about a na:me (.) Mi:ke          (.)    ] thatud give me an idea
   [((signs 'name' and then finger-spells 'M'))]
J  ((uh huh huh))=
A  =>£I thinkin< what's that Micky I thought mat-monkey[HahHahhuh huh ]
J                                                      [((smiles))    ]
A  you know what my £sphelling's like£ [((huh huhhuhhuhhuh)) ]
J                                      [      ((smiles))     ] huh
A  Mike's coming (.) [Friday   ]
J                    [((nods)) ]
```

This extract begins with prior topic closing talk by Ali (lines 01–02) before Jean initiates with vocalisations and the finger spelt 'W'. The physical holding of this letter name and the accompanying eye-gaze to Ali indicates turn completion and next speaker selection. The finger spelt 'W' is interpreted by Ali as 'Wednesday' (line 05). This, it turns out, is not Jean's intention: Wednesday in British Sign Language is conveyed through a *repeated* interlocking 'W' movement and not a single hold. Ali's interpretation is rejected by Jean who proceeds to finger spell a series of letter names: M-I-K-E (line 09).

We can see in retrospect that this series of letters spells the name 'Mike', something that both participants make explicit in subsequent talk, but at this point in the conversation Ali displays no recognition of what these finger-spelt items represent. This is in clear contrast with the talk in Extract 5 in which each of Alex's words or letter names is repeated back by Molly in next turn position.

Jean treats Ali's lack of uptake at line 10 as problematic and initiates self-repair at line 12. This time her production comprises individual letter names one turn at a time. This now operates in a similar way to Alex and Molly in Extract 5. Here Jean produces the first letter name 'M', holding her hands in position whilst looking at Ali. Ali treats this as a turn transition point, offering her interpretation of the sign with a verbally produced 'Em'. Jean then proceeds with a finger spelt 'I' (verbalised by Ali) and finally 'K'. Ali produces 'Mike' in overlap with 'K'—an anticipatory completion of the word in progress (Bloch 2011) which Jean confirms (line 18).

Following the collaboratively produced 'Mike', Jean points from Ali to another part of the room and then to herself. This finger movement, together with the vocalisation, might be referencing Mike as 'coming to me'. Jean now signs an approximation of Friday (two fingers of one hand tapping two fingers of the other) which Ali verbalises in next turn (line 23). Again, Jean confirms and again moves her hand towards herself—possibly redoing the same movement representing 'coming to me', something that Ali has not yet registered explicitly. Ali's receipt of this talk, a quiet 'okay' (line 26) prefaces what turns out to be a mild complaint.

Despite having been produced considerably earlier in the sequence, the complainable here centres on 'Mike' as the trouble source. Ali asks for a 'name clue'—stating it would help if Jean told her she was going to produce a name before the name is actually produced. The talk that follows reveals in part the nature of Ali's difficulty. Her reference to 'what's that' resonates with Molly's talk (Extract 5: line 38) where it function as an open class OIR (Drew 1997). The issue here, according to Ali, is that she could not recognise 'm-i-k-e' as a name. Ali's complaint is mitigated in part by her admission of partial responsibility, again resonating with Molly's own reference to spelling.

The repair sequence ends with Ali's recap of Jean's full utterance: 'Mike's coming Friday' (line 37). Jean nods in agreement, overlapping with 'Friday'.

Discussion

Dyads affected by dysarthria experience inevitable difficulties with (un) intelligibility, leading to an increase in other-initiated repair sequences that can take numerous turns to resolve (Bloch and Wilkinson 2011; Saldert et al. 2014). Resolution often features multiple attempts at self-repair through a variety of modalities (Bloch and Wilkinson 2013). Evidence suggests that trouble sources are not randomly distributed but may be associated with actions such as topic transition (Bloch et al. 2015). In this chapter, we have drawn attention to person referencing as another potential site for troubles.

Why Are References to Persons Problematic?

References to persons are potentially problematic in dysarthric-talk insofar as they may be used, as in all the extracts above, to identify persons not present and, as such, lack the assistance of co-present identification. They may also be problematic because the recipient may not be familiar with whomever is being talked about and/or because they may relate to knowledge not available to the recipient. Additionally, person references remove all 'categorical work' apart from what is implicit in the turn in which the person reference occurs. In this way names are unique and may not be predictable from the sequential context (i.e. both prior to the TCU in which they occur as well as the other words within that TCU). This may mean that there is a greater reliance on the phonetic 'decoding' of the word by the recipient than might be the case with other word classes.

We can see that (un)intelligibility is a significant contributor to all of the person reference difficulties displayed. A recipient needs to be able to decode a speech signal adequately in order to take an appropriate next turn. Where intelligibility is not clear, the mechanisms of other-initiation of repair are employed. However, achieving intelligibility does not necessarily mean that understanding is complete. In Extract 3, the name 'John' is heard by Pete but he seeks further clarification as to which John is being referenced, whilst in Extract 4, the letter names for 'Anne' are successfully decoded and shown to be hearable but clearly not understandable, the latter trouble being based, potentially, on the understandability of the utterance in progress and its sequential relationship with prior talk. 'Anne' has very little, if any, context, evidenced through Molly's inability to even recognise 'Anne' as a reference to person.

In terms of repair resolution, a range of practices is observable ranging from candidate understandings designed for affirmation (Extract 1: 'Vicky') and person reference recognitions (Extract 4: 'who?') to the use of shared referential information. During the 'Anne' sequence, Alex invokes 'her name' (Extract 5: line 51) in an attempt to facilitate Molly's understanding. This provides enough of a clue (that the trouble-source is a name reference) that while being initially unsuccessful, it does lead to recognition. The issue here is that participants can use whatever repair resources they have available to suit the nature of the trouble source providing they recognise the nature of the trouble itself. Molly's (Extract 5) troubles are notable given that she cannot, initially, figure out why the trouble *is* a trouble.

Responsibility for Troubles

One observation arising from this analysis relates to competence. As Robinson (2006) notes, even the subtlest forms of OIR have the potential to raise the relevance of a lapse in competence (i.e., a lapse of self-correction) by the trouble-source speaker. It may be hypothesised that the longer a trouble takes to resolve, the greater the risk of fault identification (e.g. blame) arising. What transpires in the extracts above is that there is no competency talk in Extracts 1–4, but there is in Extracts 5 and 6. In Extract 5 Molly takes responsibility for 'another one of my spelling things'—presumably a reference to the fact that she has experienced spelling problems before. Her earlier talk 'I can't work that out' (line 40) also provides insight in the ownership of the problem. In Extract 6 Ali begins with a teasing complaint—'give me a clue before you start spelling' before shifting the balance of responsibility to herself—'you know what my spelling's like'. This resonates with observations of partner responses to problematic talk by people with aphasia (Barnes and Ferguson 2015), suggesting that there are more commonalities to be found across different communication impairments than are typically assumed (see also Bloch and Beeke 2008).

Implications and Conclusions

We have previously demonstrated that topic shifts in dysarthria talk are one potential site for troubles (Bloch et al. 2015). It may be the case that references to persons are another. These may not necessarily be mutually exclusive (e.g. the trouble in Extract 6 may well be associated with a new topic initiation) but there appears enough evidence here, as with aphasia, to mark person reference as potentially more vulnerable than other actions. One general implication is that the distribution and format of trouble sources in dysarthric-talk in interaction may require as much as attention as the quality of the speech signal itself. In reality we find that intelligibility exists on a continuum. It is not an all or nothing state—largely because it is a shared accomplishment, that is, a production display and an understanding display. Additionally, we may need to develop a more sophisticated appreciation of motor speech disorders in interaction. People with Parkinson's disease, for example, often experience language-based symptoms beyond motor speech that impact on interaction (Saldert et al. 2014; Saldert and Bauer 2017). The combined interactions between motor-speech, language and cognition in a range of acquired neurological disorders is complex but there may be value in understanding how all three elements impact on interaction.

In conclusion, names provide one way in which we might consider how dysarthric talk becomes, and is treated as, problematic. To do this, the methods of CA are invaluable because they not only address the name as a problem or trouble source but also reveal how the recipient treats it as a trouble and how the participants then attempt to resolve the trouble.

References

Barnes, S. (2013). Proper noun anomia in conversation: A description of how a man with chronic anomia constructed referencing turns. *Aphasiology, 27*(1), 1–19.

Barnes, S., & Ferguson, A. (2015). Conversation partner responses to problematic talk produced by people with aphasia: Some alternatives to initiating, completing, or pursuing repair. *Aphasiology, 29*(3), 315–336.

Bloch, S. (2005). Co-constructing meaning in acquired speech disorders: Word and letter repetition in the construction of turns. In K. Richards & P. Seedhouse (Eds.), *Applying conversation analysis* (pp. 38–55). Basingstoke: Palgrave Macmillan.

Bloch, S. (2011). Anticipatory other-completion of augmentative and alternative communication (AAC) talk: A conversation analysis study. *Disability and Rehabilitation, 33*(3), 261–269.

Bloch, S., & Beeke, S. (2008). Co-constructed talk in the conversations of people with dysarthria and aphasia. *Clinical Linguistics and Phonetics, 22*(12), 974–990.

Bloch, S., Saldert, C., & Ferm, U. (2015). Problematic topic transitions in dysarthric conversation. *International Journal of Speech-Language Pathology, 17*(4), 373–383.

Bloch, S., & Wilkinson, R. (2004). The understandability of AAC: A conversation analysis study of acquired dysarthria. *Augmentative and Alternative Communication, 20*(4), 272–282.
Bloch, S., & Wilkinson, R. (2009). Acquired dysarthria in conversation: Identifying sources of understandability problems. *International Journal of Language and Communication Disorders, 44*(5), 769–783.
Bloch, S., & Wilkinson, R. (2011). Acquired dysarthria in conversation: Methods of resolving understandability problems. *International Journal of Language and Communication Disorders, 46*(5), 510–523.
Bloch, S., & Wilkinson, R. (2013). Multiple troubles and repair in voice output communication aid-mediated interaction. In N. Norén, C. Samuelsson, & C. Plejert (Eds.), *Aided communication in dialogical perspectives: Augmentative and alternative communication as action and participation within embodied social worlds* (pp. 95–126). Guildford: J&R Press.
Drew, P. (1997). 'Open' class repair initiators in response to sequential sources of trouble in conversation. *Journal of Pragmatics, 28*(1), 69–101.
Enderby, P., & Palmer, R. (2007). *Frenchay dysarthria assessment.* Austin, TX: Proed.
Ford, C. E., Fox, B. A., & Thompson, S. A. (2002). Constituency and the grammar of turn increments. In C. E. Ford, B. A. Fox, & S. A. Thompson (Eds.), *The language of turn and sequence* (pp. 14–38). New York: Oxford University Press.
Griffiths, S., Barnes, R., Britten, M., & Wilkinson, R. (2015). Multiple repair sequences in everyday conversations involving people with Parkinson's disease. *International Journal of Language and Communication Disorders, 50*(6), 814–829.
Geukes, C., & Muller, H. M. (2015). Proper name anomia after right-hemispheric lesion: A case study. *Neurocase, 21*(4), 520–528.
Heritage, J. (1984). A change-of-state token and aspects of its sequential placement. In J. M. Atkinson & J. Heritage (Eds.), *Structures of social action: Studies in conversation analysis* (pp. 299–345). Cambridge: Cambridge University Press.
Jefferson, G. (1984). Transcript notation. In J. M. Atkinson & J. Heritage (Eds.), *Structures of social action* (pp. ix–xvi.). Cambridge: Cambridge University Press.
Lee, J., & Bell, M. (2018). Articulatory range of movement in individuals with dysarthria secondary to amyotrophic lateral sclerosis. *American Journal of Speech-Language Pathology, 27*(3), 996–1009.

Makkonen, T., Ruottinen, H., Puhto, R., Helminen, M., & Palmio, J. (2018). Speech deterioration in amyotrophic lateral sclerosis (ALS) after manifestation of bulbar symptoms. *International Journal of Language and Communication Disorders, 53*(2), 385–392.

Penn, C., Frankel, T., & Wilkinson, R. (2015). Problems with the understandability of aphasic talk: Mentions of persons as a trouble source in interaction. *Aphasiology, 29*(3), 291–314.

Robinson, J. D. (2006). Managing trouble responsibility and relationships during conversational repair. *Communication Monographs, 72*(2), 137–161.

Rutter, B. (2009). Repair sequences in dysarthric conversational speech: A study in interactional phonetics. *Clinical Linguistics and Phonetics, 23*(12), 887–900.

Sacks, H., & Schegloff, E. A. (1979). Two preferences in the organization of reference to persons in conversation and their interaction. In G. Psathas (Ed.), *Everyday language: Studies in ethnomethodology* (pp. 15–21). New York: Irvington Publishers.

Saldert, C., & Bauer, M. (2017). Multifaceted communication problems in everyday conversations involving people with Parkinson's disease. *Brain Sciences, 7*(10), 123.

Saldert, C., Ferm, U., & Bloch, S. (2014). Semantic trouble sources and their repair in conversations affected by Parkinson's disease. *International Journal of Language & Communication Disorders, 49*(6), 710–721.

Schegloff, E. (1979). The relevance of repair to syntax-for-conversation. *Syntax and Semantics, 12*, 261–286.

Schegloff, E. A. (1996). Some practices for referring to persons in talk-in-interaction: A partial sketch of a systematics. In B. Fox (Ed.), *Studies in Anaphora* (pp. 437–485). Amsterdam: John Benjamins.

Schegloff, E. (2000). When 'others' initiate repair. *Applied Linguistics, 21*(2), 205–243.

Schegloff, E. (2004). On dispensability. *Research on Language and Social Interaction, 27*(2), 95–149.

Schegloff, E., Jefferson, G., & Sacks, H. (1977). The preference for self-correction in the organization of repair in conversation. *Language, 53*(2), 361–382.

Stivers, T. (2007). Alternative recognitionals in person reference. In N. J. Enfield, T. Stivers, & S. C. Levinson (Eds.), *Person reference in interaction: Linguistic, cultural and social perspectives* (pp. 73–96). Cambridge: Cambridge University Press.

Tomik, B., & Guiloff, R. J. (2010). Dysarthria in amyotrophic lateral sclerosis: A review. *Amyotrophic Lateral Sclerosis, 11*(1–2), 4–15.

Tomik, J., Tomik, B., Wiatr, M., Skladzien, J., Strek, P., & Szczudlik, A. (2015). The evaluation of abnormal voice qualities in patients with amyotrophic lateral sclerosis. *Neurodegenerative Diseases, 15*(4), 225–232.

Wilkinson, R. (2009). Projecting a reference in aphasic talk and normal talk. *Discourse Processes, 46*(2–3), 206–225.

Wilkinson, R., Bloch, S., & Clarke, M. T. (2011). On the use of graphic resources in interaction by people with communication disorders. In J. Streeck, C. Goodwin, & C. LeBaron (Eds.), *Embodied interaction: Language and body in the material world* (pp. 152–168). Cambridge: Cambridge University Press.

13

How Can the 'Autonomous Speaker' Survive in Atypical Interaction? The Case of Anarthria and Aphasia

Peter Auer, Angelika Bauer and Ina Hörmeyer

Introduction

As speakers in an interactional encounter we are never completely independent of our coparticipants; still, we can maintain an ideology of speaker autonomy because the "interaction engine" (Levinson 2006) accommodates a good deal of collaboration without endangering this autonomy. Two important reasons for this are that (1) conversation is organized in such a way that speakers are given the opportunity to say whatever they want to say by themselves; and that (2) in cases in which this is impossible, their coparticipants' cooperative actions are geared toward not making them lose control over their utterance.

P. Auer (✉) · A. Bauer · I. Hörmeyer
University of Freiburg, Freiburg im Breisgau, Germany

© The Author(s) 2020

R. Wilkinson et al. (eds.), *Atypical Interaction*,
https://doi.org/10.1007/978-3-030-28799-3_13

This applies to typical interaction. In atypical interaction of the kind we will be discussing in this chapter, one of the participants cannot function adequately as the "animator" or even the "author" (Goffman 1979) of her words. We want to argue that the principles of conversational organization mentioned above are upheld as long as possible even in such cases. The challenged participants' status as the authors and animators of their conversational contributions may be threatened—but supportive interactional partners still strive to make sure that their status as the principals of their utterances remains unaffected. The challenged speaker can at least partially save face, even though his or her lack of verbal and articulatory resources cannot be concealed.

The Autonomous Speaker

The concept of speaker autonomy—that a speaker is somebody who is able to "speak for himself" (Lerner 1996)—is a fundamental assumption of Western culture. It is deeply linked to what Goffman calls "face", i.e., a "positive social value" attributed to and claimed by any full member of society on the basis of her behavior (Goffman 1967).

Speaker autonomy is, first of all, a normative principle, and as such part of our language ideology, i.e., the beliefs about how people who are fully competent members of society should behave linguistically, and how they should be treated by others. The Western model speaker is somebody who 'has an idea' and then puts it into words. He is the linguistic embodiment of the idea of the rational individual which dominates our thinking about personhood, identity and social membership. It is the speakers' responsibility to plan and execute verbal actions; they can be held accountable for failing to comply with this responsibility. Hence, speakers are given the possibility, but are also obligated, to 'choose their words' correctly and in such a way that their intentions can be understood by the listeners. A person who lacks the words, unintentionally speaks in an ambiguous or inadequate way, or does not structure verbal contributions well—in short: someone who repeatedly and systematically fails to make herself understood—does not count as a full member of society (which applies, for instance, to small children). In Western culture, speaking 'in full sentences' is also part of this ideology, since full sentences are equated with utterances than can stand for themselves and do not depend on their context, particularly not on the coparticipants. Therefore, they are deemed to be particularly well suited to express the speaker's thoughts. For any person claiming to be a full member of society, not being able to live up to these demands on a permanent basis severely threatens face—it is a "stigma", in Goffman's terms (Goffman 1963).

But the autonomous speaker is more than an ideological notion; this notion also has correlates in everyday life, i.e., in conversational structure. The most obvious and basic correlate is the turn-at-talk (cf. Sacks et al. 1974). The turn-at-talk is the speakers' domain (cf. Jefferson 1984; Lerner 1996); it is their realm in which they can formulate und reformulate their individual contributions in interactions, typically without intervention by the other participants (see the preference for self-repair over other-repair, cf. Schegloff et al. 1977). The turn-taking system guarantees the turn's integrity. This ideal of speaker autonomy is upheld as long as possible, despite its obvious limits.

It is, by definition, true that atypical speakers cannot meet these demands. They cannot function as fully autonomous speakers. This, however, does not mean that speaker autonomy and hence an orientation toward "norm-ality" (in the sense of the above norms) is irrelevant in their case. For instance, contrary to occasional claims to the contrary (cf. Milroy and Perkins 1992), the preference for self-repair also holds for atypical (e.g. aphasic) interaction (cf. Laakso 2003; Perkins 2003).

Aphasia and Dysarthria: Two Cases of Atypical Interaction

In the following, we want to discuss two cases of what can certainly count as atypical interaction from the perspective of speaker autonomy. These are, on the one hand, interactions with people who are affected by anarthria as a consequence of severe cerebral palsy (CP) and communicate with the help of a "VOCA" ("voice output communication aid", also known as "SGD", "speech generating device"), i.e., a text- or icon-to-speech system installed on a computer, and on the other hand interactions with people who have to cope with aphasia.[1]

Bringing together atypical interaction under these two conditions might initially appear problematic.[2] From a medical point of view, the Severe Speech and Physical Impairments (SSPIs) that can ensue from cerebral palsy, and the symptoms of aphasia appear to be worlds apart. Cerebral palsy is usually acquired congenitally. The neurological damage is caused by upper motor neuron lesions, lesions in the corticospinal tract or the motor cortex, lesions in the cerebellum, the extrapyramidal motor system and/or pyramidal tract or the basal ganglia. In the severe cases we will analyze, it leads to anarthria, i.e., to the absence of speech due to articulation dysfunction. But despite this anarthria, it is often argued (although this is a debatable issue in our opinion) that people affected by severe infantile CP develop normal language capacity and are simply unable to output their linguistic competence in the form of speech. The use of speech-output systems operated, for instance, by gaze—part of so-called "Augmentative and Alternative Communication" (AAC)—are designed to overcome this limitation.

By contrast, aphasia is acquired later in life, when the individuals who are affected have already developed and used language, often for a long time. Aphasia arises due to a lesion in some or several language-related cortical regions of the dominant brain hemisphere. As a cortical lesion in the language-relevant areas in the cortex, it is per se independent of dysarthric impairment (although combinations of aphasia and dysarthria occur). It is the language itself (its vocabulary and grammar, but also

[1]The following observations are based on data and analyses that were carried out in the context of two research projects funded by the German Research Council: "Adaptationsstrategien in der familiären Kommunikation zwischen Aphasikern und ihren Partnerinnen" (Au 72/14-1, 14-2, 14-3) and "Interaktive Bedingungen Unterstützer Kommunikation bei schwerer Infantiler Cerebralparese (ICP)" (AU 72/22-1).

[2]Although we are not the first ones to point out the similarities of problem-solving across aphasia and anarthria, cf. Bloch and Beeke (2008).

semantics) that is impaired. So far, high tech communication aids have rarely been used by speakers coping with aphasia. If they are, however, their function is very different to that when used by CP speakers, since securing articulatory output is of little help to them.

Despite these differences, our work on both kinds of atypical interaction has taught us to approach medical and particularly neurological classifications of language and communication impairments and test-based assessments of a speaker's communicative capacities with some scepticism. Some people with very severe CP or aphasia can communicate quite well, while others, whose impairment is classified as light, fail in this regard. This suggests that we should take a phenomenon-oriented approach, i.e., we should start from what we can observe in interaction, not with a preconceived idea of what a certain person with a certain neurologically defined impairment should (not) be able to do.

One important finding from such a phenomenon-driven approach is that any kind of challenged interaction, be it due to aphasia or cerebral palsy, restructures the repertoire of resources available to the speakers. The restructuring is different in anarthria/CP and aphasia, of course. In the case of anarthria/CP, one of the main restructurings of resources is due to the use of a VOCA, as shown in a number of CA-oriented research papers on that topic.[3] Among other things, VOCAs delay and decelerate the production of turns by the speaker (Higginbotham and Wilkins 1999; Higginbotham et al. 2016). In addition, the process of utterance composition on the computer implies gaze withdrawal by the speaker from the interaction, which may have severe negative effects on interactional alignment (Antaki and Wilkinson 2013; Engelke 2013). This type of interactional retardation and the concomitant loss of progressivity differs from the kind of retardation and loss of progressivity observed in aphasic interaction, which it is mainly due to the extraordinary high amount of self- and other-initiated and/or -administered repair work.

[3]Cf. Norén et al. (2013), Bloch and Wilkinson (2004), Bloch (2011), Bloch et al. (2015), Hörmeyer and Renner (2013), Hörmeyer (2015), Auer and Hörmeyer (2017), Clarke and Wilkinson (2010).

The reallocation of resources also affects the multimodal nature of the interaction in different ways, although the visual channel is extremely important in both cases. When a VOCA is used by a person coping with anarthria, it is naturally the computer screen that 'augments' interaction. In addition, the minute movements that the speaker is able to execute intentionally and in meaningful ways (such as gaze or head nods) must be monitored very attentively by the coparticipants (Engelke and Higginbotham 2013). In interaction with coparticipants affected by aphasia, reliance on gestural, for instance pantomimic, compensatory resources is more important (cf. Bauer and Auer 2010; Auer and Bauer 2011).

The Autonomous Speaker and Anarthria/Aphasia

The following study is based on the in-depth analysis of interactions with five speakers with anarthria due to CP (four with spastic tetraplegic CP, one with dyskinetic [athetotic] CP), and with another five speakers with aphasia (two fluent/Wernicke type, one non-fluent/Broca type, two anomic). They were video-recorded in informal settings when interacting with spouses, parents, teachers, assistants, friends and sometimes unknown participants. The group of challenged speakers in the aphasia corpus was somewhat older (mostly above 50) than those in the CP corpus (all under 30). In the CP corpus, a second camera recorded the activities on the VOCA.

In both data sets, we found a strong orientation towards interactional norms also valid in typical interaction, and hence the challenged participants' face, even in cases where it is impossible to uphold this normality entirely. This means that the principle of speaker autonomy remains relevant, even when the costs are high, leading to communicative inefficiency, loss of progressivity, ambiguities and vagueness. There is a fundamental conflict between making the interaction work on the referential (communicating in the sense of transmitting information) and interactional (assuring progressivity and sequential structure) plane on the one hand, and enabling the challenged coparticipant to feel, and to come across, as an autonomous speaker on the other. This tension has to be dealt with by all those participating in atypical interaction. Many times, a good compromise is found.

In order to get a better grasp of the specific ways in which the conflict between speaker autonomy and referential success/conversational progressivity can be solved for practical purposes, it is useful to follow Goffman (1979 [1981]) in breaking down the notion of the 'speaker' into the role of the "animator" (the "sounding box", involved in the phonetic act of producing speech by means of the vocal articulators, even though, sometimes, a technical device such as a telephone can share this function), the role of the "author" ("someone who has selected the sentiments that are being expressed and the words in which they are encoded", Goffman 1979 [1981, p. 144]), and the role of the "principal", who is held accountable for what is said. In this latter function, speakers take specific social roles, they position themselves in a social space, they commit themselves to something, and they take responsibility for their verbal actions, in short, they become social actors. They enter into a social relationship with those for whom their words are intended and whose responses they are awaiting. As Goffman points out, the role of the principal can be split off from that of the author-animator; such as when somebody speaks for somebody else. (Of course, the role of the animator can also be split off from that of the author-principal, for instance when somebody else's text is recited.)

Participants with anarthria using a VOCA separate the role of the animator from the roles of author and principal and use the machine quite literally as their "sounding box". However, using a machine to speak is in itself the least problematic aspect of AAC in terms of speaker autonomy. The participant using a VOCA is usually in full control of the machine, i.e., it is operated by her alone. The negative effects of VOCAs are not due to the externalization of speech output from the vocal cords and articulatory apparatus of the speaker to a machine, but to the extremely slow process of putting together even one-word messages on the computer, and the withdrawal of the speaker from the interaction during this process. The precarious status of speaker autonomy rather concerns the roles of the author and the principal, and here, we find very strong parallels in aphasic and CP/AAC interactions.

In the remainder of this chapter, we will look at various aspects of the tension between orientation toward the principle of the autonomous speaker in the sense of author and principal, and the ways in which the challenged speaker's reduced communicative resources lead to a relinquishment of this principle, without abandoning it entirely.

Simple Cases of Successful Sense-Making

Let us start with the following two simple examples of sequential patterns found in both corpora that demonstrate that interactional sense-making is often quite similar (and similarly unproblematic) under conditions of anarthria and aphasia. In particular, it is not the case (as one might think) that speaking via a VOCA leads to fully-fledged sentences as we know them from unchallenged speakers, while aphasic speakers have difficulties to formulate such full sentences. There are interactional participants who more or less successfully try to do so in both types of atypical interaction, but much more frequently, utterances are produced in both cases that are in many ways 'grammatically deficient'. These fragmentary utterances are not even intended to be understood without problems but are designed, and treated by both parties, as being in need of interactional 'post-processing'. As a consequence, recipients in both cases invest work in co-constructing meaning together with the challenged participant (the collaborative model). Nevertheless, as we shall see, they also respect the challenged participants' face needs, and hence their autonomy as speakers.

In the first case, Mr. H has a diagnosis of mild anomic aphasia (according to medical classification). He is about to tell a friend (Ms. b) about his nephew who wants to go to Brazil in order to care for the three children of a German-descent Brazilian family there. (Both participants speak Alemannic dialect.)[4]

Extract 1 *Brasilien* (H61 Z. 2016)

```
01   H:   [und es hat ziemlich viel DEItsche dadr[O:]be,=
          and  there are rather many  Germans up-there

02   b:   [ja,                                  [ja],
           yes                                   yes

03        =ja,
           yes
04        (1.0)

05   H:   (jo::),
          (yeah),

06        (1.1)

07        sollt_er da    scheins  die:: äh;  (.) zwei KINder?,
          should_he there it-seems the:: uhm; (.) two kids,

08        DREI KINder sind des glaub=ich (unne) ah (        );
          three kids  they are I=think (down_there) uhm (     );

09        (-) äh; (---)
          (-) uhm; (---)

10        mer GUCKT dann halt äh:=
          one looks then PART uhm

11   b:   =beTREUT?
          looks_after
```

[4]Word-by-word interlinear translations are provided for only the utterances that will be relevant in the discussion and show structure specific to the aphasic or anarthric impairment. In the remaining utterances, the translation follows the German original as closely as possible, sometimes at the expense of more idiomatic English.

```
12   H:   ja,
          yes,

13        [ja, ]
           yes,

14   b:   [oder] unterRICHtet; (-)
            or     teaches; (-)

15   H:   dEs AU,
          that as well.

16   b:   des AU?
          that as well?

17   H:   also dass_er halt (.)(mit dene däd)  zamme   LERNT.
          well that_he  PART    (with them would) together learns
```

Mr. H is a relatively fluent speaker who is able to hide his word-finding problems with the help of various strategies. The difficulties arise when he wants to describe the tasks his nephew might have to assume in Brazil. His utterance cannot be understood without problems by his conversational partner. Formulation problems are already obvious in line 07, *soll_er da scheins die:: (.) zwei KINder,* (lit.: 'should_he there it-seems the:: uhm; (.) two kids'). The emerging syntactic structure with the auxiliary in sentence-initial position projects a full verb in last position of the sentence according to the rules of German syntax. Instead of providing this missing verb and thereby completing the sentence, as well as formulating its most important—rhematic—constituent, the speaker breaks off (cf. the glottal stop at the end of line 07) to insert a parenthesis on the exact number of children, presumably to gain time (line 08). Several subsequent pauses and a hesitation marker further inhibit the progressivity of the turn (line 09). Finally, the speaker starts a new, syntactically non-related, project: *mer guckt dann halt* (line 10, 'one then has a look') without having finished the first construction. This utterance is abandoned as well and marked as incomplete by intonation (no boundary tone) and a final hesitation particle. It remains unclear whether this impersonal construction still refers to the friend (meaning 'he then looks…' '…after them').

At this point, the recipient comes in and first suggests the verb ***betreut*** 'look after' (line 11) as a candidate for completing the first fragment (skipping back over the immediately preceding turn-unit in line 10 back to line 07). By the upward intonation contour, *betreut* is presented as a conjecture, to be confirmed or rejected by the first speaker. Mr. H confirms (lines 12 and 13). However, a prosodically neutral, non-emphatic confirmation in atypical interaction often only signals that some kind of approximation of the intended meaning has been reached. The coparticipant seems to know this and adds an alternative conjecture: *oder unterrichtet?* 'or teaches?', which is also confirmed by Mr. H (line 16 'that as well'). Ms. b now wants to check her understanding again through a question repeat (line 15: *des au?* 'this as well?'). Mr. H confirms but also slightly adjusts b's understanding by a paraphrase: he replaces 'to teach' by 'to do their homework with them'. This shows that the second reading was better than the first, although not entirely correct: Mr. H's nephew does not only intend to look after the children, but he will do their homework with them. The sequence comes to completion and Mr. H has been able to bring across a rather detailed account of his nephew's plans.

The following example from a CP speaker develops quite similarly in that an initial formulation of a verbal action by a challenged speaker results in a fragment and needs postprocessing, but can be brought to successful completion with the help of the recipient. We enter the scene as Martin (M) is being fed with chocolate by his personal assistant Mona (mo):

Extract 2 *Süß* (Martin 21.05.12_13, 06:24-07:12)

```
01   M:    ((looks to the left, see Fig.))!
02         (3.2)
03         ((looks at Mona))
04         a:::[:
05   mo:       [((feeds Martin another piece of chocolate))
```

06 M: ((looks at computer screen for 10.6 sec.))
07 Mvoca: ES
08 (12.8)
09 Mvoca: [SÜSS
cute
10 M: [((looks to the left))
11 mo: ((looks at Martin))
12 ((follows Martin's gaze))
13 [was?
what?
14 [((looks at Martin))
15 M: ((points with his chin to the left side, where Françoise is sitting, see Figure))

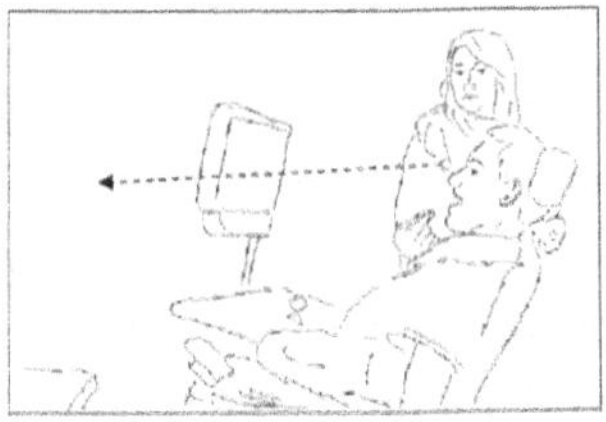

16 mo: françoise.
17 (0.5)
18 ((looks up))
19 (0.7)
20 ( ) [GOLdig;=gell?
cute;=isn't she?
21 [((looks at Martin))
22 (1.8)
23 ((puts another piece of chocolate into Martin's mouth))
24 M: häj

While Martin is chewing on a piece of chocolate, he looks in the direction of Francoise, another person in the room, who is sleeping (line 01). He turns back to the assistant and opens his mouth to be fed with a piece of chocolate (lines 03–05). After that, he directs his gaze to the screen of the laptop fixed to his wheelchair and (after roughly 10 seconds, during which he accesses the relevant letter symbols) makes the VOCA first produce the initial letter of the word *süß* ('sweet') (line 07), and then (after another 13 seconds of work on the screen) the entire word (lines 08–09). When the machine says *süß* (line 10), he looks at Françoise again, signaling that his turn is complete (Hörmeyer 2012), and Mona follows his gaze (lines 10–12). She is not sure yet what Martin wants to say (perhaps because the assessment term *süß* might also refer to the chocolate or because she has not been able to find the object Martin is looking at by gaze-following) and initiates repair (line 13: *was* 'what'). Martin now performs another deictic gesture, this time not only with his eyes, but also with his chin (line 15). This is sufficient for Mona to conjecture that Françoise is the intended referent (line 16). The conjecture is produced with falling intonation and therefore presented as a likely guess at Martin's intentions. Martin need not confirm it, and as he does not reject it either, Mona can rightfully assume that the reference has been established successfully. She moves on to add her sequentially matching second assessment (*goldig, gell?* 'cute, isn't she?'), which closes this sequence; after that, the feeding continues.

In both cases, the challenged speaker starts the sequence with a sequentially first, initiating utterance (a telling or an assessment). Producing initiating sequential actions is a difficult task for speakers who lack the full array of linguistic or articulatory resources available in typical interaction. And in fact, the aphasic speaker's utterance, just like the anarthric speaker's, is fragmentary and ambiguous. In order to understand it, the linguistic (in the first case) or situational (in the second case) context becomes a resource for the interactional partner. In both cases, recipients use this context to suggest a candidate understanding, which is—after some revisions, as in Extract 1, or immediately but implicitly, as in Extract 2—accepted by the challenged speaker. The sequence-initial action is thereby conversationally successful: it can be responded to. This success relies on the coparticipants' conjectures; the autonomous speaker has factually been replaced by a dialogical speaker: communication functions, because both participants contribute to this functioning. More precisely: although one participant is clearly the principal and responsible for the contents of what is being said, he is not fully its author, since some of the wording is provided by the coparticipant (the verb in the first case, and the referential NP in the second), nor its animator. But although autonomous speakership is to a certain degree replaced by collaborative speakership, this is done in a way that does not exceed what is typical for face-to-face interaction, and therefore does not threaten the challenged participant's face more than necessary. There are two important reasons for this.

One is that the he is given the first chance to self-repair his utterance, i.e., the preference for self-repair is in place. In the aphasic example, progressivity is already a problem in line 07. But his friend gives Mr. H time to insert a parenthesis to gain time (line 08), and also waits patiently during the pause afterwards (line 09). She even withholds an intervention while Mr. H starts a second attempt to formulate what he wants to say (line 10). Only when this second attempt also runs into trouble (cf. the hesitation at the end of line 10) does she suggest a verb as a candidate for completion of the first TCU. Mr. H's terrain, the turn, is not intruded upon for a very long time.

In the CP case, the challenged speaker produces the verbal part of his first assessment on the screen (which the assistant can probably see, since they interact in a side-by-side arrangement). His turn is multimodally constructed: the referent over whom the evaluative term is predicated must be identified by following his gaze. The multimodal package starts in line 01, when Martin looks to the left (in the direction of Françoise) for the first time. Note that he starts his turn by producing the letter sound "S", after which the assistant could already have suggested a target word. But this is not done; Martin is still visibly working on his contribution, and his coparticipant refrains from intruding into his terrain, until (after more than 20s) he makes the VOCA produce the word *süß* 'sweet' and signals—by looking away from the screen—that the turn (consisting of his gaze and the VOCA-output) is complete. Mona has failed to identify the referent, but she waits patiently until Martin's turn is marked as complete before she initiates repair in turn transition space ('what?', line 13).

The second structural feature of these extracts by which the speaker's autonomy and hence his face is protected is the fact that he is given control over the outcome of the collaboration. The recipient in the first extract suggests several verbs, and the aphasic speaker is always given a chance to accept or reject these conjectures. Equally in the second case, where the other repair (*was?*) is followed by a stronger version of a pointing gesture, and then by a conjecture (*Françoise*) which is presented to the CP speaker for confirmation or rejection.

It is not difficult to find differences between the two challenged speakers in our examples that can be linked to their specific communicative resources. Despite his aphasia, Mr. H is a fluent speaker who can conceal his word-finding problems behind a façade of continuous language production, with just the decisive (rhematic) elements lacking. He fills time with words, hoping that the semantic core elements will come. Martin, on the other hand, needs a lot of time to produce referential core elements on the VOCA, but is eventually able to have the machine produce the rhematic element of his contribution. His problem is combining nonverbal resources with minimal VOCA output (multi-word utterances on the VOCA would take even longer). He needs time to use his VOCA and therefore reduces his language output to the minimum. But despite these obvious differences, the two constructional features of collaboration discussed in this section (late onset of post-processing and speaker control over the result) hold for both examples and guarantee the challenged participants' status as the "principal" of their utterances.

Complex Post-Processing

In the two examples discussed in the previous section, the emerging problems can easily be managed by the participants. But often, much more complex post-processing is required in atypical interaction. Complex collaborative sequences emerge in which the challenged speakers have to rely more strongly on their coparticipants as a resource to compensate for the own deficits. By externalizing (dialogizing) the processes of turn-composition that are the basis of autonomous speakership—such as lemma retrieval and syntactic composition as well as articulation—, these processes of extensive and complex collaboration become efficient means for co-constructing meaning (cf. Bauer 2009, 2015; Ferguson 1998; Leiwo and Klippi 2000; Oehlschlaeger and Damico 1998; Lind 2002; Goodwin 2004; Goodwin et al. 2002). But can the challenged speaker's status as an autonomous speaker still be secured, once the non-challenged and the challenged participants' share in these post-processing activities become more and more unequal?

Here is an example in which collaborative sense-making is put to a much harder test. Mr. HC's disability was medically classified as a severe Broca aphasia; his verbal resources are restricted to a few words (*ja, nein, so* '*yes, no, so*'). Coparticipants in the following extract are his wife, Ms. FC, and the couple's daughter, T.

Extract 3 *Osterferien* (c51, S. 205, Z 544ff)

01 FC: MACHT denn die Logoschule OSCHterferien.
has PART the school-of-logopedics easter-holidays
'does the school of logopedics close for the Easter holidays?'

02 (1.0)

03 HC: <<f> NEIN.>
no

04 FC: ah ja. ((withdraws gaze))
I see.

05 (1.6)

06 HC: DOCH.
it does.

07 (0.3)

08 T: [<<laughing> eh hn h hn hn>]

09 FC: [<<laughing> hm: hm hm>]

10 HC: [<<f> ja: SO: SO: (   )>
yes so so (   )

11 [((swaying movement of upper torso, twisting hand movement))

12 (2.0)

13 FC: <<f> WEISCH es net.> (0.2)
don't you know.

14 HC: <<f> DOCH. (-) DOCH.>
I do. I do.

15 FC: <<laughing> du wie hh hn h hn>
(you like)

16 HC: NEIN.
NO.

17 hhh <<p> mensch.>
oh man.

18 (2.4)

19 ´ts °hhh

20 (2.0)

21 verDAMMte °hh
damned

22 (2.2)

23 ((coughs loudly))

24 (2.8)

25 FC: also <<allegro> FANG wer noch mal an.>
so let's start again.

26 isch die SCHUle geschlOssen?
is the school closed?

27 HC: NEIN. (0.2)
NO.

28 FC: <<f>es macht jEder EINzeln urlaub.>

```
                everybody takes his vacations individually.
29          (1.4)
30    HC:   NEIN.
            NO.
31    T:    <<f>ah nur die FEIertag> habt ihr se ZU klar.
                oh it's only over the bank holidays that they are
                closed, of course.
32    FC:   (kei       ).
            (no        ).
33    FC:   osterMONtag.
            Easter Monday.
34          osterMONtag isch geschla geSCHLOssen.
            Easter Monday is clo     closed.
35          auf JEde fall. [ne?
            definitely,    right?
36    HC:                  [ja;
                            yes;
37          SO,
38          [JA:.]
39    FC:   [JA:.]
```

When his wife asks him whether the *Logoschule* (the outpatient department of the school of speech and language therapy) is closed over the Easter holidays, she probably expects a simple yes-or-no answer, which would be within the range of her husband's possibilities and guarantee a smooth sequential development. However, the answer is more complex, as it turns out.[5] Mr. HC brings this across by answering first negatively (*nein*, line 03), and shortly after, following his wife's acknowledgement of his negative answer, positively (*doch*, line 06); this deliberate self-contradiction results in joint laughter by all participants. Mr. HC now produces a series of syllables: *ja: SO: SO:* (line 10). *So so* is

[5]This may also be due to the ambiguity of the term *Osterferien* as used by her: it usually refers to the school holidays over Easter (a two-week period), but it can also mean the much shorter period from Good Friday to Easter Monday.

a *passe-partout* word for him which he uses with multiple interactional functions. In the present case, it is combined with gestures expressing ambivalence (swaying of the torso, twisting of the hand, cf. line 10/11). Ambivalence is also one of the functions of the duplicated deictic adverb *so* in vernacular German. The multimodal package produced by HC is therefore to be understood as indicating ambivalence with regard to the answer to his wife's initial question.

But Ms. FC interprets these cues differently, i.e., in the sense of her husband not knowing the answer to her question (line 13). This reading is rejected by Mr. HC (line 14), however: he does know, but he can't express himself. About 10 seconds pass during which Mr. HC produces a series of words and sounds (such as a clicking sound and a light swearword: *Mensch*) which make his linguistic predicament 'public' and observable. It is only at this point that his wife starts to treat her husband's multimodal actions as verbally deficient. She embarks on a strictly organized sequence of yes/no questions through which she elicits the intended meaning step by step. This shift of mode is explicitly announced by "so let's start again" in line 25. Before, her husband had been treated as somebody who simply did not know the answer to her question (something completely normal); from now on, he is treated as somebody who cannot speak for himself, i.e., a person who does not qualify as an autonomous speaker.

The sequence which follows clearly deviates from the structure of typical interaction. It puts the challenged speaker in the responsive role and reduces his participation to that of an answerer in well-defined sequential slots, almost following the structure of an interrogation. However (contrary to findings by Simmons-Mackie and Kagan 1999), there is no indication in this sequence or in our data in general that such a participation framework is regularly experienced as a threat to their face by the challenged participants. The reasons are obvious: Mr. FC has first been given ample space to speak for himself; his failure is announced by himself (which can be seen as an invitation to his wife to help him out), not by his wife or daughter; and he remains the principal of the message which is jointly constructed: the final ratification is given by him (lines 36, 37, 38).

A similar case of a complex process of collaborative meaning-construction can be observed in the following example of an interaction between Nina (N), who is affected by anarthria and uses a VOCA, and Melanie (m). The topic is a former assistant of Nina's who left because Nina did not get along with her. This topic has already been established at the point where our extract starts. Melanie asks Nina whether she wants to talk about this issue now.

Extract 4 *Falsch behandelt* (Nina 30.0.09, 0050-0159)

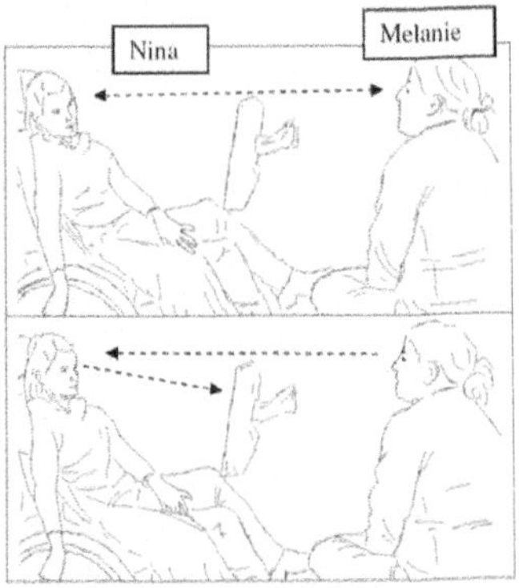


```
01   m:   ähm [wills du drüber
           REden? Figure 1))
          uhm do you want to talk
          about it?
02   N:       [((looks at VOCA
           screen, Figure 2))
03        [((nods))
04   m:   [wie du dich] damit
          FÜHLST?
          what your feelings are
05   N:   ((nods))
06   m:   dass sie jetzt WEG is?
          that she is gone now?
07   N:   ((shakes [head))
08                 [((looks at m.))]
09   m:   oder wie du dich gefühlt
          hast als die [DA(.)
          or how you felt when she
          was there
10   N:   [((nods))
```

11 m: wie als sie [DA war und du dich DA gefühlt hast;
how when she was there and your feelings then;

12 N: [((looks at VOCA screen))

13 (0.8)

14 N_{VOCA}: [falsch
false

15 N: [((looks at m.))

16 [((big nod))

17 m: [<<p>falsch;>
false;

18 du hast dich FALSCH [gefühlt;
you felt false;

19 N: [((several nods))

20 m: ä:hm falsch beHANdelt ge[fühlt?
uhm treated falsely?

21 N: [((shakes head))

22 ((several [nods))

23 m: [falsch beHANdelt ge[fühlt,
treated falsely,

24 N: [((looks at screen))

25 ((N. works on the VOCA, 9.0))

26 N_{VOCA}: PARtner

27 N: ((looks at Melanie))

28 (1.2)

29 m: mit ihr als PARtner also mit ihr als FREUND?=
with her as a partner, I mean with her as a friend?=

30 dass sie: [(.) b] nich (.)
that she didn't b

31 N: [((nods))

32 m: [so für dich DA war wie ANdere?
that she wasn't there for you like others?

33 N: [((looks away, then back at m.))

34 ((nods))

35 (0.5)

36 m: [dass:: du dich nich so] ver[STANden gefühlt][has?
that you didn't like feel understood?

37 N: [((rotating head gesture)))

38 [((nods))

39 [((looks
at VOCA))

40 (0.4)

41 m: <<p> wie bei ANderen?>
like with others?

42 N: ((nods))

43 (0.4)

44 m: <<p> is das RICHtig?>
is that what you mean?

45 N: ((nods, looks at m.))

46 m: ja?
yes?

47 N: ((nods))

The topic is negotiated in the beginning. Melanie asks several questions in order to find out exactly what Nina wants to talk about. Her turn format is that of a double expansion ("increment") of the original question 'do you want to talk about it', first by a glued-on (Couper-Kuhlen and Ono 2007) embedded question ('...how you feel about it'), then by a glued-on complement clause ('...that she is gone'). As Nina rejects the last expansion (cf. the headshake in line 07), Melanie rephrases this expansion to '...how you felt when she was there'.

After the issue to be talked about is settled in this way, Nina turns to the computer screen and makes the VOCA say the word: *falsch* 'false', which can count as an answer to Melanie's question (line 14). The turn is marked as complete by Nina's looking away from the screen and at her recipient, and by an emphatic head nod.

Up to this point, Nina is treated as a fully competent conversationalist, but now post-processing starts. It follows a similar format as in the aphasic interaction: the non-challenged participant tries to understand the fragment answer which as such does not seem to make sense to her—after all, 'false' is not a property usually associated with feelings (cf. her repetition of *falsch* in a low voice). Does Nina mean that the former assistant was false or behaved wrongly? Or that Nina felt that she was the wrong person for the job? Melanie starts a series of question/answer pairs in order to clarify the issue. First, she clarifies who falseness is predicated over by suggesting Nina as the experiencer ('you felt false' in line 18). When Nina agrees, Melanie specifies the paraphrase further by adding a verb: 'treated falsely'? Nina first rejects but then confirms this interpretation (lines 21, 22), which suggests that the paraphrase was only partly correct. Melanie repeats it once more but still does not quite get Nina's intended meaning.

At this point of near failure, Nina adds another word with the help of the computer: *Partner* 'partner' (line 26). Once again, it is Melanie's job to use this semantic cue in order to construe candidate readings which Nina can confirm or reject. She first tries to repair *Partner* into *Freund* 'friend', assuming a semantic mistake,[6] and then conjectures that

[6] *Partner* would in this context imply a love relationship.

'false partner' might mean 'that she wasn't there for you like the others' (line 32) and 'that she didn't feel understood' (line 36). Nina confirms both conjectures by head nods. The sequence is brought to completion when Melanie asks twice whether her interpretation is correct (lines 44, 46), and Melanie agrees both times by nodding (lines 45, 47), although it remains somewhat open whether Nina has made herself understood.[7] But all participants agree that 'enough is enough'.

The way in which Melanie has helped her to communicate clearly exposed Nina's difficulties to act as an autonomous speaker. However, she remained the principal of her utterance, though surely not the author or animator. The reason is again that she was given space to try to formulate her contribution, that transition into the post-processing phase is authorized by her (she marks her turn as complete by looking away from the screen and toward her coparticipant in line 14) and that every step in the post-processing phase is under her control.

Speaking *for* the Challenged Participant

So far, we have seen that exposing the challenged persons' problems does not necessarily lead to them losing the status of the principal of the utterance (see Bauer 2009; Pilesjö and Rasmussen 2011). We now turn to a third case, in which the autonomy of the speaker as an individual who can talk for himself/herself seems at an even greater risk; these are cases of multi-party interactions in which some other participant speaks *for* the challenged speaker to a third party (see Barnes and Ferguson 2014; Ferguson and Harper 2010; Samuelsson and Hydén 2017; Linell and Korolija 1995).

The first extract is taken from one of the regular interviews, we, the project members, conducted with the families who recorded their interactions for us. Mr. HK is coping with a severe aphasia classified as of the Wernicke type. The sequence starts with the interviewer asking him

[7] Her rotating head gesture in line 37 and the look at the VOCA in line 39, which usually is followed by a VOCA- produced word, might indicate that the head nods only signal partial agreement.

what he is currently doing in his speech therapy sessions. Also present is his wife.

Extract 5 *Buchstaben des Alphabets* (from Bauer and Auer 2009, p. 26) (k5i t 22:09)

```
01 Int→HK: was (.) macht denn ihre SPRACHtherapeutin zur zeit
           mit ihnen,
           on what does your language therapist work with you at
           the moment,

02         in,
           in,

03         bei der SPRACHtherapie,
           at the language therapy,

04         was ÜBT die mit ihnen?
           what kind of exercises does she do with you?

05    HK:  ja,((short look at interviewer, then away))
           yes,

06    Int: also-
           I mean-

07    HK:  also was was MACH ich denn da,
           well what what do I do there,

08         ähm,
           uhm,

09         [sie m ARbeit,
            she m work,
           [((short look at Ms. K))

10         [wie soll ich des SA,
            how should I s
           [((looks down))

11         [kannsch du mir erSÄHL bitte,
            can you tell me please,
           [((looks at Ms. K))

12    FK:  ((gentle nod, but looking down))

13    HK:  [wie wie des HEIßT da,
            what what it is called there,
      FK:  [((looking down))

14    HK:  da mUss ich etwas MAChen,
           I have to do something there,

15         und (.) ich denn werk  dann ANderst
           and (.) I   then (XXX) then  differently
```

```
            als ich äh mAchen muss,
            from I  uhm to-do   have,

16          und [dann sollte ich (.) des SAgen;
            and  then I am-supposed-to say it;
                [((turns  to  Ms.  K  by  gaze  and  upper  torso
                   movement))

17    FK:   <<nodding>ja,>
                      yes,

18          [also es geht [(.) DAdrum];
             well it's         about;
            [((looks at interviewer))

19    HK:                  [erZÄHL mal] was des-
                            tell PART what it-
                           [((keeps looking at Ms. K))

20    FK:   mein mAnn äh kriegt also jetzt von jedem buchstaben
            des alphaBETS, ((etc.))
            my husband uhm now gets each letter of the alphabet...

((FK continues to explain the therapy.))
```

Mr. HK is unable to answer the interviewer's question (lines 01–04, 06) due to his aphasic symptoms. Nevertheless, he accepts responsibility for the turn which is allocated to him by the question and produces several turn beginnings (lines 05, 07–10), before he explicitly turns to his wife and asks her to speak for him (line 11). But Ms. FK does not help immediately (which she signals by looking away, line 12), but waits (lines 13–16) to give her husband a chance to try on his own, even though she probably knows that he will not succeed. Only after this attempt visibly fails and Mr. HK again turns to Ms. FK first by gaze and body orientation (line 16), and then also verbally (line 19), does she take over and answer the question for him. During this answer (not reproduced in full here), Mr. HK remains an active participant by looking at his wife, ready to intervene in case her words were not in agreement with what he wants to say.

A very similar case of speaking for the challenged participant occurs in the following extract from our AAC corpus. Nina, who we already know from Extract (4), has a visitor from a university—Mr. Rü. Mr. Rü inquires after the assistants whose help is essential for Nina and makes it possible for her to live in her own apartment. Also present is Lutz, one of these assistants.

Extract 6 *Assistentinnen* (15.7.09 05:51-06:22, S 76)

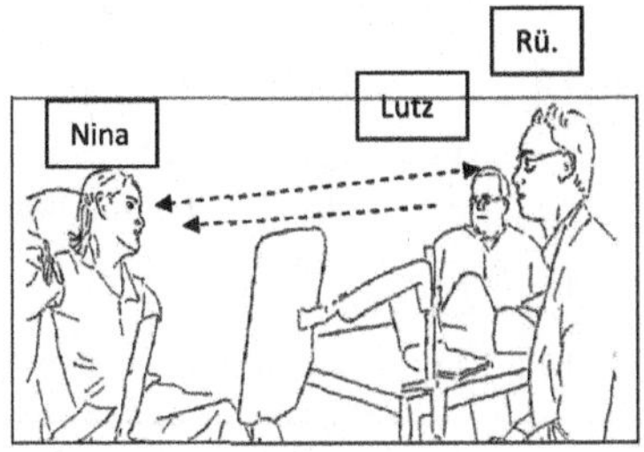

01 rü: und dann (.) würd ich jetzt mal noch frAgen wegen der (-) assiSTENZ;
and then (.) I wanted to ask about the assistants; ((see fig. 1))

02 (0.6)

03 sie ähm-
you uhm-

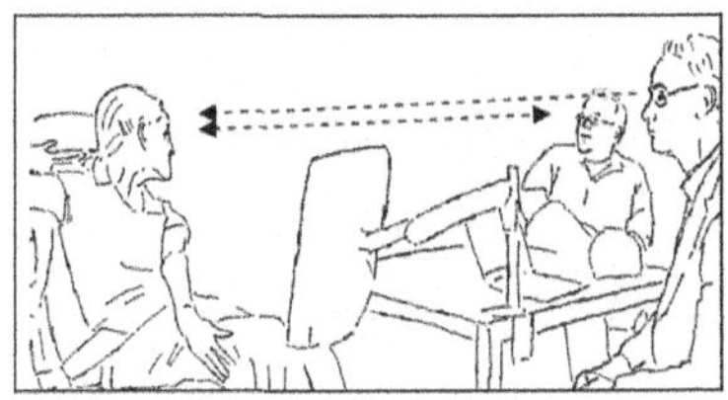

04 N: ((looks at screen))

05 slrr

06 (9.3)

07 N_{VOCA}: neun
Nine

08 ((looks at Lutz, fig. 2))

09 (1.5)

10 l: neun assis[TEN[tin[nen-*nine assistants*

11 rü: [((short gaze at Lutz))

12 N: [((nods,still looking at Lutz))

13 rü: [((several nods))

14 N: mm

15 ((looks at Lutz's belly, lowers head))

16 (0.8)

17 l: ähm °h soll ICH jetzt was dazu [sagen=
uhm do you want ME to say something about that

18 N: [((gaze at Rü.))

19 l: =neun assis[TENtinnen;]
nine assistants;

20 N: [arg mhm]

21 [((nod))

22 rü: [((nodes)

23 N: [((gaze away to right side))

24 l: dass nina (.)
that Nina

[also [ne ganze reihe von assis[tentinnen HAT,
well has a whole bunch of assistants,

25 rü: [((looks at Lutz))

26 N: [((looks at screen))

27 rü: [((looks at Nina))

28 l: ((short look at Rü.))

29 rü: [hm_[HM,

[((several nods))

30 l: [um die [NEUN,
about nine,

31 [((looks at Nina))

32 N: [((looks at Lutz))

33 da [gibt_s_n bisschen [WECHsel drin;
there is a bit of change;

```
34   rü:      [((looks at Lutz))
35   N:       [((several nods))
36            [((looks at Lutz))
37                          [((looks at Rü., Fig. 4))
38   rü:  [hm_M,
39        [((several nods))
40        [((looks at Nina))
41        ((several small nods))
42   l:   ((nod))
43   N:   hm
```

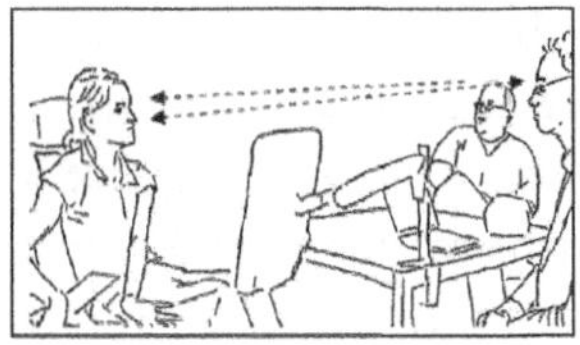

As in the previous example, a complex process of negotiation emerges between the challenged speaker—Nina—and her assistant whether he should speak for her and what he should say. Lutz, the assistant, only takes the turn *for* Nina after he has been invited to do so by her. Note that after the initial question by Mr. Rü, it is first Nina who answers (lines 04–08), just as it was Mr. HK in the previous example. She looks at her computer screen in order to compose an answer, which is given after approximately 10 seconds: the number *neun* 'nine'. As in Extract (3), line 14, this is a fragment only, not a full answer. Immediately afterwards, Nina looks at the assistant and selects him as next speaker—presumably she is already aware of the fact that the number alone is not sufficient to answer Mr. Rü's question. After a 1.5 sec silence, Lutz indeed provides a more explicit version of the answer for Nina: *neun assistentinnen* ('nine assistants'). This could be the end of the sequence ('Nina has nine assistants'), but Nina extends another invitation to Lutz to say more. She does so by looking at the belly of Lutz—a conventionalized body sign and pointing gesture between the two, meaning 'you!' (line 15). Lutz asks whether she wants him to say something about the assistants (line 17), and upon Nina's confirmation he starts to do so (lines 19, 24, 30, 33, 41, 44). While Lutz speaks for her, Nina gazes at him from time to time, monitoring his words spoken on her behalf.

She nods repeatedly, thereby confirming Lutz's words.[8] But she also looks at Mr. Rü from time to time, who is thereby given the role of *her* recipient, not that of Lutz, her porte-parole. Mr. Rü, in turn, also looks at her most of the time, as attentive recipients do, thereby also displaying her status as the speaker.

In short, we observe the pattern which we already know from the previous example with a speaker challenged by aphasia: Nina is first given a chance to speak for herself. When this becomes problematic, she turns to the person who can help (the partner or assistant), and this person starts to speak for her. While doing so, the challenged participant remains an attentive coparticipant and signals through gaze that she is still the principal of the utterance whose author and animator another person has become.

Conclusions: Balancing Speaker Autonomy and Conversational Understanding

It is perhaps the most important achievement of linguistics in the second half of the last century to have demonstrated that language is fundamentally "dialogical". And, as Linell puts it (2009, p. 13), "dialogism denies the autonomous subject who thinks, speaks and acts in and by himself. Our actions, thoughts and utterances are imbued with interdependencies with what others have done, are doing, and could be expected to do in the future". Although this is entirely true, typical interaction at the same time works in a way that supports the concept of the autonomous speaker. Face maintenance is guaranteed by conversational practices that create the illusion that we act autonomously. In a way, traditional linguistics fell prey to this illusion itself. Although we know better today, and decades of fine-grained studies on language use in its "natural habitat", i.e., face-to-face interaction, have proven the

---

[8]See Auer (2018) and Weiß (2019) for gaze and participation status in typical interactions between three or more participants.

"dialogical foundation" of talk, the analysis of interaction also needs to reconstruct the grounds on which this illusion is based.

In this paper, we have attempted to show that even in untypical interaction, participants construe the challenged speaker as somebody whose autonomy as a principal of his utterance is intact, while providing the collaborative support which she needs in order to 'survive' in interaction. While claims to speakership in terms of the speaker-as-animator and the speaker-as-author may be threatened massively, it is possible to maintain the role of the principal with the coparticipant's help. This is not an optimal solution in terms of face-work, but it is one that works: it provides a good compromise between face-needs and the need to communicate a message and to do so in a way that does not disturb the flow of the conversation more than necessary.

We looked at six successful examples (out of many more), with half of them stemming from interactions with a person affected by aphasia and the other half coming from interactions with a person affected by anarthria and using a VOCA. But of course, there are also cases in which this delicate balance is disturbed. Without going into details, we will just list a few:

- The non-challenged coparticipant may fail to respect the challenged participant's right to try on his own first. This may be the case when the coparticipant offers a conjecture or initiates repair too early, or when she speaks for the challenged person without having been invited to do so. The coparticipant then threatens the challenged speaker's rights to speakership, even on the level of the principal, and severely damages his face.
- The non-challenged coparticipant may fail to check whether his or her collaborative actions conform with the challenged participant's intentions. This may be due to lacking feedback from the challenged participant but also from a failure to take heed of or understand this feedback. In this case, the nonchallenged participant no longer speaks *for* the challenged participant, but at best *about* him.
- At the other extreme, the non-challenged coparticipant may insist on the challenged speaker's duty to provide a full utterance that can stand on its own. These coparticipants often have an explicit

anti-collaborative agenda. They believe that making the challenged speakers try hard to find the right formulation (on the screen or verbally) will help to fully restore speaker autonomy through training in the long term. However, apart from the fact that this may be an illusion, particularly in the case of aphasia, the danger of such a strategy is that it may disrupt conversational alignment and conversational progressivity entirely. Complete breakdown of communication and complete failure to understand each other may ensue.

- It can also be the challenged speaker who insists on her right to formulate utterances in a monological fashion. She then tries to keep coparticipants from interfering with their sometimes extremely long attempts to find the right words or formulations, for instance by gaze withdrawal. Again, what at first sight seems to be a good strategy to secure speaker autonomy may in the end be disruptive.
- Finally, non-challenged coparticipants may pursue a strategy of disregarding the problems they have with understanding the challenged speaker's utterances. This over-reliance on the wait-and-see principle (Garfinkel 1967, p. 41) may be a strategy of politeness and an attempt to not expose the challenged speaker's problems. However, not resorting to other-repair (Perkins 2003), hint-and-guess sequences (Laakso and Klippi 1999), scaffolding (Beeke et al. 2013) and all the other strategies of sense-making found in atypical interaction may once more lead to a complete breakdown of the interaction, as problems of understanding accumulate and the problems cannot be retrieved later.

We believe that there is something to be gained from a comparison of two conditions under which interaction becomes atypical; in particular, such a comparison can improve our understanding of how the human communication engine is able to deal with even radical damage. From the most unlikely constellations in which autonomous speakership is highly challenged, we can learn that it is a basic point of orientation, deeply linked to matters of face.

References

Antaki, C., & Wilkinson, R. (2013). Conversation analysis and the study of atypical populations. In J. Sidnell & T. Stivers (Eds.), *The handbook of conversation analysis* (pp. 533–550). Chichester: Wiley-Blackwell.

Auer, P. (2018). Gaze, addressee selection and turn-taking in three-party interaction. In G. Brône & B. Oben (Eds.), *Eye-tracking in interaction: Studies on the role of eye gaze in dialogue* (pp. 197–231). Amsterdam: Benjamins.

Auer, P., & Bauer, A. (2011). Multimodality in aphasic conversation: Why gestures sometimes do not help. *Journal of Interactional Research in Communication Disorders, 2*(2), 215–243.

Auer, P., & Hörmeyer, I. (2017). Achieving intersubjectivity in augmentative and alternative communication (AAC): Intercorporeal, embodied, and disembodied practices. In C. Meyer, J. Streeck, & J. S. Jordan (Eds.), *Intercorporeality: Emerging socialities in interaction* (pp. 323–360). New York: Oxford University Press.

Barnes, S., & Ferguson, A. (2014). Conversation partner responses to problematic talk produced by people with aphasia: Some alternatives to initiating, completing and pursuing repair. *Aphasiology, 29,* 315–336.

Bauer, A. (2009). *Miteinander im Gespräch bleiben. Partizipation in aphasischen Alltagsgesprächen.* http://www.verlag-gespraechsforschung.de/2009/bauer.htm.

Bauer, A. (2015). Miteinander im Gespräch bleiben. Partizipation in aphasischen Familiengesprächen. *Sprache, Stimme, Gehör, 39,* 129–1330.

Bauer, A., & Auer, P. (2009). *Aphasie im Alltag.* Stuttgart: Thieme.

Bauer, A., & Auer, P. (2010). Gesprächsanalyse – ein Instrument für Aphasieforschung und –therapie. *Sprache, Stimme, Gehör, 34*(2), 92–99.

Beeke, S., Beckley, F., Best, W., Johnson, F., Edwards, S., & Maxim, J. (2013). Extended turn construction and test question sequences in the conversations of three speakers with agrammatic aphasia. *Clinical Linguistics and Phonetics, 27*(10/11), 784–804. https://doi.org/10.3109/02699206.2013.808267.

Bloch, S. (2011). Anticipatory other-completion of augmentative and alternative communication talk: A conversation analysis study. *Disability and Rehabilitation, 33,* 261–269.

Bloch, S., & Beeke, S. (2008). Co-constructed talk in the conversation of people with dysarthria and aphasia. *Clinical Linguistics and Phonetics, 22,* 974–990.

Bloch, S., Saldert, C., & Ferm, U. (2015). Problematic topic transitions in dysarthric conversation. *International Journal of Speech-Language Pathology, 17,* 1–11.

Bloch, S., & Wilkinson, R. (2004). The understandability of AAC: A conversation analysis study of acquired dysarthria. *Augmentative and Alternative Communication, 20,* 272–282.

Clarke, M., & Wilkinson, R. (2010). The collaborative construction of non-serious episodes of interaction by non-speaking children with cerebral palsy and their peers. *Clinical Linguistics and Phonetics, 23,* 583–597.

Couper-Kuhlen, E., & Ono, T. (2007). Incrementing in conversation: A comparison of practices in English, German and Japanese. *Pragmatics, 17,* 513–552.

Engelke, C. R. (2013). *Technically speaking: On the structure and experience of interaction involving augmentative alternative communications.* Unpublished Ph.D. thesis, UCLA, Los Angeles.

Engelke, C., & Higginbotham, D. J. (2013). Looking to speak: On the temporality of misalignment in interaction involving an augmented communicator using eye-gaze technology. *Journal of Interactional Research in Communication Discoders, 4,* 95–122.

Ferguson, A. (1998). Conversational turn-taking and repair in fluent aphasia. *Aphasiology, 12,* 1007–1031.

Ferguson, A., & Harper, A. (2010). Contributions to the talk of individuals with aphasia in multiparty interactions. *Aphasiology, 24*(12), 1605–1620.

Garfinkel, H. (1967). *Studies in ethnomethodology.* Englewood Cliffs, NJ: Prentice-Hall.

Goffman, E. (1963). *Stigma: Notes on the management of spoiled identity.* Englewood Cliffs, NJ: Prentice Hall.

Goffman, E. (1967). *Studies in ethnomethodology*. Englewood Cliffs: Prentice-Hall.

Goffman, E. (1979). Footing. *Semiotica, 25,* 1–29. Reprinted in: E. Goffman. (1981). *Forms of talk* (pp. 124–159). Oxford: Blackwell.

Goodwin, C. (2004). A competent speaker who can't speak: The social life of aphasia. *Linguistic Anthropology, 14*(2), 151–170.

Goodwin, Ch., Goodwin, M. H., & Olsher, D. (2002). Producing sense with nonsense syllables. In C. H. Ford, B. Fox, & S. Thompson (Eds.), *The language of turn and sequence* (pp. 56–80). Oxford: CUP.

Higginbotham, J., Fulcher, K., & Seale, J. (2016). Time and timing in ALS in interactions involving individuals with ALS, their unimpaired partners and their speech generating devices. In M. Smith (Ed.), *Language learning and language use in aided communication.* London: JandR Publishers.

Higginbotham, J., & Wilkins, D. P. (1999). Slipping through the timestream: Social issues of time and timing in augmented interactions. In D. Kovarsky (Ed.), *Construction (in)competence: Disabling evaluations in clinical and social interaction* (pp. 49–82). Mahwah, NJ: Erlbaum.

Hörmeyer, I. (2012). The importance of gaze in the constitution of units in augmentative and alternative communication (AAC). In P. Bergmann, M. Pfeiffer, & W. Reber (Eds.), *Prosody and embodiment in interactional grammar* (pp. 237–264). Berlin: de Gruyter.

Hörmeyer, I. (2015). *Der Einsatz von Körper und Maschine in der Unterstützten Kommunikation: Eine konversationsanalytische Studie.* Radolfszell: Verlag für Gesprächsforschung. http://www.verlag-gespraechsforschung.de/2015/hoermeyer.html.

Hörmeyer, I., & Renner, G. (2013). Confirming and denying in co-construction processes: A case study of an adult with cerebral palsy and two familiar partners. *Augmentative and Alternative Communication, 29*, 259–271.

Jefferson, G. (1984). Notes on some orderlinesses of overlap onset. In V. D'Urso & P. Leonardi (Eds.), *Discourse analysis and natural rhetoric* (pp. 11–38). Padova: CLEUP.

Laakso, M. (2003). Collaborative construction of repair in aphasic conversation: An interactive view on the extended speaking turns of persons with Wernicke's aphais. In C. Goodwin (Ed.), *Conversation and brain damage* (pp. 162–188). Oxford: Oxford University Press.

Laakso, M., & Klippi, A. (1999). A closer look at the 'hint and guess' sequences in aphasic conversation. *Aphasiology, 13*(4–5), 345–363.

Leiwo, M., & Klippi, A. (2000). Lexical repetition as a communicative strategy in Broca's aphasia. *Aphasiology, 14*, 203–224.

Lerner, G. (1996). On the semi-permeable character rof grammatical units in conversation: Conditional entry into the space of another speaker. In E. Ochs, E. Schegloff, & S. Thompson (Eds.), *Grammar and interaction.* Mahwa, NJ: Lawrence and Erlbaum.

Levinson, S. C. (2006). On the human interaction 'engine'. In N. Enfield, & S.C. Levinson (Eds.), *Roots of human sociality: Culture, cognition and human interaction* (pp. 36–69). Oxford and New York: Berg Publishers.

Lind, M. (2002). *Conversational cooperation: The establishment of reference and displacement in aphasic interaction: A Norwegian case study.* Oslo: Unipub.

Linell, P. (2009). *Rethinking language, mind, and world dialogically.* Charlotte, NC: Information Age Publishing.

Linell, P., & Korolija, N. (1995). On the division of communicative labour within episodes in aphasic discourse. *International Journal of Psycholinguistics, 11*(2)[31], 143–165.
Milroy, L., & Perkins, L. (1992). Repair strategies in aphasic discourse: Towards a collaborative model. *Clinical Linguistics and Phonetics, 6,* 27–40.
Norén, N., Samuelsson, C., & Pleyert, C. (Eds.). (2013). *Aided communication in everyday interaction*. Guildford: JandR Press.
Oehlschlaeger, M., & Damico, J. S. (1998). Joint productions as a conversational strategy in aphasia. *Clinical Linguistics and Phonetics, 12,* 459–480.
Perkins, L. (2003). Negotiating repair in aphasic conversation. In C. Goodwin (Ed.), *Conversation and brain damage* (pp. 147–162). Oxford: Oxford University Press.
Pilesjö, M., & Rasmussen, G. (2011). Exploring interaction between a non-speaking boy using aided augmentative and alternative communication and his everyday communication partners: Features of turn organization and turn design. *Journal of Interactional Research in Communication Disorders, 2,* 183–213.
Sacks, H., Schegloff, E., & Jefferson, G. (1974). A simplest systematics for the organization of turn taking for conversation. *Language, 50*(4), 696–735.
Samuelsson, C., & Hydén, L. (2017). Collaboration, trouble and repair in multiparty interactions involving couples with dementia or aphasia. *International Journal of Speech-Language Pathology, 19*(5), 454–464. https://doi.org/10.1080/17549507.2016.1221448.
Schegloff, E. A., Jefferson, G., & Sacks, H. (1977). The preference for self-correction in the organization of repair. *Language, 53,* 361–382.
Simmons-Mackie, N., & Kagan, A. (1999). Communication strategies used by 'good' versus 'poor' speaking partners of individuals with aphasia. *Aphasiology, 13,* 807–820.
Weiß, C. (2019). Das Blickverhalten des nicht-blickselegierten Sprechers während Korrekturen und Elaborierungen. *Gesprächsforschung - Online-Zeitschrift Zur Verbalen Interaktion, 20,* 1–28.

14

Practices of Negotiating Responsibility for Troubles in Interaction Involving People with Hearing Impairment

Katie Ekberg, Louise Hickson and Christopher Lind

Introduction

Hearing impairment (HI) affects up to 65–72% of adults aged 70 years and over (Chia et al. 2007; Cruickshanks et al. 1998; Davis 1989). For people with HI, communication breakdowns are a constant concern that can significantly impact their everyday life and social relationships (Erber 1988; Lind, Campbell et al. 2010; Tye-Murray 2009). Within audiology rehabilitation, a communication breakdown is considered to have occurred when a person with HI does not recognize or understand a spoken message (Tye-Murray and Witt 1996; Erber 1988).

K. Ekberg (✉) · L. Hickson
University of Queensland, Brisbane, QLD, Australia

C. Lind
Flinders University, Adelaide, SA, Australia

© The Author(s) 2020
R. Wilkinson et al. (eds.), *Atypical Interaction*,
https://doi.org/10.1007/978-3-030-28799-3_14

People with HI experience communication breakdowns more frequently than people without HI (Lind et al. 2004). Moreover, their attempts to repair sources of hearing trouble can be more prolonged than repair sequences of people without HI, leading to significant disruption in the progress of the conversation.

Conversation analytic (CA) research has examined the details of addressing troubles of hearing, speaking, and understanding talk in naturally occurring interaction (typically with people without a HI) through the framework of 'repair' sequences (Schegloff et al. 1977; Kitzinger 2013). Within this framework, the practice of 'other-initiated repair' occurs when a recipient of a turn-at-talk has some trouble with hearing, understanding, or contextualising a prior turn, and initiates repair on that turn, usually in the next available turn slot (Schegloff 2007; Drew 1997). This then opens up a 'repair sequence' before the conversation is properly resumed. For example:

Speaker A:	Do you listen to music?	(Trouble-source)
Speaker B:	Pardon?	(Repair initiation)
Speaker A:	Do you listen to music?	(Repair)
Speaker B:	Oh, yes I do sometimes.	(Original sequence resumes)

Repair initiations can take different forms, including: open class repair initiations (e.g., "huh?", "pardon?"); category-constrained initiators ("*wh-*" questions e.g., "Listen to what?"), a partial or full repeat of the trouble-source turn, or a candidate understanding of the trouble source turn (e.g., "You mean + possible understanding") (Schegloff et al. 1977). In response, the repair solution is usually fitted to the format of the repair initiation: 'open class' repair initiations are usually responded to with (modified) repeats (see above); category-specific interrogatives responded to with (modified) repeats of the relevant categorical term (e.g., Speaker A: "Do I listen to what?", Speaker B: "Music"); and, repeats and candidate understandings are responded to by confirming or correcting the candidate, or by providing clarification (e.g., Speaker B: "Did you say do I listen to music?", Speaker A: "Yes") (Kitzinger 2013).

Most previous research into repair in conversations with people with HI has been based on data collected in experimental settings (e.g., Jordan et al. 1993; Wilson et al. 1998; Tye-Murray et al. 1995; Tye-Murray and Witt 1996; Caissie and Rockwell 1993). These studies have investigated potential causes of breakdowns in conversations with a person with HI, and effective strategies for repairing these breakdowns using simulation exercises or by setting up brief 5–10 minutes conversations for the purposes of the experimental research study. While this type of research has provided some important findings, it involves the researchers setting-up a simulated conversational environment (potentially embedding the researchers' inferences and biases into the data collection procedure) rather than inductively exploring how people with HI communicate in real-world settings.

Much less research has examined repair with people with HI within naturally-occurring interaction, although there is a growing body of CA research in this area (e.g., Laakso et al. 2019; Lind 2013; Lind, Campbell et al. 2010; Lind, Hickson et al. 2010; Lind et al. 2004, 2006; Skelt 2007, 2010, 2012; Pajo and Klippi 2013; Ekberg et al. 2017; Pajo 2012, 2013). This CA research has found that there are several ways that hearing-related problems and misunderstandings are dealt with in conversation with people with HI, including: (1) repair; (2) allowing the hearing problem or misunderstanding to pass; and (3) closing down or disengaging from the sequence of interaction (Skelt 2007, 2010, 2012). People with HI have been found to initiate repair more frequently in conversation than their conversational partners without HI (Lind et al. 2004), although there is some recent evidence that the use of hearing aids, for people with mild to moderate HI, may decrease the frequency that people with HI need to initiate repair compared with their non-HI interlocutors (Laakso et al. 2019). People with HI often initiate repair in the immediate vicinity of the troublesome portion of the talk, even if this requires an interruption (Lind et al. 2006), and also often use non-vocal actions such as gaze shifts, leaning forward, turning an ear towards the speaker, or frowning (Pajo and Klippi 2013; Rasmussen 2014). A recent study of repair sequences involving people with HI within audiology appointments found that the majority of repair initiations from the person with HI occurred when there was a lack of mutual gaze between them and the speaker (Ekberg et al. 2017). Another study found that communication partners who were accustomed to interacting with the person with HI (e.g., spouses, family members of the person with HI, audiologists) attempted to minimize the need for repair by using practices such as synchronizing their talk with the availability of gaze by the person with HI and attempting to solicit gaze before they spoke (Skelt 2010).

Rather than always disrupting the conversation, people with HI have also been found to allow hearing troubles to pass without repair (Skelt 2012). CA research has also found that people with HI often close down or disengage from the interaction altogether (Skelt 2012). These practices reflect a dilemma that people with HI have when they have trouble hearing a prior turn: they must choose between allowing the conversation to progress without sufficient understanding of what was said or disrupting the sequence of interaction to try to repair their hearing trouble. Sometimes the preference for progressivity over intersubjectivity in conversation may prevail (Heritage 2007).

These previous CA studies have shed some light on the complex structure and management of repair in interactions with people with HI. However, most of these studies have focused on open-class ("what?", "pardon?") or category-constrained ("they went where?") repair initiators as these have been found to be the most commonly used repair initiators in conversation (with both people with and without HI) (Drew 1997; Laakso et al. 2019; Ekberg et al. 2017). However, Lind et al. (2006) noted that HI adults in interaction with familiar communication partners also sometimes used meta-comments to initiate repair (initiations addressing the quality of the acoustic/auditory signal e.g., "You're fading in and out", "I'm not hearing you."). These 'meta-comments' have not been systematically analysed in the previous CA repair literature. This chapter will explore instances of repair with people with HI that involve a meta-comment either in the repair initiation or in a post-repair account. In particular, the analysis will explore how these meta-comments (sometimes in conjunction with other devices) can be used by the person with HI to negotiate responsibility for their hearing-related troubles in interaction in the course of repair sequences.

Negotiating Trouble Responsibility in Repair Sequences

When a trouble of hearing, speaking, or understanding occurs within a specific turn-at-talk, responsibility may lie with either the speaker or recipient of that turn (Robinson 2006). For example, the speaker may have spoken too softly, or the recipient may have had trouble hearing or understanding a prior turn. Furthermore, a combination of these sources of trouble is possible. Previous research has shown that there are some repair practices that communicate the stance that responsibility for the trouble belongs to the trouble-source speaker. For example, a (partial or full) questioning repeat of the trouble source turn, where one aspect of the repeat is vocally stressed (e.g., "Waiter?") has been shown to communicate that something was wrong with the production of that part of the trouble source turn (e.g., the speaker should have said "Waitress") (Jefferson 1972). In communicating that the trouble-source speaker is responsible for the repair-related trouble, these types of repair initiators may be structurally vulnerable to threatening trouble-source speakers' positive face.

Other research has shown how repair initiations sometimes communicate the repair initiator's stance that trouble responsibility belongs to themselves as repair initiator. For example, Robinson (2006) has previously shown how apology-based open-class repair initiators with upward intonation (e.g., "sorry?") can communicate the stance that responsibility for the trouble source belongs to the initiator of repair themselves, rather than the trouble source speaker (i.e., to their own trouble in hearing or understanding the previous turn). The evidence for apology-based repair initiators being understood in this way is that: (1) these repair initiations are typically responded to with verbatim repeats of the trouble source turn, rather than the trouble source speaker revising their prior turn; and (2) in instances when repair initiators subsequently provided a reason for having to initiate repair, this reason involved the 'fault' of the repair initiator themselves (e.g., their own hearing). By claiming responsibility for the trouble as belonging to the repair initiator, apology-based repair initiations can avoid projecting interpersonal disalignment and be an act of managing relationships between the participants. This previous research has demonstrated that trouble responsibility is an interactionally negotiated affair. This chapter will explore how people with HI used meta-comments within repair sequences to negotiate the responsibility for their hearing-related troubles.

Method

Data for this study come from three corpora of video-recorded audiology appointments involving adult clients with HI and a corpus of audio-recorded interactions between adults with HI and their chosen familiar conversation partner. The audiology appointment data were collected in various (public and private) audiology clinics within Australia. Data used in this study were collected as part of other studies, and detailed procedures are described elsewhere (Grenness et al. 2015a, b; Ekberg and Barr 2017). The overall corpus of data totalled 96 appointments, with 32 audiologists, and 96 adult clients. The appointment was video-recorded using an Apple iPod touch or iPhone 4 on a mini tripod placed in an inconspicuous area of the appointment room. The researchers were not present during the appointment. The familiar conversation partner data were collected in a quiet well-lit speech pathology clinic room of a public hospital in Adelaide South Australia and in each case the recorded conversation was the focal activity. Detailed procedures are described in Lind et al. (2004, 2006). The corpus comprised seven dyadic recordings each of approximately 40 minutes duration of free interaction between adults with HI and their chosen familiar conversation partners.

Ethical approval was granted by The University of Queensland Human Research Ethics Committee for all projects, and written consent was obtained from participants prior to recording their interactions. In all cases, the video/audio data were transcribed using the Jeffersonian transcription system (Jefferson 2004), and the video data included the conventions for multimodal transcription developed by

Mondada (2014). The data were analysed using Conversation Analysis (Sidnell and Stivers 2012). The corpora were first systematically analysed for all instances of other-initiated repair by the person with HI. For the current analysis, instances where the participant's hearing difficulties were made explicit were then identified within the collection for detailed analysis. The repair sequences were analysed in detail for: (1) the design of the HI participant's repair initiation; (2) the design of the audiologist's/communication partner's repair turn; (3) HI participant's post-repair accounts for the trouble (when present); and (4) how responsibility for the hearing-related trouble was negotiated by the participants across the whole repair sequence. For each of the audiology data fragments presented, C = client, A = audiologist, and F = family member. For each of the familiar conversation partner data fragments presented, HI = individual with hearing impairment, and FCP = familiar conversation partner.

Analysis

The use of meta-comments in repair sequences in conversation involving people with HI will be explored in detail in the exemplar fragments below that are representative of the corpora. Fragments (1)–(3) come from the audiology appointment data and Fragments (4)–(6) are from the familiar communication partner data.

Fragment (1) below is an example of a hearing-related repair sequence between a person with HI and an audiologist. The fragment comes from a follow-up audiology appointment. The client has already been diagnosed with HI in a previous appointment and owns hearing aids, thus his HI is known to both parties from the beginning of the interaction.

```
(1)  [20170613 0:09]

 1  A: ΔOkay s↑o what I'll do I'll st↑art with what we call
       ΔMoves away from C, turning to another computer at desk--
 2     a communication situat↑ion, u:mΔ
       ------------------------------Δ
 3  C: Now be c↑areful I- *(0.4) hearing, (0.8)* I can't hear
                           *Points to ear-------*
 4     you too well.
 5  A: ΔThat's oka:y that's- you're in the right place heh:
       ΔTurns to look at C---------------------------------
 6     SO .hh um (0.5) IN TERMS OF SITUATIONS: WHERE YOU HAVE
       ------------------------------------------------------
 7     TROUBLE HEARING, .hhh would one on one be an important
       ------------------------------------------------------
 8     situation for you?Δ
       -----------------Δ
 9     (0.7)
10  F: Yes.
```

The audiologist takes a turn at lines 1–2 where she starts to describe the next task for the appointment. Across this turn, she moves her chair away from the client to look at a computer on the desk. Following a point of possible completion of the audiologist's turn at line 2, the client takes a turn to issue a 'warning' to the audiologist: "Now be careful" (line 3). He then goes on to provide a meta-comment that accounts for the disruption in the interaction: "I can't hear you too well". In providing a meta-comment, rather than a more ambiguous type of repair initiation, the client has explicitly claimed that the disruption is due to a lack of hearing. With such an account, it might be assumed that he is thus claiming responsibility for the trouble to himself. However, by beginning his turn with a warning to the audiologist, he instead holds the audiologist accountable for this trouble for having not designed her prior turn appropriately for her HI recipient (Drew 2012). In addition, the client uses the word "can't" rather than "didn't" hear. The use of "can't hear" generalises his hearing difficulty—it is the case that he generally can't hear, rather than just not hearing certain parts of the prior turn. The client displays an expectation that the audiologist should be "careful" to adapt her interaction to make her talk 'hearable' to him as a person with HI. Thus, with this repair initiation, the client attributes responsibility for the hearing trouble to the audiologist.

In the initial part of her response, the audiologist does not accept this responsibility and instead treats the client's repair initiation as ascribing the trouble to his HI alone. She treats the client's turn as an apology by giving an absolution "That's okay" (Robinson 2004). She then cuts off another "that's-", which may have been on course to be "that's alright", a phrase that would be inapposite in a situation where the client is seeking help to better his hearing. Instead she continues by stating that the client "is in the right place". This phrase again focuses the trouble on being due to the client's hearing. When she goes on to repair her prior talk (through a modified repeat), however, she does turn to face the client and increases the loudness of her voice. She also rephrases "communication situations" from her prior turn to a more simplified phrase: "situations where you have trouble hearing". She thus adapts her talk to be more hearable to the client than in her prior turn. This revision to her turn (rather than a producing a verbatim repeat at the same volume and pitch) stands as possible evidence that the audiologist has understood the client as having communicated a stance that responsibility for the trouble lay within her speech (Robinson 2006). In other words, by adapting her behaviour to be more carefully designed for a HI recipient, she tacitly claims some responsibility for the initial trouble.

Fragment (2) comes from the beginning of another audiology appointment. This appointment is an initial hearing assessment with this audiologist, however the client has had previous hearing tests and already wears hearing aids for her (established) HI. The client's HI is thus known to the audiologist even at the beginning of the appointment.

```
(2)  [18-2 0.34]

1   A: ΔSo th↑ank you for bringing in your audiogram there,Δ
       ΔA looking down at paper-----------------------------Δ
2      ΔI've just had to enter the results here, (.) on
       ΔA looking at C-------------------------------
3      our computer system, so we can have a look [at them]Δ
       ----------------------------------------------------Δ
4   C:                                           *[ SORRY ] I*
                                                 *C leans forward*
5      can't h[↑ear yo(h)u heh heh heh]
6   A:         [Oh hah hah hah so(h)rry] hah hah hah
7      (.)
8   C: *You're talking very softly.*
       *C brings chair in closer---*
9   A: ΔOkay .hhh u::m .tch <so thank you for bringing in>Δ
       ΔA leans in, looking at C, taps paper on desk------Δ
10     your res↑ults:, um I just had to <enter that>
11     Δin the com[puter.]Δ
       ΔA gestures to computerΔ
12  C:            *[ Okay ] [yep.]*
                  *C nods---------*
13  A:                      [Yeah]
```

At lines 1–3, the audiologist begins speaking to the client about her hearing test results. At the beginning of her turn she is gazing down at some paper on her desk (line 1), before looking up at the client (lines 2–3). At line 4, the client interrupts the audiologist partway through her turn to initiate repair. The client begins with a loud prospective apology ("SORRY") (Robinson 2006) and leans forward, before providing a meta-comment concerning not being able to hear the audiologist ("I can't hear you"). The apology and account appear to claim responsibility for the repair initiation to the client's hearing, however there are aspects of the client's turn that counter this claim. Firstly, similar to Fragment (1), the client uses the term "can't" rather than "didn't", which implies a more generalised inability to hear the audiologist. Her turn also involves some laughter particles across the final part of her account and beyond the end of her turn, which mark her hearing trouble as a laughable matter (Haakana 2001). The fact that the client can't hear the audiologist is laughable because both parties already know that the client has a HI and thus has difficulty hearing conversation. In initiating repair with laughter and a meta-account, the client draws attention to this fact and thus marks the audiologist's prior talk as possibly problematic: the audiologist did not design her prior talk in a way that the client with a known HI could hear.

The audiologist enters in overlap with an "oh" change-of-state token (Heritage 1984) and an apology term of her own, in conjunction with joint laughter particles. This reciprocal apology from the audiologist displays that she has understood the client's repair initiation to have attributed some responsibility for the trouble to the audiologist. In other words, the accounting behaviour of the apology shows that the audiologist understands, or at least *claims* to understand, herself to be somewhat blameworthy for the client's hearing trouble. The client's attribution of responsibility for the trouble to the audiologist is confirmed by the client in her next turn at line 8, where she suggests that the audiologist was "talking very softly". This repair-related offence account (Robinson 2006) more explicitly places responsibility for the client not being able to hear onto the audiologist for not speaking loudly enough. With this turn, the client makes the audiologist accountable for her failure to appropriately design her prior turn for her recipient with HI (Sacks et al. 1974; Drew 2012). In response, the audiologist provides an initial acknowledgement "okay", which acknowledges, but does not explicitly accept, the offence attributed to her by the client (talking too softly), and then re-does her initial turn (lines 9–11). Across her repair turn, she leans in towards the client, maintains eye gaze, and slows her speech, thus adapting her talk to be easier for the client to hear. Adapting her talk in this way suggests that the audiologist has possibly understood that some sort of revision to her talk was needed. So again, here, responsibility for a hearing-related trouble is negotiated between the parties as potentially being the responsibility of the speaker of the troublesome talk, rather than just due to the hearing difficulties of the HI person.

A final example from the audiology appointment corpus can be seen in another appointment below. This repair sequence comes during the client's hearing assessment where she is listening, and responding, to beeps being played into a set of headphones. Although the client's HI is yet to be confirmed by the tests, the client has self-identified as "being deaf" at the beginning of the appointment. During history-taking, the client has also complained: "I really am annoyed that nobody really tries to speak clearly to me and they speak to me from other rooms and you know, that sort of thing. They don't make any allowances for my condition".

(3) [Line A1-C12 40:52]

```
1  A: Δ*This one's going to be a little bit* *louder, sorry.*Δ
      ΔGlances at C then back at computer--------------------Δ
   C: *Looking down-----------------------* *Looks up at A-*
2  C: *Sorry?*
      *Leans towards A*
3  A: Δ£That's alright.£Δ
      ΔShakes head------Δ
4  C: Hah hah .hh* *I'm deaf you know h(h)m*
      *Gaze at A-* *Gaze straight ahead----*
5  A: Δh(h)hΔ
      ΔLooking at computerΔ
```

At line 1, the audiologist informs the client that the next sound being played as part of her hearing test will be a bit louder. The client, at line 2, initiates repair on this turn. She does so by using an open class apology-based repair initiator: "Sorry?" and leaning forward across her turn, which together are suggestive of a hearing trouble. Rather than repairing the turn in response, the audiologist provides an absolution "That's alright" (line 3) and shakes his head, indicating that the trouble source turn does not need to be repeated. With this absolution, the audiologist aligns with the trouble being the client's hearing. The client then provides a meta-comment that acts as repair-related offence account (Robinson 2006): "I'm deaf you know". This turn explicitly accounts for the trouble as being a hearing-related problem (thus confirming responsibility for the trouble lies, at least in part, with the client). However, within this account, on the scale of formulations for acquired hearing loss, the client uses a strong formulation of being "deaf", which is suggestive of a high degree of HI (Bilmes 2011). With the use of this term, her inability to hear is thus positioned as being something out of her own control: she could not hear the trouble source turn because she is deaf. The implication from this term is that some responsibility for the trouble lies in the audiologist for not having adapted his talk to make his turn hearable to a "deaf" recipient. In other words, the client is holding the audiologist responsible for not adequately designing his turn to suit his intended recipient (Drew 2012; Sacks et al. 1974). This formulation is followed by the addition of "you know", emphasising that this is not new news for the audiologist, as it is mutual knowledge that she has a hearing loss. She marks the delicacy of her accusatory turn with laughter particles throughout (Haakana 2001). So, again here, across the repair sequence, responsibility for the trouble source is negotiated as being between the participants, with fault lying in the client's inability to hear the turn but also the audiologist's failure to adapt their talk to be hearable for the client with HI.

The remaining fragments below are taken from published transcripts (Lind et al. 2004, 2006; Lind, Hickson et al. 2010) of free and unstructured conversation between adults with HI and their chosen familiar conversation partners. In all cases, conversation was the focal activity, that is, there was no particular implied or overt shared action being undertaken prior to or during the recording to which the participants were oriented in their talk. The audio-recorded data fragments reflect similar patterns of the use of meta-comments to initiate repair and negotiate responsibility for the hearing-related trouble source(s). Fragment (4) provides an example:

(4) (from Lind et al., 2004)

```
1 FCP: doesn't sound very profitable I s'pose they make profit on
2      the coffee
3      (0.3)
4  HI: don't mumble what?
5      (0.9)
6 FCP: I SAID I guess they make a profit on the coffee even if
7      they don't sell the book
8  HI: even if they don't sell the book yeah
```

At lines 1–2, the FCP delivers a turn that is part of an extended telling. At line 4, the HI adult initiates repair by uttering the meta-comment "don't mumble, what?", a bald on-line utterance without redress to their FCP. With this meta-comment, the responsibility for the trouble is unequivocally attributed to an aspect of the FCP's speech, rather than the HI adult's hearing. The FCP makes no commentary in response to this other an indirect acknowledgement of the need for repair by commencing their turn, at line 6, with a louder "I SAID…." followed by a slightly rephrased version of the trouble source, substituting "guess" for "s'pose" (viz. suppose) (line 1). By contrast with the audiology appointment fragments above, there is little negotiation of responsibility: the person with HI is much more explicit about responsibility for the hearing-trouble lying with their FCP. This explicit attribution of responsibility perhaps reflects the use of on-line, immediate threats to face with varying degrees of redressive actions that reflect immediate personal/family relationships (Brown and Levinson 1987). This may be contrasted with the attempts in the client-audiologist data in which clients use various mitigating expressions aimed at more positive politeness given the more distant relationship between participants in the clinical interaction.

Fragments (5) and (6) provide further examples. These fragments arise from the same dyad in a single recording and occur some minutes apart. In these fragments, the HI adult employs more complex repair initiators, in each case combining multiple meta-comments resulting in an intricate array of implied, possibly shared, responsibility.

(5) (from Lind et al. 2010b)

```
1  HI:   /m: m: m/ I think I'd still prefer them (2.0) I mean /$m/
2        hopefully they're going to be committing themselves for the
3        full [five months]
4  FCP:       [YES    but] (0.3) but if we said (0.7) if they come a
5        little bit later
6        (1.4)
7  HI:   sorry you're dropping your voice I'm (0.3)
8        [I'm not hearing you]
9  FCP:  [if   they    come  ] a little bit later
11      (1.1)
12 HI:  [IF]
13 FCP: [if] (0.4) <THEY COME A LITTLE BIT LATER> (1.4) if they
14      don't arrive on the first of April
15      (1.4)
16 HI:  Yeah
```

In Fragment (5) the person with HI initiates repair across lines 7–8. The repair initiation begins with a prospective apology ("sorry", line 7), followed by a meta-comment directed towards the quality of the FCP's vocal volume ("you're dropping out"). This meta-comment explicitly attributes responsibility for their hearing trouble to the FCP's speech. Following a brief pause, the repair initiation turn finishes with "I'm not hearing you", bringing the responsibility back to the HI adult's hearing trouble. Across this turn, the person with HI has thus used meta-comments to orient to both his trouble with hearing and his FCP's volume of speech displaying a somewhat equal distribution of responsibility for the hearing trouble. In response, the FCP merely repeats the last part of her prior turn without altering her speech in any way. She thus does not display any claim of accepting responsibility for the trouble. The person with HI initiates repair again, following a 1.1 second gap, this time with a loud "IF" (line 12). In her second repair attempt, the FCP this time increases the loudness and slows the speed of her speech across the repaired talk, thus altering her talk to be easier to hear by the person with HI. Fragment (6) occurs several minutes later in the same conversation:

(6) (from Lind et al. 2006)

```
1  FCP: yeah (0.8) but (0.9) these are the phone calls that I have
2       to make=
3  HI:  =see you keep dropping I'm losing you
4  FCP: these are the PHONE CALLS that I have to make (1.2) so (0.3)
5       y'know (0.3) as well for (0.8) y'know work out what WE
7       want beforehand (0.5) but not in a way that makes it seem as if
8       we're (1.4) totally (0.5) y'know controlling (1.5) we don't
9       want to [to-]
10 HI:          [yes]
11 FCP: (0.4) we don't want to totally control (1.0) Beryl…
```

The person with HI initiates repair at line 3. In this case, there is a noticeable change in the structure of the repair initiator by contrast with Fragment (5). Here, the repair initiation commences with "see you keep dropping" and is followed by "I'm losing you". The use of "see you keep dropping" places the responsibility for the trouble source in the FCP's speech, and notes that the behaviour has occurred repeatedly (through the use of "see"). This meta-comment is followed by a more neutral meta-comment ("I'm losing you") which is more ambiguous in terms attributing responsibility for the trouble. The person with HI's repair initiation here does not explicitly accept any blame themselves as did the "I'm not hearing you" in Fragment (5). Once again in this fragment, the FCP, in overlap with the last portion of the repair initiation turn, repeats the final portion of their interrupted turn to repair the talk. In their repair turn, the FCP does not make much attempt to accept responsibility for the hearing trouble, although does repeat the key words "PHONE CALLS" in a louder voice.

Together these fragments suggest that adults with HI bring a complex array of meta-comments and other devices (such as apologies or warnings) to address the hearing-related trouble, attribute responsibility for its occurrence to the trouble source speaker, and then, in some cases, to mitigate these markers of responsibility. It is of note that the FCPs in these latter fragments, tend not to join in this process (although sometimes increasing the loudness of certain words in the repair), but rather address the content of the trouble source directly without joining the negotiation of trouble responsibility.

Discussion

The analysis in this chapter has examined hearing-related repair sequences initiated by a person with HI within audiology appointments and in conversation with a familiar conversation partner. The analysis has shown how the person with HI used meta-comments (sometimes in conjunction with other devices) to initiate repair and how responsibility for the hearing trouble is negotiated by the parties across these repair sequences. In each of the fragments, as it was known to the speaker of the trouble source turn (the audiologist or familiar conversation partner) that their recipient had/or at least self-identified as having a HI, responsibility for the hearing trouble was ultimately attributed to the speaker's failure to appropriately design their turn to be hearable for a HI recipient, although the person with HI sometimes also accepted partial responsibility.

Previous experimental research using 'breakdown elicitation tasks' (where the investigator uses a variety of techniques to attempt to purposely elicit communication breakdowns) has found that the three most common elicitations of breakdowns in a conversation with an older adult with HI involved the speaker: (1) having his/her back to the recipient; (2) speaking with reduced volume; and (3) speaking with his/

her head down (Wilson et al. 1998). Further, recent CA research has found that in 76% of repair initiations from clients with HI in audiology appointments there was a lack of mutual gaze between participants (Ekberg et al. 2017). These studies highlight that hearing-related troubles of people with HI often occur due to the behaviour of the trouble source speaker and support the current findings that responsibility for hearing-related troubles is a negotiated affair and can be attributed to the behaviour of either or both parties.

The findings in this study build on prior CA research on repair, and how hearing-related repair sequences in conversations with people with HI are managed. In particular, the findings build on previous research by Jefferson (1972) and Robinson (2006) on how responsibility for a trouble is managed within repair sequences. The current study has shown that, in repair sequences with people with HI, while the person with HI made their hearing trouble explicit through the use of a meta-comment (also often accompanied by non-verbal actions such as leaning forward), they also attributed responsibility for the trouble to the speech of their interlocutor. These attributions of responsibility either appeared within their repair initiation or in a post-repair turn. In this way, they held the trouble source speaker accountable for not having adapted their talk sufficiently for them to hear the original turn. In making these attributions of responsibility to the trouble source speaker, the person with HI has not only disrupted the progressivity of the interaction but also potentially threatened the interpersonal alignment between the two interlocutors. However, in the context of these sequences, the risk of interpersonal 'disalignment' (Robinson 2006) is a necessity because, unless the interlocutor alters their talk, the person with HI is unlikely to be able to hear *any* of the subsequent conversation. Negotiating responsibility for the trouble is thus a necessary dispute when the person HI is at the risk of having no intersubjective understanding of the ongoing interaction. It was also observed that the person with HI was less concerned about a threat to positive face when conversing with their familiar communication partner in comparison to their audiologist.

Within the audiology appointments, following these types of repair initiations, the trouble source speaker (audiologist) tacitly claimed some responsibility for the trouble by adapting their talk in their repair turn to make it more hearable to the person with HI (for example by typically speaking louder, speaking more slowly, emphasising specific words, meeting their recipient's gaze, and leaning forward to speak). In revising their talk in this way, rather than merely providing a verbatim repeat, they displayed a possible understanding that their original turn had not been adequately designed to meet the needs of the person with HI as the recipient of their talk. So both audiologists and the person with HI, through their interactional behaviour across the repair sequence, displayed an awareness that the audiologist should be adapting their talk when speaking to a person with HI, and are held responsible for a failure to do this if a hearing-related trouble in communication occurs.

There was almost no overt/explicit acceptance of responsibility for the trouble source among the FCPs in Fragments (4)–(6), despite various markers of their responsibility uttered by the adults with HI, other than their repetition/rephrasing in the repair turns. The FCPs sometimes repeated part of their repair turn in a louder voice but to a lesser extent than the audiologists. This is possibly a reflection of the more intimate social relation between participants and the perception by the HI adult of the relative lack of need for them to maintain their FCPs positive face as a result. Robinson (2006) suggests that if those uttering the trouble source see themselves as at fault in talk resulting in a trouble source, they more often revise the trouble source rather than repeat it. Across the samples in this study it is of note that seemingly the more familiar the conversation partners, the less likely the revision is to occur.

The findings of this study concerning the audiologists', and sometimes the FCPs', propensity to alter phonetic elements of their repair turns builds on prior CA research of this behaviour. In a study with people without a HI, Curl (2005) showed how speakers' repair turns are typically phonetically different when a trouble source has arisen in a 'fitted' sequence (i.e. repair has been initiated following a turn that is appropriately designed and placed within the sequence of talk in progress). For example, speakers repeated their turn more loudly, with expanded pitch ranges, longer durations, or changes to articulatory settings. However, within her data, she was not able to make the conclusion that this pattern displays an understanding by the speaker that the trouble was hearing-related. In a related study, Lind, Campbell et al. (2010) showed that in repair sequences initiated by people with a HI, speakers (FCPs) also made prosodic changes to their talk in their repair turns. The findings reported in a previous study by Ekberg et al. (2017) and in this chapter build on these prior studies by showing that speakers also sometimes altered their talk in their repair turn when the trouble had been explicitly displayed as a hearing-related trouble. Together with the study by Lind, Campbell et al. (2010) there is growing evidence from repair sequences with people with HI, that speakers do phonetically differentiate their repeat repair turn from their original turn when they have understood the repair initiation to be a hearing-related trouble. In this way, there is a displayed awareness that altering their talk (in pitch or speed) will make it more hearable to the person with HI.

The findings have implications for understanding how participants manage their interpersonal relationships through repair sequences more broadly, and for clinical interventions to address the consequences of HI. During the repair sequences, an expectation was highlighted that the other speaker should be adapting their talk to be easier to hear for the person with HI, and if they do not do this they are held accountable. For people with HI, the common need to initiate repair throughout their conversations has been reported as a concern that greatly impacts their daily life (Erber 1988; Lind, Campbell et al. 2010; Tye-Murray 2009). While it may also be the case that overcompensating in altering speech for someone with HI would also be held accountable, and possibly understood as patronising, the findings do suggest that people with HI expect some awareness towards the clarity of speech from their communication partners.

In terms of clinical interventions, the results of this research show support for approaches that acknowledge conversation, and hearing rehabilitation, as a 'shared responsibility' between speaker and recipient, and the important role of communication partners of people with HI in audiology rehabilitation. For example, audiologists might offer group communication programs for adults with HI and their communication partners, such as the Active Communication Education program (ACE; Hickson et al. 2007). In this type of program, all participants collaborate to problem solve situations in which hearing troubles occur and to develop effective repair strategies. The findings also lend support for the inclusion of key communication partners in audiology appointments so that clinicians can discuss hearing-related interaction troubles between them as a shared problem and mutually agree on strategies to address them (e.g., the person with HI to moves closer to the communication partner and/or the communication partner speaks more loudly). These findings build on previous research from an interview study which found that audiologists' perceived hearing rehabilitation as a shared responsibility between the person with HI and their family members, and reported the need to educate family members about different communication strategies from both sides (Meyer et al. 2015).

Overall, the findings in this study highlight the value that the person with HI places on having talk adapted to meet their hearing needs. If others adapt their talk accordingly when speaking to a person with HI, conversations are likely to progress more smoothly, and be more enjoyable for the person with HI. By sharing the responsibility for hearing-related troubles, the burden of responsibility on the person with HI is reduced, which is likely to have implications for the management of their social relationship. The findings support further community education related to how speakers can successfully adapt their talk to meet the needs of people with HI.

References

Bilmes, J. (2011). Occasioned semantics: A systematic approach to meaning in talk. *Human Studies, 34*(2), 129–153. https://doi.org/10.1007/s10746-011-9183-z.

Brown, P., & Levinson, S. (1987). *Politeness: Some universals of language use.* Cambridge: Cambridge University Press.

Caissie, R., & Rockwell, E. (1993). A videotape analysis procedure for assessing conversational fluency in hearing-impaired adults. *Ear and Hearing, 14*(3), 202–209.

Chia, E. M., Wang, J. J., Rochtchina, E., Cumming, R. R., Newall, P., & Mitchell, P. (2007). Hearing impairment and health-related quality of life: The Blue Mountains Hearing Study. *Ear and Hearing, 28,* 187–195.

Cruickshanks, K. J., Wiley, T. L., Tweed, T. S., Klein, B. E. K., Klein, R., Mares-Perlman, J. A., et al. (1998). Prevalence of hearing loss in older adults in Beaver Dam, Wisconsin: The epidemiology of hearing loss study. *American Journal of Epidemiology, 148,* 879–886.

Curl, T. (2005). Practices in other-initiated repair resolution: The phonetic differentiation of 'repetitions'. *Discourse Processes, 39*(1), 1–43.

Davis, A. (1989). The prevalence of hearing impairment and reported hearing disability among adults in Great Britain. *International Journal of Epidemiology, 18,* 911–917.

Drew, P. (1997). 'Open' class repair initiators in response to sequential sources of troubles in conversation. *Journal of Pragmatics, 28,* 69–101.

Drew, P. (2012). Turn design. In J. Sidnell & T. Stivers (Eds.), *Handbook of conversation analysis* (pp. 131–149). Boston: Wiley.

Ekberg, K., & Barr, C. (2017). *Identifying clients' readiness for hearing rehabilitation within initial audiology appointments: A pilot intervention study.* Queensland: The University of Queensland.

Ekberg, K., Hickson, L., & Grenness, C. (2017). Conversation breakdowns in the audiology clinic: The importance of mutual gaze. *International Journal of Language & Communication Disorders, 52*(3), 346–355. https://doi.org/10.1111/1460-6984.12277.

Erber, N. P. (1988). *Communication therapy for hearing impaired adults.* Abbotsfield, VIC: Clavis Publishing.

Grenness, C., Hickson, L., Laplante-Lévesque, A., Meyer, C., & Davidson, B. (2015a). Communication patterns in audiological history-taking: Audiologists, patients and their companions. *Ear and Hearing, 36*(2), 191–204. https://doi.org/10.1097/AUD.0000000000000100.

Grenness, C., Hickson, L., Laplante-Lévesque, A., Meyer, C., & Davidson, B. (2015b). The nature of communication throughout diagnosis and management planning in initial audiologic rehabilitation consultations. *Journal of the American Academy of Audiology, 26,* 36–50. https://doi.org/10.3766/jaaa.26.1.5.

Haakana, M. (2001). Laughter as a patient's resource: Dealing with delicate aspects of medical interaction. *Text: Transactions of the Society for Textual Scholarship, 21,* 187–219.

Heritage, J. (1984). A change of state token and aspects of its sequential placement. In J. M. Atkinson & J. Heritage (Eds.), *Structures of social action* (pp. 299–345). Cambridge: Cambridge University Press.

Heritage, J. (2007). Intersubjectivity and progressivity in references to persons (and places). In N. J. Enfield & T. Stivers (Eds.), *Person reference in interaction: Linguistic, cultural and social perspectives* (pp. 255–280). Cambridge: Cambridge University Press.

Hickson, L., Worrall, L., & Scarinci, N. (2007). A randomized controlled trial evaluating the Active Communication Education program for older people with hearing impairment. *Ear and Hearing, 28,* 212–230.

Jefferson, G. (1972). Side sequences. In D. N. Sudnow (Ed.), *Studies in social interaction* (pp. 294–330). New York: Free Press.

Jefferson, G. (2004). Glossary of transcript symbols with an introduction. In G. Lerner (Ed.), *Conversation analysis: Studies from the first generation* (pp. 13–23). Philadelphia: John Benjamins.

Jordan, F. E., Worrall, L., Hickson, L., & Dodd, B. J. (1993). The evaluation of intervention programmes for communicatively impaired elderly people. *European Journal of Disorders of Communication, 28,* 63–85.

Kitzinger, C. (2013). Repair. In J. Sidnell & T. Stivers (Eds.), *The handbook of conversation analysis.* West Sussex, UK: Blackwell.

Laakso, M., Salmenlinna, I., Aaltonen, T., Koskela, I., & Ruusuvuori, J. (2019). Open-class repair initiations in conversations involving middle-aged hearing aid users with mild to moderate loss. *International Journal of Language & Communication Disorders, 54*(4), 620–633.

Lind, C. (2013). Conversation repair: Ecological validity of outcome measures in acquired hearing impairment. *Cochlear Implant International, 14*(Suppl. 4), 48–51.

Lind, C., Campbell, K., Davey, A., Rodgers, L., Seipolt, C., & Akins, C. (2010). Some prosodic characteristics of repeated talk following conversation repair requests by adults with hearing impairment. *Seminars in Hearing, 31*(2), 127–139.

Lind, C., Hickson, L., & Erber, N. (2004). Conversation repair and acquired hearing impairment: A preliminary quantitative clinical study. *Australian and New Zealand Journal of Audiology, 26*(1), 40–52.

Lind, C., Hickson, L., & Erber, N. (2006). Conversation repair and adult cochlear implantation: A qualitative case study. *Cochlear Implant International, 7*(1), 33–48.

Lind, C., Hickson, L., & Erber, N. (2010). Who said what? Sampling conversation-repair behavior involving adults with acquired hearing impairment. *Seminars in Hearing, 31*(2), 104–115.

Meyer, C., Scarinci, N., Ryan, B., & Hickson, L. (2015). "This is a partnership between all of us": Audiologists' perceptions of family member involvement in hearing rehabilitation. *American Journal of Audiology, 24,* 536–548.

Mondada, L. (2014). *Conventions for multimodal transcription.* https://franz.unibas.ch/fileadmin/franz/user_upload/redaktion/Mondada_conv_multimodality.pdf. Accessed 7 Apr 2016.

Pajo, K. (2012). "One gets along enough to make it work": A case study of local contexts prior to miscommunication between a hearing-impaired man and his spouse. *Journal of Interactional Research in Communication Disorders, 3*(2), 221–249.

Pajo, K. (2013). The occurrence of 'what', 'where', 'what house', and other repair initiations in the home environment of hearing-impaired individuals. *International Journal of Language and Communication Disorders, 48*(1), 66–77.

Pajo, K., & Klippi, A. (2013). Hearing impaired recipients' non-vocal action sets as a resource for collaboration in conversation. *Journal of Pragmatics, 55,* 162–179.

Rasmussen, G. (2014). Inclined to better understanding—The coordination of talk and 'leaning forward' in doing repair. *Journal of Pragmatics, 65,* 30–45.

Robinson, J. D. (2004). The sequential organization of "explicit" apologies in naturally occurring English. *Research on Language and Social Interaction, 37*(3), 291–330. https://doi.org/10.1207/s15327973rlsi3703_2.

Robinson, J. D. (2006). Managing trouble responsibility and relationships during conversational repair. *Communication Monographs, 73*(2), 137–161.

Sacks, H., Schegloff, E., & Jefferson, G. (1974). A simplest systematics for the organization of turn-taking for conversation. *Language: Journal of the Linguistic Society of America, 50*(4), 696–735.

Schegloff, E. (2007). *Sequence organization in interaction.* New York: Cambridge University Press.

Schegloff, E., Jefferson, G., & Sacks, H. (1977). The preference for self-correction in the organization of repair in conversation. *Language: Journal of the Linguistic Society of America, 53*(2), 361–382.

Sidnell, J., & Stivers, T. (2012). *Handbook of conversation analysis.* Boston: Wiley-Blackwell.

Skelt, L. (2007). Damage control: Closing problematic sequences in hearing-impaired interaction. *Australian Review of Applied Linguistics (Special Issue: Language as Action: Australian Studies in Conversation Analysis), 30*(3), 34.31–34.15.

Skelt, L. (2010). "Are you looking at me?" The influence of gaze on frequent conversation partners' management of interaction with adults with acquired hearing impairment. *Seminars in Hearing, 31*(2), 116–126.

Skelt, L. (2012). Dealing with misunderstandings: The sensitivity of repair in hearing impaired conversation. In M. Egbert & A. Deppermann (Eds.), *Hearing aids communication* (pp. 56–66). Mannheim: Verlag für Gesprächsforschung.

Tye-Murray, N. (2009). *Foundations of aural rehabilitation: Children, adults, and their family members* (3rd ed.). New York: Delmare.

Tye-Murray, N., & Witt, S. A. (1996). Conversational moves and conversational styles of adult cochlear-implant users. *Journal of the Academy of Rehabilitative Audiology, 29,* 11–25.

Tye-Murray, N., Witt, S. A., & Schum, L. (1995). Effects of talker familiarity on communication breakdown in conversations with adult cochlear-implant users. *Ear and Hearing, 16*(5), 459–469.

Wilson, J., Hickson, L., & Worrall, L. (1998). Use of communication strategies by adults with hearing impairment. *Asia Pacific Journal of Speech, Language and Hearing, 3,* 29–41.

15

Swiss German and Swiss German Sign Language Resources in Repair Initiations: An Examination of Two Types of Classroom

Simone Girard-Groeber

Introduction

Deaf and hard-of-hearing (DHH) children can be equipped with hearing aids or cochlear implants from an early age and can thereby have an increased access to spoken language. Some of them are socialised in an environment where spoken language is the exclusive mode of communication, whereas others are given the opportunity to acquire (at least) one spoken and one signed language. These children and adolescents are *bilingual-bimodal.* This chapter explores the question of how bimodal students use their plurilingual repertoire to participate in two different kinds of classroom: a classroom in which they are encouraged to practice spoken language and a classroom in which they should practice sign language. Note that the differentiation of language settings is an etic description of the school's language policy '*one person, one language*'. This means students must speak in spoken language with

S. Girard-Groeber (✉)
University of Applied Sciences and Arts Northwestern Switzerland (FHNW), Olten, Switzerland

© The Author(s) 2020
R. Wilkinson et al. (eds.), *Atypical Interaction*,
https://doi.org/10.1007/978-3-030-28799-3_15

hearing persons, thus in the integration classroom, and sign language in the classroom with the deaf teacher. The empirical evidence highlights however, that students regularly resort to their plurilingual and bimodal repertoire in a creative and situated manner.

In the remainder of this introduction I will first discuss the 'atypicality' of the population under study here (section "A Note on Terminology"), and then review studies dealing with repair by hearing, deaf, and hard-of-hearing participants (sections "Other-Initiation of Repair in *Spoken Language Interaction*" and "Other-Initiation of Repair in *Signed Language Interaction*"). After this I state the purpose of the paper and describe the method used (section "Purpose of the Chapter and Methodology"). The analysis section "Resources Used in Different Types of Repair Initiations" gives an overview of the resources students draw upon when they initiate repair. This provides evidence for the multiple ways in which repair initiations can be designed. In the section "Fingerspelling as a Resource in Repair Initiation", I then turn to the sequential analysis of two excerpts. This analysis aims at demonstrating, by means of one exemplary resource (fingerspelling), how students design their repair initiations in a way that is contingent upon the activities at hand (see section "Fingerspelling as a Resource in Repair Initiation").

A Note on Terminology

For the population under study here, the meaning of 'atypical interaction' and of 'communicative impairment' is different according to the communication setting in which the participants are involved. DHH persons who use a signed language are necessarily *bilingual-bimodal* to some extent. They use a signed language and at least one or more modalities of a spoken language (reading and writing or more) on a regular basis. This is because they inevitably live in an environment where spoken language is the most important means of communication (Grosjean 1992). In this spoken setting, DHH bimodals experience a communicative impairment as a consequence of their restricted perceptual access to the surrounding speech. Interaction based on spoken language involving DHH participants can therefore reveal atypical patterns.

The picture is quite different when DHH bimodals act and communicate in a signed language setting. In this case the participants experience no perceptual barriers, and therefore no communicative impairment is observable. Signed conversations can nevertheless be termed 'atypical' in the sense that the accomplishment of interaction by means of a visuo-spatial language code leads analysts to reconsider interactional practices and/or formats described in CA work on the basis of spoken languages. The 'atypicality' of the interaction therefore has another significance in this context.

Previous work on persons with a hearing-impairment from a CA perspective reflects these two conceptions of atypicality. A first strand of studies focussed on specificities in spoken interactions when *adults with acquired hearing loss* participate in them. Another research strand concentrated on how the participants use a visuo-spatial language system (a sign language) and how this impacts on the organisation of interaction. Within the present chapter I intend to add to both fields by an investigation of repair initiations by students with *prelingual hearing loss*, who are *bimodal* in a spoken and a signed language, and who operate in *two different conversational settings*, namely a spoken language setting and a signed language setting. For researchers, each of these settings hosts atypical interactions. For the participants, each of these settings presents specific opportunities and challenges with respect to the design of their interactional practices.

Other-Initiation of Repair in *Spoken Language Interaction*

Repair is one of the basic interactional organisations and refers to an "organized set of practices by which parties to talk-in-interaction can address problems in speaking, hearing, and understanding the talk" (Schegloff 1991, p. 155). The focus of this chapter is on *other-initiations of self-repair*: By means of a repair initiator, a participant indicates some problem with a previous turn of a co-participant. The turn that poses a problem is called the *trouble source* (or *repairable*). The participant who produced the trouble source then carries out self-repair. Repair-initiating practices (e.g., repetition or questioning) do different interactional jobs (Dingemanse et al. 2014). First, they can locate the trouble source turn (in the just prior turn, or earlier); second, they can indicate the trouble type (hearing, understanding, speaking; cf. for example Svennevig 2008). Moreover, repair initiations can be designed to address other issues, as for example face management (Dingemanse et al. 2014, p. 9).

Early work on repair from a CA perspective has been carried out on the basis of spoken conversation and with a major focus on the vocal modality (Schegloff et al. 1977). These accounts have been broadened with new insights by researchers who have examined the multimodal unfolding of these courses of action (e.g., Egbert 1996; Seo and Koshik 2010; Mortensen 2012; cf. also Auer 1984). A recent cross-linguistic examination of 16 languages, involving one signed language, revealed that the organisation of repair is universal and that all languages use three *types* of repair initiators (Dingemanse et al. 2015):

1. *Open request* (open class repair initiators, OCRIs, as described by, for example, Drew 1997). Participants request repetition, clarification or specification of a trouble source item. They do this without precisely specifying the item that needs to be repaired. In German this can be done for example with 'what' *was*, 'pardon' *bitte*, or an interjection *hä* (cf. Egbert 1996).
2. *Restricted request.* Participants request repetition, clarification or specification of a component of the trouble source item, for example by using a question word ('who?', 'when?') (Dingemanse et al. 2015, p. 5).
3. *Restricted offer.* Participants request confirmation of a candidate understanding, for instance, on the basis of a repeat or partial repeat of a previous (component of a) turn. This may be done with an explicit 'do you mean', or just with questioning prosodic markers.

Furthermore, according to Dingemanse et al. (2015), participants in all languages follow the *strongest initiator rule* (Clark and Schaefer 1987) by choosing the most specific repair initiator that is possible at a given point (restricted offer is preferred over restricted request, which is preferred over open request).

How DHH people and their communication partners deal with problems in speaking, hearing, and understanding has long been the focus of interest of practitioners and researchers. To date, CA-inspired studies mainly focus on participants with acquired hearing impairment, more precisely on adults who grew up with a spoken language and experienced a hearing loss in later life. Evidence from these studies converges to suggest that hard-of-hearing participants other-initiate repair more frequently in comparison to their hearing communication partners (Lind et al. 2004; Pajo 2013). Moreover, Pajo (2012) shows that a micro-analytic approach taking into account the sequential organisation of repair sequences allows us to identify non-vocal resources in repair initiations (e.g., bending towards the trouble speaker) as well as resources in repair accomplishment (e.g., prosody) that appear to be related to hearing problems. Pajo (2013) further demonstrates that not all adult participants with acquired hearing loss use unrestricted repair initiations more extensively than restricted repair initiations. This calls into question earlier results that indicate that participants with hearing impairment use predominantly open class repair (i.e., unrestricted) initiators. It must be acknowledged however, that the author did not include non-vocal repair strategies. Especially due to the hearing impairment it can be assumed that the participants also initiate repair through visual means and thus the number of OCRIs may be increased. In another study, the same author and a colleague specifically examined these non-vocal resources. They were able to show that participants use such visual non-vocal actions, e.g., gaze shifts, frowned eyebrows, or leaning forward, to create intersubjectivity (Pajo and Klippi 2013). The authors did not, however, count these non-vocal actions as other-initiations of repair. This is justified by the fact that these behaviours do not occupy a conversational slot on their own. DHH participants use these visual forms of conduct (e.g., leaning forward, simultaneously to the co-participant's turn) hereby inducing self-repair by the co-participant in a smooth and non-disruptive manner (cf. also Skelt 2006).

Other-Initiation of Repair in *Signed Language Interaction*

Sign languages are fully-fledged language systems with a lexicon and grammar that make use of hands, head, eyes (gaze direction, eye aperture), or eyebrows, as well as body posture for establishing meaning. The manual sign is basically the result of a specific handshape, hand location (e.g., in front of the chest or the mouth), orientation (e.g., the palm of the hand facing down or towards the chest of the signer) and movement (e.g., linear movement from left to right or circling movement).[1] Additionally, non-manual components, such as for example eyebrow configuration or head movements, can bear linguistic meaning. In Swiss German Sign Language (*Deutschschweizerische Gebärdensprache*, DSGS), participants rely heavily on *mouthings*, or "the voiceless pronunciation of German-like words or word parts which accompany the production of manual signs" (Boyes Braem 2001, p. 100). Some sign languages use *fingerspelling*, in addition to the manual signs and non-manual components. Fingerspelling consists of a series of manual configurations, each representing one letter of the spoken language alphabet. It is a method for spelling a word in the air in front of the signer's chest (the signing space) rather than on paper, and is used for instance when no sign exists for a new object or concept, or for a person's name (Boyes Braem 1990).

Recent micro-analytic studies of signed languages as visuo-spatial language systems shed light on the universalities and specificities of the organisation and accomplishment of human interaction (De Vos et al. 2015; Floyd et al. 2014; Girard-Groeber 2015; Groeber and Pochon-Berger 2014; Manrique and Enfield 2015; McCleary and Leite 2013; McIlvenny 1995). The visuo-spatial nature of sign language also requires a rethink of the goals of conversational repair. In a purely signed setting, repair must best be termed an organised set of practice by which participants deal with *problems in signing, seeing, and*

[1]For introductions to sign language linguistics cf. Klima and Bellugi (1979) and Boyes Braem (1990).

understanding. An open question to be answered empirically is whether the practices of bimodal participants can be described in this way as well. As long as this question is not answered, one could speak of a set of practices on the basis of which speakers deal with problems *in producing, perceiving, and understanding*.

Empirical analysis of sign language data has identified two phenomena in particular. First, signers regularly design their repair-initiating turns with a turn-final hold until the resolution of the problem (Floyd et al. 2014; Groeber and Pochon-Berger 2014; cf. also Pajo 2013 on hold of the 'trouble posture' in spoken interaction). Second, the use of a steady mutual gaze (Girard-Groeber 2018; Groeber 2014 for DHH bimodals in a spoken language setting) or freeze-look (Manrique and Enfield 2015; Manrique 2017 in signed interaction) as a systematic way for initiating repair. Whether these formats are limited to this population or whether they are simply more prominently used by them remains an issue for further research.

Purpose of the Chapter and Methodology

The chapter has the following aims: (a) to *describe the resources* students use in different types of other-initiations (OIs) of teachers' self-repair in both classroom settings; (b) to *provide a quantitative overview* of the types of students' OIs in both settings; (c) to *demonstrate* how the use of OIs is contingent on the activities at hand; as an example I discuss the use of (partial) repetitions and questioning for unrestricted repair initiators.

This paper makes two empirically based points. First, I show that students use language-specific devices for other-initiation of repair, stemming from Swiss German (spoken language) or from Swiss German Sign Language. The use of these devices is, however, not strictly distributed according to the two classroom settings. This means, for example, that devices from Swiss German Sign Language do not only occur in the 'signed classroom'. Actually, devices from 'the other language' regularly go unnoticed. This means that participants do not treat them as deviant from the official language policy 'one person, one language'.[2]

Second, although the students draw on the same resources out of their plurilingual repertoire for designing their repair initiations, the data reveals important differences in the two classroom settings. First, the frequency distribution of repair types in both classrooms differs. Moreover, the excerpts presented here illustrate that students use these resources in a manner that is contingent upon the activity (and participation frameworks) at hand. It further appears that not only the use and but also the effectiveness of the same resource in both classroom settings is dependent on the activities and participation frameworks at hand.

Setting and participants. The study focusses on four hard-of-hearing bilingual-bimodal students who are enrolled on a programme of partial integration: They take classes with hearing peers and a hearing main teacher in an integration classroom (also called *the spoken classroom).* In this setting they are accompanied by a hearing assistant. All other classes involve exclusively the hard-of-hearing students and are held by a deaf teacher in sign language (*the signed classroom*). The official language policy adopted is 'one person one language'. A list of relevant characteristics of the hard-of-hearing students is presented in Table 15.1.

The DHH children's competence is understood as being fundamentally plurilingual. This plurilingualism is characterised as consisting in a proper and original competence which is different from the mere addition of monolingual competence in German to monolingual competence in DSGS.

Data collection and transcription. The data for this study were collected by the author and consist of 34 audio-video-recorded classroom lessons. All participants or their legal representatives gave permission to record and use data for scientific publication. All names are pseudonyms.

---

[2]When teachers (or students) pinpoint devices as not conforming to the classroom setting, this occurs in long repair sequences or with other non-appropriate classroom conduct.

Table 15.1 Characteristics of the hard-of-hearing students

• The participants are aged between 13 and 15 years at the time of recording
• All participants have prelingual hearing loss. All participants have hearing aids or a cochlear implant
• The participants were born into hearing families and had early exposure to spoken languages. Due to their hearing loss however, the access to these languages has been restricted and this access did not allow for a natural acquisition of spoken language as a first language (L1)[a]
• None of the participants had an early exposure to sign language. They are late learners or chronologically L2 signers. Sign language acquisition can therefore not build on a well-developed pre-existent L1
• Three of the four participants are born in immigrant families using other/additional spoken languages at home other than the surrounding spoken languages (Swiss German and German)
• The participants are bimodal, having at least one spoken language and Swiss German Sign Language (*DSGS*)
• The programme director reports that one student has attention deficit hyperactivity disorder, but no official diagnosis is available
• The students' pseudonyms are Jacob, Nikolas, Nora, and Pashali

[a]With regard to this complicated status of the acquisition of spoken language, Berent (2004) refers to it as L1.5 acquisition, suggesting that '(...) even if English is the first or only language to which a deaf child is exposed, the restricted access to the AV [auditory-vocal] modality results in English knowledge that simulates L2 knowledge' (ibid., p. 317)

- Dataset A: 21 lessons in the *integration/spoken classroom*, that is, a classroom where one to three hard-of-hearing students participate in regular classroom lessons with hearing students and a hearing main teacher. A hearing teaching assistant, Ms. Micheli, accompanies the hard-of-hearing students in this setting. The school topic is German.
- Dataset B: 13 lessons in the *bimodal/signed classroom* involving the same hard-of-hearing students with a deaf teacher, Ms. Folker, using DSGS. The school topic is German.

Transcripts and analyses are made with the help of the annotation software ELAN®. The transcription symbols are based on Jefferson (2004) with additional features specified in the conventions listed at the end of this chapter.

Analytical procedure. The analysis is built on a collection of students' other-initiations of self-repair in response to a co-participant's question (requests for information as well as display questions) or a request for action (as an invitation to accomplish something). The collection is the result of a sequential multimodal analysis of first and second pair parts and on insights from studies on repair organisation (cf. section "Other-Initiation of Repair in *Spoken Language Interaction*" and "Other-Initiation of Repair in *Signed Language Interaction*").

Resources Used in Different Types of Repair Initiations

This chapter first describes the different *resources* that students rely upon in the different types of other-initiations of teachers'/assistants' self-repair (Tables 15.2 and 15.3). It then provides a quantitative overview of the types of students' OIs in both settings (Table 15.4).

In both classroom settings students accomplish both unrestricted and restricted repair initiations. In doing so, they rely on language-specific resources stemming either from Swiss German (spoken language) or from Swiss German Sign Language. However, a range of resources cannot be straightforwardly assigned to one language or the other. This is the case for example for unvoiced production of German words when sign language productions (manually) are accompanied by unvoiced German words. Here these may count as *mouthings* and as an integral part of DSGS. The question arises, for example, whether they may still be considered as mouthings when they occur without any manual sign.

In the following tables I present the possible resources and describe how students rely upon them in unrestricted repair initiations (Table 15.2) and in restricted repair initiations (Table 15.3). Note that words in CAPITALS refer to conventionalised signs from Swiss German Sign Language, while words in *italics* are words in Swiss German.

The collection of repair initiations shows that the students in both classrooms recurrently use a combination of resources that come from both the sign language system and the spoken language. Such

Table 15.2 Resources in unrestricted repair initiations

Explicit open class repair initiation: Students request repetition or reformulation by means of questioning or interjection

The resources students use draw upon:

- *One or two hands*: palm-up gesture, lexical signs such as WAS ('what'), NICHT VERSTEHEN ('did not understand')
- *Mouth*: lexical items *was* ('what') or *wie* ('pardon'), interjections such as *hä* ('huh'); both with or without voice
- *Upper body*: head moving towards the participant, torso leaning forward
- *Face*: squinting eyes, furrowed or raised eyebrows, wrinkled nose

A characteristic of how students design explicit OCRIs is that they draw on a resource visible using the mouth (wh-word or interjection with or without voice) in combination with another visual resource of the upper body. The resources are produced simultaneously and in a synchronised manner (cf. symbol " in Example 1 below). Interestingly, the use of manual resources in OCRIs (gesture, sign) is rare. When the OCRI consists of only one resource, it is one using the upper body or the face

Example 1 (integration classroom)

Participant	***Repair***	***Translation***
1 Kar	*>hast du es gezeigt?<*	Did you show it?
2 Nik	*"wie?*	Pardon?
	"raised eyebrows	
3 Kar	*hast du das heft gezeigt?*	Did you show the booklet?

Implicit open class repair initiations: Students request repetition or reformulation with mutual gaze

The resource for this type of OCRI is mutual gaze. Students either maintain, or quickly establish, mutual gaze with the teacher in response to a question

These OCRIs occur in longish repair sequences, especially in the integration classroom. Characteristic of these sequences are issues of face-management which are dealt with by the implicit nature of the repair initiation (cf. Groeber 2014; Girard-Groeber 2018)

Table 15.3 Resources in restricted repair initiations

Restricted request: Students request repetition or clarification by questioning, or questioning + repetition, or questioning + partial repetition

The resources students draw upon are:

- *One or two hands:* wh-signs WO ('where'), WAS ('what), palm-up gesture, WIE ('how')
- *Mouth*: wh-words *wo* ('where'), *was* ('what'), *welche* ('which one'), with or without voice

Students can draw on facial and body resources (squinting eyes, furrowed or raised eyebrows, head moving towards the participant):

- These resources are deployed simultaneously with explicit questioning using wh-words or wh-signs (cf. above), thereby *adding* to the lexical questioning;
- These resources occur simultaneously with (partial) repeats, thereby *designing* the repetition as a questioning

Wh-signs or wh-words can be used alone, or with a signed or spoken repetition or partial repetition of the trouble source. (Partial) repetitions can consist of one or more signs out of a turn, or one or more fingerspelled letters out of a fingerspelled word (cf. section "Fingerspelling as a Resource in Repair Initiation")

Example 2 (integration classroom)

Participant	*Repair*	*Translation*
1 Mic	The teaching assistant explains in parallel to an ongoing explanation by the main teacher that the students have to write letters on small sheets	
2 Nor	"-und wo- ((wh-questioning))	and where?
	"palm-up gesture ((manual wh-sign))	
	"head shake	
3 Mic	((depicts a rectangle with both hands in the air, then holds one hand and points to the rectangle with the other hand))	

Restricted offer: Students request for confirmation by questioning, or questioning + repetition, or questioning + partial repetition

(continued)

Table 15.3 (continued)

The resources students draw on are:

- *One or two hands:* conventionalised manual signs, fingerspelled letters or words, gestures
- *Mouth*: Swiss German, with or without voice

Students can draw on facial and body resources (squinted eyes, furrowed or raised eyebrows, head moving towards the participant) in two ways:

- simultaneously with explicit questioning (wh-words or wh-signs, see above), thereby adding to the lexical questioning;
- simultaneously with (partial) repeats, thereby designing the repetition as a questioning.

Example 3 (integration classroom)

Participant	***Repair***	***Translation***
1 Mic	schreibe noch hin dass du gruppe b bist	Write down that you are in group b
2 Nik	"group b?	Write group b?
	"raised brows	
	"simulates writing with hand	
3 Mic	ja	Yes

Table 15.4 Overview of repair initiations in both classroom settings

Repair initiations	Integration classroom (spoken setting)			Bimodal classroom (signed setting)		
	Number	%	%	Number	%	%
Unrestricted						
Steady mutual gaze/ Freeze-look	19	40	**72**	2	7	**43**
Open class repair initiators (OCRI)	15	32		10	36	
Restricted						
Restricted request	5	11	**28**	6	21	**57**
Restricted offer (candidate understanding)	8	17		10	36	
Total	47	100		28	100	

devices from 'the other language' regularly go unnoticed, and this means that participants do not treat them as a deviation from the language policy 'one language, one person'. The repair initiation type OCRIs can be cited as an example: In the signed classroom 7 OCRIs are produced exclusively with non-manual resources (e.g., eyebrows, wrinkled nose, squinted eyes, mouthings) and only 3 OCRIs additionally contain a manual resource. In the spoken classroom only 1 OCRI contains a manual resource, while all other are combinations of spoken (but not necessarily voiced) wh-words with other non-manual resources (e.g., eyebrows, squinted eyes).

That students creatively draw on their plurilingual repertoire in both settings does not mean however that there is no difference in how they use other-initiations of repair in the spoken and in the signed classroom setting. Differences become apparent in (a) how repair types (restricted and unrestricted) differ quantitatively in the settings (cf. Table 15.4), and (b) how practices are adapted to the contingencies of the activities (cf. section "Fingerspelling as a Resource in Repair Initiation").

Table 15.4 reveals interesting distributional differences between both classroom settings. First, in the spoken-language setting, the integration classroom, there is relatively high number of unrestricted other-initiations of repair compared to restricted ones (72% and 28% respectively). Second, in the bimodal or signed setting there is a roughly equal distribution between the occurrence of unrestricted and restricted other-initiations of repair (43% and 57% respectively). This distribution is similar to that found by Manrique (2017), although her results are based on more occurrences and on ordinary conversation.

Against the background of the previous work on atypical interaction with DHH participants, it seems obvious to interpret the results as follows: the signed setting shows similar patterns due to the visuo-spatial languages, which were found for atypical interactions with sign language (section "Other-Initiation of Repair in *Spoken Language Interaction*"); the spoken-language setting, on the other hand, has similar patterns to those found for interactions between DHH adults and hearing communication partners. It could therefore be concluded from the table that the classroom type (spoken vs signed) and communication impairment are consequential for how repair initiation is organised. However, the representation of the repair initiations in the form of the current coding scheme blurs important details of their sequential embedding in activities and participation frameworks (cf. Stivers 2015). Using a sequential multimodal analysis of the following two excerpts, I would like to show that specific activities make specific resources and practices relevant (as well as efficient) for dealing with problems in mutual understanding. Thus, care must be taken to understand the practices and their dissemination as exclusively group-specific and language-specific.

Fingerspelling as a Resource in Repair Initiation

In this section I demonstrate how a resource stemming from the signed language system is used in two different types of repair initiations (restricted request and restricted offer), and show that the use and effectiveness of the same repair initiation practice (fingerspelled letter and questioning facial marking) is contingent on the activities and participation frameworks at hand.

Fingerspelling has been introduced in some sign languages by educators of the deaf to make a link between the written modality of the spoken language and sign language. Thereby fingerspelling can be used as a central resource for the acquisition of new words/signs as well as for the acquisition of reading and writing (Humphries and MacDougall 2000). Repair initiations with the use of fingerspelling occur in activities where either understanding or producing German written words is relevant. The corpus reveals how a fingerspelled letter is used as a resource in *restricted request* when it occurs with furrowed brows (section "Fingerspelling in Repair Sequences in the 'Bimodal Classroom' (Signing Teacher)"), and how as a resource in a *restricted offer* when it occurs with raised brows (section "Fingerspelling in Repair Sequences in the Spoken Language Classroom"). The use of fingerspelling in repair-initiating practices has not previously been described. The analysis of these two excerpts will show that:

a. Restricted request with fingerspelling is efficient. One fingerspelled letter singles out a whole fingerspelled word in the trouble source turn as the item to be repaired.
b. Restricted offer with fingerspelling is less efficient. A successful repair necessitates confirming not only the fingerspelled letter but also its place in a string of fingerspelled letters (i.e., a word).

Fingerspelling in Repair Sequences in the 'Bimodal Classroom' (Signing Teacher)

The following transcripts include one or two lines for the modality of the hands; the symbol both hands (BH), right hand (RH) or left hand (LH) after the participants' abbreviated names indicates a production of a gesture or a conventionalised sign in sign language; the latter is transcribed with a gloss in capitals[3] (e.g., PISTOL for the manual sign) or with capital

[3]The conventionalised manual sign is referred to with a gloss, i.e., a German word that functions as an approximate translation. Glosses are conventionally written in capitalised letters.

letters separated by hyphens for fingerspelled words (e.g., -P-I-S-T-O-L-). Another important annotation line is that of the mouth (_mth), where voiced or unvoiced words are represented. Further lines comprise annotations on gaze (_gz) and other bodily behaviour that are especially relevant for the analysis (_hd for head; _fac for face; _tor for torso). Gaze conduct is transcribed in italics and its onset is indicated with an asterisk (*) that relates it to simultaneous signs, talk or other bodily behaviour. Other simultaneity between behaviours is indicated with the symbol (“). For behaviours that occur simultaneously, the same line number subdivided with letters (e.g., 1a to 1e) is used. Each transcript is preceded by a translation into English. See Appendix for further transcription conventions.

A recurrent way for the signing students to use fingerspelling in repair initiations is to accompany them with *furrowed eyebrows* (a non-manual prosodic marker) as well as a turn-final hold, as illustrated in Excerpt 1. In this excerpt the teacher (Folker) and two students (Jacob and Nora) are engaged in a reading and word clarification activity. The students identify written German words they do not understand. The words are then explained in Swiss German Sign Language. Excerpt 1 starts when Jacob identifies the word *Pistole* ‘pistol’ as one he does not understand (l.1). The teacher, Folker, re-addresses this as a question to the second student Nora (l.3). Nora initiates repair on Folker’s turn (l.4). The teacher repairs her turn with a partial repetition of the turn, more precisely with a repetition of the fingerspelled trouble source item (l.5). Nora then answers the question by providing the conventionalised sign for ‘to shoot’ as well as for ‘pistol’ (l.6).

1 Jac:	What means +‘pistol’ (fingerspelled)+? ((addressed to Fol, the teacher)
3 Fol:	What is +‘pistol’ (fingerspelled)+ ((addressed to Nora)
4 Nor:	+‘s ? ’ (fingerspelled)+ ((addressed to the teacher))
5 Fol:	+pistol (fingerspelled)+
6 Nor:	To shoot.
7 Nor:	Pistol

Excerpt 1 (JV_BM_100518; 13:33)

(pointing to a word in the book) 'pistol' (fingerspelling)

1a	**JAC_RH**	**"IX(book) (hold)**
1b	**JAC_LH**	**"*-P-I-S-T-O-L-E- (hold)**
1c	Jac_gz	**->book(jac)->**
1d	Fol_gz	**->book(jac)->**
1e	Nor_gz	**"?*
1f	Nor_RH	*"combs her hair with her fingers*
2a		*(1.1)
2b	Jac_gz	**->fol->**
2c	Fol_gz	**->book(jac)->**

what is a 'pistol' (fingerspelled)

3a	**FOL_RH**	**"*-P-I-S-T-O-L- ^E- WAS**
3b	**Fol_mth**	**"pistol**
3c	**Fol_fac**	**"furrowed brows**
3d	Fol_gz	**->nor->**
3e	Jac_RH	^releases hold
3f	Nor_gz	**"->fol->**
3g	Nor_RH	*"combs her hair with her fingers*

Question addressed at Nora (l.3a-d) with fingerspelling, mouthing + furrowed brows

what -s-

4a	**NOR_LH**	**"*-S- (hold)->^**
4b	**Nor_mth**	**"s**
4c	**Nor_fac**	**"furrowed brows**
4d	Nor_hd	"head/chest forward quickly
4e	Jac_gz	**->nor->>*

Partial repeat of fingerspelled item (from l.3a) with fingerspelling, mouthing and questioning by means of furrowed brows (l.4a-c).

pistol' (fingerspelling)

5a	**FOL_RH**	***"-P -I-^S-T-O-L-***	
5b	**Fol_mth**	***"pistol***	
5c	Nor_LH	*-h___^releases hold* to shoot	
6a	NOR_BH		SCHIESSEN

Repetition of the fingerspelled word (l.5):

- Displays the teacher's understanding of Nora's RI (l.4) as a restricted request, singling out the whole fingerspelled word 'pistol' as trouble source
- leads to a successful closure the repair sequence.

pistol (DSGS)

7a	**NOR_LH**	***PISTOLE**
7b	Nor_gz	**->jac->>*

pistol (DSGS)

8a	**FOL**	***PISTOLE(on belt)**
8b	Fol_gz	**->jac->>*

Excerpt 1 starts with Jacob localising a word he does not understand by pointing with his right hand to the book (l.1a) and making the word visible in space by fingerspelling it with his left hand (*Pistole* 'pistol', l.1b). At this point Jacob and the teacher display shared attention in that both are gazing at his book (l.1c–d). Also Nora's head is directed towards

Fig. 15.1 Nora signing the fingerspelled letter -S-

Jacob but the focus of her gaze is uncertain (l.1e). Jacob's prolonged gaze to the teacher (l.2b) displays his expectation of a response from the teacher. Folker however addresses the question to Nora (3a–3d). In doing so, she draws on multiple resources: She first fingerspells 'pistol' (l.3a) while simultaneously mouthing 'pistol' (l.3b); she then adds a conventionalised manual sign for 'what' (*WAS*, l.3a), and simultaneously with all this she furrows her brows (l.3c). This format is a common way of formulating open questions in DSGS (Boyes Braem 1990). Precisely timed to the end of Folker's question, Nora other-initiates repair by indicating a problem with the teacher's turn (l.4). For this she combines multiple simultaneously unfolding resources: a fingerspelled 's' (l.4a), a mouthing of 's' (l.4b), furrowed brows (l.4c) and a quick leaning forward towards the teacher (l.4d) (cf. Figure 4.1).

The interpretation of the instance as a *restricted request* is based on how the teacher orients to the initiation: She repeats the whole fingerspelled word 'pistol' (l.5a) with an unvoiced mouthing (l.5b) and drops the interrogative sign *WAS* ('what'). Therefore, the teacher displays an understanding of Nora having trouble with the whole fingerspelled word 'pistol' (and not just the 's', and not the whole question). This is confirmed by how the sequence further unfolds: In overlap with the end of the fingerspelled repair (l.05), Nora provides the answer at line 6 with a first sign ('to shoot') and then a variant of 'pistol' in line 7. Folker closes the repair sequence with a variant of the sign 'pistol' (the handform for 'pistol' on the belt, l.8).

Excerpt 1 has illustrated how signers accomplish the practice of *partial repetition and questioning* as a repair initiation by using fingerspelling, a resource that is specific to sign language. Additional resources are the furrowed brows, which frame the partial repetition as a question, and the freezing or hold of the fingerspelled 's', embodying Nora's expectation for the accomplishment of the teacher's repair (cf. Groeber and Pochon-Berger 2014). This type of repair initiation makes up 4 of the 6 restricted offers in the signed setting. Other examples from the corpus provide further evidence that by means of this pattern (partial repetition with fingerspelling and furrowed brows), participants single out the whole fingerspelled word as the trouble source. Moreover, when the repair-initiating partial repetition is longer than one letter, the 'trouble source signer' can overlap the fingerspelled repair initiation and thereby display s/he does not attend to the whole sequential unfolding of the fingerspelled word but orients to the fingerspelling as pinpointing 'the fingerspelled item'. The fact that there is rarely more than one fingerspelled word in a signed sentence makes the format particularly efficient, as it becomes immediately identifiable.

In the following example, Excerpt 2, the student uses similar resources for initiating repair. On the one hand, the example will show that the student adapts the repair initiation to the activity underway. On the other hand, it also shows that the efficiency of the repair initiation practice is contingent on this activity and on the co-participant.

Fingerspelling in Repair Sequences in the Spoken Language Classroom

Excerpt 2 is part of an interaction between Jacob and the hearing teaching assistant Micheli. The interaction unfolds in parallel to the plenary activity, which for reasons of legibility is not represented here. Jacob has to write down the superlative form of the adjective 'loud' (*laut*), which is 'the loudest' (*am lautesten*). The teaching assistant rejects a prior attempt (l.1). Micheli and Jacob then launch a sequence where they accomplish the target item syllable by syllable (*am laut-tes-ten*; 'the lou-de-st') (l.2–9): Micheli pronounces the first syllable (l.2), then Jacob starts writing (l.3). Then he looks up and Micheli says the second syllable (l.4). Jacob writes again before looking up and requesting confirmation (*restricted offer*) that he has understood the second syllable correctly or has spelled it correctly (l.6). The restricted offer is based on a repeat with fingerspelling and questioning. Instead of the sequentially relevant (dis-)confirmation, Micheli now produces the whole word ('the lou-de-st', *am lautesten,* l.7). In overlap, Jacob initiates another repair: He indicates that he does not understand why a 'T' is coming at this point (l.8), and asks Micheli to produce the word from the

Fig. 15.2 Jacob signing the fingerspelled letter -E-

beginning (l.9). Micheli however refuses and asks Jacob to listen (l.10) (Fig. 15.2).

1 Mic:	no.
2 Mic:	the lou-
3 Jac:	((writes))
4 Mic:	-de-
5 Jac:	((writes))
6 Jac:	-D[-E- ((restricted offer of the syllable -de- from 'lou-de-st', *lau-tes-ten*))
7 Mic:	[the loude[st
8 Jac:	[No. What -T-.
9 Jac	Once again -L-[O-
10 Mic	[No wait, you should hear.

Excerpt 2 (JNV_IN_100624; 36:30)

no

1 Mic_hd shake

the lou-

2 Mic_mth °°am lau°°

First syllable of 'lou-de-st', ***lau**-tes-ten*

3 +(8.1) ((jacob is writing))+

-de-

4a Mic_mth tes:

4b JAC_RH -T- -h

Second syllable of 'lou-de-st', *lautesten*

5 +(1.7) ((jacob is writing))+

-D-E-?

6a JAC_LH *-T-"E- "-h

6b Jac_fac "raised brows

6c Jac_gz **->fol->**

Restricted offer (l.6), requesting confirmation of the letter E (after T)

the loudest

7a Mic_mth "am <laute"sten>

7b JAC_LH "-T-

Repetition of whole construction 'the lou-de-st', ***'am lautesten'*** (l.7) no, what -T- ?

8a Jac_hd ***shake**

8b JAC_LH ***palm-up -T- &**

8c Jac_gz **->book->**

once again, -L-A-

9a **JAC_LH &*"+palm-up -L- -A-** ((accentuates))

9b Jac_mth " (noch)mal

9c Jac_gz **->mic->**

no wait, you should hear.

10a Mic_hd "shake

10b MIC_RH "(WARTEN) "IX(ear)

10a Mic_mth "du sollst hören.

Restricted request for repetition of the whole

This excerpt provides insight into how fingerspelling can also be used in repair initiation, namely by requesting confirmation for the accuracy of one or more letters. This is done with the practice seen here, namely a (partial) repetition with questioning. The example also shows, however, how challenging it is for participants to deal with problems in spelling by means of fingerspelling: to write the word correctly, Jacob not only needs to know if *-E-* is the right letter, he also needs to locate it correctly in the sequentiality of the whole word. This is all the more challenging as the participants switch between negotiating the spelling and writing down the word. I will further argue that Jacob aims to fulfil these interactional tasks with the format of his restricted offer.

To deal with the complexity of the example, I first focus on what Jacob is doing. After Jacob seemed to have written down the first syllable (l. 2–3), we see in line 4a that Micheli continues with the second syllable (*-tes-*, -de-). Jacob displays understanding of the letter *-T-* in l.4b and then continues writing (l.5). In line 6a Jacob first produces a very short -*T*- and then a long -*E*-. This -*E*- is accentuated: Jacob raises his eyebrows, pushes his head forward and gazes at Micheli (l.6a–c). By means of this, Jacob accomplishes two things: Firstly, he asks for confirmation of the letter -*E*-, which Micheli pronounced in 4a. Secondly, Jacob locates the letter -*E*- in the sequence of the word, namely after the -T-. If all parts are put together, we see that Jacob indicates the correct sequence of letters: *lau*- (l.2–3) - *t* (4a) - *e* (6a). Micheli however repeats the construction from the beginning and accentuates the second syllable -*tes*- (l.7). This causes confusion: Jacob makes this explicit by displaying that he does not understand why a -*T*- comes now (l.8a–b). This further corroborates that his fingerspelled -*T*- was not what he asked confirmation for but rather it served as an anchor for the confirmation request. This may be reformulated as 'after T comes E?'.

All in all, this example sheds light on the particular challenges that participants have to deal with in activities with fingerspelling. While the student's design of the repair initiation addresses this challenge, the excerpt clearly shows that its efficiency is also dependent on the co-participant's understanding of these formats.

Conclusion

This chapter set out to explore how bimodal students with prelingual hearing loss other-initiate repair in response to questions and requests when they participate in two different classroom settings, a 'signed classroom' and a 'spoken classroom'. By drawing attention to *bimodal* students and their participation in two settings, this investigation complements existent studies by looking at how the same participants initiate repair in two types of 'atypical interaction'. The evidence provided in this chapter supports a position that understands the form and efficiency of repair initiations not as a consequence of the classroom or the language policy in these classrooms, but rather as something that all participants present actively accomplish depending on the situated challenges and affordances of interaction.

As a first step towards empirical documentation of students' repair initiation practices, this chapter provided a rough overview of the types of repair initiations and the resources that students combine in accomplishing them. An important point was that students in both settings combine both spoken and sign language resources. This could be seen as the first specificity that characterises the interactions of this population. Despite equal semiotic resources, differences were found between the classrooms: In line with previous research, the quantitative results of repair initiations show patterns similar to those found in spoken interactions with DHH adults on the one hand, and in sign language interactions on the other. The aforementioned findings complement these studies by pointing out some details of how bimodal students competently use repair practices and resources in a manner that is highly contingent on the activities and settings at hand. This was done with the example of *(partial) repetition + questioning with the resource of fingerspelling*. Students use this practice with furrowed brows in order to single out a whole fingerspelled word as a trouble source. By changing the questioning format, adding raised brows, students request confirmation of the accuracy of individual letters.

The micro-sequential analysis of the extracts has shown how important the shape of the eyebrows, for example, is for action formation. Future research would have to explore further systematic combinations out of the plurilingual repertoire and their sequential unfolding to provide a more complete picture of repair organization in bilingual-bimodal settings.

Acknowledgements My thanks to the editors for their constructive criticism and suggestions on earlier versions of this chapter. I particularly acknowledge the support and feedback of John Rae as lead reviewer. Any remaining errors are my responsibility.

Appendix

Conventions for the annotation lines	
mth	Articulation by the mouth, voiced or *unvoiced*, by participant Jacob
RH, LH, BH	Manual resources on the right hand, the left hand, or both hands
hd	Movements with the head (shake and nod)
gz	Gaze direction
fac	Conducts on the face (e.g., eyebrows)
->	Start and end of gaze behaviours in parallel to other behaviours
//	Simultaneously unfolding behaviours within one participant
->>	Behaviour continues beyond the end of this transcript
Conventions for the hand tier (LH left hand, RH right hand, BH both hands)	
BALL	Gloss for standardised sign of DSGS
IX(sheet)	Index/pointing towards the person/ object in brackets
-B-A-L-L-	Fingerspelling / Fingerspelled letters (B, A, L)
palm-up	Hands are held with palms oriented upwards
-h	hold

References

Auer, P. (1984). On the meaning of conversational code-switching. In P. Auer (Ed.), *Interpretive sociolinguistics* (pp. 87–112). Tübingen: Narr.

Berent, G. P. (2004). Sign language-spoken language bilingualism: Code-mixing and mode-mixing by ASL-English bilinguals. In T. K. Bathia & W. C. Ritchie (Eds.), *The handbook of bilingualism* (pp. 312–335). San Diego CA: Academic Press.

Boyes Braem, P. (1990). *Einführung in die Gebärdensprache und ihre Erforschung*. Hamburg: Signum.

Boyes Braem, P. (2001). Functions of mouthings in the signing of deaf early and late learners of Swiss German Sign Language (DSGS). In P. Boyes Bream & R. Sutton-Spence (Eds.), *The hands are the head of the mouth: The mouth as articulator in sign languages* (pp. 99–131). Hamburg: Signum.

Clark, H. H., & Schaefer, E. F. (1987). Collaborating on contributions to conversations. *Language and Cognitive Processes, 2*(1), 19–41.

De Vos, C., Torreira, F., & Levinson, S. C. (2015). Turn-timing in signed conversations: Coordinating stroke-to-stroke turn boundaries. *Frontiers in Psychology, 6,* 268. https://doi.org/10.3389/fpsyg.2015.00268.

Dingemanse, M., Blythe, J., Dirksmeyer, T. (2014). Formats for other-initiation of repair across languages: An exercise in pragmatic typology. *Studies in Language, 38*(1), 5–43.

Dingemanse, M., Roberts, S. G., Baranova, J., Blythe, J., Drew, P., Floyd, S., et al. (2015). Universal principles in the repair of communication problems. *PLoS One, 10*(9), e0136100–15. https://doi.org/10.1371/journal.pone.0136100.

Drew, P. (1997). "Open" class repair initiators in response to sequential sources of troubles in conversation. *Journal of Pragmatics, 28,* 69–101.

Egbert, M. (1996). Context-sensitivity in conversation: Eye gaze and the German repair initiator bitte? *Language in Society, 25*(4), 587–612.

Floyd, S., Manrique, E., Rossi, G., & Torreira, F. (2014). Timing of visual bodily behavior in repair sequences: Evidence from three languages. *Discourse Processes, 53*(3), 175–204.

Girard-Groeber, S. (2015). The management of turn transition in signed interaction through the lens of overlaps. *Frontiers in Psychology, 6,* 741. https://doi.org/10.3389/fpsyg.2015.00741.

Girard-Groeber, S. (2018). *Participation by hard-of-hearing students in integration classrooms: Facets of interactional competence.* Berlin: Frank & Timme.

Groeber, S. (2014). Can 'mutual gaze' be an interactional practice? Describing absence of movement as a sense-making resource. In *International Conference on Conversation Analysis (ICCA14)*, UCLA Los Angeles (USA).

Groeber, S., & Pochon-Berger, E. (2014). Turns and turn-taking in sign language interaction: A study of turn-final holds. *Journal of Pragmatics, 65,* 121–136.

Grosjean, F. (1992). The bilingual and the bicultural person in the hearing and in the deaf world. *Sign Language Studies, 77,* 307–320.

Humphries, T., & MacDougall, F. (2000). "Chaining" and other links: Making connections between American Sign Language and English in two types of school settings. *Society for Visual Anthropology, 15*(2), 84–94.

Jefferson, G. (2004). Glossary of transcript symbols with an introduction. In G. H. Lerner (Ed.), *Conversation analysis: Studies from the first generation* (pp. 13–23). Philadelphia: John Benjamins.

Klima, E. S., & Bellugi, U. (1979). *The signs of language*. Cambridge, MA: Harvard University Press.

Lind, C., Hickson, L., & Erber, N. (2004). Conversation repair and acquired hearing impairment: A prelimary clinical study. *The Australian and New Zealand Journal of Audiology, 26*(1), 40–52.

Manrique, E. (2017). Other-initiated repair in Argentine Sign Language. *Open Linguistics, 2*(1), 1–34. https://doi.org/10.1515/opli-2016-0001.

Manrique, E., & Enfield, N. J. (2015). Suspending the next turn as a form of repair initiation: Evidence from Argentine Sign Language. *Frontiers in Psychology*, 6. https://doi.org/10.3389/fpsyg.2015.01326.

McCleary, L., & Leite, T. de A. (2013). Turn-taking in Brazilian Sign Language: Evidence from overlap. *Journal of Interactional Research in Communication Disorders, 4*(1), 123–156.

McIlvenny, P. (1995). Seeing conversations: Analyzing sign language talk. In P. Ten Have & G. Psathas (Eds.), *Situated order: Studies on the social organisation of talk and embodied activities* (pp. 129–150). Washington, DC: University Press of America.

Mortensen, K. (2012). Visual initiations of repair—Some preliminary observations. In K. Ikeda & A. Brandt (Eds.), *Challenges and new directions in the micro-analysis of social interaction* (pp. 45–50). Osaka: Division of International Affairs, Kansai University.

Pajo, K. (2012). Difficulty to receive a spoken message due to hearing loss: Analysis of a private interaction between two sisters at a coffee table. In M. Egbert & A. Deppermann (Eds.), *Hearing aids communication: Integrating social interaction, audiology and user* (pp. 67–75). Mannheim: Verlag für Gesprächsforschung.

Pajo, K. (2013). The occurrence of 'what', 'where', 'what house' and other repair initiations in the home environment of hearing-impaired individuals. *International Journal of Language & Communication Disorders, 48*(1), 66–77.

Pajo, K., & Klippi, A. (2013). Hearing-impaired recipients' non-vocal action sets as a resource for collaboration in conversation. *Journal of Pragmatics, 55,* 162–179.

Schegloff, E. (1991). Conversation analysis and social shared cognition. In L. Resnick, J. Levine, & S. Teasley (Eds.), *Perspectives on socially shared cognition* (pp. 150–171). Washington, DC: American Psychological Association.

Schegloff, E., Jefferson, G., & Sacks, H. (1977). The preference for self-correction in the organization of repair in conversation. *Language, 53,* 361–382.

Seo, M.-S., & Koshik, I. (2010). A conversation analytic study of gestures that engender repair in ESL conversational tutoring. *Journal of Pragmatics, 42*(8), 2219–2239.

Skelt, L. (2006). *See what I mean: Hearing loss, gaze and repair in conversation.* Ph.D. dissertation, The Australian National University, Canberra.

Stivers, T. (2015). Coding social interaction: A heretical approach in conversation analysis? *Research on Language and Social Interaction, 48*(1), 1–19.

Svennevig, J. (2008). Trying the easiest solution first in other-initiation of repair. *Journal of Pragmatics, 40*(2), 333–348.

Index

© The Editor(s) (if applicable) and The Author(s), under exclusive license to Springer Nature Switzerland AG 2020
R. Wilkinson et al. (eds.), *Atypical Interaction*, https://doi.org/10.1007/978-3-030-28799-3

M

N

O

P

R